Curriculum for the Primary Years
An Integrative Approach

Phillip M. Wishon
University of Northern Colorado

Karen Crabtree
University of Northern Colorado

Malinda E. Jones
Colorado Children's Literacy Group

Merrill, an imprint of Prentice Hall
Upper Saddle River, New Jersey   Columbus, Ohio

Library of Congress Cataloging-in-Publication Data
Wishon, Phillip M.
    Curriculum for the primary years : an integrative approach /
Phillip M. Wishon, Karen Crabtree, Malinda E. Jones.
        p.   cm.
    Includes bibliographical references and index.
    ISBN 0-02-428762-8
    1. Education, Primary—United States—Curicula.   2. Curriculum
planning—United States.   4. Education, Primary—Parent participation—United
States.   5. Literacy—United States.   I. Crabtree, Karen (Karen D.)
    II. Jones, Malinda E.   III. Title.
LB1523.W57   1998
372.19′097—dc21   97-29461
                                                                              CIP

Cover photo: Patricia Michael Photography
Editor: Ann C. Davis
Production Editor: Julie Peters
Design Coordinator: Karrie M. Converse
Text Designer: Linda M. Robertson
Cover Designer: Russ Maselli
Production Manager: Pamela D. Bennett
Illustrations: Carlisle Communications, Inc.
Director of Marketing: Kevin Flanagan
Marketing Manager: Suzanne Stanton
Advertising/Marketing Coordinator: Julie Shough

This book was set in Optima by Carlisle Communications and was printed and bound
by R.R. Donnelley & Sons Company. The cover was printed by Phoenix Color Corp.

 © 1998 by Prentice-Hall, Inc.
Simon & Schuster/A Viacom Company
Upper Saddle River, New Jersey 07458

All photos courtesy of Patricia Michael Photography.

Printed in the United States of America

10   9   8   7   6   5   4   3   2   1

ISBN: 0-02-428762-8

Prentice-Hall International (UK) Limited, *London*
Prentice-Hall of Australia Pty. Limited, *Sydney*
Prentice-Hall of Canada, Inc., *Toronto*
Prentice-Hall Hispanoamericana, S. A., *Mexico*
Prentice-Hall of India Private Limited, *New Delhi*
Prentice-Hall of Japan, Inc., *Tokyo*
Simon & Schuster Asia Pte. Ltd., *Singapore*
Editora Prentice-Hall do Brasil, Ltda., *Rio de Janeiro*

This book is dedicated with love and respect to our loving and supportive families and to the many children and teachers who have inspired us to share with others the idea that curriculum begins with the wonderments of children.

Preface

Teachers of children in the primary years face special challenges. During this period (ages four to eight), children's attitudes and dispositions toward school and learning are shaped. This book was written for the purpose of assisting teachers with the challenge and honor of providing young children with the most appropriate, exciting, and meaningful opportunities for learning possible—learning experiences that will encourage all children to continue as learners throughout their lifetimes. Toward this goal, the authors promote the notion of developmental continuity and advance a philosophy that is child sensitive, integrative, respectful of all children, and reflective of the developmentally appropriate practices set forth by the National Association for the Education of Young Children (NAEYC).

This book reflects a response to the shift in American education away from traditional "containment" of learners across the K–6 spectrum and toward acknowledgment of children in a primary context (ages four to eight). The social, emotional, physical, and educational needs of children within this age range are distinct from those of younger preschool children and those of children nine years old and older. Implicit in the authors' motivation is the belief that children in the primary years share a body of specific developmental characteristics and general interests in response to which distinctive pedagogical, curricular, and cocurricular constructs should be designed.

Increasingly, early childhood units are being established in elementary schools to provide a unique and prescriptive pedagogy for working with children of ages four to eight years. Establishment of these early childhood units reflects the following beliefs:

- Learning for children is constructive and interactive.
- Young children learn from child-sensitive, authentic, concrete work and play.
- Young children are profoundly influenced by their families, backgrounds, and everyday experiences of living, both in and out of school.

Instructors who teach early childhood and elementary education curriculum classes can confidently use *Curriculum for the Primary Years: An Integrative Approach* to provide teachers and potential teachers with a solid foundation of research, theory, and classroom practice. The role of the teacher as mediator is rarely presented as thoroughly in early childhood or elementary curriculum or methods texts as it is in this book. This book can therefore serve as an excellent supplement for field experiences and student teaching. It includes crucial information about teaching and learning in the content areas and includes a comprehensive section on early literacy and how to support literacy development throughout the curriculum. This book provides strong support to all teachers of children in the primary years.

ORGANIZATION OF THE TEXT

Chapter 1, "Philosophy of the Primary Curriculum," views the nature of the primary learner through the theoretical lens of Lev Vygotsky. The importance of valuing the "voices" of all children is underscored, and the nature of a developmentally appropriate curriculum for the primary years is discussed. Perspectives on the role of the teacher in a developmentally appropriate primary learning environment is emphasized.

Chapters 2 and 3 provide information and perspective rarely found in curriculum texts. Chapter 2, "Developing, Delivering, and Assessing Curriculum," brings to the forefront important contemporary issues that affect teachers in today's schools. The reader is urged to examine aspects and concerns related to curriculum planning, grouping, multiage classrooms, standards, integrated curriculum, inclusion, bilingual education, the understanding and misunderstanding of developmentally appropriate practice, and the roles of the teacher within various paradigms. The reader is encouraged to be cautious about jumping on educational bandwagons, to examine all underlying assumptions, to anticipate the potential impact on children, and to determine whether a given perspective's goals for children are consistent with the reader's professional beliefs.

Chapter 3, "Planning for Children's Learning in the Primary Years," provides discussion and examples of instructional interactions and how to make and evaluate instructional decisions. The reader is provided with guidance for considering the diverse needs of all learners. The reader is encouraged to base instructional interactions on observations about what the child knows and the context within which the child knows it. Vygotsky's zone of proximal development is highlighted. Managing and designing the learning environment and planning for independent learning events and centers are also key features of this chapter.

Chapter 4, "A Cohesive, Integrated Curriculum," defines and describes integrated curriculum and differentiates it from other curriculum models such as thematic units. A step-by-step process for planning a cohesive, integrated curriculum is described. Ways to consider both mandated standards and children's interests in the process are presented. Ideas for management and scheduling are also highlighted.

Chapter 5, "Assessment and Evaluation," incorporates current information on instruction-assessment-instruction feedback loops. Sections on designing and selecting assessment tools and characteristics of effective assessment and evaluation provide practical classroom application. The reader is guided to relate assessment to specific goals and instruction, rather than to massage the curriculum to fit the assessment. A section to help novice teachers in planning authentic assessment opportunities for the beginning of the school year is included. Teachers are encouraged to be reflective practitioners and to consider professional development and self-evaluation as ongoing and critically important. Professional reading, critical friends, visitations to other classrooms, and collaborative problem solving are discussed.

Chapter 6, "Partnerships with Parents," is a comprehensive discussion of the merits and issues related to parent involvement. The reader is encouraged to consider a variety of ways to involve parents, and many hands-on examples and scenarios are provided to help beginning and practicing teachers establish and maintain rapport with parents, as well as to create successful opportunities for parents to be involved with their children's education.

Chapter 7, "Literacy Development," explores what becoming literate means and provides the teacher with a solid framework for understanding the literacy development of young children. The power of play in emerging literacy development and the characteristics of literacy-rich homes and classrooms are discussed. Stages of literacy development and appropriate materials and instructional interactions related to each are delineated. "Try It Out" opportunities encourage the reader to problem-solve along with the "teacher" to diagnose the needs and strengths of "readers" presented throughout various scenarios.

Chapter 8, "Supporting Literacy Development Across the Curriculum," describes and provides examples of the planning process used to integrate authentic literacy opportunities and instruction across the curriculum. Opportunities and protocols for qualitative literacy assessment are discussed, and examples are provided.

Helping all children think mathematically and develop mathematical power are two important features of Chapter 9, "Mathematics in the Primary Years." Criteria for including mathematics in the primary curriculum are examined. The importance of understanding the nature of young learners, how mathematics affects their daily lives, and how they construct mathematical meaning is addressed. Distinguishing characteristics of an effective primary mathematics program are identified, and suggestions for planning, implementing, and assessing primary mathematics learning experiences are explored.

A key feature of Chapter 10, "Science in the Primary Years," is a discussion of "scientific literacy" as a goal of science in the primary years. The importance of connecting science content with children's lives is stressed, along with that of helping all children become "scientists." An emphasis is also placed on effective ways to teach primary science and the characteristics of a good primary science curriculum.

Creation of a democratic learning environment is the major goal of social studies in the primary years. In Chapter 11, "Social Studies in the Primary Years," caring as a unifying theme of social studies curriculum guidelines is explored. The importance of valuing the backgrounds, interests, and abilities of all learners is emphasized. The project approach and the Reggio Emilia approach are used as backdrops for discussing suggestions about how to effectively teach social studies in the primary years.

One key point of Chapter 12, "Self-Expression in the Primary Years," is the importance of nurturing the many "voices" of children as they engage in learning experiences designed to promote self-expression. The perception of childhood as a time of enchantment is explored. Ways of helping all children learn to be freely and responsively self-expressive are examined. The Reggio Emilia approach to a self-expression curriculum is discussed. The importance of play as a medium for learning and self-expression is emphasized. The roles of the teacher in helping all children become self-expressive are explored.

ACKNOWLEDGMENTS

It is impossible to thank adequately the many people and institutions that have contributed to this book. Our experiences in numerous schools have challenged our thinking and broadened our understandings. We are particularly grateful to our own children and to the students and teachers of Accelerated Reading and of the Logan School for Creative Learning. Their willingness to share the fruits of their hard work (e.g., assessment tools, communications and planning guides) helped attach practical examples to theoretical constructs. We acknowledge the profound impact they have had on our understanding of caring, teaching, and learning. We are also indebted to the children, college students, and professional colleagues with whom we have had the opportunity to problem solve, teach, learn, search, and share insights. All have greatly affected our thinking and the concepts put forth in this book.

This book has been vastly enriched by the expertise and assistance of Dr. Don Burger, Dr. David Crabtree, and Dr. Barbara Rhine. Barbara reviewed every chapter carefully to integrate ideas and information regarding children with special needs and considerations. Dave and Don spent endless hours conversing, researching, drafting, and revising with us to conceptualize and produce the chapter on assessment and evaluation.

Amii Harmon's editorial expertise was indispensable. The combination of Amii's critical editorial eye and good humor made hours of potentially frustrating review and modification tolerable and, sometimes, even enjoyable. In this same vein, Jan Ferrari's thoughtful critiques and professional insights resulted in important changes being made; in other cases, Jan's comments affirmed the validity of viewpoints that were expressed. Jan's elegantly reasoned and practical sensibilities deserve special acknowledgment.

We offer our special thanks to our personal friends and colleagues who reviewed the manuscript, provided invaluable feedback, and offered their insights and encouragement: Lisa Davis, Annie Spalding, Mary Jo Pollman, Brenda Duncan, Leah Saidy, David Crabtree, and Nancy Harris. To the many professional colleagues who reviewed the drafts, we also extend our thanks. They include Audrey W. Beard, Albany State University; Gloria Boutte, University of South Carolina; Sandra B. DeCosta, Indiana State University; and Ione M. Garcia, Illinois State University.

We found the patience and warm assistance of Pat Grogg, our editorial assistant on this project, especially gratifying. Her good nature and timely responses to our inquiries helped us remain calm in the face of occasional uncertainty.

For her work as senior editor on this project, Ann Davis deserves special mention. From the very beginning, Ann's support and encouragement have been tireless and unflagging. Her supreme confidence in the value of this undertaking fueled our spirits throughout the project. Ann's expertise and keen professional instincts guided us from start to finish. For Ann's unyielding confidence in our work, we are deeply indebted and sincerely appreciative.

We also wish to thank Julie Peters, our Production Editor, for her professional expertise and personal support in the final stages of this book. We thank her for her neverending patience and compassionate flexibility as she worked with us to maintain the cohesiveness of this text.

The exceptional photography for this book was done by Patricia Michael who, to our amazement and delight, was able to listen to our vision for each chapter and capture its essence in photographs. Her excellent photographs honor the narrative messages in ways that reveal her deep understanding and respect for children. To Patricia and to the excellent teachers who graciously allowed her to set up a tripod in the midst of their busy classrooms, we extend our heartfelt appreciation: Lisa Davis, Jette Townsend, Nancy Babbitt, Kate Marshall-Gardiner (The Logan School for Creative Learning); Dana Collinson, Debby Cella, Diane Hoagland (The Denver Co-operative Preschool); Ruth Henson, Debbie Miller, Julia Silver-Valasquez (The Denver Public Schools); Leah Saidy (The Cherry Creek School District); and Toni Linder (Sewall Child Development Center).

Most important, we are indebted to our families and our personal friends who have been so patient with us throughout the project. They have stood beside us and given generously of their love, understanding, time, personal energy, and words of encouragement. To those who have cared for our children and loved ones when we were engaged in writing, we are eternally grateful.

Contents

Nothing is too small or too large for the enthusiastic curiosity of [young children]. They want to know about ants, worms, cars, boats, water, air, space, foreign countries, letters, machines, trees, colors, families, seeds, rocks. And their deepest concerns, played out in fantasy every day, are the timeless human ones: love, hate, birth, death, friendship, war, peace, cosmic forces, good and evil. The challenges children take on are far deeper and more complex than what is usually presented to them as "basic skills," just as the academic aims of textbooks, workbooks, and expensive learning kits are much lower than the aims of the children themselves.

(Martin, 1985, p. 24)

1

Philosophy of the Primary Curriculum

CONSIDER YOUR BELIEFS

- What do you understand about the primary years and the influences that have given rise to the current evolution of this period?
- How do you describe the nature and characteristics of young learners in the primary years?
- What are the distinguishing characteristics of the primary curriculum?
- What major theoretical tenets form the philosophical underpinnings of the primary curriculum?
- What is the role of the teacher in the primary classroom?
- What is the primary context?

The purpose of this chapter is to describe the evolving nature of the primary years and the rationale underlying the development of curriculum for children ages four to eight. An understanding of the theoretical foundations of the primary curriculum and major developmental perspectives of the learner in the primary years are emphasized. Emphasis is also given to an understanding of the critical role teachers play in facilitating learning for children ages four through eight. This chapter also acknowledges the importance of guided learning experiences designed to help young learners make connections between their current understandings and knowledge they can understand more clearly only through interactions with others.

As you read this chapter, think about the nature of young learners during this period of childhood and what aspects hold special interest for you. The age from four to eight is a fascinating time. Children in this age range provide the primary teacher with singular joys and challenges. Note how, throughout this chapter (and throughout this book), we are guided by the child—that is, how so much about what takes place in the primary classroom "keys" on (or is grounded by) the nature of the child.

WHAT IS THE PRIMARY CONTEXT?

In recent years, professional initiatives have led to a profound shift in the focus of American education, a shift of focus away from traditional philosophical "containment" of learners across the K–6 spectrum and toward acknowledgment of children in a "new" **primary context** (a learning environment designed to address the interests and needs of children ages four to eight) as having social, emotional, and educational needs that are distinct from those of both preschool-age children and children above age eight. Perhaps the most influential of these initiatives has been the 1989 National Association for the Education of Young Children (NAEYC) position paper specifying developmentally appropriate practice in the primary grades. Implicit in this document is the belief that children in the primary grades share a body of specific developmental characteristics and general interests in response to which distinctive pedagogical, curricular, and cocurricular constructs should be designed. Significantly, NAEYC is underscoring the importance of a national focus on the primary years by having developed an important position paper in which guidelines for appropriate curriculum content and assessment in programs serving *children ages three through eight* are advanced.

Consideration of Age Ranges and Organization Across Ages

Interest in the issues related to the primary curriculum has escalated because most contemporary early childhood initiatives (e.g., NAEYC position papers; *Right from the Start,* a report of the National Association of State Boards of Education Task Force on Early Childhood Education; the National Association of Elementary School Principals; the National Association of Early Childhood Specialists in State Departments of Education) are linked to the public

schools and because public attention on early schooling has been so widespread. Most states are appropriating funds for state-initiated prekindergarten programs to provide for a "nursery through grade two or three" teaching certification or endorsement option. Along with Public Law 101–476, the Individuals with Disabilities Education Act (IDEA), which provides funds for serving young children with special needs in the public schools, these factors have focused attention on the role of public schools in early childhood education. Further underscoring this new focus was the 1990 position paper of the Southern Association on Children Under Six (now called the Southern Early Childhood Association) entitled *Continuity of Learning for Four- to Seven-Year-Old Children.*

Just a few years ago, Barbara Day, past president of the Association of Supervision and Curriculum Development, affirmed the need for developmentally appropriate early childhood programs in schools for children as young as three. Speaking at a special Phi Delta Kappa invitational symposium "Educational Issues in the Nineties," Day recommended that special early childhood units be established where "a small group of teachers is responsible for children four through eight years of age"—a clear acknowledgment of the need for refocusing on the primary years.

One interesting trend in several of these early childhood units involves primary-age children and their teacher allied together in cohort groups. In a cohort arrangement, teacher and children (perhaps children of mixed ages) work and learn together for two or more years. Remaining with one's teacher and one's group of age-mates for several years is, according to Berk and Winsler (1995), very much in keeping with the importance that Vygotsky placed on history and the significance of observing and appreciating the evolution of children's social interactions and relationships over an extended period of time.

A Child-Sensitive Curriculum

At the heart of the primary curriculum is a vision for early childhood education promoted by the Early Childhood Task Force of the National Association of State Boards of Education report *Right from the Start* (1988). The foundation of this vision is reflected in one of the major recommendations of the task force:

> Early childhood units should be established in elementary schools to provide a new pedagogy for working with children ages 4 to 8 and a focal point for enhanced services to preschool children and their parents. (p. 7)

According to Shultz and Lombardi (1989), the establishment of this **child-sensitive curriculum** reflects a belief in sound developmental principles: that learning occurs best when the focus is on the whole child; that learning for children and adults is interactive; that young children learn from concrete work and play, much of which is child-initiated; and that young children are profoundly influenced by their families and the surrounding community. The task force attached no particular magic to any specific orga-

nizational structure. Just as children and families are different, so no one type of program will be effective for every community. By establishing early childhood units, however, "public schools can put renewed emphasis on goals and practices that are more appropriate to the younger child and that respond to individual developmental differences and cultural and linguistic diversity" (Shultz & Lombardi, 1989, p. 8).

The context of primary education is grounded on broad understandings that are associated with the nature of four- to eight-year-old learners and their curriculum and that form the basis of planning curriculum, designing the learning environment, and implementing teaching strategies (see Figure 1.1).

From preschool through the primary years, the growth of children is continuous, and they require educational experiences that are equally continuous (Barbour & Seefeldt, 1993). Barbour and Seefeldt coined the term "developmental continuity" to describe this relationship. They mean that, throughout this period of early childhood, "one learning experience will build on another. A thread of meaning runs through a number of experiences. Experiences, activities,

FIGURE 1.1 Broad understandings about four- to eight-year-old learners and their curriculum

- Within this age-group, the profound influences of family and surrounding community are recognized.
- Children are making the transition from the intensely physical explorations of infancy and toddlerhood toward more abstract reasoning.
- Learning experiences are largely child oriented and holistic, addressing all domains of development (social, physical, intellectual, and emotional).
- This age-group has a wide range of interests and abilities. Most responsive to this diversity are curricula and teaching practices that are developmentally appropriate in accordance with NAEYC guidelines.
- Children in this age-group learn best when they are actively engaged in investigations with concrete materials.
- Learning experiences for these children are most effective when they connect in purposeful ways to real-life experiences.
- Children in this age-group acquire new understandings best when learning experiences begin with and extend children's existing knowledge.
- To clarify the meaning of their experiences, children in this age-group rely on language as a necessary tool for learning.

and lessons are juxtaposed to enable children to see connections between the past and the present, among and between people and the objects and events of their world" (p. 13).

In the primary years, the notion of developmental continuity is respected and a philosophical approach to helping young children learn that is child-sensitive, dedicated to the development of the whole child, and reflective of developmentally appropriate practices as advanced by the NAEYC (Bredekamp & Copple, 1997) is constituted.

Learning Environments
Responsive to All Children

In many ways, schools are a reflection of society, and as society becomes more culturally and linguistically diverse, so too will the schools. Therefore, curricula must respond to and value this diversity. Language and culture are significant aspects of children's development, and curricular practices cannot be developmentally appropriate, according to Bredekamp and Copple (1997), unless they are responsive to these components. Moreover, it is imperative that teachers enable children to find relevant and meaningful linkages between learning experiences in school and their lives outside school (Akran & Fields, 1997).

Approximately 10 to 12 percent of children entering kindergarten today have some kind of special need. The Americans with Disabilities Act and the Individuals with Disabilities Education Act require that early childhood programs provide reasonable access for children with developmental delays or disabilities. The Division for Early Childhood of the Council for Exceptional Children (1994) asserts, moreover, the increasingly accepted view that young children with special needs are best served in learning environments that serve their typically developing age-mates. While recognizing that the concept of full inclusion is one of the most challenging issues in education, we (the authors) promote the spirit and principles of full inclusion, as well as the concept of inclusion as a critical ingredient of the context of curriculum in the primary years.

In many communities across the country, children are confronted with overwhelming challenges on a daily basis (e.g., poverty, family dysfunction, violence). In countless towns and cities, discrimination, prejudice, intolerance of divergent points of view, and hatred prevail over attitudes of mutual respect and acceptance. Victimized because of the color of their skin, their beliefs, or their cultural values, many young children in these communities are coming to school disenchanted, demoralized, and defensive (Allison & DeCicco, 1997). By teachers treating every child as an important and valuable member of the community of learners, celebrating the richness that diversity among young learners instills in the class, and providing a haven in which each child's wounded spirits are soothed, trust replaces doubt, and hope overcomes despair.

The early period of learning (ages four through eight) poses special challenges because this is when children's attitudes toward "formal" school and learning are shaped. If learning experiences throughout this period respond to the uniquenesses among children, as well as to patterns of children's learning within this age-group, children are more likely to discover opportunities in school to succeed, to find fulfillment, and to enjoy their childhood.

NATURE OF THE
PRIMARY LEARNER

From the time they are born, children are persistently and actively searching for meaning and comprehension from all they experience. The understandings they acquire are influenced by the chronology and history of their experiences and by their sociocultural backgrounds. Also, the way and extent to which children are able to gather meaning from their experiences vary from child to child and vary within each child according to the different developmental stages through which each child progresses.

Work of Piaget

The most sophisticated theoretical perspective on the mental development and learning of young children is that advanced by the genetic epistemologist Jean Piaget. Although multiple theories of child development and learning have been formulated, many early childhood professionals have found Piaget's ideas about the nature of human knowledge to be comprehensive, pertinent, and elegantly reasoned; his contributions to the understanding of the young child are some of those that were drawn on to inform this book.

Piaget's original and provocative research regarding how children acquire knowledge was so compelling that it transformed the understanding of how young children think, learn, and develop. Piaget's contributions to the understanding of young children's mental development, in fact, represented what is known as a *paradigm shift*— a fundamental change in a professional community's way of thinking—because it helped profoundly alter educators' views of young learners and the nature of intellectual development.

According to DeVries and Kohlberg (1987), "the central theme of this paradigm is the view of the child as active in *constructing* not only knowledge, but intelligence itself" (p. xi).

Piaget's Stages of Cognitive Development. The Piagetian paradigm shift is associated with other developmental domains, as well as with the intellectual domain. Young children's mental growth "is inseparable from physical growth, and it is widely accepted that cognitive and affective or social development are inseparable and parallel" (Piaget & Inhelder, 1969, pp. vii, 117). Thus, although young children's social, emotional, physical, or cognitive growth and development may be uneven, with one area of development surging ahead of another at any given period of a child's life, the different domains of children's development, according to Barbour and Seefeldt (1993), cannot be viewed separately.

Piaget demonstrated that children's thinking and learning develop differentially and continuously according to a sequence of hierarchical stages (see Table 1.1). Throughout his works, Piaget illustrated how children progress from a less sophisticated stage to one that is

TABLE 1.1 Piaget's views of cognitive development

Stage	Description
Sensorimotor Birth to About Two Years	Knowledge is acquired and structured through sensory and motor interactions. Children must experience things firsthand and are unable to use language or symbols. Object permanence is acquired.
Preoperational Two Through About Seven Years	Knowledge is acquired and structured through use of symbols (e.g., language, having one object represent another). Children are intuitive rather than logical, and they are egocentric.
Concrete Operational Seven to About Twelve Years	Knowledge is acquired and structured logically, but children's understanding relies on experiences and interactions with tangible (concrete) objects and events. Children have difficulty with abstract concepts but are becoming less egocentric.
Formal Operational Early Adolescence and Older	Knowledge is acquired and structured logically, and children are able to understand complex, abstract positions and to test hypotheses.

more sophisticated as they mature and are afforded opportunities to interact with the environment. It is important to note, however, that development and learning among children are characterized by wide variability and do not occur in an easily predictable, uniform, or incremental fashion (NAEYC, 1990). Because learning does not occur in a rigid sequence of skill acquisition and because wide variability is the norm, schools for young children must be able to respond to a diverse range of abilities within any group of young children, and the curriculum in the early years "must provide meaningful contexts for children's learning rather than focusing primarily on isolated skill acquisition" (NAEYC, 1990, p. 22).

Piaget's Preoperational Stage. Most children in the primary years (ages four to eight) are in the preoperational period of thinking. Their thinking is characterized by a strong reliance on perception, rather than logic, as evidenced by the inability of children at this stage to recognize the stability of an amount of liquid when the container for the liquid is changed. As Barbour and Seefeldt (1993) acknowledge, it takes many experiences before children at this stage realize there is the same amount of milk in a tall, narrow glass as there is in a short, wide bowl even when the milk is poured from one container to another.

Primary-age children are more adept than younger children at considering more than one aspect of a problem and at considering an event from the point of view of someone else. They are becoming increasingly skilled in the ability to classify objects on the basis of multiple attributes, just as they are in the ability to seriate objects—to order objects on the basis of some attribute, such as weight or roughness of texture. This is also a time when children are able to master "reversibility"—the ability to contemplate a series of events or functions and then to understand that the operation can be undone, or "reversed." They can grasp, for example, that subtraction can "undo" addition.

Four- to eight-year-olds are also growing in ability to use symbols and imagery, as reflected in their rapid growth in language. As profoundly important as their rapid growth in language is the astonishing richness of their play: It is dynamic, complex, inventive, and frequently passionate. Much of their thinking, however, is still bound to the real world. They still do not have the mental dexterity to think hypothetically or to compare the ideal with the actual (Lefrancois, 1989). Because children's learning is governed throughout early childhood by preoperational thinking, children will most likely learn best through "interactions as a result of their own social, mental and physical activity; continuity of integrated experiences; and using language in conjunction with reflection" (Barbour & Seefeldt, 1993, p. 12).

Piaget's Concepts of Adaptation and Equilibration. As the demands of the environment change, so must children's ability to deal with them—a process known as **adaptation.** Piaget proposed two processes (**assimilation** and **accommodation**) to explain how knowledge is created and changed over time (how an individual adapts). *Assimilation* refers to the process by which a person takes in information from the environment and incorporates it into an existing knowledge structure, what Piaget called a "scheme." A three-year-old who is familiar with airplanes, for example, can be said to have an "airplane" scheme, which may include loud, winged, fast-moving machines that move like birds in the sky. On seeing a helicopter for the first time, the child may call it an airplane because that's the most appropriate scheme the child has. As the child has opportunities to see more helicopters, begins to discover how they're different from airplanes, and acquires a label for them, he or she develops a separate scheme for helicopters. This process of creating new schemes or modifying old ones is called *accommodation.*

Taken together, assimilation and accommodation constitute the two subcategories of a process called **equilibration**—the child's continual process of cognitive self-correction, whose goal is a better sense of equilibrium (Krogh, 1994). Equilibration—the essence of the constructive process—is fundamental to learning, and it is "fueled" by the child's interest. In Piaget's view, the element of interest is the affective aspect that intervenes constantly in a child's intellectual functioning (DeVries & Kohlberg, 1987).

Sociocultural Theory of Lev Vygotsky

Along with the work of Piaget, the work of Russian developmental psychologist Lev Vygotsky, an early contemporary of Piaget, provides the theoretical underpinnings for the creation of a constructivist classroom community. Vygotsky advanced an innovative theory that acknowledged the importance of social and cultural experience in young children's development. In Vygotsky's sociocultural theory, social experience shapes the way individuals think about and interpret the world. One's mind, in a sense, is thus "socially formed." Because language is the major avenue by which social experience is represented, it serves a crucial role in the facilitation of thought. An essential construct of Vygotsky's theory is that sophisticated levels of children's thinking are "jointly constructed and transferred to children through dialogues with other people" (Berk, 1994, p. 30).

In recent years, new ways of helping children learn through interactions with others have been stimulated as a result of Vygotsky's ideas. These new approaches rely closely on the Vygotskian concept of the **zone of proximal development.** The zone of proximal development is "the distance between the actual developmental level as determined by independent problem solving and the level of potential development as determined through problem solving under adult guidance or in collaboration with more capable peers" (Vygotsky, 1978, p. 96). The zone of proximal development refers to a host of intellectual

Children's higher levels of thinking are constructed and extended through interactions with others.

pursuits that a child is as yet unable to handle independently but can master with the help of adults and more skilled peers. According to Berk (1992), as children engage in cooperative "dialogues" with more mature learning partners, they internalize the language of these interactions and use it to organize their independent efforts in similar fashion.

A major tenet of sociocultural theory is the notion of **scaffolding,** whereby assistance from supportive adults creates a framework for guiding children's learning, which is essential for their cognitive and psychological development. In the following examples, the interconnectedness between the concepts of zone of proximal development and scaffolding is illustrated:

Example 1. While playing outdoors, a small group of five-year-olds invites their student teacher, Ms. Laker, to join them in playing "space explorers." The student teacher accepts, asking, "Who can I be?" After conferring for a moment, the children decide that Ms. Laker can be an alien. "Let's get her, Rangers!" one child exclaims, and the children begin chasing Ms. Laker around the playground. While eluding the children, she determines that this relatively shallow level of run-and-chase play might be elevated if the children would consider an additional theme or two in the scenario. She feigns exhaustion and permits herself to be captured. The children must ponder where the "prisoner" is to be held and what she is to be fed. A bit later, the prisoner decides to attempt an escape and is "injured" while being recaptured. This unexpected turn of events requires that some of the children escort the prisoner to the "hospital" and to attend to her injuries. The remaining space explorers busy themselves building a space station and supplying it with scientific equipment.

Example 2. When Rondel's teacher, Ms. Sawyer, encouraged him to bring in a gift he received for his birthday to share with the other six-year-olds, Rondel brought his new football helmet. After talking about the colors and design on the helmet and telling about his favorite college football team, Rondel paused to see whether anyone had any questions to ask. One child wanted to know who Rondel's favorite college player was. Another asked him what position he liked to play. Before Rondel returned to his seat, Ms. Sawyer asked him to tell about the plastic bar across the front of the helmet and the pieces of padding inside the helmet. Rondel replied that the bar was "to keep your face from getting smooshed," and he thought the padding was there "so the helmet would fit smooth." Ms. Sawyer thanked Rondel and offered the other children an opportunity to share what they thought were the purposes of the bar and the padding on the helmet. Following a few minutes of lively discussion, the children agreed that the purposes of the additions to the helmet included

(1) making it fit better, (2) making it look good, and (3) making it safer to play football in.

Later that same day, Ms. Sawyer helped the children arrange themselves in groups of three and discuss other examples they could think of in which people wore or used special clothing or equipment for safety reasons. She asked the children to begin making a list of jobs or tasks around their homes for which family members made use of special safety clothes or equipment. Over a period of several weeks, the children were encouraged to work with each other and with members of their families to discover different occupations that involved the use of safety clothes or equipment. One activity in this unit provided the children with an opportunity to "invent" some useful but hazardous occupations and then to design, illustrate, and write short stories about safety clothes or equipment that might be used to make the occupations safer.

Example 3. The eight-year-olds in Mr. Toler's music class enjoyed inventing and moving to different musical themes, varying their tempo and rhythmic patterns according to their interpretations of the music being played. After a few days of exploring different ways of moving to the accompaniment of different types of music, Mr. Toler invited the children to consider other structural forms in their movement interpretations: "Can you move in different space than you've tried before?" "Can you move in low space or high space?" "How might it feel to move without your feet touching the floor?" "What's it like to move while remaining in contact with at least one other friend?" "How might it look if your movement 'partner' were a colorful streamer, a cape, or large balloon?"

Role of the Teacher

In each of these examples, adult-child (and sometimes child-child) dialogues played a crucial role in creating a context, a framework, a scaffold that enabled the children to extend their behavior and understandings. The teachers' questions and suggestions led to further information or helped the children form additional connections. The teachers served as *mediators* of childhood experiences and interactions. Teacher *communication* was sensitively adjusted to the children's momentary progress, offering the necessary assistance for more sophisticated interaction while prompting the children to embrace more responsibility for tasks as their understanding, skill, and imagination increased.

In the first example, Ms. Laker's subtle and insightful prompts enabled the children to transform the level of play from a relatively shallow run-and-chase activity to a sophisticated level of sociodramatic play rich in representational potential. In the next example, Ms. Sawyer engaged her six-year-olds in a set of cooperative learning experiences from which they were able to move from an understanding about clothing that was in large measure either comfort- or cosmetic-based to a deeper understanding about the functional or safety aspects of items sometimes worn at work or play. In the third example, Mr. Toler was able to communicate a few simple notions to his inventive children as they explored novel and multiple levels of complexity in their music/movement interpretations.

A Vygotskian-based approach to facilitating cognitive and psychological development requires that teachers "tailor" their intervention to children's current capacities and use techniques that help children regulate their own behavior while constructing new meanings. To implement intervention in this way, teachers must acquire a depth of understanding of individual children's skills and abilities and use a range of teaching strategies because the support that is appropriate for scaffolding varies from child to child. At times, the teacher may model a skill or give the child examples of strategies (e.g., "You might tell Matea, 'I'm sorry I hurt your feelings' "). At other times, the teacher may ask the child to engage in problem solving (e.g., "What could you do that might help Matea feel bet-

ter?"). In each instance, according to Berk (1994), the teacher selects a level of support that best matches the child's abilities and momentary needs and then pulls back as the child acquires new insights and skills.

The role of the teacher in a child-sensitive, constructivist, primary learning environment is outlined in a model of learning and teaching that was a feature of the *Guidelines for Appropriate Curriculum Content and Assessment in Programs Serving Children Ages 3 Through 8* (NAEYC & NAECS/SDE, 1991). As demonstrated in this model (Table 1.2), the role of the teacher is very much associated with (and responsive to) young children's behavioral cues.

CHILDREN'S CONSTRUCTION OF KNOWLEDGE

Driven by natural curiosity, children put enormous amounts of time and energy into investigating whatever environments in which they find themselves. They are natural anthropologists, linguists, and scientists, and according to Lilian Katz (1993), children naturally generate explanations and hypotheses to explain what they observe. Fueled by a boundless interest in things around them, children are in constant pursuit of understanding, of knowing. In their attempts to make sense of the world, children *mean* to mean; that is, their *intention* is to make sense. The ways children apply themselves to the process of discovering meaning in their experiences is at the heart of the theory of **constructivism**—the view that much of learning originates from *inside* the child.

In their efforts to find or build or construct meaning, children often arrive at less than fully accurate understandings; in those moments, the "misconceptions" *mean something:* They hold meaning for the children. From the constructivist point of view, little is completely misunderstood or, perhaps, fully understood. Understanding is viewed as a continually evolving process by

TABLE 1.2 Model of learning and teaching

What Children Do	What Teachers Do
Awareness	
Experience	Create the environment
Acquire an interest	Provide opportunities by introducing new objects, events, people
Recognize broad parameters	Invite interest in posing problem or question
Attend	Respond to children's interest or shared experience
Perceive	Show interest, enthusiasm
Elaboration	
Observe	Facilitate
Explore materials	Support and enhance exploration
Collect information	Provide opportunities for active exploration
Discover	Extend play
Figure out components	Describe children's activity
Construct own understanding	Ask open-ended questions, "What else could you do?"
Apply own rules	Respect child's thinking and rule systems
Create personal meaning	Allow for constructive error
Inquiry	
Examine	Help children refine understanding
Investigate	Guide children, focus attention
Propose explanations	Ask more focused questions, "What else works like this?" "What happens if . . . ?"
Focus	
Compare own thinking with that of others	Provide information when requested, "How do you spell . . . ?"
Generalize	Help children make connections
Relate to prior learning	
Adjust to conventional rule systems	
Utilization	
Use the learning in many ways; learning becomes functional	Create vehicles for application in the real world
Represent learning in various ways	Help children apply to new situations
Apply to new situations	Provide meaningful situations to use learning
Formulate new hypotheses and repeat cycle	

Source: Reprinted by permission from "Guidelines for Appropriate Curriculum Content and Assessment in Programs Serving Children Ages 3 Through 8:" [NAEYC Position Statement], *Young Children, 46*(3):36. Copyright © 1991 by the National Association for the Education of Young Children (NAEYC).

which a person proceeds from less accurate levels of "knowing" to more accurate levels (Taylor, 1996). A child's every new experience represents a quest of sorts, a quest for meaning and understanding. It would be fair to say that any methods aimed at stimulating children's constructive processes should, first, arouse children's spontaneous interest.

Learning is an *interactive process*—involving children's active engagement with the environment and with others. Children continually engage themselves in, and try to organize, experiences cognitively, whether social interactions with others or sensory experiences with objects. Through countless experiences involving interactions with others and with materials, children construct their own understanding (Piaget, 1952). The fact that they possess so many ideas they did not learn from adults is evidence that children construct knowledge (DeVries & Kohlberg, 1987). The "errors" or "incorrect" ideas (from an adult's point of view) reflect children's developing attempts to gather meaning based on their own experiences. The following vignette illustrates the attempt of a young child to construct meaning based on limited experience:

When four-year-old Valencia inquires after completing her first helping of pork chops, "Is there any more chicken left, please?" she demonstrates her construction of knowledge. No one has told her that the meat her family is enjoying for supper is pork chops. From her limited experience, she defines white meat that is kind of golden and crispy on the outside as chicken. As she continues over some period of time to enjoy servings of chicken at some meals and servings of pork chops at other meals, Valencia will come to understand that the two meat dishes are in some way different and that family members use different names to distinguish between the two.

For all children, ideas, objects, relationships, and experiences become meaningful because of the *interpretation the child gives them*. Some key points of the constructivist approach to

FIGURE 1.2 Some key points of the constructivist approach

- Children have many choices about the topics they investigate and about the direction and pace of their investigations.
- The pursuit of understanding is an active, ongoing process of engagement.
- Children gather information themselves, interpret it, and search for connections to prior knowledge and prior experiences.
- Children's learning is subjective (they make constant attempts to find meaning to their own lives) and nonlinear (not anchored to a prerequisite sequence of basic skills).
- Cooperation and collaboration are emphasized.
- Metacognitive processes are emphasized—important consideration to reflection, self-assessment, self-regulation; a concern for "what we did," "why," and "could we do it better?"
- The importance of affect is advanced; children learn to care for each other while having fun.

learning are highlighted in Figure 1.2. Knowledge that young children acquire through active engagement in these processes is most likely to stay with them for a very long while.

According to Bredekamp and Rosegrant (1992), when objects and events do not conform to the understandings that a child has mentally constructed, the child must revise the understandings or alter the mental structures to account for the new information. Throughout childhood, these mental structures are continually being reshaped, expanded, and reorganized by new experiences. The early childhood professional can facilitate young children's more refined understanding of their world by providing them with numerous real-life challenges and experiences to ponder for themselves so that they can discover inconsistencies and contradictions between their understanding and reality.

In primary classrooms in which a constructivist philosophical orientation prevails, curriculum and assessment are joined in the advancement of learning experiences that are dynamic, child-sensitive, and filled with purpose. In constructivist learning environments, the various strengths and contributions of all children are recognized, regardless of developmental differences or differences in background or culture. According to Matsumoto and Shironaka (1995), a constructivist classroom is one in which curriculum flows from children's experiences and the emphasis is on optimizing the amount of understanding children construct from the experiences they are provided. In this way, children become what Matsumoto and Shironaka call "autonomous inquirers," as well as independent learners.

NATURE OF THE PRIMARY CURRICULUM

I am not interested in a student's IQ. I am interested in his or her current understanding and what can be done to enhance it. No human understands everything; every human being understands some things. Education should strive to improve understanding as much as possible, whatever the student's proclivities and potential might be. (Gardner, 1994, p. 564)

Curriculum in early childhood is "a way of helping teachers think about children and organize the child's experiences" in the learning environment (Weikart, 1989, p. 27). Moreover, it is the curriculum teachers select and use that helps children make connections between themselves and the world. Curriculum is what happens in a learning environment, and planning for it involves ongoing observation of the children, planning for their learning, creating a climate that will facilitate learning, evaluating

the effectiveness and appropriateness of learning experiences, reflecting on what took place, and deciding how to proceed next.

Curriculum That Is Appropriate

In recent years, discussions about what type of curriculum is most appropriate for young children have focused on two major questions:

1. What do young children *need* to know (or what are the things they ought to learn)?

2. What are young children *capable* of knowing?

The underlying perspective of the first question directs one's attention to those philosophical, political, cultural, and moral issues and values that society deems important to transmit to each new generation of learners. According to Kessler (1991), for example, examining what being an American or living in a democracy means may serve as a basis for developing early childhood curricula. An appropriate curriculum based on these issues may provide opportunities for children to live democratically in the miniature world of the classroom, as John Dewey advocated.

At the heart of the second question are issues associated with the developmental level of the child; a keen understanding of child development becomes, by implication, a major determinant of the curriculum. A measure of an appropriate curriculum in this context would examine whether the content of the curriculum, for example, is too complex or abstract or trivial or disconnected from children's lives on the basis of the children's prior experiences, interests, and level of understanding. Thus, for a group of six-year-olds from suburban Colorado, planning some learning experiences around a trip to a farm or ranch as a way to appreciate the importance of the agricultural industry in that state would be more appropriate than addressing the causes of the Russian Revolution.

Bredekamp (1991) suggests that the common goal shared by proponents of both of these broad perspectives of improving curriculum and instruction for all young children will be most effectively achieved when the philosophies of both camps are joined. Likewise, Shannon (1990) acknowledges that real curriculum reform can result if proponents of these two perspectives on curriculum design come together. He cites five areas of agreement the proponents of these two positions share that provide the basis for consensus and for successful advocacy for curriculum improvement:

1. The understanding that profound and important differences exist between the social world and the physical world
2. The definition of how children learn
3. Concern for self-actualization through education
4. The importance of language in knowing and self-actualization
5. The fact that education must be based on experience

Toward the realization of combining the ideologies of the two camps discussed here, NAEYC, in conjunction with NAECS/SDE, developed *Guidelines for Appropriate Curriculum Content and Assessment in Programs Serving Children Ages 3 Through 8* (1991). In these guidelines, curriculum content (what children are to learn), learning processes (how children learn), instructional strategies (how to teach), environment (the learning context), and assessment strategies (how to know that learning has occurred and what curricular adjustments are needed) are all interrelated and constitute the education program for young children. Several key concepts from the curricular guidelines have been identified by Bredekamp and Rosegrant (1992) as essential for achieving "meaningfulness"—building conceptual development and deep understanding (see Figure 1.3).

According to Bredekamp and Rosegrant (1992), meaningful curriculum results from thoughtful planning and organization that draws

FIGURE 1.3 Key concepts essential to achieving meaningfulness in the curriculum

1. Conceptual organizers or other integrated, meaning-centered approaches (e.g., themes, units, projects)
2. Child development knowledge (normative information relevant to the cognitive, socioemotional, language, and physical domains)
3. The knowledge base of the subject-matter disciplines (e.g., science, social studies, mathematics, language arts, health, physical education, the arts)
4. The continuum of development and learning, both hypothetical and actual, of the children in the group . . . or more narrowly prescribed

Source: Reprinted by permission from S. Bredekamp and T. Rosegrant, *Reaching Potentials: Appropriate Curriculum and Assessment for Young Children,* Vol. 1. (Washington, DC: NAEYC, 1992), 66–67. Copyright © 1992 by the National Association for the Education of Young Children (NAEYC).

on at least these four concepts. Each of these concepts brings important information to the curriculum that should not be neglected.

Curriculum That Is Integrated

Although the goal of curriculum planning is meaningfulness, the strategy, according to Bredekamp and Rosegrant (1992), is **integrated curriculum.**

> During early childhood the concept of integration derives from the integrated nature of development—what happens in one developmental dimension, such as physical growth, inevitably influences other dimensions of development, such as cognitive and social development. For example, as the child acquires mobility, (the child) is exposed to a broader range of objects and interpersonal interactions, which in turn enhance (the individual's) cognition and support

language and social development. The interrelatedness of developmental domains, especially in very young children, virtually dictates an integrated approach to programming. (p. 37)

Efforts to integrate curriculum should unfold naturally and effortlessly and should be "open," rather than limiting. If a relationship between two topics is not natural, do not force it; everything does not have to relate to a specific theme or topic. At the same time, teachers should understand that basic skills development does not need to be neglected in integrated curriculum approaches. Children may not be expected to learn basic computational skills from creating, writing, and solving their own mathematics problems. The difference is that computational skills are integrated with writing and the numerous problem-solving process skills; the expectation of mastery is given later priority. In any event, curriculum for young children must provide *meaningful contexts* for children's learning, rather than focus primarily on isolated skill acquisition.

In an interview with the authors of an article addressing how young children learn, Lilian Katz described two different classes she had the opportunity to visit. In one class, children spent the entire morning making identical pictures of traffic lights. No attempt was made to relate the pictures to anything else the class was doing. In the other class, children were investigating a school bus. They wrote to the district and asked whether a bus could be parked in their school parking lot for a few days. They studied it, figured out what all the parts were for, and talked about traffic rules. Then, in the classroom, they built their own bus out of cardboard. The children had fun, but they also practiced writing, problem solving, some arithmetic, and cooperation (Kantrowitz & Wingert, 1989, p. 310).

Curriculum That Is Meaningful

Throughout integrated curriculum approaches, skills and concepts are connected to the pur-

poses, models, and larger perspectives that make them meaningful. In this way, skills and concepts are woven into a grand tapestry of flexible and functional knowledge—the big picture. This is why early childhood professionals should devote themselves to helping children discover (or "transfer") how things relate to one another. *Transfer*—how learners actually use knowledge and information—is one of the most significant outcomes of education. If children cannot make the transfer from what they are experiencing in school to life, then teachers haven't been successful in helping them make the connections they should be able to make.

Several curriculum models provide a focus on curriculum integration (problem-based learning; whole language; cooperative learning; project method; the Reggio Emilia progressive, extended project approach; curriculum for democratic living; High/Scope's plan-do-review cycle; and teacher-child interaction system, child-centered/developmental). Whether teachers adopt one of these or some other model or design one from scratch, it will ultimately be idiosyncratic—unique to a particular group of children and teacher(s) in a particular environment. Because the curriculum in many ways flows from a dynamic social milieu, prescribing a curriculum that will generalize imitatively from one context to another is inconsistent with developmentally appropriate curriculum planning (Cassidy & Lancaster, 1993).

Despite the diversity of curriculum models that emphasize integration constructs, some common components shared by most integration models can be identified, as shown in Figure 1.4. Integrative classroom learning experiences that reflect these features are dynamic, child-sensitive, and intellectually liberating. Curriculum grounded on these features is not represented by chopped-up, thirty- to forty-minute-long, bite-sized, unconnected facts that have little relationship to children's lives.

FIGURE 1.4 Common components of models of curriculum integration

- The curriculum is not bound to a text or guide, or a particular sequence (curriculum freedom).
- Activities build on information across disciplines and across content areas.
- Some degree of team teaching is usually practiced.
- Children are often organized on the basis of multiage or multiability.
- The environment and the learning experiences are characterized by novelty and excitement.
- Time is flexible; learning experiences are not restricted to 45- to 50-minute increments.
- Collaborative partnerships with other teachers, with administrators, and with community representatives are featured.

TRANSFORMATIONAL CURRICULUM

From these descriptions of integrated curriculum processes, it is clear that the learning experiences that take place in developmentally appropriate primary classrooms are dynamic, exciting, and meaningful. As changes in young learners occur, it might also be expected that changes in the curriculum would take place. To the extent that children are involved in the planning, implementation, and assessment phases of learning experiences, the curriculum can be described as being a **transformational curriculum**—"not only does a curriculum change the learner but the learner also affects and changes the curriculum" (Bredekamp & Rosegrant, 1992, p. 70). The transformational nature of the curriculum is also illustrated by the adaptations a teacher makes in the curriculum in response to changes in needs and interests of children in relation to initial curricular goals.

Fundamentally, if simplistically, teachers may measure the success of a learning experience on the extent to which the learner was able to take from it more than what he or she brought to it. The perspectives, concepts, and visions examined thus far enable educators to appreciate how important a sort of synchrony is between the nature of the young learner in the primary years and the nature of the curriculum. When the learning experiences that flow from the curriculum are "in step," so to speak, with the needs, interests, and abilities of the child, a kind of perfect dance ensues. These "dances" then become the source of relevant connections, greater understanding, and deeper, more meaningful levels of individual child growth.

Sticking with the metaphor of a dance or rhythmic interchange between the needs, interests, and abilities of the child and developmentally appropriate learning experiences, one might wonder who is orchestrating this scenario? Who brings these two fundamental bases of curricular decision making together? How are they brought together? Under what circumstances are they most likely to remain together? To these questions we now turn our attention.

ROLE OF THE TEACHER

According to Katz (1993), the central role of teachers is "helping children acquire interest in worthwhile topics and in setting the stage for children to explore and investigate topics worthy of their close attention and deeper understanding" (p. 2). In fulfilling this role, the teacher must be an evaluator, organizer, stimulator (or facilitator), and collaborator. This fourfold conception of the teacher's role is explained in further detail by DeVries and Kohlberg (1987):

> As an evaluator, the teacher must have solid psychological knowledge of the child and mental development in order to understand and assess children's spontaneous procedures, which otherwise might appear a waste of time. Then, the

implementation of a program in accordance with this psychological knowledge requires not only skills in selecting and organizing activities, and in intervening to stimulate children's reasoning, but also the ability to establish an egalitarian relationship with children and to be a companion as well as a guiding mentor. (p. 35)

It would be a mistake to conclude that teaching in a child-sensitive, constructivist setting means that the teacher has no role to play or that children should be afforded unlimited freedom to work or play on their own. NAEYC's *Position Statement on School Readiness* (1990) asserts that teachers must know how to plan and implement a developmentally appropriate curriculum that emphasizes child-initiated learning experiences, small-group activities, integrated lessons, and active, hands-on learning with a variety of materials and activities.

Teacher as Mentor and Mediator

As young learners undertake the challenges of constructing their own meaning from learning experiences and relationships, the role most properly taken by the teacher is that of a *mediator*. Instead of lecturing or transmitting ready-made solutions, the teacher patiently and thoughtfully guides children through activities that promise them opportunities for new insights and discoveries. Piaget (1948/1973) remarked that the teacher is needed "to provide counter-examples that compel reflection and reconsideration of over-hasty solutions." He added that the teacher's role "should be that of a *mentor* stimulating initiative and research" (p. 16). Some responsibilities of a teacher in a constructivist learning environment are presented in Figure 1.5.

In a constructivist classroom, the curriculum is not content, but rather an infusion of content information along with process skill development. The teacher's role as a mentor and mediator is crucial. By his or her design and coordination of all the elements involved in the educational process (materials, activities and experiences, assessments, allocation of time, classroom structure, management

FIGURE 1.5 Responsibilities of the teacher in a constructivist classroom

- To be familiar with individual children's needs, strengths, and passions
- To maintain a climate characterized by warm, responsive communication
- To equip the classroom with a rich variety of drawing, writing, and reading materials as a way to facilitate frequent communication
- To plan activities that can be extended in a host of ways through purposeful dialogue between teacher and child and among the children themselves
- To monitor and accurately assess the progress of individual children's insights and abilities
- To provide ample cultural tools (e.g., alphabet and number symbols, writing and drawing materials, reading materials, examples of environmental print, a variety of play props) and to convey the importance and excitement of their regular use
- To incorporate a variety of teaching strategies (e.g., modeling, questioning that leads to further information or that helps form additional connections, use of graduated levels of difficulty of materials, planning for multiple levels of complexity on all activities)
- To provide scaffolding of information whereby the teacher helps the child acquire knowledge or a skill that the child cannot acquire alone
- To facilitate the use of peer tutors in interactions throughout the day

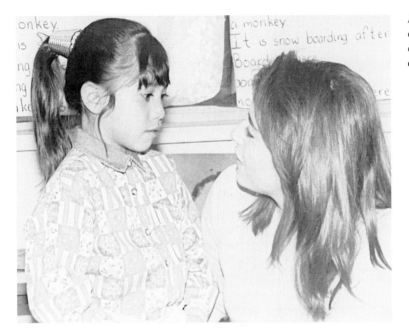

A caring relationship between child and teacher is the basis for creating meaningful learning experiences.

techniques, mediating strategies, classroom climate), the teacher creates an environment for living and learning that is both meaningful and ennobling. In such classrooms, children's minds are stretched and their sensibilities heightened; children's lives are enriched and fulfilled.

Teacher as Person

In many instances, the profession of teaching is unrealistically perceived by children, parents, and other community members as an almost exalted station in life. Perhaps this is because education (and thus teachers, who are the embodiment of this important enterprise) is often perceived as the pathway to success in life. In other words, many share the belief that to be successful in life, one must first be successful in school. To the extent that there is some truth to this notion, much faith and hope are placed in teachers and in the teaching profession.

In primary classrooms in which collaboration, shared decision making, and mutual respect between children and teacher prevail, the teacher is perceived as being simply (but importantly) human, rather than artificial, aloof, and inaccessible. When teachers are confident enough to reveal to children and parents that teachers are human—that they possess weaknesses, strengths, and emotions just as everyone else does—they help establish a basis for building caring relationships that are authentic and lasting. These caring relationships, in turn, are the basis for creating truly meaningful, treasured learning experiences. According to Ruenzel (1996), children who desire to learn *with us* want to gaze into our eyes and see *us* there. Children are looking for a collaborative adult learning "partner" made of flesh and who, like them, has feelings.

IMPORTANCE OF PLAY

Play is the most profoundly important enterprise of young children. As a rich, personal,

FIGURE 1.6 Some values of play

Emotional

Acts as a medium for expressing thoughts and feelings
Softens the realities of the world
Serves as a risk-free environment
Releases children's stress
Decreases children's anxiety
Builds well-being and self-concept

Physical

Motor development
Balancing of systems
Body command
Distance judgment
Hand-eye coordination
Testing of bodies
Self-assurance

Cognitive

Abstract thought
Divergent thinking
Creativity
Problem solving
Concept development
Perspective taking
Language development

Social

Decentering
Practicing social patterns
Encouraging social interaction
Learning to get along

Source: Data from "Wanted: Advocates for Play in the Primary Grades" by Sandra J. Stone, Ed. D., in *Young Children, 50*(6), 45–54. (Copyright 1995 by Sandra Stone. Reprinted by permission of Sandra J. Stone.)

and broadly effective medium by which learning can occur, the critical part that play should hold in the primary curriculum cannot be overemphasized. In addition, play also provides teachers with a basis for observing and assessing children's learning and behavior. Understanding the importance of play and how to facilitate play for all children is one hallmark of an insightful, child-sensitive primary teacher.

Most children in the primary years are capable of engaging in play at different levels, including the highest levels: dramatic and **sociodramatic play.** These levels of play are characterized by the player's ability to interact with objects and other children representationally, or symbolically. This means a child is able to use an object in the "real" world and conceive of a signifier, or symbol. For example, a child playing at a sand table may stick a plastic spoon into a mound of sand and, disregarding its actual function, use it as a light-house or a candle on a cake. At whatever level they are engaged, all children benefit from play.

In addition to helping children make sense of the world, play helps them develop social and cultural understanding and provides an avenue through which they can express thoughts and feelings (Isenberg & Jalongo, 1997). The relevance of play in the primary grades and its association with children's adjustment and school success is illustrated by some values of play (see Figure 1.6) identified by Stone (1995).

Even if play held no benefits for children other than the enjoyment it affords them, it would be worth including in the curriculum for the primary years. Given the host of other benefits for children's physical, psychological, and intellectual development, assertion of play's rightful place as an indelible feature of a child-sensitive primary curriculum merits the strongest support.

REFLECTIONS ON DIVERSITY

It is important for the primary teacher to remember that children have widely diverse experiences before entering school and that this will result in a wide range of possibilities regarding any particular child being at any particular level or point of development at a given age. Factors that may affect experiences include culture, gender, ethnicity, economic circumstances, disabilities, and the totality of experiences a child may have. When developmental levels are discussed in relationship to age, caution must be exercised. Specific, age-related levels may not be true for all children.

All children are learners. Many come to the classroom with understandings and information different from those expected by a traditional curriculum. Many learn at different rates. Some have hidden and puzzling learning disabilities. Some have obvious disabilities. Some have challenging behaviors. Some have a chronic illness. Some are abused and neglected. Some live in poverty. Some have a dominant language other than English. Regardless of these differences, they are children first.

The phrase "good teaching is good teaching" appears to be true. Many specialized teaching methods for children with special needs are often extensions and refinements of core teaching behaviors and skills (Ysseldyke & Algozzine, 1990). The "special" in "special education" does not refer to strange or unique methodologies, but to the specialization of instructional procedures employed to meet the needs of a specific learner. The child-sensitive primary curriculum allows teachers to plan learning activities that can meet the needs of all children on the basis of what the children *know,* rather than what they don't know; on the basis of who they *are,* rather than on who they are not.

A Learning Environment
Accepting of All Children

Creating an environment conducive to learning is a major responsibility of the teacher. In an environment in which all children are valued, in

In a child-sensitive classroom, all children are *valued* for who they are and for how they enrich the entire community of learners.

which the purposeful contributions of all children are accepted, and in which the teacher shares reciprocal, mutually respectful relationships with all children, children will feel free to make choices, take risks, question, love, and accept responsibility for much of their own learning. If teachers obligate themselves to knowing each child in their classrooms (each child's abilities, interests, fears, and passions) and then act on that knowledge by providing the richest, most responsive learning environment possible, the learning will be meaningful and long-lasting for each child.

Life can be difficult and even cruel for children who are perceived to be different in some way from most other children. Teachers will be honored by the presence in their classrooms of children who hope to find a sanctuary from the stares, the stigma, the ridicule, and the condescension to which they often find themselves subjected. In Mimi Brodsky Chenfeld's words, they, too, are gathered "in that starlit field where teachers shine" (1993, p. 75). Perhaps the best measure of teachers' success is the extent to which all children feel as fully included as possible in the experiences to be found in their classroom communities.

SUMMARY

In this chapter, the nature of the primary curriculum was introduced. We looked at the importance of responding to the common social, emotional, and educational needs of children from four to eight years of age. We also noted the profound influence of the theories of Piaget and Vygotsky on the early childhood profession. Overviews of the essential tenets of these theories provided a developmental perspective on the primary learner. In addition, the constructivist philosophy grounded on these theories let us see the young learner as being actively engaged in searching for meaning in interactions with others and with objects.

The natural integration of the curriculum for children in the primary age range was seen as a way to help children make connections between what is new to them and what they already know. Curriculum integration was also seen as a way to help the teacher associate classroom experiences with children's daily lives. Last, the crucial role of the teacher as an active mentor, a sensitive mediator, and an engaging communicator was advanced.

In subsequent chapters, many of these themes are reinforced and expanded. In particular, the focus on the role of the teacher in specific educational contexts is continual. The chapters that follow also continue to include ongoing attempts to develop a greater understanding of young learners in the primary years.

REFERENCES

Akran, S., & Fields, M. (1997). Family and cultural context: A writing breakthrough? *Young Children, 52*(4), 37–40.

Allison, J., & DeCicco, E. (1997). Creating an antidote to Beavis and Butthead: Urban young adolescents building a culture of achievement. *Childhood Education, 73*(5), 305–308.

Barbour, N., & Seefeldt, C. (1993). *Developmental continuity across preschool and primary grades.* Wheaton, MD: Association of Childhood Education International.

Berk, L. (1992). Children's private speech: An overview of theory and the status of research. In R. Diaz & L. Berk (Eds.), *Private speech: From social interaction to self-regulation* (pp. 17–53). Hillsdale, NJ: Erlbaum.

Berk, L. (1994). Vygotsky's theory: The importance of make believe. *Young Children, 50*(1), 30–39.

Berk, L., & Winsler, A. (1995). *Scaffolding children's learning: Vygotsky and early childhood education.* Washington, DC: National Association for the Education of Young Children.

Bredekamp, S. (1991). Redeveloping early childhood education: A response to Kessler. *Early Childhood Research Quarterly, 6*(2), 199–209.

Bredekamp, S., & Copple, C. (Eds.). (1997). *Developmentally appropriate practices in early childhood programs* (Rev. ed.). Washington, DC: National Association for the Education of Young Children.

Bredekamp, S., & Rosegrant, T. (Eds.). (1992). *Reaching potentials: Appropriate curriculum and assessment for young children* (Vol. 1). Washington, DC: National Association for the Education of Young Children.

Cassidy, D., & Lancaster, C. (1993). The grassroots curriculum: A dialogue between children and teachers. *Young Children, 48*(6), 47–51.

Chenfeld, M. B. (1993). *Teaching in the key of life.* Washington, DC: National Association for the Education of Young Children.

DeVries, R., & Kohlberg, L. (1987). *Programs of early education: The constructivist view.* White Plains, NY: Longman.

Division for Early Childhood (DEC) of the Council for Exceptional Children (CEC). (1994). Position on inclusion. *Young Children, 49*(5), 78.

Gardner, H. (1994). In J. Siegel & M. Shaughnessy, Educating for understanding: An interview with Howard Gardner. *Phi Delta Kappan, 75*(7), 563–566.

Isenberg, J., & Jalongo, M. (1997). *Creative expression and play in early childhood.* Upper Saddle River, NJ: Merrill/Prentice Hall.

Kantrowitz, B., & Wingert, P. (1989). How kids learn. *Young Children, 44*(6), 310.

Katz, L. (1993). Child-sensitive curriculum and teaching. *Young Children, 48*(6), 2.

Kessler, S. (1991). Alternative perspectives on early childhood education. *Early Childhood Research Quarterly, 6*(2), 183–197.

Krogh, S. (1994). *Educating young children: Infancy to grade three.* New York: McGraw-Hill.

Lefrancois, T. (1989). *Of children: An introduction to child development* (6th ed.). Belmont, CA: Wadsworth.

Martin, A. (1985). Back to kindergarten basics. *Harvard Education Review, 55*(3), 22–25.

Matsumoto, J., & Shironaka, W. (1995). Letting go: Allowing first-graders to become autonomous learners. *Young Children, 51*(1), 21–25.

National Association for the Education of Young Children (NAEYC). (1989). *Developmentally appropriate practice in the primary grades, serving 5- through 8-year-olds.* Washington, DC: Author.

National Association for the Education of Young Children (NAEYC). (1990). Position statement on school readiness. *Young Children, 46*(1), 21–23.

National Association for the Education of Young Children (NAEYC), & National Association of Early Childhood Specialists in State Departments of Education (NAECS/SDE). (1991). Guidelines for appropriate curriculum content and assessment in programs serving children ages 3 through 8. *Young Children, 46*(3), 21–38.

National Association of State Boards of Education (NASBE). (1988). *Right from the start: The report of the NASBE Task Force on Early Childhood Education.* Alexandria, VA: Author.

Piaget, J. (1952). *The origins of intelligence in children.* New York: International Universities Press.

Piaget, J. (1973). *To understand is to invent.* New York: Grossman. (Original work published 1948)

Piaget, J., & Inhelder, B. (1969). *The psychology of the child.* New York: Basic Books.

Ruenzel, D. (1996). Paradise lost. *Teacher Magazine, 7*(8), 26–34.

Shannon, R. (1990). *The struggle to continue: Progressive reading instruction in the United States.* Portsmouth, NH: Heinemann.

Shultz, T., & Lombardi, J. (1989). Right from the start: A report on the NASBE Task Force on Early Childhood Education. *Young Children, 44*(2), 6–10.

Southern Association on Children Under Six. (1990). *Continuity of learning for four- to seven-year-old children.* Little Rock, AR: Author.

Stone, S. (1995). Wanted: Advocates for play in the primary grades. *Young Children, 50*(6), 45–54.

Taylor, J. (1996). Piagetian perspectives on understanding children's understanding. *Childhood Education, 72*(5), 258–259.

Vygotsky, L. (1978). The role of play in development. In M. Cole, V. John-Steiner, S. Scribner, & E. Souberman (Eds.), *Mind and society* (pp. 92–104). Cambridge, MA: Harvard University Press.

Weikart, D. (1989). Hard choices in early childhood care and education: A view to the future. *Young Children, 44*(3), 25–30.

Ysseldyke, J., & Algozzine, B. (1990). *Introduction to special education.* Boston: Houghton Mifflin.

Variations among curriculum models reflect differences in value commitments concerning what is more or less important for . . . children to learn as well as the process by which children learn and develop, even though these value commitments frequently are not made explicit. Curriculum models . . . have varied in terms of the flexibility they grant teachers for interpreting the curriculum's conceptual template.

(Goffin, 1994, pp. 15–16)

2

Developing, Delivering, and Assessing Curriculum:
Issues to Explore

CONSIDER YOUR BELIEFS

- What do you believe children should learn?
- What do you believe about how children learn?
- Will your school or district mandate what and how you should teach, or will you be able to make your own decisions about curriculum?
- What is integrated curriculum? Do you want to plan all or a part of your daily instruction in this way?
- Should you help children become independent, lifelong learners, or should you teach them information? Can you do both?
- How will you know what children are capable of learning? How do you help them build on what they know so that they meet with appropriate challenges?
- Do you want to teach in a multiage classroom?
- Should you group children for instructional purposes? If so, on what basis should you group?
- Will you and the children be accountable for achieving established school and district outcomes or standards? If so, how will achievement of these goals be assessed? How will these outcomes/standards affect curriculum and instruction?
- How will you know whether your instruction is effective and whether the children are making appropriate progress?
- Will some children have special language, learning, physical, or emotional needs? How will you identify these needs? How will you meet these needs? How do you best use the resources of specialists? How do you nurture the children's understanding of, and sensitivity to, these diverse needs?

- How will you help children understand and be sensitive to the cultural differences that exist in their community in particular and the world in general?
- Should you discuss your curriculum with other teachers? To whom will you turn if you need help?
- How do you continue your professional development?

MAKING DECISIONS ABOUT CURRICULUM

Factors That Influence Curriculum Decisions

Curriculum consists of what is to be taught and how it is to be taught. In some instances, curriculum is specific and detailed. In other instances, broad guidelines are given for the generation and implementation of curriculum. Regardless of the design of the curriculum, the ways in which curriculum is assessed should directly reflect and influence what is taught and how it is taught. Consequently, when teachers make decisions about curriculum, they must make decisions about how the curriculum is to be developed, delivered, and assessed. These decisions are based on personal and professional beliefs about what children should learn and how they learn best. Often, decisions are directed by political mandates and strongly influenced by understandings of current educational, political, and social trends and issues.

When making decisions about curriculum, educators must determine who the key players are and what their particular investment in the decision-making process may be. National, state, and local boards frequently have standards, outcomes, or guidelines, either broad or specific, that must be considered. Current educational research, as well as the policy statements of professional educational organizations, exerts a powerful influence through the professional literature and the popular media. Special interest groups with agendas based on gender,

religion, ethnicity, social orientations, and political beliefs attempt to influence curricular decisions at all levels. At the community level, parents may voice specific curriculum preferences as advocates for their children. When teachers make daily curricular decisions, they must not only be knowledgeable about these various influences but also make decisions based on the individual and collective needs of children.

The purpose of this chapter is to bring to your attention some current issues related to the development and delivery of curriculum for children ages four to eight. Each issue has numerous perspectives. All perspectives are based on some grain of truth gleaned from research or wisdom of practice. Almost any position or perspective can be confirmed or rejected on the basis of experience or research. Although many perspectives are couched in a right-or-wrong position, other alternatives may be available. Evaluate the assumptions embedded within each perspective, anticipate the impact of these assumptions (or the interpretation of these assumptions) on children, and clarify your beliefs.

Curriculum Conflicts

Conflicts often arise as decisions are made about curriculum. Conflicts among the key players may be based on very real ideological disagreements about their expectations of the educational system. Frequently, however, disagreement among the key players may be based on misunderstandings, misconceptions, or a limited knowledge of the espoused viewpoints, opinions, and philosophical stances. In these instances, semantics becomes quite powerful. For example, the term *instruction* may carry dramatically different connotations for the key curriculum decision makers. A knowledgeable teacher must be aware that such confusion may exist and must attempt to define key terms clearly when articulating instructional decisions.

Conflicts about curriculum may also be grounded in the simplistic belief that one must choose between clear-cut alternatives–that one alternative must be right and the other must be wrong. Educational history reflects such right-or-wrong decisions, as indicated by the *swinging pendulum syndrome.* The educational pendulum has swung back and forth from totally teacher-centered to totally child-centered classrooms, from total segregation of children with special needs to total inclusion, from homogeneous ability grouping to no grouping, from direct instruction to no instruction, and from a focus on content without process to a focus on process without content. The instructional decisions resulting from these either/or swings have not always served the best interests of children. When teachers make curricular decisions, primary consideration must be given to the best interests of children.

THINKING ABOUT WHAT CHILDREN NEED TO LEARN AND HOW THEY LEARN BEST

Acquisition of Content versus Affect and Processes of Learning

With the birth of the information age, educators have come to realize that children cannot possibly learn all there is to know. They have also come to acknowledge the importance of nurturing the desire to learn (affect) and of helping children develop the tools to learn (processes). Both the affect and processes of learning are critical components for helping children become lifelong, independent learners. As teachers have grappled with "how" to teach, rather

than "what" to teach, some have come to focus on the processes of learning and the affect of learning (attitudes, emotions, self-esteem, social skills, and motivation) to the neglect of what children may or may not be learning (the breadth and depth of the curriculum).

A kindergarten teacher, for example, was overheard to say that her goal for her children for the first half of the year was to teach them social skills. She indicated that she did not believe they could learn much of anything until they learned to get along with each other, to follow directions, and to pay attention to the teacher. Other teachers have pushed to refocus on the "basics." They view a focus on affective concerns and the processes of learning as "fluff" that they believe results in the "watering down" or "total neglect" of curriculum content. The emerging issue should not be one of either/or, but rather one that acknowledges the relative importance of many aspects when making decisions about curriculum. Can't children be taught how to learn, and be helped to develop social skills, focused attention, and self-esteem *while* they are immersed in the stimulating study of content or the exploration of a theme or topic?

TRY IT OUT *Thinking About Curriculum*

As you read the following vignettes, try to identify the assumptions underlying the teachers' beliefs about what and how children should learn. Think about how those assumptions influenced the planning process. Evaluate how these assumptions were interpreted and applied. What impact do you think these decisions had on children? Was the impact desirable?

A district administrator was overheard remarking that if she walked into one more school or classroom that looked like a rain forest, she would scream. The rain forest was the thematic unit of study at many grade levels and in many schools that year. The depth of study, however, did not seem to be significantly different across grade levels. When the administrator asked how the theme was selected, teachers responded that the local natural history museum had an exhibit on the rain forest during the previous academic year. They had collected the many materials readily available and developed the unit. They decided to use the unit again this year.

In one school inundated with rain forest units, concerned parents asked several teachers of various grade levels to clarify their instructional objectives. The parents reported that the teachers were not able to articulate clearly the kinds of things they wanted the children to learn about the rain forest, nor were they able to communicate specific academic reasons for the activities in which the children were engaged. Developing children's individual math and literacy abilities did not appear to have been considered. The teachers most frequently responded that they were "doing the rain forest," "learning about endangered species," or "exploring the rain forest."

These teachers were not able to identify specifically what they were trying to accomplish or what **critical knowledge** they wanted the children to develop. The parents who conducted the informal survey subsequently petitioned the principal and the school board to institute E. D. Hirsch's curriculum (cultural literacy). They wanted clear **process objectives** (the processes and abilities that children need to develop to become increasingly proficient learners) and specific **content objectives** (a baseline of information that children will come to understand about the subject areas under study) to be established for their children. They demanded that specific curriculum materials and critical knowledge be designated.

A teacher of five- to seven-year-olds shared with a colleague her concern about the upcoming week. She indicated that she didn't know what they would study because the children had not voiced an interest in anything in particular. It was her belief that activities and themes must be based on the children's interests. She believed that only when children had a personal interest in something would the motivation for engaging in the activities be present. The children must have the personal need to know for learning to occur. If the children did not demonstrate a particular interest, she could not select a theme nor plan motivating and appropriate activities for the week.

On the first in-service day prior to the beginning of the school year, two first-grade teachers proudly announced they had nine (one for each month) thematic units for the year planned and ready to go. They had spent the entire summer working together to collect materials and plan activities for each theme. In fact, they had already prepared and laminated beautiful bulletin board displays to accompany each theme. Lesson plans were ready. They would have free weekends this year!

A second-grade teacher in the same building remarked that he, too, had his lesson plans for reading ready for the year. He had used the teacher's guide for the new literature series the district had adopted to determine which story the children in each group would read each week. He had carefully selected the accompanying activities and worksheets and planned which ones would be assigned on each day of the week.

Following Children's Interests versus a Predetermined Curriculum

The vignettes presented in the preceding section reflect some ways in which decisions about curriculum are made. At one end of the continuum is a predetermined, carefully sequenced curriculum based on a curriculum guide or model. Little, if any, consideration is given to the interests or needs of a particular child or group of children. Plans are made for the mythical average class. On the other end of the continuum is a curriculum totally dependent on the voluntarily expressed interests of children. Other curricula fall somewhere in between.

The educational pendulum has swung from the mastery learning of a sequence of isolated skills based on task analysis to a curriculum that seems to be void of instructional objectives other than keeping children actively engaged in something of personal interest to them. Both positions have some degree of merit. Teachers or schools cannot be effective if they are not able to articulate clear goals or objectives. Neither can they be effective if they do not take the interests and prior knowledge of the children into consideration. Yet, having goals and objectives does not necessarily have to result in a rigid, lockstep sequence of instruction. Nor does considering the interests of children mean that all units of study must emerge from children's overtly expressed interests. How can the two positions be merged?

A Common Direction

Teachers can organize district, school, or classroom instructional objectives around class themes that they perceive to be of interest to children or in which children have expressed an interest. Achievement of instructional objectives can be accomplished as children investigate self-selected aspects of a class theme (see sections on integrated curriculum in Chapters 4 and 8). When teachers make decisions about curriculum, they must intentionally consider both **content objectives** and **process objectives** for the class, as well as for individual children.

In many instances, the primary goal of a school or a teacher is to keep children busy with activities of interest to them. If children are actively engaged, the "teaching" is considered to be successful. Under this guise, children may explore or "do" the rain forest in first grade, second grade, third grade, and every grade beyond with a variety of fun, interesting, and exciting activities. The question is, Are children becoming increasingly more proficient in their ability to read, write, compute, problem-solve, speak, and listen or in their ability to *think* about the rain forest? What are children learning about history, geography, science, health, and other content areas as they relate to the rain forest? Are children becoming increasingly capable and knowledgeable in these many areas? Is anyone aware of what children are learning and how they are learning? *Is* there a singular, necessary curriculum for children? Should teachers have anything in mind other than keeping children busy?

Whether the curriculum is based on children's interests or on a predetermined curriculum, and regardless of whether the curriculum focus is on the acquisition of information or on the processes of learning, another issue yet remains; that is, do the school and district have a common focus? Do they know what they want a graduate of their school to know and be capable of doing? Are they working as a team across ages or grade levels to monitor the effectiveness of instructional decisions and to ensure the breadth and depth of the curriculum?

Developmental versus Maturational: An Issue of Semantics

All too often, teachers misinterpret the term **developmentally appropriate.** For example, a group of four-year-olds asked their teacher how to write the words *closed* and *open* so that they could make a sign for the pizza parlor they had created in the dramatic play area. The teacher told the children just to write the words the best they could and that whatever they wrote would be fine. This teacher was concerned that providing explicit information about words or letters was inappropriate for children at this age—at this level of maturity. She reasoned that learning about the functions of print and pretending to read and write were developmentally appropriate for four-year-olds but that learning about letters and words was a kindergarten skill and therefore developmentally inappropriate for the children in her classroom.

Many educators have assumed that the term *developmentally appropriate* is synonymous with the concept of maturation. This confusion has created major concerns regarding the role of the teacher and the expectations teachers have for children. **Developmental** indicates that a child's development in all areas occurs along various continua. It may be roughly correlated with age and *is directly related to previous experiences*. It is the teacher's responsibility to find out what understandings a child has related to a specific developmental continuum in order to support new learning in a way that a child of that particular age and maturity learns best. **Maturation** implies that the brain (or the body) has to grow, age, and/or mature for specific new learning to occur or for new concepts to be introduced—in this case, attention to print symbols.

An example of a developmentally appropriate response from the preschool teacher described above would have been to find out what the children already knew about print (and the word *open*) perhaps by asking them to write how they thought the word might look. (Many preschool teachers have been caught unaware that some children already incorporate print into their play at home and know some letters, some sounds, or may already be reading!) The teacher could then provide the children with information they were capable of understanding

("I see that you know it has an *o* in it. Do you know what comes next? It's a *p*. Do you know what a *p* looks like? It looks like this" OR "It begins with this letter. Yes, that's an *o*"). The concept of developmentally appropriate does not set limits on a child's learning ("I didn't know he could count to sixty because we only work on counting from one to ten at this age"). It directs teachers to observe what children know (no matter how limited or advanced it may seem) and to help a child construct new understandings with appropriate explorations, opportunities, and interactions.

Understanding the difference between *developmental* and *maturation* provides a framework for understanding the emerging literacy behaviors of very young children and for clarifying the types of literacy experiences and opportunities that are appropriate for four- and five-year-old children. This is particularly critical for children who have had limited literacy experiences during their early childhood years and need opportunities not only to play with and be surrounded by print but also to have an adult or more literate other help them see connections.

The debate between developmental and maturation has furthered the confusion about whether providing new skill/strategy information is an intrusion on a child's learning. Believing that children must actively construct their own knowledge has produced a fear in many teachers that verbally providing information and helping children make connections is infringing on and diminishing their learning.

This is true even for teachers who are hesitant to enter a child's sociodramatic play. For example, while playing in the housekeeping area, which had been turned into a "restaurant," none of the four-year-olds attempted to use the pencil and paper provided by the teacher to write bills or to take orders. The teacher decided to stimulate the integration of reading and writing by stepping in as a participating customer in need of her bill. This delighted the children, who immediately grasped the concept and began chattering and furiously "writing" out bills. The teacher then stepped out of the play, which was carried on by the children at a more sophisticated level than before. Teachers must sort through these concerns to make appropriate decisions about what each child is ready to learn (Vygotsky's **zone of proximal development**) and their role in how best to stimulate new learning.

This paradigm of developmentally appropriate practice also requires educators to look again at policy on retention of children in kindergarten or first grade and on keeping children from attending kindergarten for another year due to of lack of maturity. Curriculum can be adapted to meet the needs of individual children regardless of their limited experiences, knowledge, or perceived levels of achievement along the developmental continua.

GROUPING

Multiage Classes versus Grade Levels

A crucial issue for many schools is whether to group children homogeneously by age. Many schools are moving away from grade levels and toward multiage classes. They are concerned about the lockstep curriculum that has accompanied the concept of grade levels and the pressure associated with preparing children for the next grade level within the time allotted on the school calendar. Although many teachers readily acknowledge that children learn at different rates and in different ways, they still feel the need to "cover the curriculum" for the current grade so that their children will be prepared for the next grade. This approach has often resulted in teaching the *curriculum,* rather than teaching the *child.*

One hazard of the cover-the-curriculum paradigm is the underlying assumption that all children come to a grade level *at* or *very near* a targeted point on the continua of learning. Children

who have not achieved within the targeted range on the continua are often perceived as not being ready to receive the instruction that will be provided. Indeed, they will not be able to benefit from instruction if the receiving teacher continues to teach beyond what the children are able to understand (beyond the zone of proximal development).

The **zone of proximal development** (Vygotsky, 1978) conceptualizes the relationship between development and learning and represents the difference between what a child is able to do independently and what the child is able to do with the maximum support and guidance of others. Within the zone lies what the child can do with varying degrees of support (Bodrova & Leong, 1996).

Often, the child is perceived to be at fault (or even defective) when, in fact, the instruction is inappropriate. Instruction based on content goals, rather than grounded in *the child's background knowledge and current levels of achievement,* is inappropriate. The ability to integrate what is being offered in the classroom is dependent on the child's current **schemata** (background knowledge related to the topics of study) and on the child's current level of ability to listen, speak, read, write, and think as required by the instructional tasks. When a child experiencing learning difficulties is expected to interact with curricula that are too difficult for the child's cognitive structures to assimilate, the knowledge base the child constructs becomes distorted. A destructive learning cycle of reliance on rote memory and recitation often develops (Grobecker, 1996). The curriculum must be adjusted to fit the child regardless of any label the child may bring to the classroom (e.g., gifted and talented, remedial, learning disabled). The child must not be required to fit the curriculum.

It becomes a real concern for both the promoting teacher and the receiving teacher when a child is not deemed "ready" (not within the expected range of achievement) for the curriculum presented at the next grade level. The promoting teacher is often accused by the receiving teacher of being professionally incompetent. The receiving teacher often feels incapable of being successful with a child who has not been adequately prepared, who is "not ready," for the curriculum of that grade level. Both teachers perceive it to be an impossible task to provide the instruction necessary to "catch the child up" from the previous grade level and to cover the current grade-level curriculum. Given this situation, many teachers opt to cover only the curriculum of their assigned grade level. Unfortunately, this curriculum is often beyond the grasp of the children, whether because of limited content background knowledge or learning processes, and only puts them farther and farther behind (below the range).

One perceived solution to this dilemma is *retention*. Children are often retained at a grade level so that they can develop the skills deemed to be prerequisite for success in the following grade. At the kindergarten level, this is done under the guise of a "transitional first grade" that is intended to be more academically demanding than kindergarten but less structured than a typical first-grade class. In reality, these children have simply been retained for a year.

Shepard and Smith (1989), in their comprehensive work, established that the negative effects of retaining children in elementary school significantly offset any benefits. In the long term, children who are retained perform less well than their peers with similar achievement levels who were promoted for social or maturational reasons. A study by the Association of California Urban School Districts (1985) further found that only 20 percent of children who fail one of the first two grades ultimately graduate from high school. In most cases, retention is clearly not the answer and may be part of the problem.

Another perceived solution to this dilemma is the multiage classroom. Many schools have implemented multiage classrooms to give children a more flexible time frame within which to achieve. Having children of different ages in the same class may help teachers *acknowledge* that individual children have different learning needs and may encourage them to *plan* instruction and learning opportunities accordingly. The potential benefits of this developmental approach are numerous, but there are inherent dangers. Some teachers may perceive the multiage classroom as one in which children can be given extra time to "grow and develop." Consequently, teachers may become lackadaisical about providing continuous and increasingly more challenging learning opportunities. Children's levels of achievement and understandings may not be regularly monitored. The learning experiences provided may not be guided and may more frequently fall below, rather than within, the children's zones of proximal development. Children may continuously work at their independent level, and their learning may become stagnant.

Many teachers take full advantage of this multiage opportunity. They carefully monitor the development of each child's achievement and learning, plan learning experiences, select materials, and provide mediation that will be appropriately stimulating and result in the progressive development of each child's cognitive abilities and knowledge of content.

Meeting Individual and Special Needs

How do teachers who understand that children within a classroom have dramatically different levels of achievement, cognitive abilities, and degrees of content knowledge meet the needs of individual children? Does each child have to be taught individually? Is grouping ever appropriate? If so, for what reasons?

Obviously, instructing each child only on a one-to-one basis is impossible. Indeed, if one believes that learning is a social, interactive process, total one-to-one instruction would be

Working together on a common project encourages children of different ages to support each other's learning.

inappropriate. Therefore, whether children are in multiage classes or grouped by grade level, teachers must make decisions about grouping within the given classroom setting.

Whole-Group Instruction versus Achievement Grouping. Some educators are concerned that placing children in homogeneous groups based on achievement level may result in even slower progress for children in the low group than might be expected. Placement in the low group may become permanent. Consequently, many teachers have moved to *whole-group instruction*. Not only do these teachers view whole-group instruction as more manageable than other grouping alternatives, but they also believe that children will rise to the level of the teacher's expectation.

There is much truth to the self-fulfilling prophecy. Allington (1983), for example, found that many teachers have different expectations for poor readers than for good readers. They provide poor readers with fewer *contextual* reading opportunities than good readers. They expect good readers to be better at self-monitoring for meaning and self-correcting when they deviate from the printed text (**miscue**) than poor readers. Therefore, they do not interrupt good readers at the point of miscue as they do poor readers, conveying to the poorer readers that they are not capable of problem-solving through difficult portions of text. Poor readers, consequently, do not have the same opportunities to self-monitor and problem-solve as good readers. A teacher certainly will not reap more from the children than is expected.

Although whole-group instruction may appear to solve the problem of such differentiated expectations, it may create problems when teachers have inappropriate expectations. The goal is not to expect all children to perform at the same level at the same time, but rather to expect all children to progress. Whole-group instruction can benefit those children for whom the instruction falls within the zone of proximal development. For some, the instruction will obviously be above or below that range. Children at either end of the continuum will be left without appropriate challenges. Children can continue to progress only if increasingly challenging tasks accompanied by appropriate support from the teacher or others are provided within their zones of proximal development. The level of learning at which children need assistance will change as they develop. Teachers must constantly reassess children's zones of proximal development and adjust the learning opportunities and teacher support accordingly.

Needs Grouping and Individual Instruction.
Teachers can plan opportunities within each day to provide appropriate instructional interactions with individual children. Teachers may also observe common needs among children that can be addressed more efficiently and as effectively in small groups. For example, on the basis of individual writing conferences with children, one teacher noticed that several children were using dialogue in their stories but did not demonstrate an understanding of the appropriate use of quotation marks. For the next day, the teacher planned a mini-lesson on quotation marks for that particular group of writers.

A **mini-lesson** is a short, concise episode of explicit instruction of a strategy or skill related to an observed need of a group of children. On the basis of the observed specific needs of specific children, different mini-lessons may be provided to a different small group of children at different times. Mini-lessons can be related to a misunderstanding or a need for greater understanding related to literacy conventions (e.g., phonics, grammar usage, punctuation, capitalization, literary elements, strategies), math concepts, and science concepts.

For the next several days, the teacher paired the children who participated in the mini-lesson with writing buddies who had demonstrated understanding of quotation marks. During future conferences, the teacher observed that two children required additional mediation but that the others were able to make appropriate applications. The teacher worked with these two children individually during their reading and writing conferences.

Some children with special education needs may require individualized instruction in the general classroom or in the resource room during some part of the day. This individualized instruction, whether provided within the classroom or outside the classroom, must result from the collaboration between the classroom teacher and the resource teachers. For children to integrate and apply effectively what they are learning both inside and outside the classroom, teachers must work as a team. They must plan time together to establish common goals for each child, to agree on a common instructional language, and to communicate on a regular basis. The education of children is a shared responsibility of the school community and should not be regarded as the responsibility of isolated units within the school.

Regardless of the classroom setting, using fluid groupings to provide appropriately challenging tasks with teacher support is possible. It is also possible to plan time to work with some children individually each day. Offering only whole-class instruction, only small-group instruction, or only individual instruction is simply not necessary. Teachers must have a fluid organization that will permit them to meet the needs of children efficiently and effectively.

INTEGRATING CURRICULUM

The concept of **integrated curriculum** implies connections between and among disciplines, rather than isolation of subject areas. Articles about integrated curriculum, interdisciplinary curriculum, project approaches, and thematic units abound in the professional literature. Definitive descriptions of how these approaches to curriculum are similar and different are not always provided. However, educators are clearly moving away from segmenting the day into separate, limited chunks of time for each of the subject areas. They seem to be moving toward providing large chunks of time for integrated studies. Some schools integrate the entire day, every day, whereas others may choose a significant block of time each day or several times a week. Chunks of time may be organized around selected topics, novels, or themes. What is behind this trend, and why do some educators object to it?

Proponents of integrated curriculum believe that learnings connected across content areas by topics of interest to children and learnings that children have an opportunity to apply in meaningful ways are more easily understood, retained, assimilated, and applied by the children. Isolated bits of knowledge acquired through rote memorization tend to remain isolated and may be quickly forgotten. For example, children who are taught reading as isolated skills may often do better on standardized measures that test reading as isolated skills but may perform poorly on measures of strategic reading, in which they have to apply skills to construct meaning from a contextual piece of reading (a whole story or a complete informational piece).

When the curriculum is focused on a collection of facts, children may develop understandings qualitatively different from those of children who experience an integrated curriculum unit. Children may be able to associate the Declaration of Independence with July 4 but may have no understanding of the significance of this event. Children who have studied this time period as part of an integrated unit may have read or heard such books as *Adam and the Golden Cock* (Dalgliesh, 1959), *And Then What Happened, Paul Revere?* (Fritz, 1973), and *Why Don't You Get a Horse, Sam Adams?* (Fritz, 1974). These children will be more likely to appreciate the significance and understand the context of this event. They also may have used their developing reading, writing, and study skills to explore self-selected related topics that incorporated various content areas, such as the inventions of Benjamin Franklin (science), the use of stocks to humiliate wrongdoers (social issues), and Paul Revere's ill-fated ride (geography and communication systems). Younger children may have used the dramatic play area to dress and play as colonists or to read and follow the recipe for making *Stone Soup* (Brown, 1947) after sharing the story by the same name. Through integrated units such as these, children obtain a breadth and depth of understanding not possible through the study of isolated facts and subjects.

Opponents of a completely integrated curriculum are often concerned that basic skills and baseline content information may be lost within the context of integrated studies. They prefer the security of a designated time to address the curriculum of specific content areas so that important information or concepts will not be overlooked. Some are concerned that an integrated approach may tend to emphasize some content areas to the neglect of others. Some associate integrated curriculum with the absence of instruction or direction and with an overemphasis on affect, process, and children's interests. They prefer clear goals and objectives for the basics (reading, writing, listening, speaking, and computing), as well as for the specific content areas. Another concern of opponents of integrated approaches is that all learning may occur in cooperative groups or in partnerships. They fear that children will come to rely on others and may not develop the skills or abilities to function independently. They want to know that the teacher and individual children can be held accountable for achieving specific objectives.

Although these concerns may be justified by the way some teachers attempt to integrate the curriculum, knowledgeable teachers will hold themselves accountable for specific learning, content goals, and objectives. They will select broad topics to incorporate specific content goals and objectives and will provide opportunities to develop the literacy, learning, and computation skills of children. These teachers will encourage children to learn in a variety of ways, including hands-on explorations of relevant artifacts, interviews, and print/multimedia resources. They will provide opportunities for children to explore and learn both independently and cooperatively. Children will be provided with several mediums for demonstrating and sharing what they are learning. Excellent teachers will not assume that children's interest and active engagement in an activity or participation in a cooperative team will ensure that appropriate learnings are taking place. They will monitor each child's achievement of content understandings and cognitive skills and help each child use current understandings to construct new understandings.

ROLES OF THE TEACHER

Teacher as Facilitator

During the past fifteen years, educational research has clearly established that learning is an active, constructive process and that when new learning is integrated with what is already known, the strength of the learning is enhanced. The movements toward whole language, integrated curriculum, constructivism, authentic experiences, process approaches, cooperative learning,

self-selection, and risk taking by the learner have been based on these premises. In a search for professional empowerment, however, and in an effort to abandon uncomfortable roles in adult-centered classrooms, many teachers may have become the victims of insufficient professional development and a desire for long overdue change.

Many teachers who have come to embrace the affect of active and constructivist theories of learning are no longer certain of their roles in children's learning. Some teachers have gleaned (erroneously or otherwise) from conversations, workshops, conferences, and professional literature that instruction is inappropriate—that it somehow infringes on children's learning. This was the perception of the preschool teacher in the vignette about writing the sign for the pizza parlor. For some, the teacher's role has come to be viewed as merely that of **facilitator,** with the responsibility for setting up the learning environment, structuring it for independence, and staying out of the way.

Teacher as Facilitator and Mediator

Some proponents of the active learning, constructivist theories clearly urge teachers to reject the use of direct instruction with children. *Direct instruction,* as they define it, is teacher-centered, curriculum-driven, manual-dictated, skill-and-drill instruction. As defined, this type of instruction is clearly inappropriate. These educators do not, however, always clearly delineate and describe the types of child-teacher instructional interactions that are consistent with the underlying assumptions of active, constructive, and integrated learning that teachers *should* use. Therefore, some teachers are led to believe that no type of planned or "direct" (explicit) instructional interaction with children is appropriate. This is a misperception and largely a result of the semantics involved.

Implicit in these models is the need for teachers to interact with and, consequently, teach children by providing intentional as well as spontaneous *modeling, demonstrations, feedback, mediation,* and *explicit instruction as needed.* Effective teachers are assumed to make decisions about what to teach and how to teach it on the basis of their observations of what children know and how children know it. They use this information to help children build on the known by challenging and supporting children's efforts to construct new information and to solve new puzzles and problems. Therefore, the role of the teacher as mediator in each of these models is important indeed.

Teacher as Knowledgeable Observer

As process-oriented curriculum models have developed over the last decade, a strong emphasis on *kid watching* (Goodman, 1978) has emerged—that is, an emphasis on observing what children know and how they know it. Observation and informal documentation have become preferred over testing and formal assessment to provide pertinent, ongoing information for guiding instructional decisions. A concurrent emphasis has been placed on the emerging nature of children's learning within any one subject area.

Expert teachers must be able to internalize the various continua and to become skillful observers of children in order to notice what they know and how children learned it. What teachers observe children to understand (the known), combined with knowledge of the next chunk of the science, math, or literacy continuum, provides teachers with information crucial to making effective decisions about instruction (mediation). Critics of authentic assessment, however, have raised concerns about the validity of teachers' observation, indicating that a significant problem exists when teachers do not have a solid knowledge base from which to make observations and subsequent decisions. A goal of excellent teachers is to learn how to integrate effectively what is observed

with their knowledge of child development, knowledge of the various subject areas, and knowledge of effective ways to help children understand a particular content area (**pedagogical content knowledge**.

ASSESSMENT AND ACCOUNTABILITY

Seat-Time versus Performance

Standards and outcome-based education are frequently topics of debate. As more and more children pass from grade to grade and eventually graduate from high school without being able to read, write, or compute to the satisfaction of the business community, colleges, and parents, concerns are generated about graduation and promotion requirements. It is evident that seat-time (or completion of a certain number and certain kinds of courses) in school and teachers' curriculum coverage efforts do not necessarily result in children's ability to perform. In an attempt to remedy such situations, standards-based education and performance-based assessment have become increasingly popular. This means that to move to the next cluster of grade levels or to graduate, children must be able to achieve certain standards, to perform. Simply being in school for a certain amount of time and taking a particular collection of courses is not sufficient. Standards-based education and performance-based assessment can be interpreted as attempts to move accountability from making certain that teachers' lesson plans cover the curriculum to requiring that teachers' instruction results in acceptable levels of child performance.

Concurrent with the movement toward performance-based assessment is a movement toward more authentic assessments. As educators attempt to get away from worksheets, workbooks, and standardized tests, teachers much search for or develop appropriate means to assess and evaluate children's learnings, as well as the effectiveness of their instruction. In an effort to align large-scale assessment more closely with classroom instruction, performance measures are beginning to be used to assess standards.

Teachers, parents, administrators, school boards, and the general community (state and national) are all critical players in the development of standards and in the selection or design of performance-based assessments. As one might expect, there has been as much disagreement as agreement on what the standards should be and how they should be assessed. Some want to focus only on content information and basic skills, whereas others want to focus on values, self-perceptions, and self-directed learning. Still others want to combine elements from both.

When districts, schools, teachers, and parents have common, clearly articulated goals or standards, it is more likely that they will be able to achieve them. Communication among teachers across subject areas, as well as across grade levels and between divisions (elementary, middle school, junior high, and high school), must be established as standards, assessments, and benchmarks are clarified. A common vision that provides a cohesive, comprehensive profile of the desired graduate must be created.

Because assessment drives instruction, teachers must have a clear understanding of the standards and how they will be measured. They must also have a voice in determining the standards and the assessments. Once teachers clearly understand where they are going, they can develop continua of benchmarks to help guide observations, inform instructional decisions, assess child progress, and evaluate program quality. Participation in the development of benchmarks further contributes to teachers' sense of ownership of the curriculum. This may result in increased commitment to the curriculum and to the probability that they will help children be successful.

Some educators and lay persons believe that benchmarks should be clearly divided into grade-level chunks and that schools should be structured by grade levels. Others believe that benchmarks are tools that can be used to inform and support teachers as they attempt to meet the individual instructional needs of students. The importance of benchmarks is becoming especially apparent in districts where children are required to achieve in order to move from one grade level or cluster of grade levels to another. When a district, for example, requires students to pass a reading and writing assessment at grade five before being allowed to move to middle-level education, undue pressure can be put on the grade-five teachers to be certain that students can performance adequately on the assessments. Without a continuum of benchmarks, the K–4 teachers may become complacent and take less responsibility for continuously monitoring and contributing to the progress of their students.

Every teacher must bear responsibility for all children's learning. All teachers must view all children as their children. They must work together to ensure that all children continuously progress toward the established goals and achieve those goals within the designated time frames.

SUPPORTING MULTICULTURAL AND DIVERSE LEARNERS

Bilingual Instruction: Immersion versus Maintenance

In 1986, bilingual education programs were established through federal legislation. The general concept was to provide programs in which English and one other language, preferably the child's native language, were used for instruction. Obviously, providing teachers fluent in each of the languages represented in any one school is not always possible or practical. As a result of this practical consideration, many forms of bilingual, or so-called bilingual, programs emerged (e.g., transitional bilingual education, maintenance bilingual education, immersion education, two-way immersion, newcomer programs) (Peregoy & Boyle, 1997). Some forms were solidly grounded in research; others were strongly entrenched in community values and opinions.

An often heated debate revolves around the best way to facilitate the education of children who come to school monolingual in a language other than English (**English as second language children–ESL**). True to the pendulum mentality there are those who say these children should be taught only in their native language and those who insist the children should be immersed in English to the exclusion of their native language. As one might expect, research seems to support both opinions. Some proponents of English-only (**immersion**) allude to the need to speak proper English in order to be successful in the American job market. Some are concerned that speakers of other languages are often considered to be incapable of learning. They may perceive instruction in children's native languages to be a way of preventing the children from becoming active participants in the economy and in the government.

Proponents of native language education (**maintenance**) believe that it is crucial to children's cognitive development that they be instructed in their native language—that if their instruction is in English only, they will not be able to process information as effectively or to incorporate new information or concepts presented in English into existing schemata grounded in their native language. Maintenance proponents perceive immersion in English to require children to reconstruct their knowledge base from the very beginning, thus impeding their cognitive growth, rather than extending it.

Is this truly an either-or issue—either English immersion or instruction in the native language? It makes sense that teachers need some information about any language or dialect that children may speak in order to understand the children and to communicate effectively with them. It makes sense that teachers would respect a child's native language or dialect but would also provide the child with the understandings about standard English necessary for effective participation in the larger community and achievement of personal goals. Teachers do not hesitate to teach children the languages of mathematics or of computers in order for them to be successful in those areas. They help children construct or expand their current understanding of the new language (mathematics or computer languages) by negotiating (scaffolding) between the children's native language, the children's current knowledge of English, and the new language. They use any language understandings the children have (native language or standard English) to help them understand these new languages. Why wouldn't this make sense in helping them learn standard English? Why wouldn't teachers simply build on the known?

The services available for ESL children in your building may vary in purpose and quality. How you assist ESL children in the classroom will be based on your personal beliefs, values, and knowledge base. Educators in the field of ESL suggest that achievement of ESL children is greater when teachers and the educational community value the children's experiences and native language and attempt to build on these, rather than replace them (Ashworth, Cummins, & Handscombe, 1989; Ogbu, 1978; Soto, 1991; Spangenberg-Urbschat & Pritchard, 1994). They recommend that numerous opportunities for authentic use of children's own language and the second language be provided. (For more information on bilingual education, refer to Peregoy & Boyle, 1997; Spangenberg-Urbschat & Pritchard, 1994; and Tiedt & Tiedt, 1990.)

Children learn English while developing and extending concepts in their native language.

Self-Contained Settings versus Inclusion

Classrooms today are communities of diverse learners. This diversity means an increase in the numbers and types of support needed for individual children to reach their full potential (Coots, Bishop, Grenot-Scheyer, & Falvey, 1995). When children with unique needs and characteristics are a part of a classroom, the ethic and practice of collaboration must be used jointly to invent workable solutions to children's authentic problems (Udvari-Solner & Thousand, 1996). The needs of these children require the development of new roles for teachers, with increased collaboration and consultation for both general and special education teachers as needed resources are infused into a single system, rather than operating dual systems (Bishop,

Foster, & Jubala, 1993). Teachers share expertise and resources in meeting the needs of all children as teachers and children become active participants in daily decisions about teaching and learning. The success of the collaboration and consultation process depends on multiple factors that are dynamic in nature and specific to the situation. By understanding these factors and by committing to the collaborative ethic, the team members will make valuable contributions to the education of all children (Phillips & McCullough, 1990).

Two major laws define the responsibility of teachers in meeting the needs of children with individual differences: Section 504 of the Rehabilitation Act of 1973 (PL 93–112) and the Individuals with Disabilities Education Act (PL 101–476, formerly PL 94–142). Section 504 says that all children have a right to access the general education curriculum, to participate in extracurricular activities in school, and to be given appropriate instructional and curricular adaptations in general education. Children who do not qualify for special education services must still be given appropriate accommodations in the general education setting if they have been defined as having any physical or mental impairment that substantially limits one or more major life activities. These are often children with attention deficit hyperactivity disorders, health conditions, and emotional/behavioral disorders that do not qualify them for special education services but that do affect their functioning in the general education program. The 504 accommodations are the responsibility of general education, not special education, with the general education teacher accountable for planning, implementing, and documenting the accommodations that enable these children to be successful.

Originally named the Education for All Handicapped Children Act (EHA), PL 94–142, passed in 1975, was expanded and reauthorized in 1990 as the Individuals with Disabilities Education Act (IDEA). This legislation was designed to ensure that children with disabilities receive a free and appropriate public education.

The general education teacher is part of the multidisciplinary team that determines whether a child has a disability and is eligible for special education services. Other team members include the following:

- A representative of the local education agency
- The special education teacher
- Parents or guardians
- Other professionals from related services, such as social workers, speech and language pathologists, psychologists, occupational therapists, reading specialists, school counselors, school nurses, and ESL teachers
- Others who can provide information for decision making

If a child is eligible for special education services, the team develops an **Individualized Education Program (IEP)** with goals and objectives to meet the unique needs of the child. It is imperative that the classroom teacher be an active member of the team. The classroom teacher is probably more familiar with the processing and functioning of the child than are any other school personnel and will often have a major responsibility in fulfilling the goals and objectives of the educational plan. The IEP is a safeguard for planning, delivering, and evaluating an appropriate education for the child. It is an agreement to provide educational procedures that ensure an appropriate education to meet the child's needs. It is not a contract guaranteeing that the child will accomplish all the objectives in the IEP.

The IEP states where a child will receive services. IDEA states that a continuum of educational services ranging from the full-time general education classroom to a special residential facility must be available for consideration. Determination of the placement of the child is a team decision based on the principle of the *least restrictive environment (LRE)*. This principle states that children should be educated with their nondisabled peers to the maximum extent possible while receiving an appropriate education. Courts have determined that placements in other than the general education classroom must consider the following:

- Did the school attempt to maintain the child in the general education classroom?
- Will the child benefit academically and/or nonacademically from placement in the general education classroom?
- Is the education of other children in the general education classroom adversely affected? (Yell, 1995)

A recent trend in education has been that of **inclusion.** This trend has generated emotionally charged arguments in both special education and general education. Advocates of full inclusion believe that every child with disabilities should be educated with his or her nondisabled peers in the general education classroom all the time (Stainback & Stainback, 1992). Others maintain that many children with disabilities are more appropriately served along a continuum of services in settings ranging from the general education classroom to those with partial to full-time pull-out for special compensatory and remedial instruction. Some perceive that inclusion requires a teacher to focus an undue amount of time away from the learning of the group. Once again, the educational pendulum swings from one side to the other—inclusion or self-contained? Remember two important principles: (1) All children are children first, with the disability being secondary, and (2) the "special" of special education is the individualization. One size cannot fit all. Educators must consider the needs of the children.

Special needs can often be addressed in the general classroom with the support of informed and caring adults and peers.

When children with special needs spend part or all of the day in the general education classroom, the general education and special education teachers must collaborate in planning and providing individualized instruction tailored to the IEP goals and objectives. Time must be scheduled on a regular basis for this collaboration. In addition, professional development must be provided to support this collaboration in order to meet the needs of children with special needs, as well as those of the group. (For more information on inclusion, refer to Kochhar & West, 1996; and Miller, 1996.)

SUMMARY

During your educational career, you will be enticed by the excitement of innovative ideas and pendulum swing paradigm shifts. Should you jump on the bandwagon? There is no simple answer. You must be cautious of embracing or rejecting an idea or philosophy because it has attracted an enthusiastic following. You may be tempted to join the parade before you

know its destination, its origin, or its route. Before you decide to jump on the bandwagon, examine the underlying assumptions associated with a given perspective, anticipate the impact on children, and determine whether its goals for children are consistent with your beliefs. Be sure you understand how the curriculum associated with a particular paradigm is developed, delivered, and assessed. Be certain these are also consistent with what you think is best and most effective for the education of young children.

Consider also the degree to which you, as a classroom teacher, are encouraged to ascertain children's individual strengths and needs in order to provide all your children with appropriate challenges and support. The role of the teacher and the role of the child in the process of education figure prominently in any innovation. In summary, remember that all curriculum and instruction models reflect differences in value commitments regarding what children should learn and how they should learn. Consider your beliefs and use them as guides to evaluate new ideas critically.

REFERENCES

Allington, R. (1983). The reading instruction provided readers of differing ability. *Elementary School Journal, 83,* 548–559.

Ashworth, M., Cummins, J., & Handscombe, J. (1989). *Report on the Vancouver School Board's ESL program.* Report submitted to the Vancouver School Board, British Columbia.

Association of California Urban School Districts. (1985). *Dropouts from California's urban school districts: Who are they? How do we count them? How can we hold them (or at least educate them)?* Los Angeles: Author.

Bishop K. D., Foster, W. A., & Jubala, K. A. (1993). The social construction of disability in education: Organizational considerations. In C. Capper (Ed.), *Education administration in a pluralistic society* (pp. 173–202). Albany: State University of New York Press.

Bodrova, E., & Leong, D. (1996). *Tools of the mind: The Vygotskian approach to early childhood education.* Upper Saddle River, NJ: Merrill/Prentice Hall.

Brown, M. (1947). *Stone soup.* New York: Scribner.

Coots, J., Bishop, K., Grenot-Scheyer, M., & Falvey, M. (1995). Practices in general education: Past and present. In M. Falvey (Ed.), *Inclusive and heterogeneous schooling assessment, curriculum, and instruction* (pp. 7–22). Baltimore: Brooks.

Dalgliesh, A. (1959). *Adam and the golden cock.* New York: Scribner.

Fritz, J. (1973). *And then what happened, Paul Revere?* New York: Coward, McCann & Geoghegan.

Fritz, J. (1974). Why don't you get a horse, Sam Adams? New York: Coward, McCann & Geoghegan.

Goffin, S. (1994). *Curriculum models and early childhood education: Appraising the relationship.* Upper Saddle River, NJ: Merrill/Prentice Hall.

Goodman, K. (1978). Kid watching: Alternative to testing. *National Elementary Principal, 57*(4), 41–45.

Grobecker, B. (1996). Reconstructing the paradigm of learning disabilities: A holistic/constructivist interpretation. *Learning Disabilities Quarterly, 19,* 179–198.

Kochhar, C., & West, L. (1996). *Handbook for successful inclusion.* Gaithersburg, MD: Aspen.

Miller, R. (1996). *The developmentally appropriate inclusive classroom in early education.* Albany, NY: Delmar.

Ogbu, J. (1978). *Minority education and caste.* San Diego: Academic Press.

Peregoy, S., & Boyle, O. (1997). *Reading, writing, and learning in ESL: A resource book for K–8 teachers* (2nd ed.). White Plains, NY: Longman.

Phillips, V., & McCullough, L. (1990). Consultation-based programming: Instituting the collaboration ethic in schools. *Exceptional Children, 56*(4), 291–304.

Shepard, L., & Smith, M. (1989). *Flunking grades.* Philadelphia: London.

Soto, D. (1991). Understanding bilingual/bicultural young children. *Young Children, 46*(2), 30–36.

Spangenberg-Urbschat, K., & Pritchard, R. (Eds.). (1994). *Kids come in all languages: Reading instruction for ESL students.* Newark, NJ: International Reading Association.

Stainback, S., & Stainback, W. (1992). *Curriculum considerations in inclusive classrooms: Facilitating learning for all students.* Baltimore: Brooks.

Tiedt, P., & Tiedt, I. (1990). *Multicultural teaching: A handbook of activities, information, and resources* (3rd ed.). Boston: Allyn & Bacon.

Udvari-Solner, A., & Thousand, J. (1996). Creating a responsive curriculum for inclusive schools. *Remedial and Special Education, 17,* 182–192.

Vygotsky, L. (1978). *Mind in society: The development of higher psychological process.* Cambridge, MA: Harvard University Press.

Yell, M. L. (1995). Least restrictive environment, inclusion, and students with disabilities: A legal analysis. *Journal of Special Education, 24*(4), 389–404.

[T]he teacher we are asking for is aware of the complexities of the interaction between intellectual development and affective experience in the developing years. Further, the ideal teacher is aware of the differences in the social codes and styles of interaction among young children from widely different cultural groups. Finally, we are looking for a teacher who can maintain healthy, cohesive group functioning which is so flexibly enacted that individual needs can be sensed, understood and met, with suitable adjustment.

(Biber, 1988, p. 46)

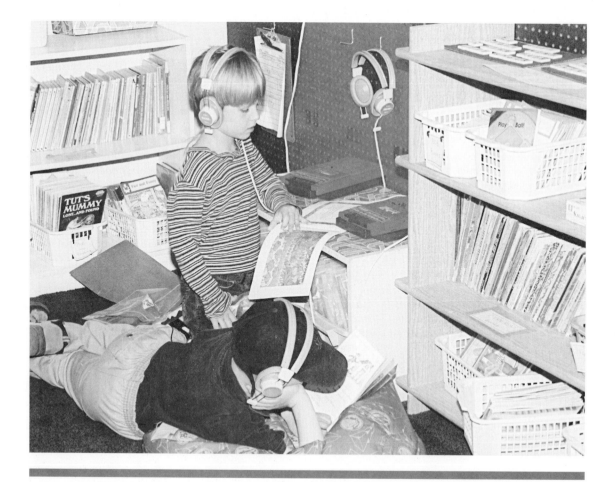

3

Planning for Children's Learning in the Primary Years:
Instructional Interactions, Management, and the Classroom Environment

CONSIDER YOUR BELIEFS

- What are instructional interactions?
- How can instructional interactions be used to help children become independent learners?
- How will you know when interacting instructionally with children is appropriate?
- Why is interacting instructionally with individual and small groups of children, as well as with the whole group, important?
- What are the roles of questions in instructional interactions?
- How can you use questions effectively?
- Why is helping children build on the "known" important?
- How will you know what children know? How will you help them build on the "known"?
- How will you organize and manage your classroom to support children's independence and in-depth learning?
- How will you organize the day to provide time to interact with individual and small groups of children?
- How will you know whether your instructional interactions are effective?
- How can you continue to improve your ability to observe and recognize children's instructional strengths and needs?

GOALS OF INSTRUCTIONAL INTERACTIONS

AT SCHOOL

Nathan, a seven-year-old, was intrigued by the movie *Balto,* the story a heroic sled dog that braved harsh Alaskan conditions to deliver an antitoxin to of a seriously ill little girl. Discussing the movie the next day with his teacher, Nathan began to ask about antitoxins: "Where do we get antitoxins?" Before the teacher could respond, Nathan asked, "How do you spell *antitoxins*? I want to look it up." He went to the computer to search a computerized encyclopedia.

As the teacher assisted with the spelling, she wondered aloud whether some antitoxins might be found in nature. As they examined the Encarta information, they discovered together that some antitoxins can be made synthetically and that some are also found in nature. The teacher said, "I wonder whether any of the edible plants you have collected so far contain antitoxins." (Nathan was studying edible plants that grow in Colorado.)

Nathan replied that he didn't know and asked whether any plants containing antitoxins grew in Colorado.

"I don't know," replied the teacher. "How can we find out?" Together, they made plans to extend Nathan's unit on edible plants to include determining whether some of Colorado's native plants contained antitoxins and, if so, how he could go about locating them.

AT HOME

As Lisa's toddler brother carried his Easter basket to the car, Lisa, age six, picked up the pieces of candy that had escaped from the swaying basket. As she pondered the tidbits she was retrieving from the sidewalk, Lisa began to ask her mom questions about the goodies. "How come some candy is orange and some is red? Where do we get candy from? How do you make candy? What makes some candy hard and some candy chewy?" She stopped her questioning abruptly and addressed her mom, "I think I'll study candy for my next unit at school."

Both Nathan and Lisa attend the same school. Their curiosity, self-direction, and confidence in themselves as learners reflect the school's goal of nurturing children's enthusiasm for learning both inside and outside the classroom. Empowered by their school experiences, both children naturally generated genuine questions about their world and viewed themselves as capable investigators and problem solvers. The kinds of wonderment questions they generated were the kinds of questions they heard and were encouraged to pose every day at school. Their questions and their confidence reflected the cumulative effect of interactions that had taken place daily throughout the year between teachers, teachers and children, teachers and parents, and children and children. The children exhibited the habits of mind that the school had intentionally set out to help the children internalize.

Long-Term Instructional Goals

Teachers need to establish **long-term instructional goals** to help children develop certain **habits of mind** (Marzano, 1992). These goals should reflect the "mission statement" or underlying school philosophy that has been delineated by the school community. All decisions about curriculum and instructional interactions should then be examined to determine how they will contribute to the development of these habits of mind. Teachers should ensure that four-to eight-year-old children

- Are excited about learning at school and outside school

- Are curious about the world and initiate investigations independently

- Are capable of generating and investigating questions

- Think critically, creatively, and in a problem-solving manner

- Think like scientists, artists, mathematicians, social scientists, and authors

- Know how to tackle and solve problems independently and collaboratively

- Perceive (and are capable of using) reading, writing, listening, speaking, and thinking as tools for investigating and sharing their learning

- Reflect on the goals they have established for themselves and monitor their efforts to achieve, and possibly extend, those goals as appropriate

- Perceive learning as continuous, developing, and never ending

- Develop conceptual understandings about their world, as well as the information needed to support those understandings

- Develop a familiarity with many aspects of their world while also having ample opportunities to explore areas of personal interests in depth

These expectations and habits of mind should be a consistent focus as teachers plan curriculum, design instructional interactions, assess children's achievement, and evaluate the educational program.

Short-Term Instructional Goals

Short-term instructional goals are those that reflect the daily curriculum goals established by

teachers, sometimes in conjunction with the children and sometimes independently, so that the children acquire a broad knowledge base while developing the skills and strategies they need to become self-regulated learners. The short-term goals established by teachers for young children are influenced by many factors. Besides the curriculum goals established by the school or district, national and state standards and mandates must also be addressed (refer to Chapter 4). These must be considered when determining the short-term goals of instructional interactions. Immediate instructional goals and instructional interactions for individual children are determined by the current achievement level of each child and the ways each child processes information.

CONTEXT OF INSTRUCTIONAL INTERACTIONS

Expectations Teachers Have for Children and Themselves

As teachers interact with children each day, they make moment-to-moment decisions about the types of interactions they believe will help the children *acquire new knowledge* and *become self-regulated learners.* Teachers also hold the same expectations for themselves. They expect themselves to acquire new knowledge and to be self-regulated learners. They communicate both their expectations for children and their expectations for themselves to their children. The types of interactions that teachers should ultimately use are also grounded in the following personal and collaborative beliefs.

Teachers Should Be Excited About Learning. Effective teachers express and demonstrate a genuine enthusiasm for learning. They are interested in what children are learning. They value and acknowledge the expert status of individual children about topics that may be unfamiliar to them. They pose questions about a topic that re-

In effective classrooms, teachers and children communicate the expectations they have for each other and for themselves.

Teachers expect children to set goals, work hard, and do their very best.

Children expect teachers to set goals, work hard, and do their very best.

flect personal curiosities. They continue to extend children's learnings. Teachers share personal explorations and learnings with children. Teachers and children conduct mutual explorations often to learn about areas of common interest. Teachers are co-learners in many ways.

Teachers Should Support Children's Development as Learners. Effective teachers strive to increase children's "understanding of the world around them and to strengthen their dispositions to go on learning," (Katz & Chard, 1989, p. 5). Teachers provide the type and amount of guidance, instruction, mediation, and support to help *all* children become self-directed, self-regulated, and self-monitoring independent learners. They use *questions* to clarify, stimulate, and extend child's questions and thinking and to model thought processes, not merely to assess understanding.

Instruction Should Develop and Build on What Each Child Knows. Both explicit instruction and mediation play crucial and active roles in leading and guiding children's development. Effective teachers do not wait for a child to "mature" before teaching him or her. Rather, they identify, celebrate, and build on "the knowns" (knowledge, understandings, and experiences the child already has). Instructional interactions must lead a child from the known into the unknown. The *unknown* is that which is somewhat beyond the child's current level of understanding but within immediate reach with support from the teacher. For example, a child may not have experienced book reading at home. The teacher could therefore assume the child is not ready for reading instruction and choose to defer instructional interactions until the child has had sufficient experiences with literature. A more effective teacher, however, would begin to draw the child's attention to how print works (its form and functions) both in the environmental print familiar to the child and through **literacy events** (e.g., in the dramatic play center "restaurant," or as the teacher records the experiences the child dictates individually or as part of the group). Concurrently, the teacher would ensure that the child has opportunities to hear many wonderful stories read aloud.

Instructional Support Must Be Within the Child's Zone of Proximal Development. Effective teachers take responsibility for tasks that are beyond the reach of the child—that is, beyond the understanding of the child even with the assistance of others. It is also the professional responsibility of teachers to identify what an individual child knows and is capable of learning next with instructional support; that is, teachers identify each child's zone of proximal development. Teachers provide instructional interactions to support children's efforts to accomplish tasks just within their reach and let children take full responsibility for tasks that can be accomplished independently (Trawick-Smith, 1994).

Instructional Interactions Must Focus on Developing Conceptual Understandings and Searching Behaviors. Effective teachers' intent is not to identify, teach, and assess isolated pieces of information devoid of conceptual understanding (e.g., teaching multiplication facts before children understand the concept of multiples and the functions that multiplication can serve). Rather, it is to help children develop or recognize connections, patterns, structures, functions, purposes, and relationships. Teachers then encourage and assist children to search for other examples or applications of the concept.

Instructional Interactions Should Help Children See Connections Across the Curriculum and Across Life Experiences. Effective teachers strive to construct a **cohesive curriculum** that makes sense to children and helps them make sense of their world. When interacting with children, teachers intentionally help them make connections across disciplines, make connections with other personal experiences, and apply to other situations.

Teachers Should Encourage and Celebrate Risk Taking. Children (and teachers) who make no mistakes are those who take few risks. Although teachers encourage and assist children to make thoughtful hypotheses and to ask thoughtful questions, teachers also understand that children learn as much or more when hypotheses are not corroborated and the answers to questions are not accurately anticipated. Effective teachers understand that children can learn from puzzling situations and mistakes, as well as from successes.

Learning Should Be Supported by Social and Collaborative Interactions. Effective teachers plan opportunities for children to learn from one another, as well as independently or with the teacher. Learning is supported through opportunities for children to identify topics to explore collaboratively, to design a plan for investigating their questions, to gather and analyze information, and to share what they have learned. Teachers understand that learning is supported by the social context and therefore plan opportunities for collaboration. Teachers also understand that children at all levels need guidance on how to collaborate effectively.

Teachers Should Encourage and Model Problem Solving. Effective teachers reflect *in action* and *on action* (Schon, 1983). They expect children to learn to reflect and to become increasingly more reflective. Teachers are problem solvers and expect children to become problem solvers.

INSTRUCTIONAL INTERACTIONS

Explicit Instruction

Instructional interactions are interactions between teacher and children intended to help the children construct new knowledge and become self-regulated learners.

MR. GLASER: EXPLICIT INSTRUCTION

Mr. Glaser regularly observed the children as they read instructional-level books. As a result, he had determined that John, Abby, Nicholas, and Wendi (ages six and seven) relied primarily on sounding out as a strategy to figure out new words. He planned a small-group session with them *to demonstrate* other possible strategies to use when they encounter a challenging word. Mr. Glaser selected a Big Book new to the children that would serve the instructional purposes. He chose three words that had several possible substitutions and that the children might find challenging if they tried to sound them out. He covered the selected words with self-stick notes before introducing the book to the children.

During the preview of the text, the children responded to the covered words with surprise. Mr. Glaser *explained* that they were to try to guess the word the author used. When the children encountered the first covered word as they read the book aloud, Mr. Glaser took a turn. As he read the sentence containing the covered word, he *thought aloud* as he *demonstrated* the strategies he wanted the children to be able to use. He read up to the covered word and stopped to look at the picture. Then he reread the sentence, skipped the covered word, and read on to the end of the sentence. He *hypothesized* what word he thought the author had used, *explained why,* and then invited suggestions for alternative words. After each child had an opportunity to contribute a word, Mr. Glaser *encouraged the children to think* of the letter the word might start with. Then he uncovered the first letter of the word in the book and *thought aloud as he cross-checked* his guess with the exposed letter. He invited each child to do the same. The word was then completely exposed, and the children cross-checked it with the suggested words that started with the same letter as the covered word. The children confirmed or rejected each word.

As Mr. Glaser *reviewed* the specific strategies they had used, he wrote the strategies on a chart and drew a simple picture beside each to represent the strategy. He *explained* to the children that these were strategies that good readers used to figure out hard words and *encouraged children to use them when they read on their own.* The children repeated this process as they encountered the other covered words. (*Individual strategies charts were provided* for each child to use when reading independently at school and at home.)

In this vignette, Mr. Glaser used demonstrations, modeling, thinking aloud, explanations, and reviewing *to provide the children with new information.* He then provided immediate opportunities to try out the new learning with his support and encouraged the children to apply the new learning independently. Instructional interactions intended to teach specific information, strategies, or skills directly are called **explicit instruction.**

Mediation

MR. GLASER: MEDIATION

A few weeks later, Mr. Glaser was helping Abby read a new book. Abby previewed the book with Mr. Glaser by reading the title, examining the pictures of the entire text, identifying some unfamiliar vocabulary related to the illustrations, and predicting what the book might be about. Abby began to read. She paused at an unfamiliar word and then looked at Mr. Glaser. Mr. Glaser waited silently for a few moments.

Mr. Glaser: What are some things you can do when you come to a hard word?

(Abby responded by listing several possible strategies.)

Mr. Glaser: What will you try first?

Abby: I can skip it and read on.

Mr. Glaser: Try that.

(Abby reread the sentence from the beginning and skipped the difficult word to complete the sentence.)

Mr. Glaser: Did that help?

Abby: No.

Mr. Glaser: What else can you do?

(Abby looked at the picture.)

Abby: I could get my mouth ready to say the word.

(Abby suggested the appropriate word and again looked up at Mr. Glaser.)

Mr. Glaser: Try it out. Read it like that.

(Abby reread the sentence, using the correct word.)

Mr. Glaser: What do you think? Did that work? Did you get it?

(Abby confirmed that the word made sense and matched with the print.)

The dialogue between Mr. Glaser and Abby reflects another category of instructional interactions, called **mediation.** Mr. Glaser used wait time, questioning, prompting, and scaffolding to help Abby apply what she knew to new situations and *become a capable, self-regulated learner.* Teachers intentionally use instructional interactions referred to as mediation to help children learn to control and guide their attention and thinking, to monitor understandings, to formulate solutions to problems, and to self-evaluate (Trawick-Smith, 1994).

Considering the Possibilities

Instructional interactions consist of two categories of teacher-child interactions: **explicit instruction** and **mediation.** Teachers recognize that both types are integral to children's learning. All decisions that teachers make are consistent with and support the expectations they have for children and for themselves. The purposes and specific types of explicit instruction and mediation are described in Table 3.1.

Making Effective Instructional Choices

To make good decisions about instructional interactions, you must know a lot about the children. You must know what the children know (knowledge and strategies), how the children learn, and how the children are able to use the knowledge and strategies they possess. You gather this information by watching the children in action and as you interact with them over time, not through formal testing or in a single day of observation.

For a conscientious teacher, this task may seem overwhelming at first, but as you begin to observe and document your observations on a regular basis, you will begin to internalize the continua of child knowledge and strategies you want to observe. You will learn not only to create authentic learning events that lend themselves to observation but also to take advantage of spontaneous opportunities. You will develop habits of mind that will allow you to focus easily and intentionally on gathering this information while interacting with the children and while watching them engaged in learning events. You will learn to observe the children carefully and to document your observations as a basis for making effective decisions about instructional interactions.

What Do Children Know? Whether you are planning a literacy mini-lesson with a small group,

TABLE 3.1 Instructional interactions

Explicit Instruction	*Mediation*
Purposes:	**Purposes:**
To provide new information	To help the child think about and use what he or she already knows to solve problems and/or to construct new knowledge
To provide opportunity for immediate application of new information	To help the child monitor (cross-check) his or her understandings to see whether they make sense
To encourage independent application	To increase the child's independence and to decrease the child's dependence on the adult to identify problems, generate solutions, and evaluate the product and process of the problem-solving effort
Types of Interactions:	**Types of Interactions:**
Demonstrating/Modeling to show application of a process or strategy or how to do something	**Prompting** to help the child call up and build on the known
Thinking aloud to make audible the thinking process that you use and that a child can use to solve a problem	**Questioning** to encourage the child to clarify, extend, and diversify his or her thinking
Explaining to make clear to the child a process or specific information the child most likely will be unable to construct independently or without support	**Wondering aloud** to model and extend thinking processes
Reviewing to help the child recognize and organize the most important points of explicit instruction	**Restating** to help summarize, clarify, or confirm your understanding of the child's thoughts
Providing feedback and support as the child attempts to apply the new information or process to other situations	**Answering questions by posing new questions** to clarify or extend, to stimulate thinking, and/or to promote self-discovery and self-evaluation
	Responding to help the child appreciate his or her own accomplishments and attempts, to pose his or her own questions, and to reinforce a process

introducing a new unit of study with the class, or assisting an individual child with a math computation, you must know what knowledge the children already have and what strategies they can apply. You must have this information to work within the children's zones of proximal development (to know what is within their grasp). Only when you have this information can you decide what new information or explicit instruction, if any, to provide. Only when you have this information can you decide how to prompt and question an individual child or group of children to help them use what they know to construct new knowledge or solve a problem—to mediate.

How Do Children Learn? As you observe and interact with the children, you must also attend to how each child learns. You must notice and document the following:

- The type and amount of teacher support each child needs in order to internalize a concept or strategy

- How each child responds to various instructional mediations
- Whether the child is able to generalize a concept or strategy from one situation to another
- The degree of concrete support (e.g., manipulatives, self-help tools, aids to making visual comparisons) a child needs in order to begin to manipulate concepts mentally (abstractly)
- The contextual factors (e.g., specific kinds of learning events, topics of study, types of explicit instruction or mediation, noise level, visual distracters, independent or collaborative learning) that seem to result in the child's engagement or disengagement
- How the child seems to process information and to make connections
- How much wait time the child needs in order to solve a problem (to generate possible solutions, cross-check the possibilities, and evaluate the selected solution)
- The length of time a child needs to complete a task and the amount of refocusing he or she may need to complete a task at all

Are Children Able to Use the Knowledge and Strategies They Possess? The easiest task for teachers is observing what children know. Observing how children learn is more difficult. Recognizing whether children are able to use independently the knowledge and strategies they have developed to solve new problems and to construct new understandings within and across disciplines is even more challenging but equally important. For example, if a child has learned to say /ch/ when attempting to read the word *chair,* does the child write the letters *ch* when attempting to write the word *chair* or any other word beginning with /ch/? If the child has been taught to figure out unknown words independently in storybooks by cross-checking

alternative choices of words with different sources of information, does the child also apply the concept of cross-checking when independently reading informational books? If the child has learned the value of thinking about what he or she already knows about a topic before reading in history, does the child also do this when reading in science or when reading a fictional story? If the child is a problem solver in the classroom, is the child also a problem solver on field trips, on the playground, and at home? Does the child exhibit behaviors that indicate you have helped him or her develop the habits of mind that are the long-term goals of instructional interactions?

ADJUSTING TO INDIVIDUAL ABILITIES AND NEEDS

Children within any one classroom will demonstrate a wide range of responses to the learning environment. Some responses may be directly related to physical characteristics (e.g., vision, hearing, allergies) or to injuries resulting in processing difficulties. A child in your classroom may have been identified as being in need of special education or as having unique learning considerations. This identification may imply a need for certain instructional approaches or for instructional acceleration, extension, or enhancement. Your responsibility is to adjust instruction for each child. Adjustments should be based on your observations and documentation. Your modifications must also incorporate the information and suggestions you have gathered from various resource specialists to ensure that you are able to assist each child regardless of how the child learns or whether the child comes with a special education designation. You must adjust instruction to ensure that each child meets with academic success while progressing toward the short-term and long-term instructional goals established for all children.

To address individual needs effectively, enlisting the assistance or professional expertise of others may be helpful or necessary—for example:

- Visit with the school counselor to determine how to interact with a child who has experienced a personal trauma

- Inquire about specific cultural norms that may affect your interactions with the child or the child's interactions with others

- Seek information from an audiologist or occupational therapist to adjust the learning environment or event appropriately

- Meet with a specialist (e.g., remedial, gifted and talented, learning disabilities) to determine collaboratively how to challenge and support the learner appropriately

- Discuss in advance with a paraprofessional how and when to refocus a child who has difficulty staying on-task

- Engage the assistance of a special education aide to help a child with specific physical needs

- Invite a special educator to collaborate and co-teach with you to determine effective instructional interactions for a particular child or group of children

Cultural and Linguistic Differences: Implications for Instructional Interactions

Are Teaching and Learning Interactions Affected by Culture? Culture can affect the achievement of children in the primary years. A risk factor is often created by the mismatch between the cultural interaction style of the learner and that of the teacher (Trawick-Smith, 1997). Cultures differ in the ways children learn to learn. The Navajo, for example, are taught to learn through careful observation of demonstrations, by those competent in the desired skill, over an extended period of time (John, 1972). They observe extensively before they attempt to try out the skill. Such children would be at risk in classrooms of teachers who require active, hands-on exploration and learning prior to demonstrations. In various cultures, making eye contact with an adult has different implications. For some, it signifies honesty, integrity, and self-confidence; for others, it is considered disrespectful behavior. Consequently, "Cultural differences can lead teachers to misunderstand children, to assess incorrectly their developmental competence, and to plan incorrectly for their educational achievement" (Bowman & Stott, 1994, p. 121). However, teachers must not assume that all children of one culture have the same interaction and communication styles. Although a child has ties to a certain cultural heritage, he or she may not have assumed the values and behaviors of that culture. For a simple example, consider that a child with a surname common to a particular cultural or linguistic group may not speak the related language, nor may the child's immediate or extended family. Indeed, all may be native speakers of a different language.

It is your responsibility as the teacher to be knowledgeable about the interaction and communication styles related to the cultures represented by children in your classroom. This may require that you do some reading and that you do some firsthand research by actively participating in the communities served by your school. You must observe your children carefully to determine whether interaction styles are a result of cultural experiences or individual personalities (Kendall, 1996). The information you gain provides one more piece of crucial information as you plan appropriate instructional interactions for all the children.

As you become knowledgeable about various cultural interaction and communication styles, do not overlook the fact that these styles are also affected by the gender of the child. Even children who share a similar cultural heritage exhibit interaction and communication styles that reflect gender differences. Any culture has different expectations of behavior for children and adults of different genders (King, Chipman, & Cruz-Janzen, 1994; Sadker, Sadker, & Long, 1997). These expectations can significantly influence the interactions and communication between children and between children and teachers (and other adults) (Tannen, 1990, 1994). Teachers must be aware of how gender and gender stereotypes in various cultures, including their own, may influence their interactions with and expectations of children. Teachers can take steps to counteract gender stereotypes in the classroom: (1) become knowledgeable about and sensitive to gender roles assigned within and across cultures and existing stereotypes, (2) intentionally intervene when children reflect or express gender stereotypes in their activities and conversation, (3) become aware of children's personal gender stereotypes and adjust their expectations and verbal interactions accordingly, (4) provide opportunities through play for children to participate in activities that may be stereotypically assigned to one gender, and (5) read stories (fiction and nonfiction) to children about persons in roles or professions that defy traditional gender stereotypes (American Association of University Women, 1994; Derman-Sparks & A.B.C. Task Force, 1989; Robles de Melendez & Ostertag, 1997; Streitmatter, 1994).

What Vocabulary Terms Are Children Able to Use? It is crucial that you pay attention to the vocabulary terms a child uses to express what he or she knows or wants to know. It is also crucial that you pay attention to the language *you* use during instructional interactions and daily conversations with children. The vocabulary terms you use can support or confuse a child. Every individual brings a personal understanding to a word or intends to relate a certain meaning when using a certain word. The same word can cause children from different cultural or linguistic backgrounds to call up different concepts, images, or thoughts. For example, the word *slippers* in Colorado implies warm foot coverings used as house shoes, whereas in Hawaii the word *slippers* brings to mind rubber thongs for daily wear.

Some children may not have certain vocabulary terms because the related concept does not exist within their cultures. A person from the Rocky Mountain area knows that snowmen cannot be easily made with *dry snow*. A visitor from Hawaii, however, on hearing the term *dry snow*, may consider it an oxymoron.

The same word can cause children (and teachers) from the same culture but with different background experiences to bring different meanings to a word. In the field of education, the terms *whole language, direct instruction, skills, comprehension, authentic, phonics instruction* and *developmentally appropriate* conjure up dramatically different concepts to different teachers, administrators, and parents. They are *semantically charged!*

Some children may not be familiar with certain vocabulary terms common to their cultures because they have not had the personal opportunity to experience or develop understanding of the concept. Children with limited literacy experiences may not be familiar with the terms *word, letter,* or *sentence* and certainly may not have developed the related concepts. Children from small rural towns may not be familiar with the term *escalator.* Therefore, even encouraging such a child to use the accompanying illustration may not help the child identify the unknown word in print.

Whether the new learning situation is previewing or reading a new book, beginning a new unit of study, or engaging in a friendly conversation or instructional interactions, you must know the concepts and vocabulary the child has available and the meaning the child may or may not have for specific vocabulary terms you or an author may use. You must know when to provide new experiences or explicit instruction to help a child construct new concepts and develop related vocabulary if the child is to benefit effectively from the learning event. If you know the language the child has available, you can effectively help the child see relationships between the familiar and the unfamiliar.

THE LEARNING ENVIRONMENT

The learning environment consists of, and results from, interaction of the following:

- The expectations the teacher has of the children and of him- or herself
- The underlying beliefs the teacher has about teaching and learning
- The kinds and quality of learning taking place
- The types of learning events, explicit instruction, and mediation routinely provided by the teacher
- The types of interactions demonstrated and encouraged
- The management system designed by the teacher to facilitate independent learning, collaborative learning, and teacher/child interactions
- The affective atmosphere of the classroom
- The quantity and quality of learning materials available to both the teacher and the children
- The physical arrangement of the classroom

The learning environment should be designed and structured to promote self-regulation, independence, collaboration, mutual respect for alternative thoughts and suggestions, appreciation for all efforts (including those that may not result in success), questioning, investigations, conversations, problem solving, reflection, and self-evaluation by children and teachers.

Affective Environment

The *affective environment* refers to the tone, feeling, and atmosphere of the classroom and school. It is something you sense the moment you walk in the door. You notice the ways children interact with each other and with the teacher. You notice constructive activity or distracting noise. The affective environment clearly communicates the shared beliefs about how children learn best, the common expectations held for all children, and the habits of mind that are valued and promoted as long-term goals of instructional interactions. Figure 3.1 lists what you would expect to see and hear in an appropriate and effective environment for children ages four to eight.

Physical Arrangement

The *physical arrangement* of the learning environment also reflects the teacher's beliefs about how children learn and the expectations the teacher has for children. The physical arrangement of appropriate and effective classrooms for children ages four to eight reflects the experiential nature of learning that teachers value and contributes to the affective tone of the classroom. Ongoing, in-depth explorations are evident by projects throughout the room; experiments in progress accompanied by charts, graphs, and diagrams; individual cubbies brimming with field journals and collections; artifacts displayed and labeled; and materials for reading and writing in every nook and cranny. Materials such as microscopes, scales, metersticks, tools, computer software, art supplies, and literacy resources are easily accessible to children and are coded to allow the children to return them to the proper locations.

FIGURE 3.1 The affective environment: What you see and hear

When you walk into an appropriate and effective classroom for children ages four to eight, you will see the following:

- Busy, engaged, and focused children and teacher
- Children working independently
- Children working collaboratively
- Children sharing their learning with peers and adults
- Children conferencing with the teacher or other adults
- Teacher interacting instructionally with individual children and groups of children
- Children making choices
- Evidence of teacher's organizational system designed to promote child independence (e.g., labeled containers and spaces, responsibilities chart, sign-in sheets, daily schedule, individual daily plan sheets, visual reminders to regulate the number of children in any one learning area at a time, daily news, instruction charts for use of materials, signals to transition from one situation to another)
- Children independently gathering and returning materials and resources needed to construct a project
- Completed projects and projects in process
- Material written by children (e.g., books, stories, labels, signs, lists, personal dictionaries, journals, captioned pictures and diagrams, charts, announcements)
- Books, magazines, reference materials, dictionaries, thesauruses, pamphlets, brochures, and other print resources
- Computers, word processors, VCRs, tape recorders, and so forth
- Children using materials and self-help tools to assist them in their work
- Teacher and children listening to one another
- Teacher observing children and documenting the observations

When visiting in this classroom, you will hear the following:

- The hum of purposeful conversations and the quiet of personal thought and reflection
- Teacher and children asking wonderment questions and thought-provoking questions
- Teacher and children identifying problems, puzzles, or questions
- Teacher and children generating alternative ways to solve problems or to address questions
- Teacher and children encouraging one another in their efforts and attempts
- Teacher and children reflecting on the choices they have made
- Teacher and children evaluating learning processes and products

---

Primary classrooms should be intentionally designed to invite explorations and to facilitate the independent functioning of children. The physical arrangement, the organizational system, and the management system should work together to (1) empower children to be more independent in their learning, (2) provide teachers with the time necessary to interact instructionally with individual children, as well as with small groups of children, and (3) allow teachers the time and opportunities to observe and document progress.

Effective and appropriate classrooms are purposefully arranged to provide for *independent pursuits* (e.g., quiet corner, personal project area), *conversations and collaborative work* (e.g., sharing table, project corner, group area), *quiet work* (e.g., library/reading area, listening

Effective classrooms are intentionally designed to provide a warm and comfortable setting that invites explorations and encourages independence.

FIGURE 3.2 Oganizing for independence (disaster prevention)

1. On the basis of the ages and ability levels of your children, consider what materials to make accessible for children's independent use. Even messy materials can be made accessible to children if (a) appropriate containers are used (e.g., plastic containers with lids for premixed paints) and (b) the "mess" is limited to the appropriate area.

2. Organize the materials sensibly so that they are easily accessible to children in the areas where the materials are most frequently used. Discuss with children the rationale underlying the organization of the materials.

3. Use shelving, tables, and other storage units that are at levels accessible to children.

4. Use symbols, colors, pictures, and words to label shelves, baskets, containers, and storage cabinets to indicate placement of materials.

5. Demonstrate and explain the appropriate use of materials and equipment (e.g., tape recorders, workbench tools). Create accompanying how-to charts to place with the materials to serve as reminders to children.

6. Clearly separate quiet areas and active areas, dry areas and wet areas. For example, do not put the reading area next to the workbench.

7. Carefully consider the traffic patterns resulting from the physical arrangement. Large, open areas and long, straight walkways may encourage more fast-paced activity than may be desired.

center, writing center, mathematics area, quiet corner, carpeted areas), *active or noisy events* (e.g., reader's theater area, dramatic play area, workbench, block center, music area, gross motor area), and *messy activities* in need of a sink (e.g., science area, art center, snack area, water play, sand table). Areas for both teacher and children to organize and care for their personal materials and belongings are also provided.

Not every effective classroom contains all the areas listed above as discrete areas. Selected areas may be permanent, whereas others may change to accommodate a particular exploration. The permanent areas that you select for your classroom, however, should be discretely defined areas designed for specific purposes. These purposes should be made clear to the children. Guidelines for using the areas must be clearly explained and the appropriate use of the materials demonstrated. Suggestions for organizing the room and materials to facilitate independence and to prevent unnecessary disasters are described in Figure 3.2.

Management System

Classrooms can be managed in a way to facilitate the independent functioning of children. A well-managed classroom creates the time for sustained explorations by children, as well as the time necessary for the teacher to observe and interact instructionally with individuals, as well as with small groups of children. When you think about classroom management, consider several factors.

General Schedule. What kinds of learning events do you want children to engage in on a *daily* basis (e.g., morning message, read aloud, sustained independent reading, readers' and writers' workshop, mathematics computation and problem solving)? What kinds of learning events do you want to schedule on a *regular* basis but not necessarily on a daily basis (e.g., independent or class study of a topic, buddy reading, journal writing)? How much time will be allotted each day to independent learning, for large- and small-group instruction, and for the teacher to observe children as they are engaged in learning? What blocks of time will you need each day or each week for these events? What time is available to you? What time frame is imposed by the school (e.g., music, art, technology, physical education, recess, assemblies) or by the administration (e.g., minutes required for various content areas, bus schedules, field trip allotments)?

Children who are at risk or who have special needs often do better if they know the schedule of the day beforehand. Discussing and posting the daily schedule with both words and picture cues may help them to be comfortable with the environment and the activities. Some children with more severe needs often benefit from a schedule that pictures them engaged in the activities. For example, photographs of general learning events can be sequenced in a page from a photograph album with separate compartments for each event.

Routines. What routines can you establish to facilitate the efficient functioning of the classroom? Will you schedule certain learning events for certain times each day? Will a daily block of time be allotted to language arts or mathematics? Will children expect to find a mathematics word problem on the chalkboard immediately after recess each day or to have a read aloud every day after lunch? Will you help children learn to go to the group area and sit quietly when the lights go off? Children with special needs may need extra time and mediation (e.g., modeling, discussion, role playing, self-help tools or cues) to become independent in the classroom routines.

On the basis of the ages of the children and the amount of responsibility they can manage, you can help children share the responsibility for some clerical and maintenance tasks. For example, on their arrival at school in the morning, you can help children sign in or check off their names (perhaps initially accompanied by their picture for very young children), indicating they are present. Classroom attendance helpers can then be taught how to post the absentee list on the door or to carry it to the office.

Expectations for Behavior. Has the school community defined core values and long-range goals to guide the behaviors of children and teachers? Has the school community described expectations for behavior that will facilitate the values and goals set by the community? Are the expectations consistent across ages so that children know what is expected of them and what they can expect from others regardless of whether the teacher or another adult is present? Are the expectations based on mutual respect for each other? Have the expectations and consequences, as well as the rationale behind them, been clearly communicated to children? Do children know the consequences of decisions they make? Are consequences consistent from child to child, from situation to situation, and from teacher to teacher? A committee of teachers, parents, and children from one K–8 school collaborated to construct the **rubric** shown in Table 3.2 to communicate common values, goals, and expectations as they related to the mission statement of their school.

TABLE 3.2 Rubric of goals and expectations for students

TIME MANAGEMENT		
Beginning	*Developing*	*Skillful*
I often leave tasks to the last minute or do not allow enough time to complete a task.	I sometimes put things off but usually plan my work to accomplish tasks. I sometimes need to be reminded to get started on a task, and sometimes I misjudge the time required to complete a task.	I budget enough time to successfully complete tasks. I begin promptly without being reminded and work diligently. I also take into account setup and cleanup time.
DEPENDABILITY		
Beginning	*Developing*	*Skillful*
I rarely fulfill my responsibilities and need to be reminded repeatedly.	I attempt to find ways to remember my responsibilities and sometimes fulfill them.	I usually remember to do what was promised. Others can count on me.
WORK ETHIC		
Beginning	*Developing*	*Skillful*
I only do things that I find easy or already know how to do; I rarely consider the quality. I don't pay enough attention to directions. I choose behaviors that are counterproductive to getting started and continuing work on a task. I allow myself to be easily distracted and distract others with irrelevant discussion or behavior.	I try to produce just enough to get by; quality is not always a consideration. I sometimes pay close attention to directions. Sometimes I set unrealistic goals. I usually work on my assignments but sometimes stop if I get stuck. I occasionally digress from the task at hand and talk with others about irrelevant topics.	I make each task my own by asking appropriate questions when problems arise, negotiating with the instructor, and striving toward the highest possible quality in my work. I follow directions. I set realistic goals. I stay on-task and ask questions when I get stuck. I limit my discussion with others to areas relevant to the task.
GROUP PARTICIPATION		
Beginning	*Developing*	*Skillful*
I am inattentive and unfocused when a group activity is held. I offer little or nothing, even when I am expected to be prepared. I may distract others with verbal or physical behaviors. My own opinions are not supported with sound reasoning.	My contributions to a group activity are inconsistent, depending on my level of focus, preparation, or interest. I rarely distract others. I sometimes support my opinions with sound reasoning.	I always prepare well for any planned group activity and participate in impromptu activities as well. Throughout the activity, I make valuable contributions. My opinions are supported with sound reasoning. I listen to support or contradict others in a respectful manner. I value creative inspiration both in myself and in others.

TREATMENT OF OTHERS

Beginning	*Developing*	*Skillful*
My behavior is inconsiderate. I act without regard for the feelings of others, including those I say are my friends. I don't use polite words like *thank you, please,* and *excuse me.* Neither my words nor my actions shows care and concern for others.	I show some attention to caring about others. Sometimes I can show serious attention to being respectful and polite, especially with close friends or teachers I know will demand it, but I do less with those I don't know or care about.	I show complete control of my behavior by using polite words with everyone and giving support to friends and others with words and actions. I use no putdowns and make some attempt to tell others to stop their use as well.

RISK TAKING

Beginning	*Developing*	*Skillful*
Only when directed will I try a new activity. Sometimes I won't even try. I will experiment only when assured of success. I am unable to overcome my fears.	I will try some new challenges when shown all the steps (given a lot of support). I will try to experiment when the probability of success is high. If my work does fail, I try to find excuses for it, rather than deciding just to try again.	I will try new things often, and when I fall short, I will try again. I am motivated to find new challenges that aren't the usual thing done. I like to experiment and to be surprised by the outcome. When I take challenges, I do my personal best and don't rely on excuses for failing something tried.

OWNERSHIP OF BEHAVIOR

Beginning	*Developing*	*Skillful*
Nothing is ever my fault. Even after discussion, I rarely take responsibility and am usually indifferent to the effect my behavior has on myself and others.	Sometimes I take responsibility for my actions; at other times, I can only take responsibility after discussion. I am sometimes swayed by the behavior of others. I am learning to see and care how my actions affect myself and others.	I take responsibility for my actions. I choose to act appropriately. When I do not, I make the necessary amends. I accept the consequences of my behavior and can discuss its effects on myself and others. I learn from my mistakes.

Source: *Relating the Rubric to Our Mission,* by the Logan School for Creative Learning, 1995, Denver, CO: Author. Reprinted with permission by Linda Baie, The Logan School for Creative Learning.

Independent Work Time. At times during each day, you will be engaged with individual children or with small groups of children. It is important that you and the child or children not be needlessly interrupted. Others will have to work independently of the teacher. You must plan carefully for this to happen. For these time periods, you must plan learning events that children are capable of, and prepared for, doing independently. This is not a time for them to interact with new materials or activities that require extensive introduction, information, or assistance from the teacher in order to stay effectively engaged. The vignette entitled "Preparation for Independent Learning Events or Centers" describes how one kindergarten teacher helps children identify available choices during independent learning time.

PREPARATION FOR INDEPENDENT LEARNING EVENTS OR CENTERS

During morning group time, Miss Yamana shared with the kindergartners some of the choices they would have during independent center time while she worked with a small group in the writing center. She began by showing the class a flannel board with a figure of a gingerbread man on it.

Miss Yamana: Here is someone from a story we have read many times and know very well. What story do you think it is? What other characters from the story do you think I might have to put on the flannel board?

(Children enthusiastically offered names of other characters in the story. Miss Yamana put each character on the flannel board.)

Miss Yamana: Today, the book and the flannel board with all the characters from *The Gingerbread Man* will be in the reading area. When you are in the reading area, you can put the figures on the flannel board as you tell the story to yourself or to a friend. Maybe a friend will want to read the book to you as you put the characters on the flannel board, or you can use the book to remind yourself of the story. Please be sure that all the characters are on the flannel board when you leave the reading area so that your friends can also enjoy the story.

If you choose to work in the science area today, remember to look at your corn plant to see whether it's grown since the last time you measured it with your number line. Don't forget to color in the number line next to your name on the chart to show how tall your plant is. You may also want to draw and write in your science journal about any changes you see in your plant. Who measured

their plants yesterday? What changes did you see? Who would like to share what they recorded in their journal?

(Children related what they had observed, and several shared their journals. Miss Yamana then showed the class a clear plastic box filled with parquetry blocks. She demonstrated for the group how she could use different configurations of the blocks to make squares of different sizes.)

Miss Yamana: How many squares do you think we could make out of all twenty-four of these blocks?

(Miss Yamana recorded each child's prediction on a chart. This gave her an opportunity to model how to use the chart.)

Miss Yamana: When you go to the math area today, try to make as many squares as you can. When you have made as many as you can, count them and record on this chart the number of squares you made. See if you were able to make as many squares as you predicted. After you are finished, put all the blocks back into the container so that others can have a turn. Now, if you see your name on my Special Group chart, meet me in the writing center. If you are not on my chart and your name ends with *N*, you may choose the center you want to start with today. If your name ends with *E*, you may choose your center . . .

(She continues this process until all the children have gone to a center to work.)

Depending on the ages and abilities of your children, independent time may be a time that they are asked to reflect by writing about and illustrating an experience such as a field trip, a science experiment, a guest speaker, a read aloud, or a reading related to their current investigation of a topic. You might ask them to re-spond in their journals to specific questions you have posed. Even emerging readers and writers are capable of independently communicating their thoughts in writing, especially if you have demonstrated for them various ways young chil-dren write (e.g., scribble strings, discrete scrib-ble marks, letterlike forms, random letter strings, sound spelling; see Chapters 7 and 8). This op-portunity for independent construction of writ-ten language, regardless of their developmental level, helps children build new understandings about the conventions and authentic functions of print.

Other learning events that children *can be prepared* to engage in independently and that are designed to provide opportunities *to apply* newly acquired skills or strategies include cen-ter events, buddy reading, literacy or mathemat-ics games, independent-level reading, emergent storybook reading (pretend reading), listening to tapes with books, independent writing associ-ated with writer's workshop, using computers, and independent or collaborative investigations. Your choice of independent learning events for the children will, of course, be based on their ages and capabilities.

Whichever independent learning events you select for children to do, it is crucial that you have (1) clarified where all necessary materials, including self-help tools, are located, (2) demon-strated how to play the available games or how to use the available equipment, (3) provided clear and simple guidelines and timelines for so-cial interactions, (4) ensured that any reading the children are to do is at their independent level, (5) determined that children have the prerequi-site abilities and understandings to participate successfully in the events for a sustained amount of time, (6) clarified the choices and amount of time available for independent learning events, (7) considered the time that children can be expected to work independently, on the basis of their capabilities, and (8) communicated to

Thoughtful planning by the teacher can help four-year-olds become independent.

the children how they can appropriately seek your assistance when you are interacting with others, and (9) planned time to interact with children to review what they have done during independent time. Collaboration with special service providers such as special education teachers, bilingual education teachers, and reading specialists will help you in planning adaptations for the diversity of children in your classroom.

You can, and should, provide appropriate self-help tools to assist children with indepen-dent functioning and learning. **Self-help tools** are materials that children can independently refer to or use to locate or figure out information

Editor's glasses, editing checklists, letter/sound charts, and personal dictionaries all serve as self-help tools.

they want or need to accomplish a task. Children must be taught where to find and how to use each self-help tool prior to its use during independent time. Some self-help tools are tailored to individual children; others are designed for group use. Some self-help tools must be available at each child's workspace (e.g., personal word banks, personal dictionaries, alphabet strips, editing guides, letter/sound charts, number lines, time management menus); others are visually or physically accessible to all (e.g., word charts, word rings, mathematics manipulatives, letter tiles, how-to reminders). Some self-help tools are commercially prepared; others are constructed by teachers and/or children.

Many self-help tools, such as dictionaries, thesauruses, alphabet charts, and editing guides, should be available both at individual workspaces and for group use. Some children must be able to see, touch, or manipulate the self-help tools to benefit from them; others are able to access the same information from a wall chart or bulletin board. Some children can effectively use commercially prepared self-help tools; others require self-help tools prepared especially for them on the basis of personal connections. Selecting or designing and making appropriately accessible the self-help tools each child requires to function independently is your responsibility.

Some children have difficulty remaining involved in independent learning events. A checklist with the words *yes* or *no* or pictures of a thumb up/thumb down or of a smiley face/sad face is useful for children to monitor their involvement. Discuss with the children which behaviors reflect acceptable and appropriate engagement with an activity. Demonstrate how to use self-talk, such as, "Am I doing what I am supposed to be doing?" and how to check the appropriate word or picture on cue. Initially, monitor the children as well and help them check the appropriate word or icon. Use a touch, a look, a soft sound, a physical token, or other unobtrusive way to alert the children to ask themselves the monitoring question. (For information on external mediation of cognition, see Bodrova & Leong, 1996.)

Collaborative Work Time. Why do new teachers plan opportunities for children to learn collaboratively in the classroom? What does collaborative learning mean? *Collaborative (cooperative) learning* is a learning situation in which two or more people work together toward the same goal (Hill & Hill, 1990). The advantages associated with engaging children in collaborative learning are many. When used appropriately and effectively, collaborative learning opportunities can

- Provide children with enjoyable ways of exploring ideas and information with other children (Hill & Hill, 1990)
- Lead to more advanced cognitive development and promote higher academic achievement (Doise & Mugny, 1984; Johnson, Maruyama, Johnson, Nelson, & Skon, 1981)
- Help children develop leadership skills (Johnson & Johnson, 1983, 1987)
- Result in children being more positive about school, subject areas, and teachers

(Cooper, Johnson, Johnson, & Wilderson, 1980; Johnson & Johnson, 1981, 1983, 1987)
- Promote children's care and respect for others (Hill & Hill, 1990)
- Increase children's sense of belonging within the classroom (Hill & Hill, 1990)
- Help children develop the skills necessary to collaborate effectively with others outside the classroom
- Result in positive effects for achievement, interpersonal relations, self-perception, and social development (Maheady, Sacca, & Harper, 1991)

Effective collaborative learning activities have two characteristics in common: (1) Children involved have similar goals for the activity or project, and (2) each child involved recognizes that his or her learning will result in success only if all contribute and work together. Children cannot be expected to participate successfully in collaborative learning simply by being required to work as a group. The teacher must help children learn how to work together collaboratively.

It is the teacher's job to define the specific roles involved in cooperative learning (e.g., observer, recorder, questioner, timekeeper) and the designated responsibilities of each role. It is the teacher's responsibility to teach children the skills they need to be successful in their role and to provide opportunities for them to practice these skills with support and guidance. It is also the teacher's responsibility to assist children to recognize that the roles are interdependent and to manage conflict effectively if it occurs. Children must recognize that the individuals in each role must function effectively if the group goals are to be achieved. The teacher must model how to reflect on personal efforts in the collaborative process and to provide each group member with thoughtful and constructive observations.

When planning a cooperative learning experience for children with disabilities, consider the following:

- Which children will work well with the special needs child without detriment to their own learning?

- What roles will be given to the special needs child?

- What criteria will be used to assess this child's performance?

- Which social skills will be emphasized within a lesson (Johnson & Johnson, 1989)?

- How will the activity be structured for successful engagement by this child (Mainzer, Mainzer, & Slavin, 1993)?

(For more information on how to facilitate effective collaborative learning in the classroom, refer to Hill & Hill, 1990.)

EVALUATING THE EFFECTIVENESS OF YOUR INSTRUCTIONAL INTERACTIONS

It is not uncommon for a teacher to try a new instructional activity or instructional strategy described in a teacher's guide, methods text, or professional journal. After using the activity or strategy, the teacher may often wonder, Did I do it right? The appropriateness of instructional interactions cannot be determined by whether you follow each step as it was described. Neither can you turn to an outside observer for verification of the procedure. You must instead reflect on the children's responses to the instructional interactions to determine both appropriateness and effectiveness. This reflection must occur during, as well as after, the instructional interactions (Schon, 1983).

During instructional interactions, you must observe how children are responding. Do they seem to be confused or frustrated? Is the task too difficult? Is it beyond their zones of proximal development? Are your comments themselves confusing? If so, are you able to adjust instruction to clarify the confusion and to increase children's successes? Do the children seem to be accomplishing what was set out to be accomplished? Do the children generate hypotheses, initiate problem solving, and self-evaluate? Do they seem to look consistently to you for information, direction, and confirmation? Are you noticing what they know and how they are making new connections? Are you able to integrate this information into your instructional interactions?

After providing instruction, you must reflect back on the entire process, asking yourself many of these questions. As you reflect, are you able to anticipate future instructional interactions and to plan mentally the needed adjustments? Are you able to identify new information about children's understandings and ways of learning? If the children appeared confused or frustrated, disengaged, and disinterested, or if their responses reflected that they were already familiar with the concepts being presented, reflect on (1) whether the goal you selected was appropriate and (2) whether the strategies and interactions you selected were appropriate both to the goal and to the children. Was the goal or task too challenging or too easy?

SUMMARY

The long-term effectiveness of the planning you do and the decisions about instructional interactions you make is determined by whether children are clarifying and extending understandings and whether they are becoming more self-regulated learners. Are children developing a broad knowledge base by exploring many areas and constructing new understandings within many disciplines? Are children developing new concepts and habits of mind and applying them across the disciplines inside and outside school? Is the design of the classroom and of your systems of organization and management supportive of the goals you have established for yourself and the children? Are the processes of reflection and self-evaluation becoming natural for both you and the children? These are questions you should never stop asking. They are part of the reflection process in which excellent teachers engage throughout their lives as they plan for the continuation of their own learning and the learning of children.

REFERENCES

American Association of University Women. (1994). Equitable treatment of girls and boys in the classroom. In E. Nunn & C. Boyatzis (Eds.), *Child growth and development* (pp. 67–72). Guilford, CT: Dushkin.

Biber, B. (1988). The challenge of professionalism: Integrating theory and practice. In B. Spodek, O. N. Saracho, & D. L. Peters (Eds.), *Professionalism and the early childhood practitioner* (pp. 29–47). New York: Teachers College Press.

Bodrova, E., & Leong, D. (1996). *Tools of the mind: The Vygotskian approach to early childhood education.* Upper Saddle River, NJ: Merrill/Prentice Hall.

Bowman, B., & Stott, F. (1994). Understanding development in a cultural context. In B. Mallory & R. New (Eds.), *Diversity and developmentally appropriate practices* (pp. 119–133). New York: Teachers College Press.

Cooper, L., Johnson, D., Johnson, R., & Wilderson, F. (1980). The effects of cooperation, competition, and individualization on cross-ethnic, cross-sex, and cross-ability friendships. *Journal of Social Psychology, 3,* 243–252.

Derman-Sparks, L., & A.B.C. Task Force. (1989). *Antibias curriculum: Tools for empowering young children.* Washington, DC: National Association for the Education of Young Children.

Doise, W., & Mugny, G. (1984). *The social development of the individual.* New York: Pergamon.

Hill, S., & Hill, T. (1990). *The collaborative classroom: A guide to cooperative learning.* Portsmouth, NH: Heinemann.

John, V. (1972). Styles of learning–styles of teaching: Reflections on the education of Navajo children. In C. Cazden, V. John, & D. Hymes (Eds.), *Functions of language in the classroom.* New York: Teachers College Press.

Johnson, D., & Johnson, R. (1981). Effects of cooperation and individual learning experiences on interethnic interaction. *Journal of Educational Psychology, 73,* 454–459.

Johnson, D., & Johnson, R. (1983). The socialization and achievement crisis: Are cooperative learning experiences a solution? In L. Bickman (Ed.), *Applied social psychology annual IV.* Beverly Hills, CA: Sage.

Johnson, D., & Johnson, R. (1987). *Cooperation and competition.* Hillsdale, NJ: Erlbaum.

Johnson, D., & Johnson, R. (1989). Cooperative learning: What special education teachers need to know. *Pointer, 33*(2), 5–10.

Johnson, D., Maruyama, G., Johnson, R., Nelson, D., & Skon, L. (1981). Effects of cooperative, competitive, and individualistic goal structures on achievement: A meta-analysis. *Psychological Bulletin, 89,* 47–62.

Katz, L., & Chard, S. (1989). *Engaging children's minds: The project approach.* Norwood, NJ: Ablex.

Kendall, F. (1996). *Diversity in the classroom: New approaches to the education of young children.* New York: Teachers College Press.

King, E., Chipman, M., & Cruz-Janzen, M. (1994). *Educating young children in a diverse society.* Boston: Allyn & Bacon.

Logan School for Creative Learning. (1995). *Relating the rubric to our mission.* Unpublished document.

Maheady, L., Sacca, M. K., & Harper, G. T. (1991). Peer-mediated instruction: Review of potential applications for special education. *Reading, Writing, and Learning Disabilities, 7,* 75–102.

Mainzer, R., Mainzer, K., & Slavin, R. (1993). What special education teachers should know about cooperative learning. *Teacher Education and Special Education, 16,* 42–50.

Marzano, R. (1992). *A different kind of classroom: Teaching with dimensions of learning.* Alexandria, VA: Association for Supervision of Curriculum and Instruction.

Robles de Melendez, W., & Ostertag, V. (1997). *Teaching young children in multicultural classrooms: Issues, concepts, and strategies.* Albany, NY: Delmar.

Sadker, M., Sadker, D., & Long, L. (1997). Gender and educational equality. In J. Banks & C. Banks (Eds.), *Multicultural education: Issues and perspectives* (3rd ed., pp. 131–149). Boston: Allyn & Bacon.

Schon, D. (1983). *The reflective practitioner: How professionals think in action.* New York: Basic Books.

Streitmatter, J. (1994). *Toward class and gender equity in the classroom.* Albany: State University of New York Press.

Tannen, D. (1990). *You just don't understand: Women and men in conversation.* New York: Morrow.

Tannen, D. (1994). *Gender and discourse.* New York: Oxford University Press.

Trawick-Smith, J. (1994). *Interactions in the classroom: Facilitating play in the early years.* Upper Saddle River, NJ: Merrill/Prentice Hall.

Trawick-Smith, J. (1997). *Early childhood development: A multicultural perspective.* Upper Saddle River, NJ: Merrill/Prentice Hall.

When you are out walking, nature does not confront you for three quarters of an hour only with flowers and in the next only with animals.

(Elvin, 1977, p. 29)

4

A Cohesive, Integrated Curriculum

CONSIDER YOUR BELIEFS

- What is a cohesive, integrated curriculum?
- How is an integrated curriculum different from a thematic approach to teaching and learning?
- What are the benefits of integrating curriculum?
- Is addressing all school standards, curriculum objectives, and individual learning needs solely within an integrated curriculum feasible?
- How may curriculum be integrated in different ways?
- Must all subjects be included during each integrated unit?
- How will you plan and schedule an integrated curriculum? Will you integrate all day?
- How can you document and evaluate the development of individual children's learning?

Curriculum consists of what is to be taught and how it is to be taught. When teachers make decisions about curriculum, they must consider how it is to be developed, how it is to be delivered, and how it is to be assessed. As always, the decisions teachers make about curriculum are based on their personal and professional belief systems about *what children should learn and how they learn best*.

THE TIME-CLOCK CURRICULUM

With increased demands for additions to the curriculum (e.g., technology, safety, problem solving, self-esteem, drug awareness) and accountability for specific standards within each discipline, teachers have more difficulty scheduling everything adequately. The perception is that everything must be squeezed in even if this results in superficial coverage. Some coverage seems better than no coverage.

Trying to schedule seat-time for each identified discipline and each content objective is an overwhelming task for teachers. Once recesses, lunch, and specials are scheduled, teachers struggle to plug the required subjects and content into the remaining time slots simply to get them recorded as covered on the lesson plans. For some teachers, getting through the day successfully comes to mean simply getting to everything that was on the daily plan, often without regard for the amount or quality of learning that may or may not have occurred. The focus is more on the cooperation and management of children to get through the day's ac-

tivities efficiently, rather than on concern for children's enthusiasm or lack of enthusiasm for learning. The habits of mind that should provide direction and purpose for teachers are not even on the horizon.

For children, the activities of a time-clock curriculum such as the one described in Figure 4.1 are viewed as independent and unrelated except by time and/or day (If it is 11:00, this must be mathematics). Different activities have different appeal to different children. Some children are better at some activities than they are at others. The challenge for many children becomes one of completing the day's activities

FIGURE 4.1 The time-clock curriculum

The substitute teacher for Ms. Allen's six/seven-year-old children examined the plans left for the day. This is what she saw scheduled for the morning. Her afternoon would be filled with PE, safety session with a counselor, and a science lesson on measurement.

8:45 Pledge, attendance, lunch count, calendar, and a poem (p. 15 of handwriting workbook)

9:55 Handwriting: Demonstrate upper- and lowercase Rr. Have children make 2 rows of uppercase and 2 rows of lowercase *R*'s on handwriting paper.
Have children copy poem in best handwriting—will be graded

9:15 Reading
Whole Class: Mini-lesson on Story Grammar (see attached story map)

    Group 1   (with teacher) Shared Reading (Mrs. Wishy Washy) and Innovations of a Text (independently—use prepared booklets)

    Group 2   Phonics Workbook pages 25, 26, and 27/Independently select and reread three Level 6 books

    Group 3   Independent Reading and Literature Response Logs (check logs)

10:15 Spelling   10 high-frequency words (have children independently write a story using these words—underline the words)

10:40 Recess

11:00 Math (see worksheets)

    Group 1   Addition Computation with Regrouping

    Group 2   Addition Computation without Regrouping

    Group 3   Math Facts to Ten

11:30 Computer lab

12:00 Lunch

(with varying attention to quality) without getting into trouble. For some children, the daily reward for successfully completing activities is a sense of personal accomplishment. For others, the reward is acceptance, and sometimes praise, by peers, parents, and teachers, with the grand prize being promotion to the next grade level. If the tasks are too difficult and too unappealing to a child, however, the results can be disastrous.

When activities are segmented and presented in isolation, children may learn bits and pieces of information and develop certain skills, but some of them may have difficulty understanding how the information or skills might be used in other contexts. They may not see the relevance of, or be able to apply independently, the information and skills they are learning in their daily activities, inside or outside school.

A COHESIVE, INTEGRATED APPROACH TO TEACHING AND LEARNING

For learning to make sense to children, it must be introduced, taught, put together, and applied in ways that make sense to them and in ways that help them make sense of their world. Learning should encourage children to "pose questions, pursue puzzles, and increase their awareness of significant phenomena around them" (Katz & Chard, 1989). This can be accomplished in the classroom by integrating curriculum.

Integrated curriculum means "providing an organizing topic or concept within children's range of experience [and understanding] that allows children to explore, interpret, and engage in learning activities that draw on goals from one or more subject-matter disciplines" (Bredekamp & Rosegrant, 1995, p. 168). When the topics of investigations reflect the concerns, interests, experiences, and environments of children, the curriculum will be cohesive as well as integrated. An integrated and cohesive curriculum (Beane, 1995) is the goal.

Supporting Diverse Learners Through Integrated Curriculum

Children with learning disabilities often have difficulty gleaning concepts from isolated experiences and do not readily transfer understandings and information between activities that are not unified. They often are not able to connect new understandings and experiences developed at school to their real world without mediation. Integrated curriculum as described in this chapter builds in natural connections for children and provides time for teachers to mediate as needed.

Integrated curriculum provides an appropriate and supportive approach to learning for children with unique abilities or special needs (Wood, 1997). Flexibility in the ways made available for children to gather and share information enables all children to participate actively, to be appropriately challenged, and to be successful. Children are encouraged to gather information from a variety of sources, including videos, audiotapes, print resources, interviews with experts, and computer software. They may also share their learnings in a variety of ways, including demonstrations, constructions (e.g., models, dioramas, graphs, charts), videos, dramas, written reports, poetry, stories, brochures, simulations, music, and art. Integrated curriculum is an effective way to address the cognitive needs and creative abilities of all children.

An additional benefit of integrated curriculum is flexibility of time and scheduling. For example, some children may be required to spend time out of the classroom with specialists, thus missing portions of the school day often used by the teacher to present new learnings. Because investigations within an integrated curriculum can be conducted over a period of time, these children are not penalized by their absences. Investigations can be conducted at other times of the day or on other days.

Children who may not be proficient readers and writers are encouraged to gather and share information in creative ways.

Planning for Integrated Curriculum

Integrated curriculum is a planning model that can be used by all teachers, including special educators, to achieve both short- and long-term goals. It can be used to address a broad range of content and processes, to enhance children's enthusiasm and dispositions for learning, to stimulate personal inquiry and research, to nurture problem-solving abilities, to develop self-regulation, and to facilitate independence. Integrated curriculum requires that the teacher identify where the content within the various **disciplines** (e.g., science, social studies, mathematics, language arts) overlaps or is related (integration can occur here) and where it does not (content must be addressed separately). Therefore, teachers who are planning integrated curriculum should frequently ask themselves (1) which content and process objectives from

the various disciplines overlap, are related, and can be taught simultaneously; and (2) which aspects must be addressed separately (Bredekamp & Rosegrant, 1995)?

It is not necessary or even desirable for all disciplines to be addressed in each unit of study within an integrated curriculum. The content and processes of certain disciplines should be integrated only *as they make sense* or *are required* to pursue investigations within a particular unit of study. Sometimes the particular structures, processes, concepts, and skills of a discipline cannot be addressed to the degree necessary for efficient and effective application within an integrated unit. Blocks of time may need to be dedicated to the explicit study of discipline-specific concepts, skills, or processes. For example, although the application of mathematics concepts and skills (e.g., graphing, ratios, place value, computations) may often be required for pursuing investigations, these concepts and skills may need to be explicitly taught, and time provided for guided practice, prior to the actual application within an investigation.

The topic under investigation should determine which disciplines are integrated and how—that is, which disciplines will contribute to the investigation. Disciplines, content, and processes must be integrated in a sensible way. Disciplines should be included only as they work together to serve the purposes of an investigation. Facilitating investigations that make sense to children (which by nature requires integration) is the goal. Integration is the means, not the end.

Thematic Approach versus Integrated Curriculum

When planning curriculum, some teachers use the terms *thematic approach* and *integrated curriculum* synonymously. In reality, a "thematic unit" often reflects the inclusion of all disciplines but does not reflect the characteristics of a cohesive, integrated curriculum. A cohesive, integrated curriculum

- Is organized around topics within children's understanding and that help children make sense of their world
- Is organized around topics that provide opportunities to explore a broad range of content areas (disciplines)
- Encourages in-depth exploration of a topic within an integrated unit
- Integrates the content and processes of many disciplines into an integrated unit but only as they contribute to the investigation
- Stimulates and facilitates personal inquiry, problem solving, self-regulation, and independence

BEARS: A THEMATIC UNIT

The door to Mrs. Roby's classroom looks like an entrance to a cave. Inside the entrance is a bookshelf where the five- and six-year-old children have set teddy bears they brought from home. The walls are covered with drawings, posters, and photographs of bears. The calendar has bear cut-outs to mark the date. The helpers' chart is filled with construction paper bears mounted on craft sticks, each containing the name of a child.

The "cave" is filled with happy, engaged children. Some children are in the art area making bears out of paper plates and construction paper. They culminate their efforts by adding a blue pocket (to follow up the teacher's reading aloud of *Pocket for Corduroy* [Freeman, 1978]). Some children are in the mathematics area, working on addition. They are attempting to match two groups of felt bears by counting the dots on one group and matching them with the corresponding numerals written on the other set. In the reading area, children select from a group of bear books, the favorite being *Brown Bear, Brown Bear, What Do You See?* (Martin, 1983). Some children choose to read from a teacher-made chart of *Going on a Bear Hunt* (Rosen, 1989), a chant the teacher introduced earlier in the day during music time. The teacher is helping a small group of children with a cut-up activity that requires them to match text and pictures from *Going on a Bear Hunt*. Stimulated by their recent trip to the zoo, children in the block area are building a zoo, with special attention to construction of a habitat for their plastic bears—polar bears, brown bears, black bears, and so on. In the dramatic play area, children are acting out *Goldilocks and the Three Bears* (Ziefert, 1994).

Bear-shaped books are available in the writing area, along with bear stamps and animal stickers to encourage the production of a version of *Brown Bear, Brown Bear* or an original bear story. In the science area, a swatch of bear fur and a piece of honeycomb are available for children to touch and to examine with a magnifying glass. At snack time, children are treated to cupcakes covered with gummy bears.

BEARS: AN INTEGRATED UNIT

Across the hall, five- and six-year-old children in Mrs. Amdur's classroom are also learning about bears. The door looks like an entrance to a cave, just like Mrs. Roby's. The walls are covered with charts and pictures constructed and organized to indicate what the children have learned and are investigating about bears. Questions to guide new investigations are posted. A large wall map of the world depicts where different kinds of bears live. Special events, including a trip to the zoo, are highlighted on the class calendar. Choices that children have for pursuing their investigations of bears during the day are recorded in the morning message.

These children are also happy and engaged. The dramatic play and block areas have been consolidated to form a zoo complex. Various kinds of bears are placed in corresponding habitats created by the children. Several children are dressed as, and are reenacting the roles of, tour guide, veterinarian, nursery attendant, zookeeper, zoologist, and concessionaire observed during their field trip to the zoo. They each wear teacher-made pins indicating job titles.

In the art center, some children are constructing dioramas of habitats appropriate to a bear of their choice. The teacher is helping several children in the mathematics center compare their heights and weights with the heights and weights of various types of bears charted on the wall (see the table "Are All Bears the Same?"). They are also trying to determine the number of children (and which combination of children) it would take to balance on a teeter-totter with a panda.

At the science center, children are examining several swatches of different kinds of bear fur on loan from the zoo and are documenting their observations in their science journals. Other children are playing a teacher-made game in which they attempt to match labeled pictures of bears with pictures of the appropriate habitat and diet. In the reading center, children are engaged with nonfiction and fiction books about bears. Even the fiction books (e.g., *The Biggest Bear* [Ward, 1973], *Blueberries for Sal* [McCloskey, 1976]) selected for this center implicitly relate information that describes the behaviors and habits of bears. Some children are listening to nonfiction books on audiotapes as they examine the illustrations. A paraprofessional is assisting several children in the writing center. Some children are writing tall tales about bears, inspired by the ones the teacher read to them from *Fat Man in a Fur Coat* (Schwartz, 1984). Other children are working on informational books about the type of bear they have chosen to study. Posted in the center are charts of bear words.

Connected versus Cohesive

Although both vignettes above represent each teacher's attempts to "connect" children's learning throughout the day, it is obvious that each of

Are all bears the same?

	panda	polar	Kodiak	grizzly	(choice)
habitat					
diet					
color					
height					
weight					
endangered?					

these teachers has a different idea about what children should be learning and how they should go about learning it. The goals identified and the planning each teacher did to reach those goals were very different.

Mrs. Roby created a thematic unit (see Figure 4.2) using the topic of bears. One of her goals was to help children develop an awareness of bears, an animal of interest to them. Another goal was to include all the disciplines within the theme by somehow connecting bears to each center and to each large-group activity. She wanted to keep the children actively engaged with interesting and fun activities.

Mrs. Amdur clearly designed all activities to help the children develop *understandings* (critical knowledge) about the habitats, diets, characteristics, and behaviors of different types of bears. She wanted the children to have opportunities for personal explorations within the study of bears. She also wanted to provide the children with opportunities to develop and use their literacy, science, and mathematics skills to *learn about bears.* The long-term goals of initiating inquiries, problem solving, and self-regulation were evident in her choice of learning events. She wanted children to be enthusiastic about learning and to be actively engaged.

Both teachers attempted to address curriculum mandates and content standards. Both teachers selected topics that would be of interest to children and attempted to design activities and learning events that would result in active engagement. Both teachers attempted to connect activities and learning events through a common theme. The planning models and the assumptions that guided their decisions, however, were quite different. Mrs. Roby used a planning model that resulted in all curriculum areas being addressed and connected to the theme. Even though the activities were loosely "bear related" (e.g., mathematics problems on bear cut-outs, bear-related literacy activities, bear shapes for the calendar, a song about a bear

hunt), these "connections" were not authentic in that they did not contribute to the children's further understanding of the topic—bears. If her goal had been a cohesive, integrated unit, the key question Mrs. Roby should have asked herself about each learning event was, How does the children's engagement in this event contribute to their further understanding of bears? It is evident that Mrs. Amdur posed this question about each learning event she designed. She used a planning model that helped her in planning a cohesive, integrated unit (see Figure 4.3).

The Project Approach

Similar in philosophy to integrated curriculum is the **project approach** (Katz & Chard, 1989). The project approach to the teaching and learning of children ages four to eight, like integrated curriculum, seeks to "engage children's minds" in ways that deepen their understanding of their own experiences and environment. Katz and Chard, authors of *Engaging Children's Minds: The Project Approach,* refer to the "mind" not merely as knowledge and skills but also as emotional, moral, and aesthetic sensibilities.

Teachers using this approach encourage children to identify topics from their environment for in-depth independent or collaborative study. Project work activities generally consist of investigations, constructions, and dramatic play. **Investigations** include both active and receptive opportunities for children to develop new understandings and ideas. Active strategies may include asking questions, interviewing, and looking up things in books. Receptive strategies may include listening and reading.

Constructions, planned and built by children, often involve woodworking, drawing, painting, cutting, and pasting. Constructions may include models of props for dramatic play themes, (e.g., operating room, store, post office, zoo) or smaller scale models for display, such as charts, books, or graphs. The quality of the constructions

FIGURE 4.2 Sample planning web. Thematic unit: Bears; Ages 5–6; Wednesday, Day 3 of one-week unit

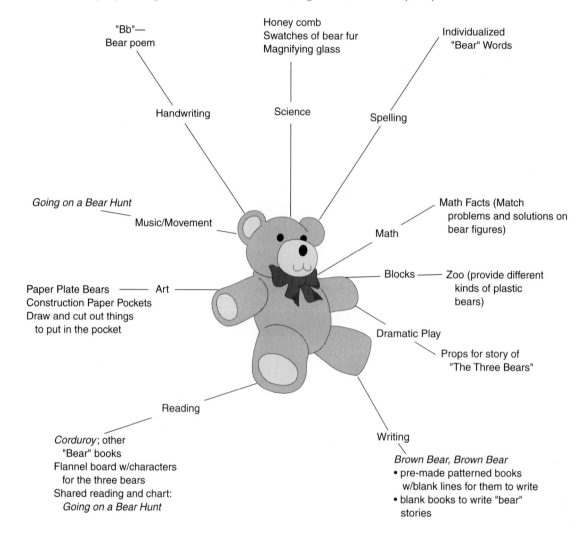

"Bb"—
Bear poem

Honey comb
Swatches of bear fur
Magnifying glass

Individualized
"Bear" Words

Handwriting

Science

Spelling

Going on a Bear Hunt

Music/Movement

Math

Math Facts (Match
problems and solutions on
bear figures)

Paper Plate Bears
Construction Paper Pockets
Draw and cut out things
to put in the pocket

Art

Blocks

Zoo (provide different
kinds of plastic
bears)

Dramatic Play

Props for story of
"The Three Bears"

Reading

Corduroy; other
"Bear" books
Flannel board w/characters
for the three bears
Shared reading and chart:
Going on a Bear Hunt

Writing

Brown Bear, Brown Bear
• pre-made patterned books
w/blank lines for them to write
• blank books to write "bear"
stories

Read Aloud: Corduroy
Snack: cupcakes with gummy bears

FIGURE 4.3 Sample planning web: A three-week integrated unit: Bears; Ages 5–6

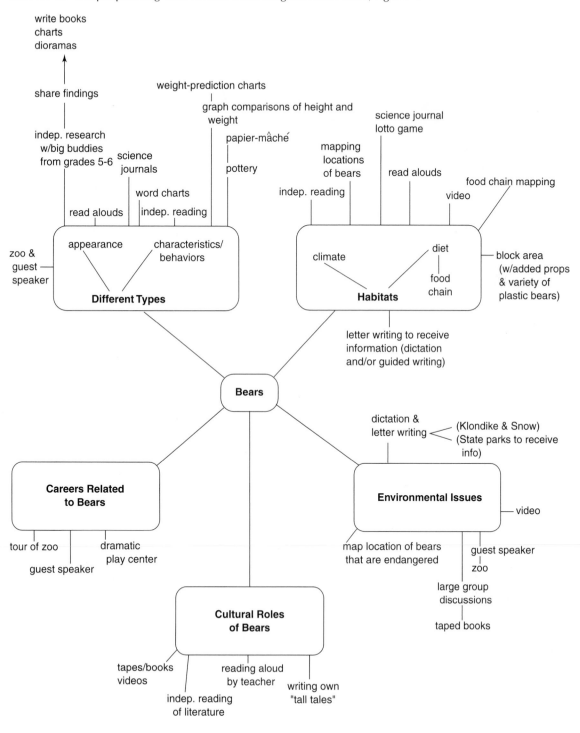

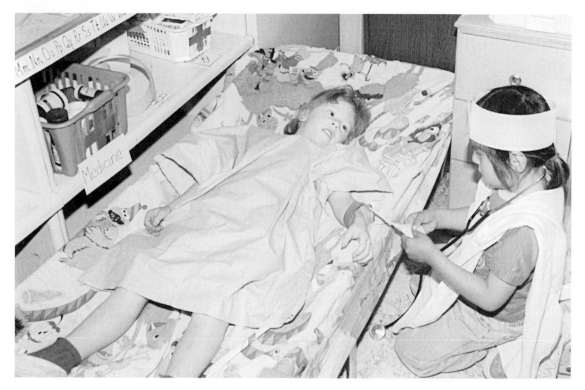

Young children reflect their current understandings and construct new understandings about the world of the hospital.

are directly related to the quality and in-depth nature of the investigations.

Dramatic play activities include acting out roles associated with the topic under study (e.g., operating room physicians, store clerks and customers, post office employees and customers, zoo workers). "Dramatic play helps children to integrate newly acquired information with what they already know. It enables participants to apply their new understandings appropriately in script representations. They can find out from interacting with other children where they differ in understanding and experiences" (Katz & Chard, 1989, p. 72). Although younger children typically spend most of their time in dramatic play activities, they can also participate in construction activities and investigations.

A COHESIVE, INTEGRATED CURRICULUM

Establishing Goals and Coordinating Curriculum for Learning

As always, when establishing goals for children, excellent teachers initially sift everything through the lenses provided by their long-term and short-term goals. They are focused on what children learn, as well as how they learn—on the content as well as the process. They carefully select a range of topics that will provide exposure to a broad range of **content subjects** (e.g., science, geography, history). They select topics that will facilitate children's achievement of specific standards within various content subjects. They design learning events that will enhance children's skills in, and ability to use, **process subjects** (e.g., reading, writing, mathematics, technology, art). The specific learning goals established in relationship to specific content or process subject goals must be based on documented observations of where individual children and groups of children are in relationship to those specific goals: What benchmarks have already been achieved? Where do we go from here?

Planning and coordinating a cohesive, integrated curriculum require that teachers first examine curriculum mandates and priorities to determine which can be taught or applied together. They then have to identify topics for investigations that will be meaningful to the children. Finally, they have to determine which of these topics and which overlapping learning goals will be mutually supportive. The intended result is the achievement of learning goals through explorations that make sense to children and that will help children make sense of their world.

Integrating Curriculum Mandates

The terminology used to label, organize, and define curriculum mandates of critical knowledge and skills is specific for each school district. Most, however, use a hierarchy of terms to distinguish general and specific expectations for achievement. The following terms are examples. They are used to describe a sample scope and sequence of curriculum integrated into a study of the earth's changes (see Figure 4.4).

- *Standards* are specific for each discipline. They describe mandated *general* critical knowledge and skills required of each child.
- *Outcomes* describe in somewhat *more specific* terms the skills and critical knowledge that each child needs to develop to master the set standards.
- *Specific child outcomes* are *very specific* critical knowledge and skills specific to

each grade level and related to helping children master the general outcomes and standards.

After reviewing the standards and outcomes presented in the curriculum guides for each discipline, a teacher of seven- and eight-year-olds selected a broad science topic with which to integrate specific child outcomes from science, language arts, and mathematics. The selected outcomes would contribute to the investigation or would be needed to pursue the investigation. Examples of the curriculum standards and specific child outcomes the teacher chose to integrate into the study are listed in Figure 4.4.

The teacher proceeded to plan learning events that would

- Facilitate children's achievement of the curriculum standards
- Increase the breadth and depth of the children's knowledge regarding how the earth changes
- Increase the children's knowledge of, and ability to apply, process subjects (reading, writing, mathematics, and technology)
- Nurture problem solving, personal inquiry, independence, and self-regulation
- Be intriguing and meaningful to children
- Contain adaptations to meet the needs of a variety of learners

🌿 TRY IT OUT *Planning Learning Events*

Select and combine other standards and outcomes from Figure 4.4 and use the planning chart in Figure 4.5 to generate additional learning events for a class of seven- and eight-year-olds.

Scheduling

Scheduling "integrated" curriculum is perceived as a simple task for some teachers and somewhat more complex for others. For some, the

FIGURE 4.4 Integrating mandated outcomes

Integrated Study Topic: How the Earth Changes

SCIENCE Curriculum

Standard 4: Earth Systems: The learner understands the processes and interactions of Earth's systems and the structure and dynamics of Earth.

Outcome 4.1: The learner knows the composition of Earth, its history, and the natural processes that shape it.

Grades 2–3 Specific Child Outcomes:
- The learner will describe processes and explain the causes of natural events that change Earth's surface, such as erosion, mountain building, and volcanic activity.
- The learner will recognize that humans are affected by natural events such as volcanoes, earthquakes, and floods.

LANGUAGE ARTS Curriculum

Standard 3: The learner gathers and organizes information from a variety of sources for diverse purposes.

Outcome 1: The learner develops skills in gathering information.

Grades 2–3 Specific Child Outcomes:
- The learner will share information from a speaker.
- The learner will gather information from audiovisual sources.
- The learner will identify the organizational features of the printed text.
- The learner will list or web information from subject-specific books, encyclopedias, and/or dictionaries.

Standard 4: The learner exhibits an understanding of a variety of genre forms and produces a variety of modes of discourse.

Outcome 2: The learner produces various types and modes of writing.

Grades 2–3 Specific Child Outcomes:
- The learner will publish an expository paper.
- The learner, when prompted, will draft the piece, use word source tools, solicit feedback, reread and revise the piece, and edit for appropriate conventions.

MATHEMATICS Curriculum

Standard 3: Statistics and Probability: The learner uses data collection and analysis, statistics, and probability to solve meaningful problems.

Outcome 1: The learner finds a pattern, makes a graph, and uses logical reasoning.

Source: Adapted from Portscheiler et al. (1995). *Eagle County School District: Draft of curriculum standards.* Eagle, CO: Eagle County School District. Reprinted by permission of Millie Hamner, Director of Curriculum, Instruction, and Staff Development.

FIGURE 4.5 Planning learning events

Content Understandings	Process Skills	Possible Learning Events

task seems as simple as dividing the year into an equal number of two-, three-, or four-week segments and determining a theme for each segment. Scheduling the day means identifying a unit of time to address each content area and relating it to the theme. It may also mean ensuring that children have time to visit each learning center that is also related to the theme. Some teachers attempt to coordinate theme topics with other teachers in their school to share materials or perhaps to avoid an overlap of themes.

A cohesive, integrated curriculum means something quite different; therefore, scheduling is a bit more complex. Once the topics of exploration for each integrated unit have been identified, teachers must estimate the amount of time that may be required to develop the targeted concepts and processes and for children to pursue personal interests and inquiries within the topic. Some topics may require only two weeks; others may require more than four weeks, possibly even a semester. Beginning stages of the investigation may require more time than later stages. More time may need to be provided initially for developing and practicing new skills within a single discipline prior to applying them to one investigation rather than another.

Time will be needed to collaborate with other teachers so that necessary resources can be shared. Teachers will plan to ensure that children are provided with opportunities within their school experiences to address a broad range of topics from the perspective of a broad range of disciplines. Teachers will also plan for children to have the opportunity to apply thinking and learning processes and skills in a wide variety of contexts. The planning will be thoughtful, thorough, and comprehensive.

Teachers must determine which process subjects and standards must be individually and specifically addressed (e.g., mathematics concepts and computations, reading and writing skills, technology skills). Time must be scheduled for explicit instruction in these areas. Teachers must also examine priorities and determine which areas to provide time for in addition to what may occur during an investigation (e.g., opportunities for self-selected independent reading and writing, reading aloud by the teacher, physical education, music). The daily schedule may vary from investigation to investigation. An example of a schedule for one week of a four-week investigation is provided in Figure 4.6.

STEP-BY-STEP PLANNING FOR INTEGRATED STUDY

Consider the steps outlined in Figure 4.7 when planning for integrated learning.

Curriculum-Level Planning

One goal of excellent teachers is to ensure that children have the opportunity to conduct inves-

FIGURE 4.6 Daily schedule with integrated curriculum

DAILY SCHEDULE

	9:00-10:30	10:30-11:30	11:30-12:05	12:05-12:18	12:20-12:50	12:50-1:10	1:10-2:00	2:00-3:00	3:00-3:15	3:15-3:20
MONDAY / SESQUIPEDALION WORD	RDG/ WRITING SPEAKING LISTENING	MATH INSTR. PRACTICE / BUDDY MATH	LUNCH	SSR	SPECIALS	READ ALOUD	INTERDISCIPLINARY UNIT			CLOSURE CLEAN UP
TUESDAY	RDG/ WRITING SPEAKING LISTENING	MATH INSTR. PRACTICE / BUDDY MATH	LUNCH	SSR	SPECIALS	COMPUTER LAB		INTERDISCIPLINARY UNIT		CLOSURE CLEAN UP
WEDNESDAY	RDG/ WRITING SPEAKING LISTENING	MATH INSTR. PRACTICE / BUDDY MATH	LUNCH	SSR	SPECIALS	READ ALOUD	ART	INTERDISCIPLINARY UNIT		CLOSURE CLEAN UP
THURSDAY / IMPONDERABLE	RDG/ WRITING SPEAKING LISTENING	MATH INSTR. PRACTICE / BUDDY MATH	LUNCH	SSR	SPECIALS	READ ALOUD	KEYBOARDING	INTERDISCIPLINARY UNIT		CLOSURE CLEAN UP
FRIDAY / COMMON KNOWLEDGE	TEAM WRITING / INTER-DISCIPLINE UNIT WRITING	MATH QUIZ / BUDDY MATH	LUNCH	SSR	SPECIALS	INTE-GRATED THEME STORY PROBLEM	KEYBOARDING	INTERDISCIPLINARY UNIT		CLOSURE CLEAN UP

Source: Reprinted by permission of Shelly Lantz, Teacher, Weld County District #6, Dos Rios Elementary School, Evans, Colorado.

FIGURE 4.7 Planning for integrated learning

I. Curriculum-Level Planning
  A. Review Mandates: Content Standards and Curriculum Goals
  B. Identify Possible Topics
  C. Match A and B for Cohesive Integration
II. Conducting Investigations
  A. Immersion
  B. Generate Purposes for Investigations
  C. Collect and Organize Information
  D. Express and Share Learning
III. Evaluation

tigations within a broad range of topics. They want children to develop familiarity with many aspects of the world while having ample opportunities to explore areas of personal interest in-depth. They want children to develop habits of mind that will enable them to become independent, self-regulated learners who can identify questions, problems, or interests and who can conduct investigations independently or collaboratively to answer questions, solve problems, or pursue interests.

Selecting a Focus for Integrated Study. A topic for an investigation or a focus for an integrated unit of study can be identified in several ways. As mentioned previously, teachers can review the curriculum standards and other mandates to determine where overlaps or relationships between content and processes exist. With these clusters of standards in mind, teachers can readily determine topics through which these clusters can be addressed. Teachers must always keep in mind, however, variety and breadth. A primary goal is to broaden children's interests, knowledge base, and understanding. With this primary goal and the clusters of standards in mind, the topics and areas of focus available and appropriate are limited only by the imagi-

nation. To generate possible topics, teachers can consider the following:

- Interests generated by books children have read
- Children's interests and experiences
- Teacher's interests and experiences
- Current events and issues
- School events
- Local exhibits or events
- Subjects within disciplines (e.g., science: pond life, plants, volcanoes, invertebrates, natural disasters, weather, genetics)
- Objects brought in by a child or group of children
- Curriculum requirements

At this point, you may be thinking that a teacher should establish all topics before the school year begins. Not so. A teacher should have in mind possible or probable topics and possible curriculum clusters. At times, children may suggest topics for investigations or the teacher may generate topics that were not anticipated early in the school year. When this occurs (and it will), the teacher will evaluate whether a topic can be used to contribute to the depth of a study currently under investigation, to the breadth of children's knowledge related or unrelated to the topic, and whether the topic can be used to address curriculum clusters. If the topic is appropriate and the teacher decides to use it, the teacher will then need to reevaluate the topics selected for future studies. Perhaps the newly selected topic (e.g., pond life) will simply replace a future topic (e.g., rivers and streams), or perhaps because the children have already studied the ocean, the future broad topic of rivers and streams needs to be changed to something related to history or geography rather than science. Excellent teachers are careful to provide for a breadth of topics to be investigated.

An interest in mining led to a productive study that integrated standards from geology, literacy, math, geography, and history.

Conducting Investigations

As teachers consider the investigations to be conducted with and by the children, they must consider how each related learning event, whether designed by the teacher or initiated by the children, will contribute to the long-term and short-term goals identified by the teacher. What knowledge will children glean from each learning event? What specific skills do they need in order to participate in each learning event? What learning processes and thinking processes will the event encourage children to use? Teachers must consider what children can do independently and when they may require assistance. Teachers must decide whether the processes, skills,

and content are within children's reach (zones of proximal development). Each potential learning event and the ways the learning events interact are filtered through these lenses. Every learning event is selected or designed with purpose and intent.

Immersion. The first learning events a teacher must plan are those that will occur within the **immersion stage of an integrated unit.** This stage occurs at the beginning of the integrated unit for a designated period of time, ranging from a few days to two weeks. The immersion stage of the investigation is designed for several purposes: (1) to determine what the children already know, (2) to create enough familiarity and curiosity about the topic that the children are able to generate thoughtful and interesting questions to pursue, (3) to build common language and concepts based on shared experiences, and (4) to determine and teach any new skills the children will need to conduct the investigations.

During the immersion stage, the teacher creates opportunities to determine what the children already know about the topic to be investigated (the known). This helps the teacher know what new information the children are capable of learning and how the content might best be acquired. The teacher can do this directly by asking the children what they know about the topic, jotting their comments on chart paper, and then organizing the shared knowledge into a web. The teacher can also do this indirectly by observing and listening as children respond to shared experiences such as field trips, guest speakers, videos, and read alouds. With shared experiences come opportunities for the teacher to help children develop common vocabulary and concepts related to the topic.

Generating Questions for Investigation. Many times, teachers ask children to develop questions for personal investigations before the children know enough about a topic to develop interesting and researchable questions. Excellent teachers intentionally help children become familiar with the breadth of the topic and the many ex-

Teachers can assist children in developing guiding questions for their investigations by using a K-W-L to elicit their prior knowledge.

plorations available within a topic prior to having them develop research questions. Excellent teachers ensure that children have enough information to peak their curiosity and to identify specific areas of personal interests. This strategy allows children to develop questions that will lead them to in-depth explorations.

One way in which teachers can help children select a specific area and develop questions for personal investigations is by dividing the topic (e.g., the ocean) under investigation into several subtopics (e.g., plant life, animal life, industry, tides and currents, pollution). Children select one subtopic to explore as part of a small group. Each small group is provided with opportunities to view related videos, take related field trips, listen to and visit with guest speakers, and im-

merse themselves in reading about the selected subtopic. Children record what they are learning in personal journals and on wall charts available to the entire class. On a regular basis, each group reports to the class what they have learned and any new questions they have developed. Any child in the class can contribute information to any chart at any time. On completion of the small-group study of the topic, children identify the subtopic they want to pursue further and the specific questions they want to research. They may then work in small groups, individually, or as a whole class.

Another way to help children develop questions for investigations is to use a K-W-L chart (What We *Know* About _____; What We *Wonder* About _____; How We Can *Learn*

About _____; Davies, Politano, & Cameron, 1993; Ogle, 1986). K-W-L can be used when the focus of the integrated unit is introduced to make children aware of what they already know about the topic. The questions they develop in the "What we wonder about" segment become the initial broad areas of exploration for individuals, small groups, or the whole class during the immersion stage. On completion of the initial explorations, children dictate or record on the chart what they have learned. Another K-W-L chart is then created to identify questions for a more in-depth study of the topic.

Collecting and Organizing Information. The in-depth questions generated during immersion guide the investigations and provide direction as teachers plan appropriate learning events. Teachers must determine whether the investigations will be conducted as a whole class, in small groups, or by individual children. They must consider the age and maturity levels of the children, their skills, the degree to which they are able to self-regulate, and their experience with research.

Because teachers' expectations increase and the necessary research skills become more complex as children progress, teachers of children of all ages may choose to begin the year with whole-class investigations. During these initial investigations, teachers model and demonstrate needed skills and processes for the entire class.

Investigations can be conducted with children of all ages and ability levels, even those who are not yet reading and writing independently. Teachers of young children help them gather information through read alouds, shared readings, videos, taped books, field trips, guest speakers, in-class demonstrations and experiences, research buddies (upper-level children or adult volunteers), and mentors from the community. Children can record or share information with drawings, dictated language experience, their current form of writing (which may or may not be accompanied by dictated language experience), projects, oral reports, and/or demonstrations.

If children are to conduct investigations successfully, teachers must not only help them establish a clear focus (questions) but also provide

Research buddies can help younger children gather and record information, as well as design a way to share learnings from their investigation.

TABLE 4.1 Data chart on tigers

	Diet *What do they eat?* *How do they eat?*	*Habitat* *Continents?* *Environments?*	*Enemies* *How do they* *protect themselves?* *Who are their* *enemies?*	*Ancestry* *Predecessors?* *Other related* *animals?* *How have they* *evolved?*
#1 Book: *Jungle Animals*				
#2 Book: *Tigers*				
#3 Magazine: *Ranger Rick*				
#4 Guest Speaker: Zoologist				

them with effective and efficient formats for gathering information in a systematic and organized manner. Visual organizers can be used to help children of all ages collect and organize information. Teachers can use visual organizers such as K-W-L, question cards, data charts, semantic feature analysis charts, and webs (Moore, Moore, Cunningham, & Cunningham, 1994) with whole groups or individuals. The data chart shown in Table 4.1 helps children use multiple resources to answer questions. It can be modified for use with young children by substituting drawings for print.

Collecting information requires that children set goals and remain focused. This can be a challenge to children of any age. Some may not be able to get started and remain focused; others may find it difficult to stop gathering information and begin synthesizing it. Knowledgeable teachers recognize these challenges and help all children self-regulate by providing and/or helping them formulate a timeline with appropriate checkpoints. Agendas or menus can be devised to help children monitor their progress with center work or project work on a daily or weekly basis (Figures 4.8a and 4.8b). The teacher routinely conferences with children to monitor their progress jointly.

If working collaboratively will be an option, teachers need to prepare children in advance and provide guidance for successful collaboration. Excellent teachers will make certain that the children are focused on clearly defined group goals. The children will be assigned a role (e.g., recorder, questioner) and will understand the contributions of each role to the success of the group (Johnson & Johnson, 1989).

Expressing and Sharing Learning. It is important that children have opportunities to express and share their learning with classmates and others. Several long-term goals are supported by providing children with these opportunities. Knowing at the beginning of an investigation

FIGURE 4.8a Menus: Helping children help themselves

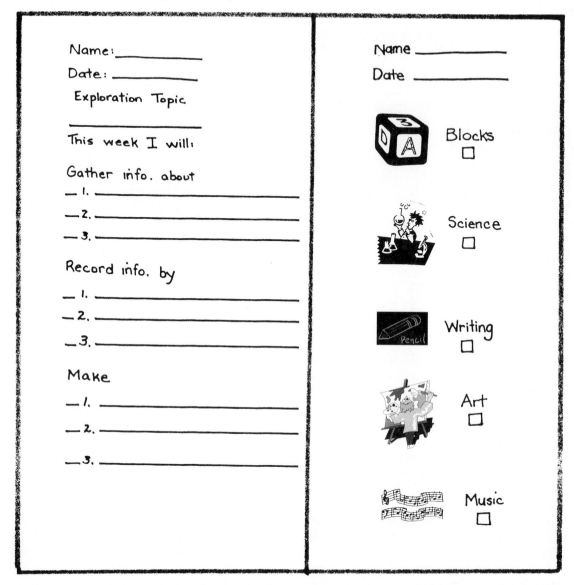

that they will have the opportunity, and be expected, to share their learning with others motivates children and provides an additional focus for their learning.

Considering how they might share information (e.g., visual display, written report, oral presentation, demonstration, or a combination of these) often contributes to the direction children's investigations will take and the ways information will be synthesized. The genuine interest and positive responses that children receive from an audience and the personal

FIGURE 4.8b Center planner

CENTER PLANNER

NAME_____   DATE_____

	Monday	Tuesday	Wednesday	Thursday	Friday
Blocks					
Playhouse					
Table Toys					
Art					
Literacy					
Science					

Source: Reprinted by permission of Ruth Hensen, Early Childhood Teacher, Denver Public Schools, Denver, Colorado.

satisfaction they feel from sharing contributes to their self-esteem. They will perceive themselves as learners capable of initiating and completing investigations.

Opportunities for sharing need not be confined to a single, culminating event. Indeed, younger children must have frequent opportunities to express and share the current status of their learning. Children of all ages benefit from similar opportunities throughout an investigation. By sharing the processes and results of their pursuits, children provide each other with in-depth information about a broad range of topics. Ensuring that children develop breadth and depth of knowledge is a defining characteristic of an effective, cohesive, inte-

grated curriculum and an important long-term goal.

Evaluation

Regardless of how children decide to share their learning, teachers must establish (with the children) a **rubric,** or set of criteria that establishes critical expectations. The rubric will be used to evaluate the learning and sharing. This use ensures that the content and process goals identified by the teacher, as well as the children's self-selected purposes, are achieved.

Investigations that occur within an integrated curriculum provide innumerable opportunities for the teacher to observe children as they initiate questions, employ problem-solving strategies, and use literacy, mathematics, and technology skills to pursue investigations. The teacher uses these authentic opportunities to document children's progress toward the identified long-term and short-term goals. This use allows the teacher to determine what a child has learned and can apply (the new known) in order to provide appropriate learning opportunities and instruction necessary for the next investigation.

A critical component of the evaluation process is a child's self-evaluation of the investigation process, of her or his personal efforts, and of the quality of her or his learning. Evaluating the various stages of the investigation, particularly if it was conducted independently, not only leads to the child's self-discovery of her- or himself as a learner but also provides the child with information to guide future investigations. Questions that might help the child evaluate the effectiveness of an investigation would include the following:

- I learned the most when I . . .
- The most interesting part of this investigation was . . .
- The most difficult part of this investigation was . . .
- I worked hardest on . . .
- I could have improved my investigation by . . .
- If I could do this again, I would . . .

The teacher also responds to similar stems (e.g., I noticed that you worked hardest on . . .). Both child and teacher will use the rubric created prior to the investigation to establish critical expectations for judging whether the criteria for learning and sharing were met.

The evaluation process is not complete until the teacher creates the opportunity to conference with each child individually. During the conference, both teacher and child share their perceptions of the child's efforts, the obstacles encountered, and the child's successes. The child is often her or his own worst critic. The teacher can take this opportunity to point out growth and achievements the child may not have noticed. The conference may also provide an opportunity for the teacher to suggest areas for improvement the child may not have noticed. The conference is a time filled with teachable moments. As the child identifies the obstacles and possible improvements, the teacher can provide new information or suggestions that may assist the child in future endeavors.

SUMMARY

Creating and using a cohesive, integrated curriculum supports the efforts of teachers to achieve the long- and short-term goals they have established as priorities for the children. A cohesive, integrated curriculum enhances children's enthusiasm for learning by providing meaningful topics and processes for investigations. Topics and learning events are thoughtfully selected to address a broad range of curriculum content and processes. The immersion stage peaks curiosity and stimulates questions to be pursued in-depth through investigations. Opportunities for personal inquiry nurture problem-solving abilities, develop self-regulation, and facilitate independence.

Even though it is more complex and requires more thought than a time-clock curriculum, a cohesive, integrated curriculum constructed by thoughtful teachers can solve many problems created by a time-clock curriculum. A cohesive, integrated curriculum acknowledges, identifies, and builds upon the known within each child, whether addressing content or processes. It is designed to work within each child's zone of proximal development. Each investigation begins at each child's level of conceptual development. Children are encouraged to gather information and construct concepts by using a variety of print and nonprint resources. Learners are encouraged and taught to organize, express, and share newly acquired concepts and understandings in a variety of ways. A cohesive, integrated curriculum, therefore, naturally accommodates the wide range of ability and knowledge levels of the diverse learners found in every classroom.

REFERENCES

Beane, J. (Ed.). (1995). *Toward a coherent curriculum.* Alexandria, VA: ASCD.

Bredekamp, S., & Rosegrant, T. (Eds.). (1995). *Reaching potentials: Transforming early childhood curriculum and assessment* (Vol. 2). Washington, DC: National Association for the Education of Young Children.

Davies, A., Politano, C., & Cameron, C. (1993). *Making themes work: Building connections.* Winnipeg: Peguis.

Elvin, L. (1977). *The place of common sense in educational thought.* London: Unwin.

Johnson, D., & Johnson, R. (1989). Cooperative learning: What special education teachers need to know. *Pointer, 33*(2), 5–10.

Katz, L., & Chard, S. (1989). *Engaging children's minds: The project approach.* Norwood, NJ: Ablex.

Moore, D., Moore, S., Cunningham, P., & Cunningham, J. (1994). *Developing readers and writers in the content areas K–12* (2nd ed.). White Plains, NY: Longman.

Ogle, D. (1986). K-W-L: A teaching model that develops active reading of expository text. *Journal of Reading, 33,* 170–176.

Portscheiler, P., et al. (1995). *Eagle County School District: Draft of curriculum standards.* Eagle, CO: Eagle County School District.

Wood, K. (1997). *Interdisciplinary instruction: A practical guide for elementary and middle school teachers.* Upper Saddle River, NJ: Merrill/Prentice Hall.

Children's Books

Freeman, D. (1978). *Pocket for Corduroy.* New York: Viking.

Martin, B. (1983). *Brown bear, brown bear, what do you see?* New York: Holt, Rinehart & Winston.

McCloskey, R. (1976). *Blueberries for Sal.* New York: Puffin.

Rosen, M. (1989). *Going on a bear hunt.* New York: McElderry.

Schwartz, A. (1984). *Fat man in a fur coat.* New York: Farrar, Straus & Giroux.

Ward, L. (1973). *The biggest bear.* Boston: Houghton-Mifflin.

Ziefert, H. (1994). *Goldilocks and the three bears.* New York: Tambourine.

…assessment should improve performance, not just audit it.

(Wiggins, 1993, p. 11)

5

Assessment and Evaluation

CONSIDER YOUR BELIEFS

- What is the difference between assessment and evaluation?
- What is the difference between formal and informal assessment?
- How do goals influence assessment and evaluation?
- Who determines the assessments used in your classroom, school, and district?
- Will the assessments reflect what you teach?
- Why are assessment and evaluation so important to school administrators and local community members?
- How will you know that the children are progressing as they should be?
- Whom will you talk with if you think a child may need special services? What is the process for referring a child?
- What records will you keep to document a child's progress?
- How can you know whether your instruction is effective?
- Will you be evaluated by your principal? your colleagues? parents? children?
- How do you plan for effective self-evaluation to guide your professional development?

At the end of the school day, teachers often give a sigh of relief, "Well, this was a good day!" When asked what made it a good day, the comments offered are, "I made it through the day," "There were no major problems," "The children stayed on-task," "We had a lot of fun," "The children really enjoyed the activities we did today," "We made the neatest gifts for Mother's Day," and "I got everything I planned to do done." Comments about new understandings that children developed or how they solved an interesting problem or researched an area of interest are sparse. In the majority of schools, common, explicit, and measurable learning goals are still rare (Schmoker, 1997) and infrequently discussed.

Novice teachers are especially prone to addressing the issues of classroom management as a primary goal. To become excellent, novice teachers must establish goals that focus on achievement and dispositions toward learning, rather than on getting through the day. Long- and short-term goals are based on the basic beliefs and assumptions that teachers hold about teaching and learning. All subsequent instructional decisions are filtered through these beliefs and goals. If teachers are not proactive in establishing such goals, these goals will be established for them.

At the end of the instructional day, excellent teachers reflect on how the instructional interactions and learning events of the day contributed to developing the habits of mind (Marzano, 1992; Wiggins, 1993) they established as long-term goals for the children. Excellent teachers also reflect on the progress each child is making toward the short-term goals. Excellent teachers reflect on the progress the class as a whole is making toward the academic standards established by the school and district. They refer to samples of the children's work that were collected and the observations that were recorded throughout the day.

It is not possible to be an effective teacher without creating and using an effective assessment plan. First, you have to know where you are going (goals), and then you need a way of knowing whether you are getting there (assessments and evaluation) (Calfee, 1996). Assessments must be planned. They cannot be haphazard, but they can be informal. Just as there are unplanned "teachable moments," there are unplanned "assessable moments." The information gathered from these assessable moments, together with the information gleaned from structured assessment opportunities, provides the information necessary for making effective instructional and program decisions.

Just as you set priorities for the learning goals you have for the children, you must also set priorities for assessments. Just as too much teaching gets in the way of learning, too much formal assessment may get in the way of teaching and learning. You must design a *balanced* system of instruction and assessment that will provide you with the continuous information you need to help the children achieve the established goals.

DISTINGUISHING ASSESSMENT AND EVALUATION

Assessment is the process of collecting information and gathering evidence about what a child knows and/or is able to apply. *Classroom assessment* refers to any method, strategy, or tool a teacher may use to collect evidence about a child's progress toward achievement of the established goals—to collect evidence about what a child knows, the context within which the child has learned it, and how the child uses what is known. Assessments may take a variety of forms, depending on the type of information needed. Assessments can be spontaneous or structured (planned), formal (standardized/normed) or informal, published or teacher designed. The purpose for which the teacher is gathering information should determine the form of the assessments, as well as the content of the assessments the teacher selects or designs.

The terms *assessment* and *evaluation* are not synonymous. Whereas assessment is the gathering and recording of information, assessment is not an end in itself. Assessment is of no value unless the data are used to help the teacher reflect on previous data and instructional decisions, as well as guide future instruction. Drawing conclusions about what children know, what they need to learn, and how they learn cannot be based on a single assessment.

Good instructional decisions must be based on many sources of data, or **bodies of evidence,** collected in a variety of contexts and over a period of time (Burger, 1996).

Evaluation implies bringing meaning to those data through "interpretation, analysis, and reflection and includes the kinds of instructional decisions that are made by careful examination of the evidence" (Routman, 1991, p. 302). Consequently, the knowledge base of the teacher directly determines the quality of the interpretations, analysis, and reflection, as well as the quality of the resulting instructional decisions. The ability to transform data into instructional strategies that result in individualized learning plans and increased student learning determines whether teachers are dispensers of information or facilitators of learning.

PURPOSES OF ASSESSMENT AND EVALUATION

To Benefit the Children

The primary purpose of assessment and evaluation must be to benefit the children. Assessment and evaluation must be designed to individualize and improve the quality of instruction provided to children (Bredekamp & Copple, 1997) to maximize the children's learning (short-term goals) and to help the children become self-monitoring, self-regulating, and independent learners (long-term goals) (Routman, 1991). Assessment is used to ensure the continuous progress of each child toward the established goals.

To Plan, Inform, and Evaluate Instruction

Just because something is taught, does not mean it is learned (McAfee & Leong, 1994). The information gleaned from assessments helps teachers know what has been learned—that is, determine whether the children are moving along the various continua toward the established goals

(Waters, Burger, & Burger, 1995). Unfortunately, this information is often used to judge a child, rather than to reflect on the quality of the instructional support provided to the child. The underlying and false assumption is that "If I taught it and the child did not learn it, then there must be something wrong with the child." If the primary purpose of assessment is to benefit the child, then the underlying premise must be that if the child does not learn, the teacher must re-examine and change instruction so that the child does learn. Assessment must result in the improvement of instruction, rather than the allocation of blame to the child. Assessment can and should be used to determine whether the what, when, and how of instruction are appropriate.

Building on the Known. Effective instruction helps children make connections between what they currently know and the new information they are experiencing. Effective teachers use assessment to determine what a child knows and to focus instruction on the child's strengths, rather than on what the child doesn't know (the *holes*) and the child's weaknesses. An effective teacher uses assessment information to provide immediate instruction within a child's zone of proximal development, rather than to teach material and skills based on grade-level criteria regardless of whether they are within the child's grasp. The child's current understandings, discovered through assessment, become the basis for instructional decisions.

To Determine Progress Toward Goals

In addition to providing information that teachers can use in adjusting day-to-day instruction, assessment provides information about the extent to which children are progressing toward the established long-term and short-terms goals (Schmoker, 1996).

Teachers. Teachers use assessment to determine whether they are successfully helping their children meet learning goals. They use assessment information to individualize and adjust their instruction so that all children continue to progress toward the goals. They use assessment information on a daily basis to determine what to teach and how to teach.

Parents. Parents want teachers to share assessment information that helps them understand how their child is doing on an individual basis. Parents want information about their child's personal progress, as well as about how their child is doing relative to other children in the same age range. To demonstrate for the parents the child's personal progress, the teacher must select or design assessments that will provide information about how the child has progressed from one point in time to another on the various continua toward the long-term and short-term instructional goals. For this purpose, the teacher may choose to share dated samples of the child's work, accumulated over time, that can effectively demonstrate to the parents their child's academic development and achievement in many areas across the curriculum. For example, the teacher may keep a sample of the child's writing each week or each month to share with the parents. This will allow the parents to see how the child's writing has changed or progressed over time.

The teacher must also select or design assessments that will provide information related to a child's personal performance or development compared with that of peers. For this purpose, the teacher may also share a continuum of early writing development or a rubric of performance standards used to evaluate writing in the classroom, as Table 5.1 illustrates. The teacher can provide samples of papers (without names, of course), called *anchor papers,* that are representative of various stages on the rubric. On the continuum, the teacher can highlight the range of writing behaviors most common to the child's age-mates.

By receiving this kind of assessment information, the parents can become active participants in the evaluation process. They can interpret and see for themselves their child's personal progress. For too long, educators have treated parents as passive participants in the assessment process. Parents are interested in any information they can use to gauge their child's progress. They are also interested in knowing the teacher's perceptions of their child's strengths and weaknesses. When provided with the opportunity, they are willing to contribute information and perceptions they may have about their child's learning and progress.

Children. Children want to know how they are doing. Teachers can simply provide the children with assessment information, or they can involve them in the assessment process. If a long-term instructional goal is to nurture self-regulated, independent learners, then children must be active participants in the assessment and evaluation process. Teachers must guide children to collect and evaluate information about their personal progress. When children are involved in the assessment process, they are more likely to take ownership of their learning and to internalize the processes of self-monitoring and problem solving.

Teacher and parents should discuss the broad goals set for the child that are within the child's zone of proximal development. The child should then be involved with establishing specific goals. When children are able to establish personal learning goals and to self-monitor their progress toward those goals, they have taken those first crucial steps to becoming problem solvers and lifelong learners. Children are more motivated to learn when they participate in the establishment of goals, can make decisions about which learning strategies and tasks will best enable them to succeed, and can be supported in their attempts to assess and evaluate their progress.

TABLE 5.1 Writing process rubric for young children

	The Emergent Writer	*The Early Writer*	*The Fluent Writer*
Basic Attitude Toward Writing	Likes to play at writing. Has confidence that personal meaning is expressed in own writing. Encouraged by own success. Finds writing enjoyable and rewarding.	Likes to write on a variety of topics. Willing to look for meaning in own work and seeks help from others to clarify it. Confident in own skills to express thought immediately. Expects own writing to be enjoyed by others. Attempts several genres.	Satisfaction using many genres. Feels confident encountering challenges in writing. Respects reader needs in relation to topic and purpose of writing.
Concepts About Print	Orients a page to start writing. Writes left to right. Spaces between words. Uses upper- and lowercase letters.	Begins to understand reasons for print conventions. Starts to use periods, capitals, question and exclamation marks correctly.	Uses most print conventions correctly (e.g., commas, quotation marks, parentheses, line breaks, colons).
Revising and Drafting	Adds to, and reads back, own story. Begins to see writing can be reworked. Begins using word processor to compose text.	Inserts information in text. Uses others' questions to clarify own writing. Reads own work to check for meaning. Willing to revise own work. Refines keyboard skills. Makes changes on screen.	Strategically places relevant information. Revises text to accommodate new ideas. Understands reasons for revising. Continually betters own writing. Seeks constructive comments from others. Sophisticated word processing.
Structure	Draws pictures and scribbles to generate and express ideas. Explains orally about own pictures. Begins to use simple sentence forms. Links own story title to own story. Developing an understanding of how books and stories work.	Draws, discusses, jots to fix initial structure ideas. Talks freely about a topic, using language to develop ideas. Makes use of appropriate headings. Understands middle, beginning, ending in different genres.	Uses notes and plans to help express ideas. Has repeated discussions to develop ideas. Uses complex sentence forms. Writes in paragraphs and sections. Uses titles and subheads appropriately. Starts to build plot, characters, setting, purpose, suspense, and climax.
Spelling	Attempts spelling of unknown words. Begins to realize words are always spelled the same. Shows some knowledge of ABCs through writing letter forms to represent a message. Develops sound/letter relationships. Recognizes some key words.	Attempts unknown words. Knows spelling is consistent. Knows alphabet. Knows sounds are represented by letters. Knows letters are ordered to make words. Starts to self-correct text. Getting familiar with dictionaries. Going from sound/letter to visual cues.	Attempts unknown words. Knows alphabet. Uses sound/letter relationships when uncertain. Develops spelling based on syllabification, patterns, etc. Has large body of known words. Uses dictionary when proofreading.

Source: Selected by Susie Carrol from *Dancing with the Pen: The Learner as a Writer.* Published by Learning Media Limited on behalf of the Ministry of Education, New Zealand. Copyright © Crown, New Zealand 1996. Reproduced by permission of the publishers.

To Plan, Inform, and Evaluate
Curriculum and Special Programs

At the School Level. Building administrators and faculty work together to assess and evaluate the curriculum and special programs under consideration or currently in place within the school. Initially, they work together to establish long-term goals. They collect data to identify child needs (academic intervention and/or enrichment programs, extended care programs, parental education opportunities), to design a curriculum that will facilitate achievement of established goals (integrated curriculum, departmentalized subjects, cultural literacy focus), to determine the macrostructure of the school (multiage classes, early childhood units, teams), to select or create subsequent instructional and extracurricular programs (early intervention programs, technology labs, and enrichment programs), and to design the professional development needed to support the teachers. Prior to implementing curriculum or special programs, administrators and faculty design an assessment and evaluation plan to monitor curriculum and program effectiveness. Evaluation of the data provides information that can be used to modify existing programs and curricula or to indicate a need to seek alternatives.

At the District Level. District policymakers use the information gleaned from building-level assessment and evaluation plans to determine how schools are meeting the goals the schools have established for themselves. In addition, district policymakers often require certain assessments of students to monitor the effectiveness of the curriculum and special programs in their schools over time; that is, districts use the data to examine trends over time in evaluating whether the schools are successfully helping students achieve district and state goals. The data may be disaggregated and evaluated on the basis of ethnicity, socioeconomic status, gender, and special educational needs to determine how well schools are serving various student populations within the district. This information may be used in making decisions about the allotment of resources (human and monetary) to schools and special programs. It may also serve to initiate the modification of district goals, curriculum, or assessments.

At the State Level. Most states have established broad academic expectations for students and have an assessment plan for evaluating over time how well districts are helping students achieve these goals. Statewide assessment plans vary widely. Some states feature traditional standardized norm-referenced testing. Other states use combinations of traditional assessments and the newer, performance-based assessments. In addition to the different types of assessment tools that states may use, they may also devise different methods for generalizing information from a sample of students to the entire student population. Some states use matrix sampling to test only a sample of students representative of the state population demographics, rather than test all students in the state. The data may also be disaggregated and evaluated on the basis of ethnicity, socioeconomic status, gender, and special educational needs to determine how well districts are serving various student populations within the state.

In addition to monitoring the general effectiveness of the educational system, evaluation of statewide assessment data is used to

- Establish and/or modify statewide goals
- Establish performance standards on selected assessments
- Set priorities for goals and subsequently the allocation of resources
- Place sanctions and related demands on individual schools or districts
- Inform and guide the legislature and other policymakers as they establish and/or modify the assessment and evaluation plan

For example, on the basis of evaluation of assessment data, legislators in Colorado passed a bill in 1996, mandating that all students in the state be given a reading assessment at the end of third grade (Fox, 1996). Those students not passing the test are to be retained in reading. This bill has major implications for the modification of goals and the allocation of resources within school districts.

Informing the Taxpayers. Taxpayers want data that will indicate whether each school is meeting their expectations—that is, whether they are getting their money's worth from the educational system (Pearson, 1997). Public opinion is a very real part of assessment and evaluation. Public opinion translates into financial resources and support.

CHARACTERISTICS OF GOOD ASSESSMENTS

Assessments Should Be Aligned with Established Goals

Teachers, administrators, and policymakers must work together to establish common goals and to select assessments that will help all parties involved determine progress toward those goals. Establishing common goals is the most difficult part of this process. Once the goals have been established, appropriate assessments can be designed or selected (Schmoker, 1996). Because an assessment tool may be valid for one purpose but not for others, several different assessments may be required to determine whether the goals are being achieved.

Assessments Should Reflect Instructional Practices

To be valid, assessments must not only measure the established goals and standards but also reflect classroom instructional practices (or be selected to have a desired influence on classroom instructional practices). For example, if reading instruction in a classroom focuses on using multiple strategies to construct meaning from text and the assessments selected by the district or state assess reading by asking readers to identify a series of words presented in isolation, there is a mismatch between instructional practices and assessment practices.

As long as a mismatch exists between the two, the effectiveness of classroom instruction cannot be fairly evaluated by using data from the selected assessments, and the assessments will not be recognized as valid by the teachers. This type of dilemma has played a significant role in the move away from more traditional standardized assessments and toward assessments that have been labeled as alternative, authentic, and/or performance-based because the latter are more inclined to reflect classroom practices. Many states and districts have developed or adopted these types of assessments to provide summative data for program and curriculum evaluation. Although these assessments were initially used to resolve the mismatch between classroom instruction and summative assessments, the unexpected result has been to initiate positive changes in classroom instruction.

Teachers must examine school, district, and state assessments to determine whether they reflect instructional goals and instructional practices—to see whether they are valid. If teachers identify a mismatch, they must work toward achieving alignment; that is, they must work toward an alignment of instruction and assessments that is consistent with their professional beliefs. First, however, teachers must examine the alignment among the established goals, instructional practices, and assessments they choose to use to inform instruction *within their own classrooms.* If classroom instruction is to be focused and effective, alignment is not optional. If programs and curriculum are to be focused and effective, alignment must extend from daily instructional practices to annual district assessments to periodic state assessments.

Evaluation Should Include Authentic Assessment Tasks. Authentic assessment tasks are used to observe and document the children's application of knowledge and skills as they engage in contextual learning events. One important goal that an excellent teacher strives toward is the alignment of meaningful assessments with meaningful instruction. As the teacher uses instructional strategies, she or he must look for signs from the children that the instruction has been successful. The teacher is constantly reflecting on the children's performance or responses to the learning event, as well as to instruction or mediation. The teacher's evaluation of these data is then used to guide subsequent instruction. Authentic assessment often cannot be differentiated from teaching or mediation because excellent teachers continuously integrate observation (assessment) into their interactions with children. Instruction becomes an assessment tool, and assessment becomes an instructional tool.

Assessments Should Always Be Developmentally Appropriate

The past decade has seen considerable debate on teaching, learning, and assessment for four- to eight-year-olds. The National Association for the Education of Young Children (NAEYC) has provided a framework considered to be exemplary and a model for educators. **Developmentally appropriate practices** are those practices that consider the aspects of teaching, learning, and assessment that change with the age and experience of the learner. For example, administering paper-and-pencil, multiple-choice tests to young children is developmentally inappropriate. Play-based assessment (Linder, 1990), work sampling, portfolios, and teacher observation are appropriate assessment tools for young children.

When selecting or designing assessments that are developmentally appropriate, teachers must consider not only how to assess but also what to assess. Sometimes teachers allow

Observing young children at play is an appropriate and authentic opportunity for assessment.

what they assess to be governed by a child's age, rather than by the child's actual cognitive development. This error often results in limiting assessment to a narrow range of information, skills, or abilities on any one continuum. For example, the teacher may ask a three-year-old to count to ten in order to assess the child's ability to count, when indeed the child may be able to count far beyond ten. The teacher's perception of what is developmentally appropriate was unduly limited. In a similar situation, the teacher may assess an eight-year-old on tasks that are too difficult and not provide the opportunity for the child to demonstrate the skills she or he may have on the easier end of the continuum.

Assessment should be conducted in a variety of ways and in a variety of contexts.

Assessment Should Be Conducted in a Variety of Ways and in a Variety of Contexts

Just as children read, write, and compute for a variety of purposes in a variety of contexts, assessment data should reflect children's ability to apply their knowledge and skills for a variety of purposes and in a variety of contexts. To develop a complete picture of a learner, the teacher should assess the child in a variety of learning situations, with more than one assessment and with more than one type of assessment. Some assessments should focus on process, others on product. Some should be based on observation alone, others grounded in interactive situations with the teacher. Some may be conducted with time constraints, others without. Information from formal and informal assessments can be integrated.

Assessments Should Be Ongoing Over an Extended Period of Time

What a child understands and is able to do should change continuously when she or he is placed in an effective learning environment and provided with appropriate instruction. Assessment, there-

fore, must be continuous so that the teacher can obtain the information necessary to make ongoing and appropriate decisions about instruction and curriculum for each child.

Assessment Should Provide Information in a Timely Fashion

If assessment information is to affect instruction or curriculum significantly, it must be made available to the children, teachers, parents, and administrators within a relatively short amount of time. If too much time elapses before results are made available, the information cannot be used productively. The less formal and the more spontaneous the assessment, the shorter the feedback loop. The shorter the loop between assessment and feedback, the greater the direct impact on teaching and learning.

USING ASSESSMENT AND EVALUATION TO ADDRESS SPECIAL NEEDS

In the usual processes of assessment and evaluation, classroom teachers will become aware of children who are not developing at the usual rates or within acceptable ranges of academic or social development. Teachers should carefully reflect on the instructional decisions they have made and the instructional practices they have used with these children. Contact should be made with the parents to share information and to problem-solve together. Parents can often provide important insights and possible strategies for meeting a child's needs. Relevant information from these parent-teacher contacts should be recorded.

On the basis of professional reflections and information from parents, teachers should adjust what they teach, as well as how they teach, in order to facilitate and accelerate an individual child's progress. Assessment data should be collected to evaluate the effectiveness of each adjustment. If the *many* instructional adaptations do not seem to facilitate a child's learning, teachers should consult with specialists in the school to determine whether other classroom adaptations can be made and whether the child should be referred for testing for a possible specific learning disability (see Figure 5.1). Most districts have teacher assistance teams that meet on a regular basis to discuss problems that children are having and to develop adaptations to facilitate learning for these children. Teams are usually composed of both general and special education teachers.

Each district has a specific procedure for making a referral. A referral form from the classroom teacher that includes a clear statement of the observed problems and the adaptations that have been tried will be required. A multidisciplinary team then meets to determine whether classroom adaptation is sufficient or further testing is required. If additional testing is recommended, the parents are notified. Signed parental permission must be received for the assessment process to begin. The assessment process is complex and may involve many professionals. Both formal and informal assessments will be conducted to explore all suspected problem areas. All measures must be nonbiased, given in the child's dominate language, and administered by trained personnel.

Assessment is usually conducted in the areas of physical development, academic achievement, classroom behaviors, and intelligence. The professionals involved may include special education teachers, reading specialists, nurses, speech-language pathologists, psychologists/psychometrists, physical/occupational therapists, other specialists, and the classroom teacher. When a child is a second-language learner or has unique physical needs, specially trained district personnel will be designated for many of the assessments.

The classroom teacher is responsible for providing information about the child's academic and social functioning in the classroom, including anecdotal records, classroom assessments, and work samples. The special education teacher may also observe the child in the classroom to collect additional information. All assessment information, both formal and informal, will be used in a multidisciplinary team meeting. This team will consist of the

- Principal
- Parents or guardian of the child
- Special education teacher
- Classroom teacher
- Persons trained to administer and interpret the formal assessments
- Personnel with expertise in areas of concern (e.g., nurse, counselor)
- Other professionals who interact with the child in the school setting and who can contribute pertinent information

The multidisciplinary team will review and discuss the initial referral and all available assessment information (1) to determine the child's needs and abilities; (2) to decide whether special services should be provided to the child; (3) to determine what categorical label, if any, best fits the child; and (4) to write an individualized education program (IEP). The IEP consists of

FIGURE 5.1 Individuals with Disabilities Education Act (IDEA) 1991

In 1975, Congress passed the Education for All Handicapped Children Act (Public Law 94–142), which was reauthorized and expanded in 1990 as the Individuals with Disabilities Education Act (IDEA; Public Law 101–476). This legislation provides for the right of all children between the ages of three and twenty-one with disabilities to receive a free and appropriate public education in the least restrictive environment. (Infants and toddlers with developmental delays and sensory disabilities are also eligible to receive early intervention services through Child Find.)

Children with disabilities are defined in IDEA as children with mental retardation, hearing impairments including deafness, speech or language impairments, visual impairments including blindness, serious emotional disturbance, orthopedic impairments, autism, traumatic brain injury, other health impairments, or specific learning disabilities (IDEA, Sec. 1401). States may use different terms for the disabilities in the state regulations but must address all disability categories in the implementation of IDEA.

The definition of specific learning disabilities in IDEA consists of four major components:

1. A disorder in basic psychological processes involved in understanding or using spoken or written language

2. Difficulty with listening, thinking, speaking, reading, writing, spelling, or doing mathematical calculations

3. A discrepancy between intellectual ability and achievement

4. The discrepancy is not the result of a visual, hearing, or motor disability; mental retardation; emotional disturbance; or environmental, cultural, or economic disadvantage.

What actually constitutes the discrepancy is not stated in IDEA. State regulations provide a description of the accepted process for determining whether a significant discrepancy exists between a child's academic achievement level and the child's expected level of performance based on formal tests of intelligence. Because the exclusionary clause in IDEA states that a specific learning disability is not the result of mental retardation, all children with specific learning disabilities have normal or above intelligence.

IDEA defines a *serious emotional disturbance* as a condition existing over a long period of time or to a marked degree that adversely affects educational performance. Characteristics include one or more of the following:

- An inability to build or maintain satisfactory interpersonal relationships with peers and teachers
- Inappropriate types of behaviors or feelings under normal circumstances
- A general pervasive mood of unhappiness or depression
- A tendency to develop physical symptoms or fears associated with personal or school problems

written statements regarding the child's current levels of educational performance, annual educational goals, short-term instructional objectives, specific educational services to be provided, and the extent to which the child will be able to participate in the general education program (the least restrictive environment, LRE).

If parents disagree with the findings of the team, they have the right to bring in outside assessments that must be considered by the team. Parents have the ultimate right to determine whether their child will be served through a special education program. If the parents agree with the IEP and sign the written document, special education services may begin. The IEP is reviewed yearly to monitor the child's progress and to develop the IEP for the following year. An extensive review of the IEP is conducted every three years.

MAKING DECISIONS
ABOUT ASSESSMENT TOOLS

Designing and Selecting Assessment Tools

Assessment tools can take a variety of shapes and forms. Each kind provides varying kinds and degrees of information for helping the classroom teacher gather and record data about a specific aspect of a learner during a particular time in that learner's development. Each assessment tool has strengths and limitations. To select or design appropriate assessment tools, the teacher must carefully match intended purposes for assessments with the strengths and limitations of the instruments available.

During your teaching career, you will be asked to interpret the results of, or to react to, the validity of various assessments. Understanding the purposes, strengths, and limitations of each measure is therefore crucial. You must be able to determine and articulate the appropriateness and usefulness of each to inform classroom instruction and to communicate your interpretation of the results to parents, administrators, and other educators.

Assessments can be compared and contrasted on the basis of the type of learning being assessed (process skills, recall of specific information, application of knowledge) and the criteria used to evaluate a child's progress (e.g., progress toward common goals, personal growth, comparison of children within grade levels).

Formal Assessments

Most assessments considered to be **formal measures** are norm-referenced or standardized. These measures typically yield little information to inform daily classroom instruction. They are used instead for accountability purposes, to evaluate curricula and programs, and to dispute or support the need for educational reform. *Norm-referenced* means that a student's score is interpreted in rela-

tion to how that student achieved, compared with other students. **Norm-referenced assessments** are typically objective tests. They usually have a traditional multiple-choice (forced-choice) question format. They are considered to be objective because no subjective judgments are made in the scoring process. The norming sample of children creates a normal bell-shaped curve, with most of the scores falling in the average range. Tests such as these are more likely to be appropriate measures of pure knowledge (rote memory) and are a poor choice for assessing process skills.

Norm-referenced tests require a large sample and are commonly used by districts and states to judge curriculum and instruction. These tests are considered to be cost-effective ways of assessing the achievement of basic skills of students within each grade level tested. The degree of alignment between the established goals and the actual goals tested, however, may vary. Therefore, unless both the established classroom academic goals and the goals measured on the test have been aligned, the relationship may be only moderate. Examples of norm-referenced tests are the Iowa Test of Basic Skills, the Comprehensive Test of Basic Skills, the Stanford Achievement Test, the Metropolitan Achievement Test, and the California Achievement Test.

Indicating that an assessment is *standardized* means that students participate in the assessment under the same controlled conditions. Various types of assessments can be standardized. For example, both norm-referenced tests (e.g., an achievement test) and a performance-based assessment task that uses a rubric scoring guide (a measure of process skill development, e.g., writing) can be considered standardized if the conditions under which each "test" is administered are the same for all students.

Standardized assessments are used to create a level playing field on which to gauge and compare student learning. A standardized assessment can be norm-referenced or criterion-referenced and may consist of objective questions, an essay, a performance task, or a project. Standardization is important when data will be aggregated across schools.

Requiring all students to participate under exactly the same conditions may not elicit all a student knows or can do regarding the academic goal. Decisions to abandon large-scale performance assessments in California and Arizona, however, indicate that the public puts more stock in formal objective measures regardless of how appropriate (or inappropriate) the assessments may be to measure the academic goal.

Important formal measures for teachers to be aware of include the National Assessment of Educational Progress (NAEP) and the International Assessment of Educational Progress (IAEP), two assessments that are commonly used to indicate student achievement of basic skills on a national level. The NAEP is a standardized assessment that measures a child's skills in reading, writing, mathematics, science, and geography. The NAEP tests use a variety of item formats including forced choice and constructed response. Children across the country are selected to participate in a state and national sample. The NAEP tests are scored by using three levels: Below Basic, Proficient, and Advanced. The Proficient level is the target for all children. States receive scores expressed as the percentage of children scoring Proficient or above. Because multiple versions of the test are equated, longitudinal results provide a glimpse at how child preparation changes over time. Even during times when national assessments are not in favor, the NAEP program has enjoyed considerable success.

The IAEP is a standardized assessment that uses forced-choice and child-constructed response (essay) formats. Based on results of this assessment, judgments are made about how well children in the United States are academically prepared when contrasted with children of other countries.

Formal and Informal Assessments

Some assessments can be designed as formal or informal measures. **Informal assessments** are designed to inform classroom instruction. They are usually not standardized or norm-referenced, but they can be structured. The following can be constructed as either formal or informal measures:

- **Performance sampling** is an assessment procedure that requires children to be actively engaged in carefully designed, open-ended learning activities that they find interesting and meaningful. Systematic observation and evaluation of both the process and the product of these activities are conducted to draw conclusions regarding a child's level of development and instructional needs.

- **Standards-referenced assessments** are used to measure the progress a child is making along a continuum toward established goals or standards.

- **Criterion-referenced assessments** have a predetermined level of mastery and are used to measure the extent to which a child is mastering specific content regardless of the achievement of other children. Textbook and curriculum publishers frequently provide a variety of assessment tools that are criterion-referenced and therefore aligned with the curricular materials. If the curriculum is presented to children as the publisher directs, then the publisher's test can be an appropriate tool.

- **Diagnostic assessments** are designed to provide in-depth understanding of a child's strengths and needs in specific areas such as literacy, mathematics, and oral language development. Diagnostic assessments can be used to identify characteristics within an individual child that inhibit learning. Teachers can use the results of diagnostic assessment tools to inform their instruction for a particular child or to create a learning environment more conducive to learning. Formal diagnostic assessments are typically administered by specialists in the various fields.

Informal Assessments

Informal assessments, as stated previously, are used primarily by the classroom teacher to provide qualitative and/or quantitative information about an individual child's learning processes and achievement that can be used to inform instruction and shared with parents and children. Informal assessments can be guided (structured) or open-ended, planned or spontaneous.

Informal assessments are used to evaluate children while they are engaged in actual or authentic learning or teaching/learning events. These events may occur naturally in the classroom or can be intentionally created by the teacher for assessment purposes. Teachers use **authentic assessment** tasks to observe intentionally the processes children go through to tackle challenging problems, to construct new understandings, as they encounter frustration or as they help others grasp new constructs. Because the task is aligned with, and may actually consist of, what children usually do in the classroom, it provides a valid measure of what children know and can apply, as well as information about the effectiveness of the teacher's instructional decisions.

While conducting authentic assessments, teachers can use observation guides such as checklists and rubrics to help them focus on desired points of learning, or they can use open-ended formats such as anecdotal records and audio- or videotapes, which allow them to document what they are observing about children's learning and to evaluate the data at a later time.

Informal Assessment Tools

Anecdotal records are factual narratives or notes written by the teacher to document an observation of a child's behavior as the child engages in learning. The purpose of anecdotal records is to provide a complete picture of the child's behavior in a variety of educational and social learning situations. Notes should include cumulative and sequential recordings of a child's behavior in a variety of learning situations throughout the school day. Each record should identify the learning event, clearly describe the child's behavior, and include the time and date of the event. Anecdotal records can be planned and structured to aid in assessing a targeted social issue or academic area or can be spontaneous to provide general assessment information. If the anecdotal records are planned for a specific purpose, self-stick file folder labels, self-stick notes, or note cards are helpful. The teacher writes the purpose for the record and the name of the targeted child on each card or label in advance of the observation. At the end of the observation period or at the end of the day, the labels or cards with notations are placed in the child's folder or working portfolio. Figure 5.2 is an example of a planned anecdotal record and the instructional implications that were added later upon reflection.

Checklists are one of the easiest ways to record the progress of an individual child or group of children. A checklist can be developed or selected to reflect observable child behaviors or performances that serve as benchmarks of progress toward an identified classroom, school, or district goal. Although checklists are subjective and difficult to aggregate across schools or even across classes, they can provide the informed and astute observer with valuable information on which to base instructional decisions. Checklists related to oral reading, for example, can help focus a teacher's observations on the reader's strengths and can be easily translated into future instructional interactions. As with

FIGURE 5.2 Planned anecdotal record

> 9/6/96 Science hands-on experiment using magnets
>
> Jon was an active participant in group. He first tried to discover whether items were magnetic and then recorded information in his journal.
>
> He helped Bob and Juanita decide how to test for magnetic qualities by showing them how to touch items to magnet.
>
> His recordings stated object's description and why he thought it was or was not magnetic. Accurate readings. Language reflected knowledge of content vocabulary.
>
> Not patient with Bob, who did not grasp concepts as readily.
>
> **Instructional Implications:** Jon developed plan to extend understanding by going around school and testing things he thought were magnetic on the basis of his hypothesis about what magnets would be attracted to. Determined equipment he would need and responded in his journal. I will have Jon work in a lab situation where he will have opportunity to apply the concept of magnetism.

Source: Printed with permission of Nancy Harris.

anecdotal records, the use of checklists can be planned and structured or spontaneous.

Rubrics are used to evaluate a child's performance in a given area (e.g., social development, mathematics, writing). Rubrics consist of clear descriptions of child behaviors or performance standards organized along a continuum with assessment guidelines. Rubrics clearly describe performance expectations and the criteria to be used for assessment. Whether used to assess behaviors, processes, or products (e.g., research papers, constructions), rubrics should be provided in advance to children and parents to serve as a guide and to assist in self-evaluation. Rubrics can also be used during conferences with children and/or parents to "note strengths and weaknesses, discuss differences in perceptions, and to set realistic goals" (Routman, 1991, p. 333) for future performance. Children helped create the rubric for writing on demand presented in Table 5.2.

Audiotaped and videotaped records are excellent ways to assess and evaluate complex performances and deep understandings. Audiotapes and videotapes of learning events can document child accomplishments and can assist the teacher in assessing a child's growth from one taped episode to the next. They can complement report cards or the results of more formalized assessments. Audiotapes and videotapes can be powerful for parents as they review the growth of their child.

As with other informal measures, audiotaped and videotaped documentation can be planned and structured or spontaneous. In either circumstance, when recording is incorporated into the classroom on a regular basis, the probability that the tapes will provide natural, rather than staged, documentation is increased. Tapes should always be dated and the specific event noted on the cover for later reference.

Assessment portfolios are collections of a child's work samples over a period of time and include planning documents, drafts, and final products. Each child and the teacher select documents they think demonstrate the child's learning and

TABLE 5.2 Rubric for writing on demand (with time limitations)

FOCUS		
1	*2*	*3*
No! The piece goes all over, or it's too wordy.	Focus is pretty clear. Only a few things don't fit.	Very clear focus. It stays on track and isn't too big.
DETAILS		
1	*2*	*3*
Very few details (1 to 3).	Some good details (4 to 6).	Many great details (7 plus).
LEAD		
1	*2*	*3*
Uninspiring, needs work.	Just okay, but good try.	Great! It catches my reader's attention and gives a clue to what's coming.
ENDING		
1	*2*	*3*
No end in sight. It just stops.	Pretty good. I can tell it is finished without "The End."	Terrific! The end is tied to the beginning and pulls the whole piece together.
SPELLING		
1	*2*	*3*
Tons of mistakes.	A few mistakes.	Very few mistakes.
PUNCTUATION AND CAPITALIZATION		
1	*2*	*3*
Lots of missing periods, capitals, commas.	Only a few missing periods, capitals, commas.	Almost no errors on periods, capitals, commas.
USE OF LANGUAGE		
1	*2*	*3*
Little evidence of change in use of words and phrases.	Tried some different ways of saying things.	Use of words and phrases shows creativity and attempt to say things in different ways.

Source: Reprinted by permission of Linda Baie of the Logan School for Creative Learning, Denver, Colorado.

progress. The children must engage in self-evaluation as they select items to include in their portfolios and consider the rationale for inclusion. Electronic portfolio systems are available that include video and audio products, as well as more traditional contents. Conferences are held regularly throughout the year with each child and with parents to discuss the processes and products demonstrated in the portfolios and to evaluate growth toward established goals. Although portfolios are excellent tools for presenting individual accomplishments, aggregating data across schools and districts can be difficult.

Working portfolios, as opposed to assessment portfolios, are folders that teachers create about each child. Working portfolios contain observations such as anecdotal records and findings regarding the most appropriate instructional and mediational strategies to use with each child. Work samples may also be included to indicate strengths and needs.

Student portfolios are organized and maintained by the children themselves. The children select the work samples to be included. They often include self-evaluations or learning process journals that help them reflect on their personal learning strengths and needs. Student portfolios can be collected in boxes, pillowcases placed on the backs of children's chairs like backpacks, or folders.

The Instruction-Assessment-Instruction Feedback Loop

In the classroom, assessments should be so integrated into the instructional weave that distinguishing between instruction and assessments becomes difficult. Excellent teachers automatically and intentionally gather information about children while interacting with them and while observing as they engage in learning events. Excellent teachers use this information as a basis for making effective decisions about instructional interactions, goals,

materials, and future learning events. A teacher's observations of a child's responses during instruction may prompt the teacher to adjust the immediate goals of the interaction, to change the type of mediation used, or to provide new information. The following vignette about Hannah is an example of this process called the **instruction-assessment-instruction feedback loop.**

HANNAH: INFORMAL AUTHENTIC ASSESSMENTS

Hannah is just beginning first grade and is new to the school. After a visit to the neighborhood fire station, Hannah drew a picture of her adventure. The teacher watched Hannah as she drew.

Purpose: To assess Hannah's current literacy understandings and prior experiences with the reading process.

Observations: Hannah seemed relaxed and involved in her drawing. She drew an age-appropriate picture of herself but did not include the setting of the fire station. I had to prompt Hannah to get her to add details about her trip.

The teacher asked Hannah to tell him what she would like him to write down about her trip to the fire station. The teacher began to write Hannah's dictation clearly and deliberately, saying each word as he wrote it.

Observations: The wording of Hannah's story was very stilted. "I go to the fire station," was her first sentence. I had to prompt her to generate more sentences. She added the sentence, "It's fun." I asked her what was fun, and she said, "To put on the boots and hat." Hannah dictated a disjointed collection of phrases and sentences (see copy attached). Hannah does not seem to have a well-developed sense of story. She did not pay close attention to the print as I wrote it down.

The teacher read the story to Hannah. He then asked her to take a turn and to point as she read.

Observations: Hannah seemed happy to read. She read the first sentence correctly. She tried to read the other sentences from memory, but the rest of her "reading" deviated from the actual story. Her voice-print match was inconsistent. Her reading was not always grammatically correct. For example, she read, "I have fun to go to the fire station."

Reflections: It seems as if this was a new experience for Hannah. She had difficulty telling about the trip in complete sentences. I wonder whether she's heard many stories or whether she's been asked to express her thoughts like this before. I need to find someone to read extra stories to her on a daily basis—maybe my teacher's aide or a volunteer.

Her stilted language and lack of connection between the story and the drawing made it difficult for Hannah to remember the story. It's interesting that she did not attempt to self-correct using voice-print match and what she may know about phonics. I need to model how to use both of these strategies to "read" dictated stories. (I need to find out what she does know about phonics!)

As illustrated above, the information gathered from a carefully facilitated instruction-assessment-instruction feedback loop informs instruction in a seamless, continuous way. All children learn differently on the basis of their own strengths and weaknesses. The feedback loop helps the teacher be continuously aware of what children know and are able to apply, which allows the teacher to provide appropriate, timely, and effective instruction.

BEGINNING THE SCHOOL YEAR: PLANNING OPPORTUNITIES FOR AUTHENTIC ASSESSMENTS

Prior to the beginning of the school year, consider the long-term goals you will establish for the children. The children will not arrive with manuals that indicate where each child is functioning along the continua of skills and understandings that will lead to the achievement of these goals. Thoughtful teachers never consider planning the specifics of curriculum and instruction before they know the children and determine what they know (the zone of proximal development). Curriculum and instruction must be grounded in the known and lead children's development. Before you plan what to teach and how to teach, you will have to identify the kinds of information you must know about the children and how you will gather it so that you can make decisions about curriculum and instruction. During the first two or three weeks of school, your *primary responsibility* is to observe, interact with, and learn about the children. To make effective instructional decisions, you must plan to collect information about the following:

- Children's interests, knowledge, and understanding related to specific content areas
- Children's skills and abilities in process subjects (reading, writing, listening, speaking, computation, and mathematical problem solving)
- Children's abilities to work independently, collaboratively, and in instructional groups
- How children learn most effectively
- How children respond to various types of mediation and teacher interactions

Opportunities for initial authentic assessment and informal observation can be embedded naturally within the exploration of a topic if learning events are intentionally and thoughtfully designed for this purpose. You can collect data to inform all of the above areas while you carefully observe the children as they listen, read, write, compute, solve problems, and discuss what they are learning in various contexts (e.g., large group, independently, collaboratively) and as they interact with you.

The following steps provide a guide to planing learning events within an integrated study that will allow you opportunities to gather the necessary data on which to base future instructional and curricular decisions:

Prior to the Beginning of the Year

1. Select a topic for whole-class exploration to take place during the first two or three weeks of school.

   The first unit (e.g., endangered species) is intentionally planned to provide opportunities for children to explore what being learners in this particular classroom environment means and for you to observe them as learners. The topic itself can be generated and selected prior to the school year through information gleaned from correspondence with families and parent-teacher-child conferences (see Chapter 6).

2. Determine how you will assess and record information related to children's prior knowledge, interests, and wonderments related to the topic.

   Perhaps you will begin the unit by reading aloud a fiction or nonfiction book related to the topic and then simply asking the children what they know about the topic. As you record the information on the chalkboard or chart paper, jot down the name or initials of the child who contributed the information. Younger children can be asked to illustrate and "write" about their prior knowledge of the topic and then to talk about the information revealed by their drawing and accompanying script. Collect or copy the children's work. Attach your notes related to the children's discussion of their illustrations. These suggestions will provide you with information about their knowledge of the relevant content subjects, as well as about their oral language (and possibly written language) development. After an immersion period, you can easily identify the personal interests and wonderments of individual children (see Chapters 4 and 8) to guide the more individualized explorations.

3. Determine the information you wish to know about each child in relation to the process subjects: reading, writing, mathematical computation, mathematical problem solving, and communication skills. Select or design assessment tools that will allow you to document this information.

   You must be aware of various aspects of each process subject (e.g., reading: interest in reading, favorite types of books, concepts about print, reading strategies known about or in place) and be knowledgeable about the continua of development for each aspect. This information is imperative for you to be able to effectively focus observation, evaluate data, and make subsequent instructional decisions. Numerous developmentally appropriate observation guides, checklists, and rubrics abound in teacher's guides and the professional literature. You can use these resources not only to record your observations but also to guide your observations of children as they apply personal understandings within the exploration of a theme. With time, effort, and practice, you will internalize this information, and having a paper in hand to make comprehensive observations will not be necessary.

4. Design learning events that will immerse children in content about the topic while at the same time require them to use their process skills.

As you immerse the children in the topic under study at the beginning of the unit, you will undoubtedly provide them with a variety of print resources related to the topic and the time to read them. This procedure will create an opportunity for you to collect information about how children choose books, search for interesting information in books, tackle unknown words, and organize and share information they have found. If a guest speaker interacts with the class, you can evaluate the children's communication skills and perhaps their depth of understanding of the content. By posing guiding questions prior to a videotape and asking children to respond to these question in their journals, you create an opportunity to assess their ability to focus their attention and independently reflect on the content and their understandings about the form and conventions of writing. As children work in teams to conduct science experiments, you can observe collaborative decision making, problem-solving abilities, related math process skills, and concept knowledge (see Figure 5.3).

5. Schedule blocks of time for unit exploration. Include time for guided observation when children are working independently and/or with you.

Because effective assessment requires the collection of data over time and in a variety of contexts, decide which learning events can be designated for independent learning, group instruction, and collaborative learning. Determine how independent learning and small-group time facilitate interacting with individual children to observe how they construct new concepts and respond to your mediation and interactions (see Chapters 3 and 4 for further information about scheduling time for unit explorations).

After the First Week of the Unit

6. With the children, plan opportunities for sharing what they have learned and for culminating projects. Include the children

FIGURE 5.3 Planning and recording authentic assessment

Process Skill	Learning Event	Dispositions/ Attitudes	Knowledge/ Concepts	Strategies/ Skills	Comments/ Observations
Reading	1.				
	2.				
	3.				
Problem Solving (Mathematics)	1.				
	2.				
	3.				

in designing or selecting assessments for self-evaluation.

You may be able to glean some of the information you want to learn about the children from past student portfolios, test results, report cards, and teacher observations. Keep in mind, however, that children's skill development, knowledge, interests, and behaviors may have changed over the summer. Do not let this dated information or previous teachers' comments determine or limit the expectations you have for any one child. Simply consider what the information can contribute as you collect new information about the children at the beginning of the year.

PROFESSIONAL SELF-EVALUATION

Excellent teachers use assessments and evaluation continuously to improve instruction. The primary focus, of course, is on whether the children are progressing appropriately toward the established goals. If even one child is not progressing toward the goals at the expected rate, the excellent teacher begins to problem-solve.

Some teachers tend to blame the child, a particular instructional strategy, or a set of instructional materials when children are not making progress. This tendency reflects a *mastery* attitude toward teaching. Authors of curriculum materials, publishers, and researchers often contribute to this attitude by attempting to "teacher proof" materials (e.g., some authors write down strategies or activities step by step for teachers to follow). Researchers often supplement instructional materials with data to indicate the probability of child achievement if teachers follow the outlined steps, use a particular set of materials, or conduct a certain set of activities in the prescribed format. Consequently, when children do not progress, teachers have every reason to believe that something is wrong with the children

or with the methodology being used. They do not have reason to examine their own instruction beyond determining whether they have followed the procedures in the book.

Excellent teachers are problem-solving teachers. The first step they take when children are confused or not progressing is the critical examination of their previous instructional decisions. Even when children are progressing adequately and everything seems to be going smoothly, excellent teachers examine their instruction to see whether they can make improvements that would further enhance children's achievement of the short-term goals and their progress toward the long-term goals. Teachers can engage in a reflective, problem-solving process in several ways.

Reflect on the Purposes for Instructional Decisions

As you reflect on specific instructional interactions, teaching/learning events, your instructional day, or your weekly curriculum, are you able to articulate why you did what you did (Fenstermacher, 1994; Richardson, 1994; Schon, 1983)? Were teaching/learning events selected or designed to address specific short-term or long-terms goals? Can you explain how specific events and interactions facilitated the progress of specific children? Do you have evidence that your instructional decisions were based on current assessment information or that they contributed to child growth? Excellent teachers filter all instructional decisions first through long-term and short-term goals and then through the assessment data they have about what children know, what they can learn next, and how they learn best. Excellent teachers know and are able to articulate why they are doing what they are doing and why they are doing it in a certain way.

Although written records of instructional events and interactions can be used as stimuli for reflection, videotapes of the same events may be more helpful to the novice teacher. Viewing a videotape will allow you to observe the event without the pressure of participation. As you watch the event you videotaped, you may want to verbalize the rationale for your decisions and to observe whether your attempts accomplished what you had hoped to accomplish. You can watch how the children responded to your decisions and how you responded to the children.

Read Professional Literature

As you reflected on the purposes for your instructional decisions, were you able to provide a theoretical or research base for what you did? For how you did it? Do you know why some things seem to result in learning for most children and others do not? Are you able to change or modify your instruction to make it more effective? Reading current professional journals and educational texts can help you understand why certain instructional decisions result in greater child engagement and achievement than others.

Reading professional literature can provide you with new ways of thinking about teaching and learning, with new or modified perspectives. Observing through a broader lens can help you observe with a new eye—a different mindset, if you will. When you reread professional material, you will notice things you did not notice the first time you read them and understand concepts in ways you did not understood them before. These new understandings and perspectives not only can increase the instructional alternatives immediately available to you but also will increase your ability to more easily and effectively adjust your instructional decisions and interactions to help individual children achieve specific goals. A professional, by definition, is a person who strives to be well grounded and current in the related professional literature.

Examples of journals to consider for professional reading are *Educational Leadership, Kap-*

A professional, by definition, is a person who strives to be well grounded and current in the related professional literature.

pan, Young Children, Childhood Education, Primary Voices K–6, Reading Teacher, Language Arts, Remedial and Special Education, Theory Into Practice, Teaching Children Mathematics, Social Studies and the Young Learner, Social Education, and *Science and Children.*

Visit Other Classrooms

Create opportunities to visit other classrooms in your school and in other schools. Visit situations that are dramatically different from, as well as similar to, your own in philosophy. You will see examples of what you want to do and of what you do not want to do. You will glean ideas that you can modify within your own instructional schema to benefit your students. Talk with the teachers about why they do what they do and why they do it in a certain way. Describe to them a particularly puzzling or problematic instructional episode or event. What insights, suggestions, or alternatives can they provide? Do they have suggestions for professional reading that might contribute information about the event you shared or that they have found particularly helpful or enjoyable?

Make Critical Friends

Critical friends are individuals you respect and value enough to invite into your classroom to observe and listen, to ask thought-provoking questions, to reflect with you, to provide information and insights about what was observed, and with whom to consider alternative instructional interactions (Costa & Kallick, 1993; Kroath, 1990). Critical friends are helpful, rather than destructive. They are part of the professional problem-solving team, not evaluators. School environments must be "safe" enough for teachers to establish critical friend relationships. If all teachers view all children as their children and are responsible for the learning of all children, then the entire faculty should be a team of critical friends.

A critical friend can be used to improve technique and strategy and to observe and respond to children. Critical friends flourish in school environments where teachers are collegial and facilitating child learning through excellence in instruction is valued. Critical friends help colleagues develop and hone skills. You should not wait for an annual evaluation from the principal to determine the quality of your instruction. Examine the progress of the children and reflect on your instructional interactions to improve the children's progress continuously. Initiate critical friend relationships to provide additional data for your professional self-improving system.

Successful teachers take responsibility for their own professional development by asking, What do I know and what do I need to know to better facilitate the progress of the children? Teachers who constantly search for ways to improve, who constantly engage in professional problem solving about the teaching and learning processes, are more resistant to burnout and are more successful in the classroom than teachers who attempt to master and use specific instructional strategies, methods, or sets of activities.

SUMMARY

There was a time in the recent past when teachers entering the field could reasonably expect to spend most of their career behind the closed doors of their classrooms, isolated from the rest of the educational world—at least in terms of instruction and assessment. With limited knowledge about assessment and evaluation, teachers performed their expected responsibilities. That time is now gone, however, and is not expected to return any time in the near future. Assessment is not optional.

REFERENCES

Bredekamp, S., & Copple, C. (Eds.). (1997). *Developmentally appropriate practice in early childhood programs.* Washington, DC: National Association for the Education of Young Children.

Burger, D. (1996). *Designing a sustainable, standards-based assessment system.* Aurora, CO: Mid-continent Regional Educational Laboratory.

Calfee, R. (1996). Assessing critical literacy: Tools and techniques. In M. Graves, P. vandenbroek, & B. Taylor (Eds.), *The first R: Every child's right to read* (pp. 224–249). New York: Teachers College Press.

Costa, A., & Kallick, B. (1993). Through the lens of a critical friend. *Educational Leadership, 51*(2), 49–51.

Fenstermacher, G. (1994). The place of practical argument in the education of teachers. In V. Richardson (Ed.), *Teacher change and the staff development process: A case in reading instruction.* New York: Teachers College Press.

Fox, P. (1996). *Brief CASE, 92*(2). Englewood, CO: Colorado Association of School Executives.

Individuals with Disabilities Act. (1991). Washington, DC: Government Printing Office.

Kroath, F. (1990). *The role of the critical friend in the development of teacher expertise.* Paper presented at the international symposium on Research on Effective and Responsible Teaching, Universite de Frigourg Suisse, Fribourg, Switzerland.

Linder, T. (1990). *Transdisciplinary play-based assessment: A functional approach to working with young children.* Baltimore: Brookes.

Marzano, R. (1992). *A different kind of classroom: Teaching with dimensions of learning.* Alexandria, VA: ASCD.

McAfee, O., & Leong, D. (1994). *Assessing and guiding young children's development and learning.* Boston: Allyn & Bacon.

New Zealand Ministry of Education. (1992). *Dancing with the pen: The learner as a writer.* Wellington, N.Z.: Learning Media, Ministry of Education.

Pearson, P. (1997, February). *Advances in reading assessment: Keeping our promises.* Paper presented to the Annual Conference of the Colorado Council of the International Reading Association, Denver.

Richardson, V. (Ed.). (1994). *Teacher change and the staff development process: A case in reading instruction.* New York: Teachers College Press.

Routman, R. (1991). *Invitations: Changing as teachers and learners K–12.* Portsmouth, NH: Heinemann.

Schmoker, M. (1996). *Results: The key to continuous school improvement.* Alexandria, VA: ASCD.

Schmoker, M. (1997). Setting goals in turbulent times. In A. Hargreaves (Ed.), *ASCD yearbook: Rethinking educational change with heart and mind.* Alexandria, VA: ASCD.

Schon, D. (1983). *The reflective practitioner: How professionals think in action.* New York: Basic Books.

Waters, T., Burger, D., & Burger, S. (1995). Moving up before going on. *Educational Leadership, 52,* 35–41.

Wiggins, G. (1993). *Assessing student performance: Exploring the purpose and limits of testing.* San Francisco: Jossey-Bass.

A lot of people start trying to involve parents and wonder why it doesn't happen.

(Stacey, 1991, p. 37)

6

Partnerships with Parents: Informative, Collaborative, and Empowering

CONSIDER YOUR BELIEFS

- How do you think a child's home experiences affect teaching and learning in the classroom?
- What can you do as a teacher to ensure that all children, regardless of home experiences, achieve in your classroom?
- What kinds of involvement should you encourage from parents?
- What should you communicate to parents? What are effective ways to communicate with parents?
- What factors should you consider when you communicate with parents about the progress their children are making?
- What should you do when parents' expectations and beliefs about teaching, learning, and curriculum are different from yours or those of the school administration?
- How can you help parents locate and use the resources they may want or need to provide for the overall well-being and cognitive development of their children?

CONSIDERING PARTNERSHIPS WITH PARENTS

Making Decisions about Parent Involvement in Education

The professional guidelines of many national organizations (Bredekamp & Copple, 1997; National Association of Elementary School Principals [NAESP], 1990; National Association of School Boards of Education [NASBE], 1988), the regulations for federal programs like Head Start and Title I, many state standards, and the professional literature (Berger, 1995; Day, 1988; Johnston, 1982) have made it clear that schools and teachers should attempt to involve parents in the education of their children. The NAEYC position statements (Bredekamp & Copple, 1997) describe the following appropriate practices for teachers regarding parent-teacher relationships:

- Teachers work in partnership with parents, communicating regularly to build mutual understanding and ensure that children's learning and developmental needs are met. Teachers listen to parents, seek to understand their goals and preferences for their children, and respect cultural and family differences.

- Teachers and parents share decisions about children's education. Teachers listen to parents and seek to understand their goals for their children. Teachers work with parents to resolve problems or differences of opinion as they arise and are respectful of cultural and family differences.

- Teachers and administrators view parents as partners in the education process. Teachers have time for periodic conferences with each child's parents; conferences may include the teacher, parents, and the child. Parents' visits to school are welcomed at all times, and home visits by teachers are encouraged and supported. Opportunities for parent participation are arranged to accommodate parents' schedules. Goals and celebrations of learning are shared with all who are involved.

- Members of each child's family are encouraged to participate in the classroom in ways that they feel comfortable. For example, family members may take part in classroom activities (sharing a cultural event or language, telling or reading a story, tutoring, making learning materials, or playing games), contribute to activities related to but not occurring within the classroom (designing or sewing costumes, working in the school library) or participate in decision making. (Bredekamp & Copple, 1997, pp. 134, 176–177)*

Kostelnik, Soderman, and Whiren (1993, p. 373) reported guidelines of the National Association of School Boards of Education (NASBE) for the dispositions that public schools are to have toward parents:

- Promote an environment in which parents are valued as primary influences in their children's lives and are essential partners in the education of their children.

- Recognize that the self-esteem of parents is integral to the development of the child and should be enhanced by the parents' positive interaction with the school.

- Include parents in decision making about their own child and the overall early childhood program.

- Assure opportunities and access for parents to observe and volunteer in the classrooms.

- Promote exchange of information and ideas between parents and teachers which will benefit the child.

- Provide a gradual and supportive transition process from home to school for those young children entering school for the first time. (NASBE, 1988, p. 19)**

Consequently, determining whether to involve parents is not a decision you will have to make. Understanding why it is important to involve parents and deciding how to involve parents effectively will be your primary concerns.

The strength of the commitment you make, as well as the time and energy you allocate, to involving parents in the education of their children will be based on your beliefs about what parents are willing and capable of contributing.

What is your concept of parent involvement? Do you perceive it to mean that parents should help their children with homework, provide cupcakes and coupons for the class, directly participate in classroom instruction, or be active members of policy-making committees? The strength of your commitment to parent involvement will also reflect your perception of your role as teacher or educational specialist. To what degree can you share the responsibility of a child's education with someone who may not have teaching credentials but who continues to be the child's teacher and who can contribute much information about the child as a person and as a learner?

Your ability to engage a majority of parents effectively in their children's education will depend on your concepts of parents and family and reflect any stereotypes or biases you may have. Do you consider parents to include only biological or stepparents, or do you include any significant other in the child's life who is willing to participate in the child's education? To what degree do you accept, reject, or empathize with diverse family units? What is your personal comfort level with families from diverse ethnic, cultural, linguistic, and economic circumstances? What effort have you made to increase your understanding of the customs, values, and communication patterns of these diverse groups? All of these beliefs and factors will influence what you do to involve parents and how effectively you do it.

As you read the following scenarios, consider the beliefs and assumptions that both the teachers and the parents may hold. Consider the conversations the teachers and parents may need to have and the issues they may need to resolve to form partnerships that will benefit the children.

I send books home every night with Abbie. I send books for her to read to her parents and a library book for them to read to her. They never do read with her. Don't they understand that she is behind because they don't help her at home? I bet her younger brothers and sisters will have problems in first grade too.

I had such a wonderful turnout for the open house last night! Almost all of the parents came. Of course, the ones that really need to be there never show up.

Troy did such a wonderful report on the Anasazi Indians. He brought all sorts of brochures, books, and artifacts in to share with the class. He and his family spent three weeks on an archaeological dig at Mesa Verde this summer. You're going to love having Troy in your class next year!

You have homework again tonight? We've spent at least two hours every night this week on homework. Doesn't your teacher understand that we have other commitments as a family in the evening? We need to go to your sister's basketball game this evening and won't get home until 9:00. Let's just take it with us, and I'll help you with it at the game.

I make Angela work on her homework every evening from 5:30 to 6:30. She sits at the kitchen table while I fix dinner so I can make sure she's working. She tries so hard. Sometimes she asks me questions about her work, but I don't know how to help her. What do you do when David asks you for help?

School Success: Who's Responsible?

When a child is not succeeding in school, the teacher often points to the home environment as the source of the problem. Perhaps the child's parents are high school dropouts. Perhaps the child's parents are illiterate and are unable to read books aloud to the child or to help with homework. Perhaps the child's parents are destitute and do not have the resources to provide the child with summer vacations, trips to museums, and a personal computer. Perhaps the parents are both professionals and away on business trips most of the time, unable to attend the child's school and extracurricular activities. What can the teacher do?

Home Environment and School Success

Without question, the home environment influences the physical, social, emotional, cognitive, and linguistic abilities and dispositions that a child brings to the classroom. Teachers know that children who are read to (Briggs & Elkin, 1973; Clark, 1976; Durkin, 1966; Holdaway, 1979; Plessas & Oakes, 1964; Taylor, 1983; Teale, 1978, 1984) and conversed with (Applebee & Langer, 1983; Cochran-Smith, 1984; Flood, 1977; Roser & Martinez, 1985; Taylor & Strickland, 1986) prior to entering school are likely to learn to read without difficulty. Children who have a myriad of language-rich opportunities such as attending plays, participating in sports events, traveling with their parents, visiting museums, and participating in other extracurricular activities are likely to learn easily and develop rapidly in the academic setting. Children whose parents provide appropriate support and supervision are more likely to succeed. When parents are involved in school activities, the teacher treats them with respect and demonstrates positive attitudes toward their children (Lyons, Robbins, & Smith, 1983). When parents are supportive and involved, the teacher has high expectations for their children and confidence in the children's ability to learn.

Conversely, when the teacher perceives the home environment to be deficient and views the parents as nonsupportive and uninvolved, the teacher may knowingly or unknowingly limit expectations for the children and lack confidence in the children's ability to learn. If a child is not succeeding in school, it is easy for a teacher to place blame on the home environment. Such a teacher often feels incapable of helping a child who lacks parental support to succeed. A sense of professional helplessness and hopelessness prevails.

TRY IT OUT *Challenged or Hopeless?*

As you read the following vignette, determine the expectations you would have for Theresa as her first-grade teacher. What expectations would you have for the contributions her parents could or would make toward her education? Would you try to get them involved? Why or why not? If so, how?

MRS. CHACON AND THERESA

The kindergarten teacher shared with Mrs. Chacon, the first-grade teacher, what she had observed about Theresa during the previous year. Theresa had been very quiet in class and did not often respond in group activities. In general, she seemed to have limited background experiences and vocabulary concepts. When she entered kindergarten, she did not know any letters, numbers, or colors. According to the kindergarten teacher, Theresa's parents rarely attended school functions or parent conferences, did not respond to notes or assignments sent home, and did not seem to take much interest in her academic development. At the end of the year, Theresa was at the bottom of her class.

As predicted by the kindergarten teacher, Theresa came to first grade with limited knowledge about print and numbers. As reflected in her language, her experiences were limited to the immediate community surrounding her home and school, not necessarily those typically deemed crucial for school success.

Did You Consider?

- The various reasons why Theresa was quiet and did not often participate in class

- That Theresa's parents may have limited literacy skills

- That English may not be Theresa's first language

- That Theresa's parents may have had valid reasons for not attending school functions
- That Theresa's parents may have been interested in her academic development
- Alternative strategies for contacting the family to answer some of your questions about Theresa's previous lack of success in school and to evaluate the type of parent involvement you can expect or create in the future
- How you could determine and build on the knowledge and experiences Theresa did bring to the classroom to ensure classroom success and achievement

---

Mrs. Chacon could easily have been discouraged by Theresa's limited experiences and language base, as well as by the apparent absence of parent involvement or support. Rather than become dismayed by what Theresa did not know, Mrs. Chacon determined what Theresa did know so that she could plan learning events to extend Theresa's knowledge and language base. Mrs. Chacon did not perceive herself as helpless, nor did she perceive Theresa as hopeless. Mrs. Chacon based her actions on more positive assumptions: (1) *All* children can succeed with appropriate classroom support and instruction, and (2) even minimal parental support further enhances children's achievement and their perceptions of themselves as capable learners. Rather than focus on what Theresa's family was not providing, Mrs. Chacon sought to increase Theresa's chances for success by enlisting the support her family was capable of providing.

Mrs. Chacon must consider, however, that some families are incapable or unwilling to give support. Physical addictions, emotional stress, mental incapacity, economic circumstances, and health-related problems sometimes render par-

ents incapable of providing any degree of support. Teachers must not take this as a sign that the child is incapable of learning. Nor must they see themselves as incapable of teaching a child who does not have parental support. Teachers must recognize that they can significantly affect a child's achievement and perception of him- or herself as a capable learner independent of parent involvement and home circumstances.

The Power of Instruction

On the basis of their research, Snow, Barnes, Chandler, Goodman, and Hemphill (1991) concluded that *classroom support* is the most important factor in the academic achievement of at-risk children. Children with low home support but high classroom support were shown to achieve. In contrast, children with high home support but low classroom support did not always achieve. Teacher support and instruction do make a difference! Allen and Mason (1989) suggested that educators need to shift their focus away from looking at the child as at-risk and toward searching for ways to reduce the risks for children in the classroom; that is, educators often focus more on how deficits in the home environment prevent a child from benefiting from instruction, rather than on how to adjust or modify instruction and support to build on what the child does know and to increase success.

MRS. CHACON AND TERESA (CONTINUED)

Mrs. Chacon began to plan ways to ensure that Theresa would achieve in the classroom. She also began to create ways for Theresa's parents to support her learning. For Theresa, she located books reflecting familiar concepts to use for reading instruction. During a home visit, Mrs. Chacon discovered that Theresa's family had a rich oral language heritage, a heritage of storytelling. With Theresa's help, she transcribed several of the family's favorite stories to include as initial reading materials for Theresa. Mrs. Chacon used these stories to help Theresa develop concepts and generalizations about print. She also paired Theresa with a parent volunteer who came to the classroom twice a week to read books and converse with her.

Mrs. Chacon extended Theresa's experience base, as well as that of the rest of her classmates, by frequently reading books aloud and facilitating rich conversations about the content and illustrations. During the class investigations, she provided Theresa and the other children with opportunities to use taped books, to use filmstrips accompanied by tapes, videos, and interactive videodiscs, as well as to go on field trips to extend their background and vocabulary related to the theme. On the field trips, she made certain that a parent volunteer accompanied Theresa and other selected children, with specific instructions to "language" through the experiences with the children. This volunteer provided appropriate language labels related to whatever the children were observing or experiencing and stimulated their thinking with thoughtful questions.

PARTNERSHIPS: PARENTS AND TEACHERS TOGETHER

Why Involve Parents?

Effective teachers know that children can learn, succeed, and achieve without parent involvement if the classroom environment provides appropriate support and instruction. Teachers cannot overlook, however, the positive benefits of parent involvement for the children, the parents, and the school.

Parent involvement can provide important support for children at risk for dropping out of school (those from deprived environments, children with mild disabilities, and underachievers) and can increase the likelihood that they will become a part of the learning community. More effective support will be forthcoming if the teacher's concept of *parent* involvement includes the extended *family* (e.g., grandparents, uncles, aunts), as well as other significant adults in a child's life.

Benefits to Children

Parents' involvement in their child's education has been shown to contribute significantly to the child's academic success and emotional well-being. When parents take an active interest in their child's education, the child's cognitive and physical development is enhanced, the child develops greater problem-solving abilities, and a significant increase occurs in the child's receptive and expressive language skills. Further, when children view their parents as a dynamic part of their schooling, they demonstrate a greater level of awareness of, and responsiveness to, both their school and home environments (Coleman, 1991; Eastman, 1988; Meier, 1978; Miller, 1978; Powell, 1989; Rich, 1985).

Benefits to Parents

Important benefits also accrue to parents who participate in their child's education. These parents seem to develop more positive attitudes toward themselves, including greater feelings of self-confidence, competence, and self-worth (Boren, 1973; Donofrios, 1976; Hereford, 1963; Herman & Yeh, 1980; Lane, Elzey, & Lewis, 1971; Powell, 1989; Radin, 1972; Rose, 1974). Through their participation in their child's school, parents tend to better accept the individual differences in children and to better understand their own child's development and needs.

This helps them become better teachers of their child at home, to find more enjoyment in their child, and to become more positive and flexible in their parenting (Andrews et al., 1982; Meier, 1978; Olmsted, 1977; Risley, 1968).

Benefits to Teachers

When parents and the teacher begin to communicate about a child, to exchange information about the child, and to develop common goals, the teacher also benefits. When the teacher listens to parents and visits with them about their child, he or she acquires a greater insight into the child. As a result, the teacher often becomes more sensitive to the individual needs of the child and more willing to adjust curriculum and instruction to meet those needs. The teacher who becomes involved with parents becomes less text and curriculum oriented and more child oriented. When parents are involved and the teacher perceives the parents to be concerned and engaged in their child's learning, the teacher is more likely to spend personal time on instructional matters to continue as an effective player in the child's education (Benyon, 1968; Hedges, 1972). The teacher and the parents become team members, and being a member of a team requires commitment.

Benefits to Schools

It is well worth the time and energy for teachers and schools to reach out actively to parents. When parents become involved with the school and the education of their children, they develop a more accurate understanding of the school's and teacher's goals for the children and the plan for achieving those goals (Umansky, 1983). As parents and the teacher communicate about a child, a more complete picture of the child emerges that permits them to support each other as they work toward common goals. This

Parents who participate in the classroom by listening to children read aloud benefit the children, the teachers, and themselves.

cooperation results in a greater identification with, commitment to, and understanding of classroom and school goals.

Consequently, involved parents are more likely to communicate the importance of what the teachers are providing for their children to the school, to the community, and to their children (Bronfenbrenner, 1977; Nedler & McAfee, 1979; Revicki, 1982; U.S. Department of Education, 1986). These parents tend to be more inclined to support school policies, to generate financial assistance, and to become advocates for programs within the community.

Obstacles to Parent Involvement

If parent involvement has so many benefits, why don't more parents participate in their child's education and with their child's school? Significant misperceptions of teachers and parents may be a primary reason. "The teacher may be viewed as less helpful and less interested in the family than he or she really is, and teachers are likely to underestimate parents' strong desire to be included in their children's education (Hess, Block, Costello, Knowles, & Large, 1971)" (Kostelnik, Soderman, & Whiren, 1993, p. 376).

Results from various polls and research studies have yielded interesting glimpses into the misperceptions that parents and teachers have regarding parents' involvement (or lack of) in the schools. Of 21,000 teachers surveyed by the Carnegie Foundation for the Advancement of Teaching (CFAT), 90 percent indicated not enough parent involvement in their classrooms. A subsequent survey, however, found that half the teachers polled believed that efforts to encourage parents to become involved in program-related activities would be useless. Teachers indicated that parents of today's children (particularly low-income, single-parent, and two-working-parent families) would be unwilling or unable to participate. Therefore, they would not exert the effort to try to get the parents involved (CFAT, 1988).

Surveys of parents, in contrast, indicated different perceptions. Up to 90 percent of parents polled indicated they were very interested in their children's social and academic development in school and would be interested in learning ways to support the teacher's efforts in the home (Epstein, 1986; Lightfoot, 1980; Snow, 1982). Although only 20 percent of parents indicated they were currently involved, an additional 70 percent indicated they would like to become more active in their children's schooling.

MRS. CHACON AND ROBERT

Because Robert's home had no telephone, Mrs. Chacon asked the parent liaison to arrange a home visit. The parent liaison consequently learned that Robert's parents spoke very little English. Being bilingual, she offered to accompany Mrs. Chacon on the home visit. During the visit, Mrs. Chacon discovered that both parents worked long shifts and frequently left Robert in the care of Alicia, his ten-year-old sister. She also discovered that the parents relied on Alicia to translate all information from the school and to do any follow-up communication. Much of the communication, however, required more understanding than Alicia was able to interpret. Mrs. Chacon also found out that Robert's mother set aside a time each evening for both children to work on school assignments. The mother could do little to assist them, however.

For Robert's parents and other parents with similar needs, the parent liaison was asked to make an audiotape in Spanish to explain what the children were studying and what parents might do at home to help develop concepts related to the theme. Tape recorders were sent home with the audiotapes. Parents were encouraged to record any comments or questions they might have for the teacher.

Most parents do want to be actively involved in their children's schooling in some way. There are many possible reasons for the discrepancy between parents' desire to participate and their absence from classroom and school activities. Teachers can take steps to address this lack of participation. Table 6.1 identifies possible roadblocks to parental participation and what teachers can do to remove those roadblocks.

GUIDELINES FOR SUCCESSFUL PARENT INVOLVEMENT

Developing Rapport

When teachers value and elicit parents' knowledge about their children and demonstrate genuine respect for the contributions the parents make to their children's development, they are able to see parents as partners (Stacey, 1991). When teachers focus on what parents neglect to do and devalue what parents are able to contribute, teachers alienate parents. When teachers criticize the child, they criticize the parents. When they support the child, they support the parents.

When you were in elementary school, what was your first reaction when your parents said your teacher had called? More than likely, your first response reflected some form of anxiety. For many parents, the first contact with the teacher or school, besides an open house or PTA meeting, is initiated when something is not going well—perhaps when the child is struggling academically or socially. In either case, parents typically respond in one of two ways. One is to become anxious about what they might be doing wrong as parents and about what they need to do to correct the situation. The other is to become defensive toward the teacher or school and protective of the child and/or of the family's personal values. In either case, the result is more detrimental than beneficial. If, however, the teacher has developed a positive rapport with the parents, a call from the teacher is viewed as a call from a concerned, friendly professional who has the well-being of the child at heart. When parents feel valued and respected by the teacher, they are more likely to work in partnership with the teacher to benefit the child.

Developing a positive rapport with each family takes extra time and effort by the teacher, but it is not a difficult task. The basic guidelines are simple: Emphasize the positive and demonstrate that you genuinely care about the child and the family. Initiate this process before the school year begins and continue throughout the year. Here are some things you can do.

Before School Begins

1. *Get to know the community you serve.* What is the cultural makeup of the community? What are the social norms? Is poverty a concern? Is ethnic diversity the norm? Do families have strong or limited language skills in English or another language? Is the community predominantly a professional community with at least one "stay-at-home parent," or do both parents work, with the children cared for by a nanny or in a day care facility? Would parents be more comfortable visiting with you at the school, in their home, on their front stoop, or in a nearby coffee shop? What are the culturally appropriate ways to interact with the parents in your community? Should you shake hands, nod, or simply extend a personal greeting? Should you maintain eye contact? Should you stand or sit close to the parent or at a certain distance? It is important that you understand the families you serve. Make it a point to become well informed before the school year begins. (For suggestions, see Chapter 10 in Robles de Melendez & Ostertag, 1997, pp. 319–355.)

TABLE 6.1 Roadblocks to parent participation

Roadblocks	Solutions
Negative school experiences of parents as children	• Make a personal visit to the home or another place outside the school suggested by the parent. • Organize family activities such as picnics, especially at the beginning of the school year. • Call the parent to share positive things the child is doing in school. • Personally invite the parent to participate. • Continue to personally contact the nonparticipating parent.
Not confident in their ability to contribute	• Value and acknowledge what parents already do informally at home to contribute to the child's education. • Alert parents to topics of study. Invite them to share related artifacts, information, hobbies, and experiences. • Invite parents to participate in classroom activities such as cooking, constructing, and reading with children. • Provide detailed descriptions of ways parents can contribute. • Provide home-based alternatives to volunteering in the classroom. Participation can be as diverse as cutting and pasting, working with children, and curriculum development. • Allow parents to choose the ways they will be involved. • Provide opportunities for parents to observe, ask questions, and get feedback about specific tasks they will do.
Offers to volunteer not acknowledged Feeling unwelcome	• Consider the type of parent involvement you wish to solicit. Do not send out generic surveys. Be specific in your requests. Immediately acknowledge responses. • Warmly greet any parents. Express how glad you are to have them in the school. • Acknowledge their contributions. • Maintain an open-door policy. Welcome parents at any time. • Send invitations for special activities and events. • Create a parents' lounge and provide a parent bulletin board.
Scheduling difficulties	• Schedule meetings at different times of the day and evening. • Negotiate with employers to provide release time for parents to attend meetings or to participate in the classroom. • Ask parents about the best times for them to participate.
Lack of child care	• Provide child care at the school. • Make home visits. • Work with community agencies to assist with child care.
Lack of transportation	• Coordinate a car pool or school transportation. • Make home visits.
Inability or unwillingness of parent to participate	• Solicit nonparent volunteers such as senior citizens, service organizations, or significant others.

2. *Contact each family personally through a letter or a telephone call* once children have been assigned to your class (see Figure 6.1 for an example of a letter to parents). Let parents know how much you look forward to having their child in your class and how much you look forward to meeting them. Tell them you would like to schedule a visit with them and their child at a mutually convenient time at the school, at their home, or in another designated place. Explain that the purposes of the visit are

- For them to share with you important information about their child
- To learn about the child's and the family's special talents and interests
- To learn about their goals for their child
- To tell them about your classroom
- To answer any questions they may have about their child's educational development

3. *Contact the child personally through a note or telephone call.* (Remember to use

FIGURE 6.1 Correspondence with parents prior to the school year

August 1, 1997

Dear Families,

Summers can be wonderful, especially for teachers! We get the chance to shift gears and enjoy a different routine for part of our year. But thoughts of Logan are never too far away, and the anticipation of a new school year builds as July fades. Now it is time for us to begin to work together to give your child the best opportunities for growth in the coming year.

I look forward to meeting with you during our August conferences. I hope that you bring your child, as well as your questions and concerns. I will tell you more about my plans and expectations for this new school year. I have enclosed a list of ways in which I hope you can be involved in the life of our group. Please complete it and bring it with you to our conference. Your child should receive a note from me in the next few days with something to fill out as well.

In addition, I am asking you to write a letter to me about your child. Even if your child has been in my class before, please write. Each year brings changes as our children grow academically, socially, and emotionally. Goals and priorities often change with a new year. Find a few quiet moments and describe your child as you see him or her at this point. Tell me what you think will be most important in your child's learning this year. Talk about the hopes and goals you have for your child. Tell me what you believe I need to know in order to be a good teacher for your child.

I want to thank you in advance for taking the time to write. I hope it is the beginning of a year of open and frequent communication between home and school that supports each child's growth.

Thank you.
Lisa

Source: Reprinted by permission of Lisa Davis, The Logan School for Creative Learning, Denver, Colorado.

FIGURE 6.2a Correspondence with children prior to the school year: Postcards

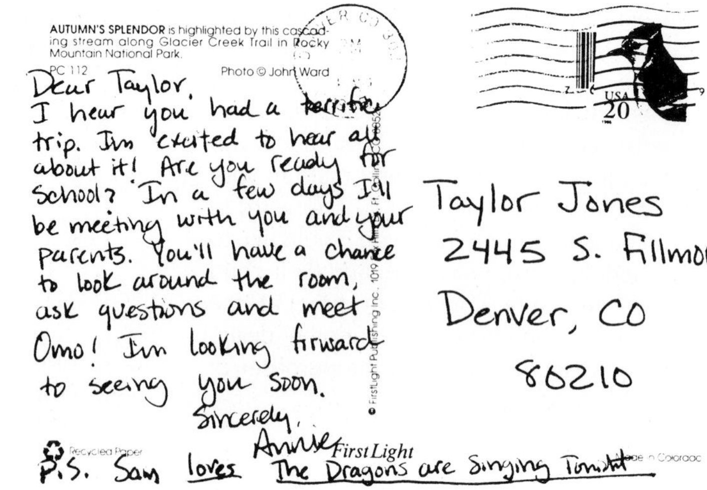

AUTUMN'S SPLENDOR is highlighted by this cascading stream along Glacier Creek Trail in Rocky Mountain National Park.
Photo © John Ward

Dear Taylor,
I hear you had a terrific trip. I'm excited to hear all about it! Are you ready for school? In a few days I'll be meeting with you and your parents. You'll have a chance to look around the room, ask questions and meet Omo! I'm looking forward to seeing you soon.
Sincerely,
Annie
P.S. Sam loves The Dragons are Singing Tonight

Taylor Jones
2445 S. Fillmore
Denver, CO
80210

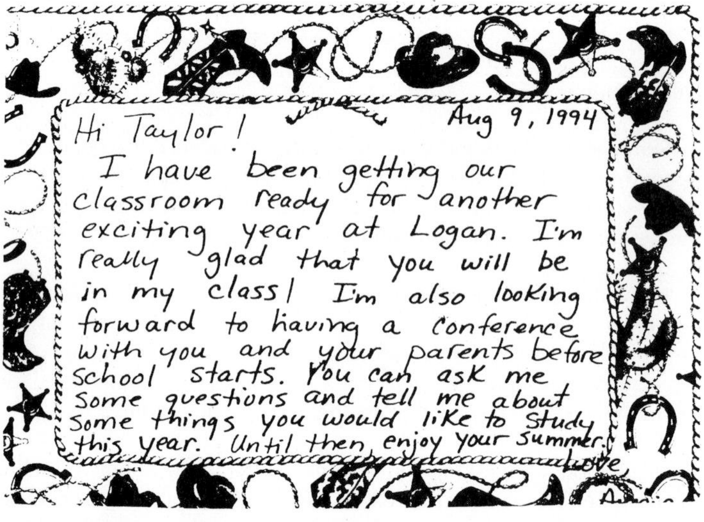

Hi Taylor!   Aug 9, 1994
I have been getting our classroom ready for another exciting year at Logan. I'm really glad that you will be in my class! I'm also looking forward to having a conference with you and your parents before school starts. You can ask me some questions and tell me about some things you would like to study this year. Until then, enjoy your summer.
Love,

Source: Reprinted by permission of Annie Spalding, The Logan School for Creative Learning, Denver Colorado.

print or cursive as appropriate; see Figures 6.2a and 6.2b for examples.) Tell the child how pleased you are that he or she will be in your class. Share with the child something about your interests, a trip you have taken over the summer, or something you enjoyed about school when you were the same age. Tell the child you have scheduled a time to meet him or her and the family and how much you look forward to visiting with them. Mention some special door decoration or any other special ways the child will be able to recognize the classroom and

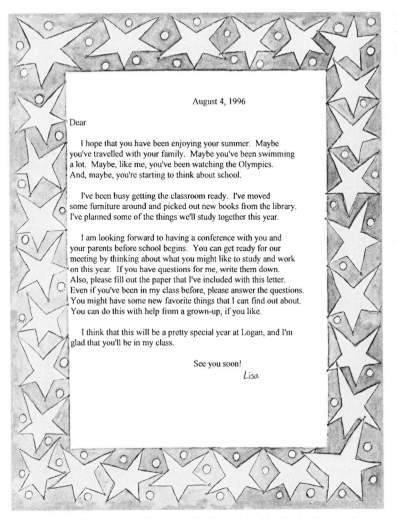

Source: Reprinted by permission of Lisa Davis, The Logan School for Creative Learning, Denver, Colorado.

FIGURE 6.2b Correspondence with children prior to the school year: Letter

his or her desk or cubby when the family arrives at school.

4. *Schedule and conduct a conference with the parents and child.* Clarify how much you respect the roles the parents play in their child's education. Encourage the child to share any personal interests, and mention how these may be addressed in the classroom. For example, if the child loves dogs, mention stories or books you will be reading about dogs or suggest a book that may interest the child as independent reading (be certain to have the book and other related materials on the child's desk the first day of school).

Share with the parents and the child some things the class will be exploring throughout the year. Also describe the routine of a typical day or week, including any special classes (e.g., music, art) that will be offered on a regular basis. Use a conversational tone. Welcome and invite questions and input from both parents and child.

Throughout the School Year

1. *Be observant.* Talk with the child. Know the child well. This will allow you to identify even the smallest achievement in the personal, social, or academic realm.

2. *Celebrate positive steps.* Perhaps you have observed some specific progress in the child or perhaps you have simply appreciated the child's contributions to class discussions or enjoyed the child's sense of humor. Send a note home or call the parents to share this information (Berger, 1991; Bundy, 1991; Freedman, Aschheim, Zerchykov, & Frank, 1990). When the parents tell the child about your call or show the child your note, positive parent-child interactions ensue. It was a most memorable occurrence for one of the authors and her son when the middle school art teacher called just to say how much he enjoyed having her son in class and to comment on the child's pleasant personality. Her son had never been in trouble at school and made good grades, but this was the first and only time a teacher ever made an effort to contact the parent outside regular school activities.

3. *Demonstrate genuine interest in the family.* Acknowledge happy family events or demonstrate empathy regarding family loss or tragedy with a card, telephone call, or personal visit. Recall the special interests and hobbies of the family. Share with the family any related books, brochures, snapshots, or newspaper clippings.

4. *Acknowledge all family contributions* to the child's personal and academic growth (Berclay, 1977). Share your enthusiasm with the child, as well as with the parents. Reinforce the benefits of time the parents spent with the child, whether cooking, taking the child on a hike, reading to the child, or teaching the child a skill.

5. *Advocate for the family.* As you observe the needs of the family or child, help the family connect with appropriate resources. If a child breaks his glasses and the family is unable to afford a replacement pair, help the family connect with the appropriate charitable organization. If a child demonstrates artistic talents, provide the parents with information about related opportunities. If parents have confided in you that home discipline is an issue, provide them with related books, articles, and videos, as well as information about available parenting classes.

COMMUNICATING ABOUT THE CLASSROOM

As School Begins

For parents to be active partners in their children's education, it is important that you share with them relevant information about the goals and functioning of your classroom. Rapport is more easily maintained when parents understand what you are doing and why you are doing it. Providing this information to parents at the beginning of the year, whether via a conference, home visit, handbook, or letter, helps circumvent potential problems later in the year. When parents are not well informed, confusion and misunderstanding may result that will interfere with your partnership. Figure 6.3 identifies general information parents need to know to support their children's efforts to succeed.

Throughout the School Year

It is important that you maintain rapport and sustain communication with parents throughout the school year. As the year progresses and the

Schedules, Routines, and Guidelines (School and Classroom)

Arrival and departure information
Daily and weekly classroom schedules

- Instructional blocks
- Snacks, lunch, and recess
- Designated sharing/show-and-tell day
- Specials—art, music, P.E., computers, drama
- Regularly scheduled assemblies

Calendar of upcoming classroom and school events
Codes of conduct and dress
Class rules and expectations for behavior: rewards and consequences

Information About School and Classroom Curriculum

Philosophy

- Child goals
- Samples and explanations of in-class assignments
- Explanations of instructional methods and materials
- Methods of assessment

Upcoming investigations

- Topics of study (e.g., change, transportation, endangered species)
- Related special events

Focus of academic units

- Mathematics (e.g., time, money, place value)
- Language arts (e.g., author studies, genre studies)
- Science (e.g., scientific method, magnetism)

Methods of reporting child progress

- Report cards
- Portfolios
- Written narrative summary of progress
- Conferences

Expectations About Homework

Will homework be assigned? Rationale?
Types of homework
Amount that will be assigned
When it will be assigned

- e.g., Never on Friday, always on Monday
- Regularly scheduled tests (e.g., spelling)

Degree of assistance required of parents
Expectations of quality

FIGURE 6.3 What parents need to know

FIGURE 6.3 *continued*

Ways Parents Can Contribute to Classroom Learning

In class (e.g., read to children, conduct demonstrations, assist teacher)

Outside class (e.g., field trips, collect materials, coordinate guest speakers)

Communication Between School and Home

Times and days parents can reach you at school
Times and days parents can call you at home
Ways you will communicate with parents (e.g., newsletter, notes, telephone)
Importance of communicating concerns to teachers or to parents
Communication channels in case of emergency

Visitation Policy

Requirements to check in at the office?
Must visits be scheduled in advance?
Should visitors interact with teachers and children?

---

calendar becomes more and more cluttered, it is easy to forget to communicate important information to parents. It is also tempting to maintain communication only with those parents who have outwardly demonstrated appreciation or who have become actively involved in the classroom. The importance of continuing to communicate with parents who are or appear to be unresponsive or uninterested is crucial. You never know when your continued efforts will attract their attention. And the child will know that you have not given up on him or his family.

Ways to Communicate with Parents about the Classroom

Handbook. Compile a handbook to distribute to each family at the beginning of the school year. Keep a copy in the classroom and one in the Parents' Lounge. Include such information as the school's philosophy, standards, and procedures pertaining to curriculum, discipline, child responsibility, and parent involvement. Also include information about any after-school activities or on-site day care, emergency information,

a map of the school, names and telephone numbers of important school personnel and PTA officers, and other crucial information. This will minimize frantic telephone calls to the school and circumvent potential miscommunication.

Open House. Schedule an open house for the early part of the school year. Provide time for parents to tour the classroom, examine children's work and related projects, and talk informally with you and with other parents. Plan a short group presentation. Share with parents your goals and expectations, as well as the types of learning events their children will engage in during the year. Plan opportunities for parents to experience the types of learning the children will regularly experience in the classroom. Suggestions follow:

- Invite parents to respond to questions the children have written to them in their journals. (How did you like our model of Warwick Castle? Were you scared by our Halloween cavern? What did you think of my endangered species story? Did you notice the model of the airport in the block area? I made it!)

- Provide hands-on mathematics activities for parents to engage in (e.g., Venn diagrams, guessing jars containing unknown quantities of objects). Have them record the process they used to solve the problems, as well as the outcome, in the children's mathematics notebooks.

- Guide parents as a group (as you would children) to compose a written piece reflecting the genre the children are currently exploring. Write it on chart paper to share with the children the next day. For example, after reading their children's innovations of *The Important Book* (Brown, 1949), one K–1 teacher had the parents break into pairs, interview each other, and construct similar innovations to reflect the important things they learned about each other. One parent wrote about another, "He likes practicing law. He loves playing baseball with his sons. He makes his own root beer. But, the important thing about Bruce is that he is Taylor's dad."

- Encourage parents to make and record their predictions regarding the outcome of a science project the children have conducted.

For parents, having opportunities to experience the types of learning their children experience every day in the classroom removes some of the mystery surrounding the time the children spend at school. For the children, having parents engage in these experiences sends the message that they are interested in their life at school and provides common experiences that can serve as stepping stones to empathy, understanding, and rich communication.

Personal Conference or Home Visit. Conferences and/or home visits should be scheduled at the beginning of the school year and continued throughout the year both as regularly scheduled semester or quarterly updates and as needed throughout the year. Conferences and home visits are discussed in detail in the sections "Developing Rapport: Before School Begins" and "Conferencing with Parents."

Class Newsletter. Send a class newsletter home to parents on a regular basis. The newsletter may contain information about the topics the class is investigating, requests for materials or artifacts to enhance topics, special class and school activities, samples of children's work, acknowledgment of parental contributions, ideas for things parents can do at home with their children, titles of books children may enjoy, references to resource books for parents, and opportunities to participate in the classroom and in other school activities. It is also important to incorporate information, ideas, and events related to the various cultures represented by the families in your classroom (Robles de Melendez & Vesna, 1997). An example of a newsletter is provided in Figure 6.4.

An efficient way to compile a newsletter is to keep a clipboard on your desk to record items as they occur to you. The children can be invited to contribute pieces for the newsletter and to suggest what they think is important for their parents to know. Some children may choose to dictate pieces; others may choose to write independently, or on a word processor or other computer software. Some children may choose to contribute artwork. Be certain to provide a bilingual edition of the newsletter, as well as other class documents, if appropriate. A parent who is bilingual may be willing to assist with the translation.

Class Calendar. Use a blank calendar to record scheduled events such as field trips, guest speakers, parties, standardized or academic testing, PTA meetings, parent conference dates, deadlines for book orders or fund-raising, holidays and vacation times, and designated units of study. Distribute a monthly calendar to each family at

January 27, 1997

Dear Families,

The boiler's working again, the sun is shining, and we had a three-day weekend! Back to school, there's much to do . . .

TUE. JAN. 21—Thanks to the helpful presence of Elaine and Judi, Lisa met with two book groups during quiet reading this morning. The "Amelia Bedelia" readers finished reading this silly book together today. The "Molly's Pilgrim" group had their first discussion and agreed to meet again on Friday, having marked sections they want to talk more about. Mid-morning was a time to come back together for a special story and a treat for Emery's birthday. Tina read "The Family Reunion." After snack and recess, Lisa met with seven children who are writing captions for photos taken during unit trips. The rest of the group worked independently. In the afternoon, we had Myg, [Gym], with Justine.

WED. JAN 22—It's our library day today. After sharing time, half-groups visited in the library with Fran, most checking out a new book. After snack and recess, we had a busy project time with buddies. Many unit projects were begun as we approached the home stretch to EXPO. After lunch, we had a story and then Myg with Justine. We worked a lot on our dance about games for the Kids-to-Kids Matrix sharing next week.

THU. JAN. 23—A major focus of our morning was a different view of how people might use measurement in their daily lives. Bill, a runner, came in to teach about how he uses an opisometer to measure distance in inches along a map and then divide the inches by the scale of the map to determine the miles along a particular route. Each child spent time with Bill and Sharon throughout the morning, finding his or her home on an enlarged map of the Denver metro area and then rolling the opisometer along a route to the Logan School. The children went on to calculate the distance, in miles, from their homes to school. When they were not measuring, the children worked in math notebooks, spent time reading or writing, had snack in small groups, and worked on a variety of unit tasks. When I called for lunch cleanup around 11:45, they were amazed at their "marathon" worktime of 2 hours, 15 minutes. In the afternoon, we added comments to a thank-you letter to Chris's parents and had Myg. At the end of the day, we were treated to a special reading of "Wump World" by Molly's mom in honor of Tu B'Shevat, a Jewish holiday that honors the birthday of all trees. Thanks, Terry!

FRI. JAN. 24—After this morning's meeting, we went up to the theater with the rest of primary to meet Paul Stewart, the founder of the Black American West Museum. He shared his experiences as a young boy being told that there were no such things as black cowboys and then coming to Denver and finding out that there were. He told about traveling and interviewing and collecting artifacts and stories and eventually starting a museum here in Denver so that many people could learn the history of black cowboys in the West. We returned to the room for snack and recess and then had a reading and writing time until lunch. Some reading and writing related to units; some did not. After lunch, Sam, Molly, and Emery went to the Stock Show with Suzann. Emery and Sam planned to meet with a beekeeper there. Molly planned to see the rabbits. At school, we read "A Lion Named Shirley Williamson" by Bernard Waber and then had a long math and project worktime. At the end of the day, we wrote a thank-you note to Bill Davis for his map-measuring lesson.

Thanks,
Lisa

Source: Reprinted by permission of Lisa Davis, The Logan School for Creative Learning, Denver, Colorado.

least several days before the beginning of each month. Post a copy in the classroom so that you, the children, and the parents can refer to it as needed.

Bulletin Board for Parents. Maintain a special bulletin board just for parents. Post information such as that listed above in "Class Newsletter." Also post the activities and achievements of the PTA, minutes of parent committee meetings and school board meetings, and any other related information. Encourage parents to maintain the bulletin board and to share information and resources.

Mailboxes for Parents. Establish individual mailboxes for parents at schools where parents visit or pick up children on a regular basis. This makes communication simple and efficient. Having a personal mailbox at the school also increases parents' sense of partnership and membership in the learning community.

Parents' Lounge or Resource Center. Create a friendly, warm, attractive space especially for parents. This should be a place where parents can go to relax when they are volunteering in the school and to visit informally with other parents (Cochran & Henderson, 1986; Powell, 1989) and school partners. This is an excellent place to maintain a **lending library** of books, magazines, videotapes (include videotapes of past class and special school events), computer programs, educational games, and other resources especially selected for parents (Bundy, 1991). Establishing a special place for parents indicates their special status in the school community.

Parents feel that they are welcomed and contributing members of the school community *when they are invited to share their interests and talents.*

Personal Telephone Calls or Calling Tree. Consider contacting parents personally to relate information that is detailed or that may pertain to only a few families. Establish a calling tree with several branches to remind parents of special events or to provide them with updated information about classroom activities. Each parent can pass along information to one or two other families.

CONFERENCING WITH PARENTS

As the school year begins, parents appreciate conferences relating general information about the classroom and the school. During this initial conference, parents are interested in knowing about the general goals and in sharing their aspirations for their children. As the year progresses, however, of utmost importance and interest to each set of parents is specific information about their own child. They want to know how their child is doing. They want to know whether the child is performing successfully in the classroom and getting along with other children. Parents will want to know what they can do at home to help their child be successful. They may also express concerns when the child does not seem to be performing in accordance with their expectations. To sustain an effective partnership with parents, you must be skilled as a professional educator in the art of conferencing with parents and should consider the following guidelines (Berger, 1991; Kostelnik et al., 1993; Stacey, 1991).

Preparation for the Conference

1. *Contact parents to schedule the conference at a mutually convenient time and place.* Provide the parents with several options. Discuss with each set of parents whether their child should be included in the conference. Post sign-up sheets to schedule periodic conferences at the school. Make the purpose of the conference absolutely clear to parents. In some cultures, a request from the teacher to visit with parents is interpreted to mean their child has misbehaved. In these instances, the parents may punish the child for misbehavior prior to the conference (Robles de Melendez, 1992).

2. *Schedule enough time for the conference.*

   - Allow enough time immediately prior to each conference to organize your thoughts and any materials you want to share with parents.
   - Schedule ample time with parents so that neither you nor they feel rushed.
   - Keep to the schedule. If you sense that a conference requires more time than you allotted, reschedule for a later time, rather than encroach on the time scheduled for the next parents. Be respectful of each parent's time.
   - Plan to use a few minutes after the conference to reorganize your materials and to jot down your reflections.

3. *If the conference is held at school, reserve a place that accords some privacy and can be made comfortable and pleasant for the parents.* Plan to sit where you can see parents arriving or, if conferences are held behind closed doors, devise a system that allows you to determine when parents have arrived.

4. *Contact the parents prior to the conference to verify and remind them of the time and place of the conference.* This task can be done in writing or by telephone.

5. *Carefully think through the purposes of the conference.* What do you want to discuss with the parents? What do they want to discuss with you? For the initial conference at the beginning of the school year, it may be helpful to provide parents in advance with samples of questions you might ask

them and they might want to ask you. Regardless of how well you plan, parents may ask questions for which you are not prepared. Keep notepads and pencils available for jotting down notes and questions that will require your attention later. As you jot down these questions, indicate to the parents when you will get back to them with the requested information. Parents, as well, will appreciate having paper and pencil available for note taking.

6. *Review the purposes of the conference* and any goals for the child the parents have previously shared. Collect any relevant materials and information you may wish to share with the parents. Refer to your anecdotal records. Gather representative samples of the child's work. Talk with any other teachers the child may have during the day to collect pertinent information and to consider their perceptions of the child.

Consider interviewing the child prior to the conference and sharing the child's responses with the parents. Pose such questions as: What do you enjoy doing most during the school day? What are you working on that seems the easiest? the most challenging? If you could change one thing about the school or the classroom, what would you change? What do you like to read about most? Who are your favorite friends to work with? What are you currently reading and writing about?

Some children will have foster parents, stepparents, or other full-time caregivers. Be certain to contact the legal custodial caregiver to determine who will attend the conference. In some instances, one conference with all interested parties will be sufficient. Under other circumstances, separate conferences may be requested or required.

It is not uncommon for children to come from homes in which a language other than English is the primary language of the parents. If you do not speak this language, be certain to arrange for an interpreter. When parents have limited English proficiency, avoid the use of figurative language in your conversation. Figurative language is frequently culture bound and may be difficult to interpret. If a parent is hearing impaired, determine the parent's preferred mode of communication and plan accordingly.

Consider in advance whether children will participate in the conferences. In some instances, it may be desirable for children to participate in all or most of the conference. The children may share their portfolios and their perceptions of areas in which they have made personal growth and areas in which they would like to improve. At times, it may be important to conduct all or a portion of a conference with only the parents or caregivers. Child care may be necessary at the school for the children and their siblings during all or part of the conferences.

During the Conference

1. *Greet parents in a warm and friendly manner.* Begin the conference with a positive statement or anecdote about the child.

2. *Review the purposes of the conference with the parents and see whether they have anything to add.*

3. *Maintain a conversational stance with parents.* Be a good listener.

   - Listen with the intent to understand.

   - Lean forward to reflect attention, and nod to indicate agreement.

   - Maintain eye contact if culturally appropriate.

   - To check for accuracy, restate what you think was said.

   - Ask clarifying questions. Avoid putting answers in a parent's mouth.

   - Be patient. Do not interrupt.

The child shares samples of her work with her mother to demonstrate the progress she has made.

4. *Be sensitive in your communication.* Empathize with the parents.

   - Recognize possible feelings of the parents. Avoid accusatory or judgmental terms.

   - When there are concerns about the child, focus on how to address the concerns. Do not attribute blame.

   - Use language the parents can understand. Avoid jargon.

   - Encourage parents to ask questions. Answer the questions they ask.

   - At key points throughout the conference, ask parents to share personal observations related to the point at hand. This will allow you to determine whether further clarification is necessary.

   - Provide parents with specific or concrete examples. Do not converse in generalities or abstractions.

5. *Be professional in your comments.* Avoid negative comments or personal information about other children, parents, teachers, and administrators.

6. *Collaboratively discuss future goals and strategies.* Problem-solve together. Admit that you do not have all the answers.

7. *Summarize what has been discussed and agreed upon during the conference.*

8. *End the conference with a positive comment.* Review the achievements the child has made. Express your appreciation for the continued partnership with the parents.

After the Conference

1. *Record what you discussed with the parents and the decisions you made together.*

2. *Contact the parents to provide any information they requested at the conference.*

3. *Communicate to the parents any steps you have taken and any progress you have made toward the goals established together during the conference.*

4. *Continue to express appreciation for their partnership.*

THE SCHOOL-HOME PARTNERSHIP

Helping Parents Help Their Children

Specific parent-child interactions and home routines have a very positive impact on children's success in school. Conversely, children of parents who are unaware of, or seldom emphasize, these interactions and routines tend to experience less success in school (Kellaghan, Sloane, Alvarez, & Bloom, 1993). Some parents naturally incorporate many of these positive behaviors into their lifestyles. Others will seek your professional advice regarding what they can do at home. For some, you may need to bring to their attention the significance of these parent-child interactions and home routines to the success of their child in school. For still others, your professional guidance or even a parent education support system may be required to help parents develop the skills and understandings requisite to providing these experiences for their children.

The following characteristics perceived to be common to educationally supportive home environments have been identified by Kellaghan et al. (1993).

The Educationally Supportive Home Environment

Work Habits of the Family. A certain amount of routine and structure in the home is essential if children are to develop good work habits in school as well as outside school. It is easy to understand why children from homes with (1) set routines, (2) shared responsibilities, (3) emphasis on timeliness of tasks, (4) established plans for work and play, (5) identified space for various activities, (6) a relatively quiet place to study or work, (7) a balance between play and educational activities, and (8) parents who value and give priority to educational opportunities will have an easier time internalizing and adjusting to the expectations and demands of the school environment. Consider sharing the following suggestions with parents to help them reflect on home dynamics.

- Establish routines to support your child's well-being. Make certain your child is well-nourished and in good health. It is difficult for a child to focus on learning when he or she is hungry or does not feel well. It is equally difficult for your child to benefit from even the most stimulating learning environment when he or she is tired or feels rushed and unsettled from arriving late. Establishing regular bedtimes and morning routines is important.

- Establish a time each day to visit with your child about what has happened during the school day. Avoid questions that require only yes-and-no answers. Ask about specific aspects of the day, rather than the whole day.

- Have appropriate materials at home for your child to use when doing homework. Locate a pleasant place for the child to work away from the television and other distractions. Designate a regular time each day for your child to do homework and to seek any necessary assistance from you. Your job is not to do the work for your child, but to be available to problem-solve with your child.

- Help your child learn to organize (notebooks, schedules, assignments, and time).

- Model positive attitudes toward learning and helpful work habits for your child.

Academic Guidance and Support. Support and enthusiasm for a child's learning helps the child maintain interest in, and commitment to, learning. Each day, the child is involved in exciting learning experiences at school. Some of these experiences may be perceived by the child to be fun and relatively easy, others as interesting and challenging, and yet others as unfamiliar and difficult. It is important that parents communicate to their children that they have confidence in them as learners. Suggestions for parents to help support their children's efforts in school follow:

- Review any papers or projects your child brings home. Demonstrate a genuine interest in what your child is learning.

- Share with your child what learning was like for you when you were in school and how learning continues to be exciting for you.

- Make certain your child has the materials and supplies necessary to participate fully in classroom activities. (Community resources are available to support parents in this matter.)

- Encourage your child to become responsible and independent. Allow your child to experience the natural or imposed consequences of personal choices and decisions.

- Help your child think through ways to solve a problem, but don't provide the "right" solution. Provide clues to, or think aloud about, the factors to consider. Help the child generate and evaluate alternative solutions.

- Participate in your child's classroom or in other school functions. When you do, you are communicating to your child that he or she is important to you and that what he or she is doing at school is important. Your participation and presence demonstrate to the child and to the teacher that you are part of the learning team.

- Initiate and maintain communication with the teacher. Communicate with your child's teacher on a regular basis through notes, telephone calls, and informal conversations. Don't forget to share insights and successes, as well as anxieties. Do share problems or concerns, however, as soon as they occur, rather than wait and worry.

Stimulation to Explore and Discuss Ideas and Events. Children perceive themselves as capable lifelong learners when learning and stimulating opportunities are experienced and discussed as a family on a regular basis. Opportunities for families to learn and to discuss their learning together outside the structured school environment not only helps children develop positive habits and attitudes toward learning but also expands their conceptual knowledge, vocabulary, habits of thinking, and conversational abilities. Suggestions for parents follow:

- Encourage all family members to talk about and share their interests, hobbies, and other activities that have educational value. New interests and learning can be stimulated and enjoyment heightened when shared.

- Play games as a family that develop and reinforce your child's reading vocabulary, concept development, mathematical skills, and problem-solving abilities.

- Encourage all family members to read frequently and to view educational television programs together. Encourage frequent discussion of books, magazine and newspaper articles, and television programs, accepting and encouraging each family member's contribution.

- Make frequent visits to museums, zoos, and cultural activities as a family. Encourage conversations and thought-provoking discussions related to the exhibits or demonstrations prior to, during, and after each visit.

Consider the home context when you explain the general idea of each point. Be nonthreatening and collaborative. Problem-solve with the parents as they consider possible ways to incorporate each characteristic, given their particular set of personal circumstances and their particular home context. In some instances, parents may need outside resources or further support. Help parents consider the suggestions at a level that will allow them initial success, consequently opening the door for more sophisticated applications.

🌿 TRY IT OUT   *Partnerships with Parents*

As you read the following vignettes, try to identify home factors that may be negatively affecting the child's success at school, as well as factors that may be influencing the behaviors of the parents. Consider ways you might work with each parent to help increase the child's school success. What suggestions would you make?

🌿 🌿 🌿 🌿 🌿 🌿 🌿 🌿 🌿 🌿 🌿 🌿 🌿 🌿 🌿 🌿 🌿 🌿 🌿 🌿

Sun-Hi, a four-year-old, is always late to school, sometimes as much as an hour late. When Sun-Hi enters the classroom each morning, she has difficulty separating from her mother. When she attempts to join in other children's activities, she is often disruptive and says things to seek attention or to cause conflict.

Jeffrey, a six-year-old, is already an accomplished athlete. Every day after school, he has karate, gymnastics, or soccer. On Saturdays he takes ice-skating lessons, and on Sundays he plays tennis. His mother is wondering whether to give him music or art lessons because she wants his activities to become more balanced. Academically, Jeffrey is struggling with learning to read and is just beginning to develop basic concepts about print and to recognize some letters of the alphabet.

Martin, an eight-year-old, has difficulty sticking with and finishing even the simplest assignments. Requiring him to plan ahead and to turn things in independently usually results in disaster. To help him stay on-task and to remember what needs to be accomplished within a certain time frame, you have designed a simple menu (or planner) for him to track the assignments he has completed and to keep aware of those that are still incomplete or in progress.

When you meet with Martin's parents, his mother tells you that she has trouble getting him to complete household chores and to take responsibility for getting homework completed or materials ready for school the next day. She wants to know what she can do at home to reinforce the habits you are helping him develop in the classroom.

TEAMING WITH PARENTS AT SCHOOL

Encouraging Parents to Participate in Classroom Activities

The benefits of parental participation in a child's school activities have been clearly established. The obstacles to their participation have been discussed and solutions suggested. If you decide to encourage parents to contribute to classroom or school endeavors from home or in the classroom or school, certain steps will increase the possibility of successful partnerships:

Know Your Parents. Through parent conferences, open houses, and informal contacts, get to know parents' interests, talents, hobbies, and areas of professional expertise. Consider any obstacles that parents may encounter if they choose to participate in the classroom. Use this information to identify a variety of opportunities espe-

TABLE 6.2 Teaming with Parents: Opportunities

Classroom Opportunities	*School Opportunities*
IN CLASS	
Read with children	Serve on parent advisory committees
Manage publishing center	Serve in parent-teacher organizations
Work with individual children	Manage parent lending library
Work with small groups of children	Serve on curriculum committee
Serve as room parent	Conduct study groups and workshops
Share theme-related talents	Assist with fund-raisers
Assist teacher	Assist with extracurricular programs
Accompany class on field trips	
Serve as a guest speaker	
Share talents, hobbies, and interests	
FROM HOME	
Gather resources for integrated studies	Assist with mailings
Collect resources for class activities	Constructing and assembling fund-raising materials
Coordinate room parents	Collect materials for fundraisers
Coordinate guest speakers	Coordinate school volunteers
Coordinate calling trees	

cially designed to use their unique abilities. Table 6.2 lists some opportunities that can be created for parents to assist with classroom activities.

Provide scheduling options and services that will circumvent identified obstacles. Be aware of the comfort level of parents in working with children, other adults, and school personnel. Take steps to increase their comfort level. Above all, let parents know how much you and the children need and appreciate their help—their partnership.

Clearly Describe the Opportunities Available. Some parents hesitate to volunteer when surveys are sent home that do not clearly identify what they will be expected to do. *What does being a room parent mean? Will organizing parties be the primary responsibility? Does the job involve teaching children? How often is a room parent expected to be in the classroom? What does listening to children read mean? Will any teaching be involved? Will the children be reading familiar books or new books?* Parents will be more likely to volunteer if they know enough about the expectations of the task to assess their own ability to assist competently. Berger (1995) suggests the use of a Help Wanted sheet that playfully describes jobs and the necessary qualifications—for example, "Good-Will Ambassador: Help us make everyone feel like an important part of this school. Be in charge of sending get-well cards or congratulatory messages" (p. 150). Figure 6.5 is an example of a letter sent home to encourage parents to participate in the classroom.

FIGURE 6.5 Letter to invite parent participation in the classroom

Throughout the school year, we welcome parent involvement in the classroom in many different ways. Please complete this form so that we can include you in the life of our group.

Thanks,
Lisa

CHILD'S NAME _____

PARENT'S NAME _____

PHONE (H) _____ (W) _____

OCCUPATION _____

Call me if you need . . .

_____ someone to listen to children read at quiet reading time

_____ someone to come in to read or tell a story to the group

_____ someone to drive on a trip (How many children can be safely seat-belted in your car? _____)

_____ someone to gather materials for projects

_____ someone to cook with a small group of children

_____ someone to play a musical instrument for the group or to teach a new song or game

_____ someone to . . . _____

_____

My interests/hobbies/special skills include _____

_____

_____

I could share a family tradition with the class this year. (Please describe briefly) _____

_____

_____

_____

Source: Reprinted by permission of Lisa Davis, The Logan School for Creative Learning, Denver, Colorado.

Preparing Volunteers to Participate in the Classroom

Many parents remain in awe of professional educators and forget that parents, too, are teachers. Remind parents of the teaching experience and skills they already possess by virtue of raising their own children. Some opportunities for working with children, however, may still be unfamiliar or seem a bit threatening to some parents. Inviting parents in to observe you do what would be expected of them may be helpful.

Give them the opportunity to observe as much as they like before deciding to volunteer for that particular job.

Concurrently with the observation, set aside time to go over in detail the materials, procedures, and interactions involved. Give the parents time to verbalize any remaining concerns and to ask questions. Respond to questions and concerns in an honest and open way. Do not pressure parents to take a role, but do provide them with enough information to reach a decision with which they will be comfortable.

If parents are recruited to assist with instructional interactions with children (e.g., assessment, individual tutoring, small-group instructional activities), it is important that you provide appropriate in-depth preparation. The amount of preparation required will be directly proportional to the volunteer's background experience and the task the volunteer is being asked to do. Do not ask parents to do things for which they are not adequately prepared.

Provide Volunteers with General Information. All volunteers in the classroom should be provided with a daily schedule and be informed of classroom routines. Prior to their actual participation, set up a time to tell volunteers what the expectations and rules are for classroom behavior. This will help them know how to support you, as well as what to expect of the children. Discuss with parent volunteers any potential behavior problems and ways to respond appropriately. Provide school guidelines regarding disciplinary interventions, as well as your professional suggestions for how to deal with such issues should they arise.

For safety purposes, inform volunteers of the health needs of specific children (e.g., seizures, allergies, asthma). Be certain that volunteers know what to do in case of a health emergency. Provide them with information about other emergency procedures such as fire and tornado drills.

All classroom volunteers should be informed of the school policy on confidentiality. Caution them about discussing any child's academic progress or social behaviors with anyone other than yourself or appropriate school personnel. Model appropriate behaviors by keeping your conversations about children, parents, and school personnel on a professional level inside and outside the school setting.

Opportunities for Parents to Contribute to the School

As Table 6.2 reflects, parents have many opportunities to contribute to the school as a whole. Just as with classroom opportunities, parents need to be well informed about what they will be expected to do in any particular position. Some opportunities may be familiar to you. The responsibilities and expectations of other positions may not be as familiar. Visit with school administrators and veteran teachers to know what schoolwide opportunities are available. Request printed information about the functions of the various advisory committees, the time commitment required, and the responsibilities of the position. Provide this information to parents and refer them to the appropriate committee chair or appropriate administrator for additional details. Indicate the need for interested and dedicated parents to serve in such positions. Voice appreciation for their willingness to consider accepting such schoolwide responsibilities.

WHEN EXPECTATIONS AND BELIEFS DIVERGE

Managing Conflicts with Parents

During your professional career, your understandings, beliefs, expectations, and values will be different from those of some parents. If you know the community and the parents well, you can anticipate and take steps to avoid conflict. The best way to circumvent conflict is to develop a positive rapport with parents, keep them well informed, and support their children. Know what subjects are controversial in your community. Be certain to let parents know when, why, and how these topics will be addressed in your classroom or in the school. Clarify your positions on these topics in your own mind and be prepared to explain and support your position.

If you are unable to avoid conflict, address the conflict in a professional manner. The following suggestions are recommended:

- Listen calmly and carefully. Be certain you understand the source of the conflict.

- Respond calmly and honestly to what the parents are saying.

- Gather necessary information, suggestions, and advice from colleagues, counselors, and administrators.

- Be informed about related school policies and procedures.

- Explore reasonable alternatives and compromises with the parent. Do not attempt to resolve irresolvable conflict.

- Address the source of the conflict, not the personalities or emotions involved.

- If necessary, suggest an impartial mediator. (Stacey, 1991, pp. 33–34)*

When you experience conflict with parents, remember that you do not have to agree on everything. You do have to listen to understand and communicate effectively and to be understood. The focus must be on the child. You must respect the role of the parent in the child's life and expect equal respect from the parent for your role in the child's life. You must collaborate with the parents for the benefit of the child. As Stacey (1991, p. 99) so aptly reminds teachers and parents in conflict, "It is not friendship but a viable working partnership that you are seeking."

---

*Adapted from *Parents and Teachers Together* by M. Stacey, Copyright 1992 by Open University Press. Reprinted by permission of Open University Press.

Responding to Suspicions of Child Abuse

During your teaching career, you will probably encounter children who are victims of abuse or neglect. All states have definitions of child abuse and neglect, as well as regulations that require teachers to report all suspicions (usually within twenty-four hours). All states have laws that hold teachers personally liable for unreported abuse or neglect; the laws clearly delineate the consequences for failure to report suspected abuse or neglect. It is crucial that you understand your legal responsibilities. You must understand the guidelines that must be followed in your state to report suspicions of child abuse or neglect. You must also consider your ethical responsibility to provide a safe, nurturing, and respectful environment inside the classroom for all children. This safe environment is especially crucial for the abused or neglected child.

Teachers must be aware of signs of abuse and neglect. In Lowenthal's article "Educational Implications of Child Abuse" (1996), Brodkin and Colman (1994) and Stone (1994) describe signs of various types of abuse and neglect. The following descriptions have been extracted and adapted from Lowenthal's article:

Signs of Physical Abuse

1. The child has unexplained bruises, cuts, welts, bite marks, burns or fractures.

2. The child's explanation of an injury is inconsistent with the nature of it.

3. The child reports an injury inflicted by his or her caretaker.

4. The child appears extremely fearful or startles easily.

Signs of Sexual Abuse

1. The child demonstrates an abrupt change in behavior.

2. The child displays seductive behavior with other youngsters and adults.

3. The child demonstrates extreme behavior in regard to touching, such as inappropriate sexual touch or reluctance to be touched by an adult.

4. The child has knowledge of sex that is age inappropriate.

5. The child consistently appears isolated, depressed, and angry.

6. The child complains of itching, bleeding, or bruises around the genital area.

Signs of Neglect

1. The caretaker demonstrates a lack of supervision of the child for long periods of time.

2. The child has unattended medical problems.

3. There is evidence of caretaker drug or alcohol abuse.

4. The child exhibits inappropriate dress, hygiene, or an unkempt appearance.

5. The child is chronically hungry or fatigued.

Signs of Emotional Abuse

1. The child demonstrates an impaired sense of self-worth.

2. The child displays a failure to thrive.

3. The child exhibits intense fears, anger, and/or depression.

4. The child demonstrates delayed physical, emotional, or intellectual development.

5. The child exhibits extremes of behavior, such as being extremely compliant and passive or extremely aggressive. (Lowenthal, 1996, 21–22)*

Although a child may demonstrate signs of abuse, the parents may not be the perpetrators. Other relatives, friends, or child care providers may be the source. Regardless of the source, all

suspected abuse or neglect must be reported, and it becomes the job of the Department of Social Services, not the teacher, to determine whether abuse has actually occurred and who, if anyone, is responsible.

Teachers must carefully consider interactions with the family of abused or neglected children. A teacher's first response to abusive parents may be to shun all interaction. Positive parent involvement, however difficult, should be attempted and encouraged for the sake of the child and to help the parents break their cycle of abuse (or to help prevent a cycle of abuse from starting). Abusive (or potentially abusive) parents may not have knowledge of child development or age-appropriate expectations of their children. To attempt to alter the perceptions the parents may have of their children's abilities, teachers should relay positive feedback and compliments to parents regarding their children's accomplishments. Many parents, but especially abusive parents, need more knowledge about positive and appropriate parenting skills. Teachers should be cognizant of parent services available in the community so that they can make appropriate referrals (Lowenthal, 1996).

Contemporary Issues

In recent decades, parents have begun to take a more active role in their children's education. The general tone of parent involvement has shifted dramatically from parents serving as room parents and PTA fund-raisers toward more equal partnerships between home and school. In practice, legal mandates and the political aspects of parent involvement seem to have created some divisions between parents and schools. With the emphasis on parents' rights, parents have taken on more the role of the consumer. And, as business practices have us believe, the consumer is always right. The historical perception of teachers and schools as the

---

*From "Educational Implications of Child Abuse" by B. Lowenthal, 1996, *Intervention in School and Clinic, 32*(1), 21–25. Copyright 1996 by PRO-ED, Inc. Adapted and reprinted by permission.

education experts seems to be significantly weakening.

With the onset of school restructuring efforts and site-based management philosophies, more and more parents have become active members of parent advisory committees, parent councils, and school boards. As parents have increased their participation in policy-making positions, often dramatically divergent beliefs and values between and among parents, teachers, and schools have emerged. Not only are these conflicts between parents and teachers, but they are also between teachers, between teachers and schools, and between schools. The conflicts have not always been anticipated, circumvented, negotiated, or resolved satisfactorily. As a result, strong movements toward voucher systems, charter schools, magnet schools, and schools of choice have developed.

These movements and many of the conflicts you will experience will be out of your immediate control. You will not be able to avoid or resolve all the conflicts you encounter. As a professional, you must know what you believe, be able to articulate your beliefs clearly, and be able to provide a solid rationale for your beliefs. When conflict arises, you must make a value judgment that is compatible with your belief system, make your voice heard, and work as a change agent within the system to change what you can as an advocate for children.

SUMMARY: EMPOWERMENT THROUGH PARTNERSHIPS

Collaborative partnerships with parents potentially have many benefits for the children, the parents, the teacher, and the school community. The commitment of time, energy, and resources necessary to develop rapport and working partnerships with parents requires a strong belief in the value of such relationships on the part of the teacher and the school. The roles that parents

can or are willing to take will differ from classroom to classroom, from school to school, and from community to community. Each context provides unique social, political, cultural, and economic circumstances. The mix of beliefs, values, and influence of individual personalities within each context will affect the nature and quality of partnerships with parents (Delgado-Gaitan, 1991; Epstein, 1986, 1992). You will play a key role within your particular context. You can radiate and generate hope or hopelessness. Consider your beliefs.

REFERENCES

Allen, J., & Mason, J. (Eds.). (1989). *Risk makers, risk takers, risk breakers: Reducing the risks for young literacy learners.* Portsmouth, NH: Heinemann.

Andrews, S., Blumenthal, J., Johnson, D., Kahn A., Ferguson, C., Lasater, T., Malone, P., & Wallace, D. (1982). The skills of mothering: A study of parent-child development centers. *Monographs of the Society of Research in Child Development, 47*(6, Serial No. 198).

Applebee, A., & Langer, J. (1983). Instructional scaffolding: Reading and writing as natural language activities. *Language Arts, 60,* 168–175.

Benyon, M. (1968). Parents in classrooms: Hope for the future. *The Times Educational Supplement, 2788,* 897.

Berclay, G. (1977). *Parent involvement in the schools.* Washington, DC: National Association for the Education of Young Children.

Berger, E. (1991). *Parents as partners in education: The home and school working together.* Upper Saddle River, NJ: Merrill/Prentice Hall.

Berger, E. (1995). *Parents as partners in education: Families and schools working together.* Upper Saddle River, NJ: Merrill/Prentice Hall.

Boren, J. (1973). *A family program: Analysis and difficulties in implementation.* Paper presented at the meeting of the Association for Advancement of Therapy, Miami, FL.

Bredekamp, S., & Copple, C. (Eds.). (1997). *Developmentally appropriate practice in early childhood programs* (Rev. ed.). Washington, DC: National Association for the Education of Young Children.

Briggs, C., & Elkin, D. (1973). Cognitive development in early readers. *Developmental Psychology, 9,* 279–280.

Brodkin, A., & Colman, M. (1994). Has this child been sexually abused? *Instructor, 103,* 25–26.

Bronfenbrenner, U. (1977). *Who needs parent education?* Paper presented at the working conference on parent education, Mat I Foundation, Flint, MI.

Brown, M. (1949). *The important book.* New York: Harper & Row.

Bundy, B. (1991). Fostering communication between parents and schools. *Young Children, 46*(2), 12–17.

Carnegie Foundation for the Advancement of Teaching (CFAT). (1988). *The conditions of teaching: A state-by-state analysis.* Princeton, NJ: Author.

Clark, M. (1976). *Young fluent readers.* Portsmouth, NH: Heinemann.

Cochran, M., & Henderson, C., Jr. (1986). *Family matters: Evaluation of the parental empowerment program.* Ithaca, NY: Comparative Ecology of Human Development Project.

Cochran-Smith, M. (1984). *The making of a reader.* Norwood, NJ: Ablex.

Coleman, J. (1991). *Planning for parent participation in schools for young children.* Bloomington, IL: ERIC Digest.

Day, B. (1988). *What's happening in early childhood program* (pp. 3–31). Alexandria, VA: Association for Supervision and Curriculum Development.

Delgado-Gaitan, C. (1991). Involving parents in the schools: A process of empowerment. *American Journal of Education, C, 1,* 20–46.

Donofrios, A. (1976). Parent education versus child psychotherapy. *Psychology in the Schools, 13,* 176–180.

Durkin, D. (1966). *Children who read early.* New York: Teachers College Press.

Eastman, G. (1988). *Family involvement in education.* Unpublished manuscript prepared for the Wisconsin Department of Public Instruction.

Epstein, J. (1986). Parents' reactions to teacher practices of parent involvement. *Elementary School Journal, 86,* 277–293.

Epstein, J. (1992). School and family partnerships. *Encyclopedia of Educational Research, 6,* 1139–1151.

Flood, J. (1977). Parental styles in reading episodes with young children. *Reading Teacher, 30,* 864–867.

Freedman, S., Aschheim, B., Zerchykov, R., & Frank, R. (1990). *Parent-school collaboration: A compendium of strategies for parent involvement.* Quincy: Massachusetts Department of Education, Office of Community Education.

Hedges, H. (1972). *Volunteer parental assistance in elementary schools.* Unpublished manuscript, Ontario Institute for Studies in Education, Toronto, Canada.

Hereford, C. (1963). *Changing parental attitude through group discussion.* Austin: University of Texas Press.

Herman, J., & Yeh, J. (1980). *Some effects of parent involvement in schools.* Paper presented at the annual meeting of the American Educational Research Association, Boston. (ERIC document Reproduction Service No. ED 206 963)

Hess, R., Block, M., Costello, J., Knowles, R., & Large, D. (1971). Parent involvement in early education. In E. Grotberg (Ed.), *Daycare: Resources for decisions* (pp. 265–298). Washington, DC: Office of Economic Opportunity.

Holdaway, D. (1979). *The foundations of literacy.* Sydney, Australia: Ashton Scholastic.

Johnston, M. (1982). *How to involve parents in early childhood education.* Provo, UT: Brigham Young University Press.

Kellaghan, T., Sloane, K., Alvarez, B., & Bloom, B. (1993). *The home environment and school learning.* San Francisco: Jossey-Bass.

Kostelnik, M., Soderman, A., & Whiren, A. (1993). *Developmentally appropriate programs in early childhood education.* Upper Saddle River, NJ: Prentice Hall.

Lane, M., Elzey, E., & Lewis, M. (1971). *Nurseries in cross-cultural education (NICE).* San Francisco: San Francisco State College.

Lightfoot, S. (1980). Families and schools: Creative conflict or negative dissonance? *Journal of Research and Development in Education, 9,* 34–43.

Lowenthal, B. (1996). Educational implications of child abuse. *Intervention in School and Clinic, 32*(1), 21–25.

Lyons, P., Robbins, A., & Smith, A. (1983). *Involving parents in schools: A handbook for participation.* Ypsilanti, MI: High/Scope.

Meier, J. (1978). Introduction. In B. Brown (Ed.), *Found: Long-term gains from early intervention.* Boulder, CO: Westview.

Miller, S. (1978). *The facilitation of fundamental motor skill learning in young children.* Unpublished doctoral dissertation, Michigan State University, East Lansing.

National Association of Elementary School Principals (NAESP). (1990). *Early childhood education and the elementary school principal: Standards for quality programs for young children.* Alexandria, VA: Author.

National Association of School Boards of Education (NASBE). (1988). *Right from the start.* Alexandria, VA: Author.

Nedler, S., & McAfee, O. (1979). *Working with parents.* Belmont, CA: Wadsworth.

Olmsted, P. (1977). *The relationship of program participation and parental teaching behavior with children's standardized achievement measures in two program sites.* Unpublished doctoral dissertation, University of Florida, Gainesville.

Plessas, G., & Oakes, C. (1964). Prereading experiences of selected early readers. *Reading Teacher, 17,* 241–245.

Powell, R. (1989). *Families and early childhood programs* (Research Monographs of the National Association for the Education of Young Children, Vol. 3). Washington, DC: National Association for the Education of Young Children.

Radin, N. (1972). Three degrees of maternal involvement in a preschool program: Impact on mothers and children. *Child Development, 43,* 1355–1364.

Revicki, D. (1982). The relationship among socioeconomic status, home environment, parent involvement, child self-concept, and child achievement. *Resources in Education, 1,* 459–463.

Rich, D. (1985). *The forgotten factor in school success— The family: A policymaker's guide.* Washington, DC: Home and School Institute.

Risley, R. (1968). Learning and lollipops. *Psychology Today, 1*(8), 28–31, 62–65.

Robles de Melendez, W. (1992, July). *Creating the multicultural environment.* Paper presented at the Conference of the Florida Department of Education, Tampa, FL.

Robles de Melendez, W., & Ostertag, V. (1997). *Teaching young children in multicultural classrooms: Issues, concepts, and strategies.* Albany, NY: Delmar.

Rose, S. (1974). Group training of parents as behavior modifiers. *Social Work, 19,* 156–162.

Roser, N., & Martinez, M. (1985). Roles adults play in preschool responses to literature. *Language Arts, 62,* 485–490.

Snow, C., Barnes, W., Chandler, J., Goodman, I., & Hemphill, L. (1991). *Unfulfilled expectations: Home and school influences on literacy.* Cambridge, MA: Harvard University Press.

Snow, M. (1982). *Characteristics of families with special needs in relation to schools.* Charleston, WV: Appalachia Educational Laboratory.

Stacey, M. (1991). *Parents and teachers together.* Bristol, PA: Open University Press.

Stone, D. (1994). *Stop it now.* Everett, WA: Open Door Theatre.

Taylor, D. (1983). *Family literacy.* Portsmouth, NH: Heinemann.

Taylor, D., & Strickland, D. (1986). *Family storybook reading.* Portsmouth, NH: Heinemann.

Teale, W. (1978). Positive environments for learning to read: What studies of research tell us. *Language Arts, 59,* 555–570.

Teale, W. (1984). Reading to young children: Its significance for literacy development. In H. Goelman, A. Oberg, & F. Smith (Eds.), *Awakening to literacy.* Portsmouth, NH: Heinemann.

Umansky, W. (1983). On families and the revaluing of childhood. *Childhood Education, 59*(4), 259–266.

U.S. Department of Education. (1986). *What works: Research about teaching and learning.* Washington, DC: Government Printing Office.

If children live associating reading only with repetition of skill, drill, teach, and test, they will never reach for a book on their own. If, on the other hand, children live in an environment that associates reading with pleasure and enjoyment as well as with skill development, they are likely to become voluntary readers. How children live and learn at home and in the classroom ultimately determines whether they will live their lives as literate or alliterate individuals.

(Morrow, 1985, p. 20)

7

Development of Literacy in the Primary Years:
The Interdependence of Reading, Writing, Listening, Speaking, and Thinking

---

CONSIDER YOUR BELIEFS

- What is your concept of literacy?
- How do listening, speaking, reading, writing, and thinking interact as a child becomes literate?
- How do you recognize, support, and extend children's understandings about literacy?
- Some young children have experienced literacy-rich environments since birth; others have had limited literacy opportunities. How can you find out what children know about literacy? How do you adjust instruction accordingly?
- How do you know whether your literacy instruction is helping children become literate?

WHAT BECOMING LITERATE MEANS

Becoming literate is a lifelong developmental process. The literate adult has learned to use oral and written language effectively to reason and think within the context of her or his culture. The literate adult has learned to use language to accomplish personal goals and to meet the demands experienced within various contexts (e.g., home, personal relationships, workplace, community, society). The literate adult continues to refine and expand language in response to life experiences. Although at a different point in this lifelong process, the literate child, like the literate adult, continuously *seeks* to use and *learns* to use language (reading, writing, listening, and speaking) effectively to

- Communicate effectively with others
- Think
- Regulate thoughts and behaviors

- Explore her or his world
- Create
- Express personal needs and feelings
- Solve problems
- Function effectively in society
- Nurture her or his personal interests
- Reflect on her or his experiences
  (Bodrova & Leong, 1996; Halliday, 1975)

Learning to read is crucial to becoming literate. Children who do not learn to read by the end of third grade tend to have difficulty becoming readers. Teaching children to read by the end of third grade is considered by many to be the single most important task assigned to elementary schools (NCITE, 1996). The National Assessment of Education Progress (NAEP) 1994 reading assessment report found that 42 percent of fourth graders in U.S. schools were reading at "below basic" level. Some of these children had disabilities, some were from disadvantaged homes, some had second language problems, and many simply had not learned to read. The NAEP found that 32 percent of fourth graders reading below basic level had parents who had graduated from college. How can this be? What factors and life experiences affect whether one becomes literate?

Beginnings

Children's literacy journeys begin at birth as they respond to the voices, touches, and physical presences in their environments. Most infants soon learn that crying results in feeding or attention or both and that cooing or babbling (*emergent speech mechanisms*) result in pleasant responses from those around them. Toddlers quickly learn that the word *no* can be used to control behavior, just as they learn that certain utterances result in the appearance of certain objects (e.g., bottle, ball). The motivation for learning and using language comes from the functions language can serve. As children be-

come increasingly mobile, their needs, desires, interests, and worlds expand. The demands on their language faculties, both listening and speaking, expand concurrently.

As with other aspects of human development, oral language learning is a result of interactions between *nature* (what children bring to the task by way of biological endowment) and *nurture* (the conversations they experience, particularly those in which they participate; Wells, 1986). Children learn the oral language of their community as they interact with more language-proficient others. They modify their language interactions and behaviors according to the responses they receive from others to their efforts. If responses are positive and their attempts are successful, they maintain the modifications. If responses are negative or the attempts are unsuccessful, children construct new hypotheses and try them out in future language interactions.

This process is also true for written language development. As children begin to notice that written symbols are used to represent messages, concepts, and ideas, they naturally begin to attempt to make sense of the purposes of print in their environment and to decipher the code. As with oral language, the quality of responses and the encouragement children receive from more literate others to their attempts affects the quality of children's literacy development.

When entering school, children's initial participation as listeners, speakers, readers, writers, and thinkers in the classroom directly reflects their prior literacy experiences. Children's self-perceptions and participation will be reinforced or modified by the teacher.

EMERGENCE OF LISTENING (AURAL) AND SPEAKING (ORAL)

Children seem to learn language in a somewhat intuitive way. Language learning is a systematic problem-solving process, however, governed not merely by imitation, but by the patterns and grammatical rules the child subconsciously extracts from language interactions—a built-in ability that is theorized to be common to all humans and that allows young children to learn the language primary to their environment (Chomsky, 1968). Young children are frequently overheard referring to "two *foots*," rather than "two feet," or saying "I *petted* the kitty," which is a clear indication that a grammatical pattern has been extracted and is being applied, even if overgeneralized.

As children use language to attempt to get their needs met, they learn about the form and functions of language. They develop understandings about the abstract and complex systems that undergird language:

- *Phonology* (sounds and cadence specific to the language)
- *Morphology* (rules governing word construction)
- *Semantics* (meanings of words)
- *Syntax* (grammatical structures)
- *Pragmatics* (appropriate use of language in various social contexts)

Impact of Early Aural/Oral Language Interactions

Language learning occurs through interdependent **aural language** (listening, receptive) and **oral language** (speaking, expressive) interactions with more literate others. Children who are provided with rich and varied models (demonstrations) of language, as well as with encouraging **scaffolded interactions** (in which the child's current competence is acknowledged and gradually extended), will develop a greater knowledge of, and facility with, the functions and forms of language than those who have more limited opportunities (Bloom, 1972; Brown & Bellugi, 1964; Brown, 1973; Bruner, 1976; Cazden, 1972; Chomsky, 1965; Halliday, 1975; Lennenberg, 1967; McNeil, 1970; Menyuk, 1977).

Children come to school with varying degrees of experience with having been spoken with and listened to. Researchers (Heath, 1982; Wells, 1986) have observed vast differences in the extent to which families (or cultures) encourage children to be conversational partners. In some homes, children are expected to be seen and not heard; in other homes, children are expected to participate in rich, open-ended conversations in which their thinking is stimulated as they express and support their opinions. In many homes, the expectations and opportunities for children's language lie somewhere between. It is important to be cognizant of these differences because a child's passivity or talkativeness in the classroom may stem from this prior "language conditioning" but may be misconstrued as slowness or misbehavior.

Preece (1992) identified several important language skills that support the academic and social success of young children (see Figure 7.1). Children must be provided with opportunities to develop these language proficiencies.

Teachers recognize that children often require demonstrations of how to use language effectively in specific situations and explicit explanations of why effective use is important. Examples of how a teacher might accomplish this follow:

Example: Prior to a visit from a marine biologist, the teacher of the five-, six-, and seven-year-olds modeled how to greet and introduce a visitor to the classroom. The children were then given the opportunity to role-play both the role of the visitor and the role of the greeter. The teacher also modeled appropriate audience behaviors, such as how and when to ask a question, the types of questions the children might ask, and how to listen while the guest or a member of the audience is speaking.

Example: A teacher of six-, seven-, and eight-year-olds anticipated that he would frequently use brainstorming sessions to determine the children's background knowledge about concepts under study. To ensure that these sessions would

FIGURE 7.1 Learning the pragmatics of language use

Young children need to learn—

- how to initiate conversation;
- how to observe turn-taking rules;
- how to sustain a conversation;
- how to gain and hold the floor;
- how to initiate a play encounter;
- how to gain access to an ongoing play activity;
- how to address adults;
- how to talk to and with peers;
- how to ask for help or information;
- how to explain;
- how to verbally express feelings;
- how to greet and take leave;
- how to argue;
- how to talk on the phone;
- how to anticipate the needs of the listener in order to adjust the communication accordingly; and
- who is allowed to speak, to whom, when, and how.

Source: Reprinted from "Oral Language Competence and the Young Child," by A. Preece in *Emergent Literacy: Preschool, Kindergarten, and Primary Grades* by L. Ollila & M. Mayfield, Eds., p. 49. Copyright 1992 by Allyn & Bacon. Reprinted by permission of Allyn & Bacon.

be positive, productive experiences, he modeled for the children when and how to share their ideas during a brainstorming session.

Example: Observing that several children expressed angry feelings by physically striking out, a teacher of four- and five-year-olds demonstrated ways to verbally express anger: "It hurts my feelings and makes me angry when you say that"; "I don't want to do it that way. I want to do it my way this time"; and, "May I have a turn now? I've been waiting a long time." She also suggested ways to respond when physical aggression by a peer seems eminent: "Tell me why you're mad"; "Remember, the teacher said, 'When you hit, you sit. Use your words.' " The teacher provided opportunities for children to role-play what they could do in several anger-provoking scenarios.

Developing Aural/Oral Language Proficiency

Children's oral language (speaking, expressive) and aural language (listening, receptive) faculties will continue to develop within the home and school environments in direct response to the following:

- The variety of contexts in which a child must use language to function and/or to solve problems
- The variety of "needs to use language" the child experiences (see Figure 7.1)
- The number of opportunities the child has to use language (social and collaborative interactions)
- The quality of language the child listens to and tries to make sense of
- The quality of conversations in which the child participates
- The responses the child gets to attempts to use language for various purposes
- The acceptance and encouragement the child gets as she or he emerges toward a more proficient use of language—as the child tries out her or his hypotheses about language
- The degree to which others in the child's world expect her or him to express her- or himself and to be a conversational partner
- The types of thinking with language that others model for the child and expect her or him to use

Creating a Rich Language Learning Environment

Language usage and development is highly sensitive to context (nurture). Consequently, before evaluating the language abilities of children, first examine the language-learning environment created in the classroom. If ample and appropriate opportunities to use language are not provided for children, then limited language performance may reflect inadequacies in the curriculum, rather than in the children (Preece, 1992). Examine your curriculum. Have you created an environment conducive to language learning? Have you developed instructional habits that encourage and support language use and experimentation? Use the following questions to guide your reflections:

- Do I listen and respond to the children?
- Do I remember what the children have told me?
- Do I think about what children say?
- Do I show by my facial expression and body language that I am listening?
- Do I encourage children to listen to one another?
- Do I listen more to one group or type of children than another?
- Do I interrupt or otherwise discourage children's talk?
- Do I dominate class discussions?
- Do I look at children when they are speaking to me or to others?
- Do I make certain that I have everyone's attention before I begin to talk or to read aloud? Do I tend to repeat what I have said, which may discourage good listening?
- Do I plan for conversations and social interactions to be a critical part of the daily learning process?
- Does the physical arrangement of my classroom encourage communication?
- Do I plan frequent opportunities for children to share with each other the things they are experiencing, learning, and thinking?

- Do I plan a variety of contextual situations in which language can or must be used for a variety of purposes?
- Do I respond to the children and interact with them in ways that stimulate thinking and elaborate discussions?
- Do I encourage and acknowledge each child's contribution to a discussion?
- Do I respond to each child's contribution to a conversation in a way that encourages the child to say more?
- Do I give children enough time to think through what they want to say? (Yellin & Blake, 1994, p. 143)*

EMERGENCE OF READING AND WRITING

Impact of Early Literacy Experiences

As with oral language, children's appreciation of, and interest in, print develops in response to the models provided in the environment, especially within the initial and primary environment, the home. If the models in the home are primarily functional (e.g., grocery lists, directions, telephone messages), children may view print as purely functional. If others in the home value reading and writing as sources of pleasure, excitement, new ideas, and information, children may approach print with more enthusiasm.

The power of play for young children cannot be disputed or overemphasized. Through play, children develop social, intellectual, and emotional understandings about themselves, their relationships with others, and their world. As children play, they use language to scale down

---

*Adapted from *Integrating the Language Arts: A Holistic Approach* by D. Yellin & M. Blake, pp. 7–8. Copyright 1994 by HarperCollins College Publishers. Reprinted by permission of Addison-Wesley Educational Publishers, Inc.

Children who are read to frequently in the home grow to enjoy books and are more likely to become successful readers.

the world in order to manipulate it, control it, and understand it.

Play provides a supportive medium for literacy to naturally emerge in the daily lives of young children. For example, children who are read to frequently and begin to acquire favorite stories often incorporate reading-like behaviors into their play by pretend reading (**emergent storybook reading;** Sulzby, 1985) to themselves, to others involved in their play, or to dolls and stuffed animals. Holdaway (1979) indicated that this reading-like behavior is one of the most important variables affecting literacy acquisition.

Children's continued interest in the meanings of words and how print works and is used is related to the following:

- The opportunities they have to use and explore print materials in their play
- The quality of the responses they receive to their questions about the written language in their environment

- The enthusiasm and interest more literate others demonstrate toward their attempts to "read," "write," and understand the many forms and functions of print
- The enthusiasm and frequency with which adults invite children to "figure out" and use print in their day-to-day lives

Young children who are lucky enough to be immersed in literacy-rich home environments initiate their own exploration of written language as they incorporate print into their play (e.g., menus for their "restaurants," prescription pads for their "doctors' offices," chalkboards and chalk in their "classrooms"). Literacy materials that reflect life outside the classroom help children see the purpose and necessity of reading and writing (Patton & Mercer, 1996). The richer and more nurturing the literacy environment, the more likely children are to explore language and print and the more creative and competent children's literacy usage will become.

When literacy materials are readily available, children may naturally mimic the functions of print in their play.

Nowhere in the research is this point more evident than in Dolores Durkin's now classic observations of the home environments and daily interactions of pre-first-grade children who learned to read "naturally"—that is, without direct or formalized teaching (Durkin, 1966). When Durkin interviewed the families of these children, it became obvious that none of the children had learned to read all by themselves. Durkin and others found that parents played a vital role in their children's learning to read, not by "instructing," but by doing the following:

- Serving as literacy role models
- Reading a variety of books aloud to their children frequently
- Sharing and discussing real and vicarious experiences with their children
- Responding positively to their children's emerging attempts to read and write
- Directing their children's attention to print in the environment, intentionally pointing

out the function it served, and incorporating attention to its form as children developed understandings

- Making available to their children a wide variety of print materials to play with and to use in their play (e.g., storybooks, writing materials, maps, cookbooks, letters, magazines)
- Answering children's questions about print

These conclusions emphasize the necessity of parents, teachers, or more literate others to serve as literacy mediators, as well as literacy models.

The most common thread throughout all the home literacy experiences of children who learned to read "naturally" was frequent one-to-one reading of storybooks. Other studies (Bus, vanIJzendoorn, & Pellegrini, 1995; Taylor, 1983; Wells, 1986) that have attempted to determine predictors of school achievement have also found that early childhood experiences with print sharply affect later achievement and that *the frequency with which children have been read to in the home during their early childhood years is the most significant predictor of later school success.*

Emerging Literacy

Knowledgeable teachers no longer see their job as getting young children "ready to receive" formal reading and writing instruction (reading readiness). Children should not be perceived as either ready or not ready, readers or nonreaders, writers or nonwriters, or literate or nonliterate. Careful observation and research have clearly indicated that learning to read and write is a *process* that begins to emerge as children begin to grasp the concept that written symbols in their environment hold meaning—an awakening that begins early in childhood—well before a child enters school. Once children begin to hypothesize about the purposes and power of print, they begin actively to construct knowledge about the rules that govern *the use* (function) of written language in many different contexts and with many different people on a daily basis. They do this informally as they

- Cruise the cereal aisle, searching for a favorite cereal, waffling between the one with the large *P* on the front and the one with the *Where's Waldo?*
- Write the names of friends they want to invite to a backyard campout
- Try to put the video of *Jungle Book* back into its correct container by matching the titles
- Write a pretend speeding ticket for a friend
- Peruse the menu at the dramatic play area restaurant to find just what they're hungry for

Recognizing What Children Know

When children begin school, observing and acknowledging the understandings about language these emerging readers and writers have constructed becomes the teacher's responsibility. It is important for teachers to understand and share with administrators, parents, and the children themselves how such conceptualizations are emerging toward conventional understanding and usage of written language, no matter how "incomplete" those behaviors and conceptualizations may appear to the uninformed observer.

Figure 7.2 shows a letter written at preschool by Taylor (age four). The teacher observed Taylor busily writing at a table and asked him about his message. He indicated that he was writing a letter to Santa and needed help making an *M*. She provided dots in the form of an *M* where he indicated it was to go and watched as he traced over the *M* and proceeded to finish his letter. After he had finished, she asked him to read his letter aloud to her. Taylor read, "Dear Santa, please bring me a Alien. Please bring me a capture claw." The teacher observed that Taylor had written his message from left to right and from top to bottom. Additionally, he had used the appropriate letter to represent the initial consonant sound of each word in his message. The teacher had been unaware that Taylor knew so much about the function and form of written language. This experience encouraged her to provide other children with similar opportunities to demonstrate their literacy understandings and to consider ways in which she could help them build on what they already knew.

It is important for you as the teacher to understand how children learn language and become literate. It is also important for you to become familiar with the stages of reading, writing, and spelling development so that you know what to look for and how to help children build upon what they already know. The information in this chapter is provided specifically for these reasons.

FIGURE 7.2 Letter to Santa by Taylor, age four

Even within what seem to be homogeneous communities, children who enter your classroom will have vast differences in their knowledge of, and abilities with, written language. Some children enter school having been read to practically every day of their lives. They may have had more than one thousand hours of informal literacy experiences before they enter your classroom (Adams, 1990). Others have had virtually no interactions with storybooks or other print (Allington & Cunningham, 1994). Others fall somewhere between, perhaps experiencing an occasional story with Grandma or a baby-sitter. Both the quality and quantity of these interactions will significantly affect what children notice and understand about print.

Just as children's experiences with storybook reading vary, children's other literacy experiences vary significantly both in quantity and quality. Some children have had many opportunities to see and try out print for a variety of purposes and in numerous forms. In some homes, children are encouraged to be involved in writing grocery lists, messages, notes, and letters. In some homes, writing materials are not present or available to the children.

Foundations of Literacy: Concepts About Print

Children who have had frequent and rich storybook reading and other literacy experiences may have already developed some important **concepts about print** (Clay, 1979, 1991; Ollila & Mayfield, 1992; Wells, 1986):

1. *Children may be familiar and comfortable with the structures and cadences of written language,* recognizing that they are distinctly different from those of spoken language. These children often "read" to their dolls or stuffed animals, using the language patterns and intonations of "storybook talk."

2. *Children discover that the print, not the picture, carries the author's message.* When pretend reading, children often track the

print with a finger as they "read" even though there is little relationship between their spoken words and the print.

3. *Children may be familiar with many functions of print.* They may have discovered that, with books, they can learn about dinosaurs, dangerous animals, trucks, and the moon. They may begin to understand that they can experience feelings of silliness, love, anger, success, failure, hope, loss, and happiness through stories. They may have learned that written language can help them make pancakes, find a friend's house, or select favorite foods from a menu (Ollila & Mayfield, 1992). They may have come to appreciate the value of leaving a note for a parent when the baby-sitter has taken them to the park or on an errand.

4. *Children may be familiar with some of the many forms of print.* They may have noticed how preparing for a trip to the grocery store requires a column of words (a list), whereas a letter to Grandma is written left to right and top to bottom in "sentence" form (connected text) with a greeting at the beginning and at the end.

5. *Children may have begun to hypothesize about some conventions of print.* As they observe parents writing and/or rereading familiar books, children begin to develop the concept of a "word" and that words are separated by spaces. They may begin to observe the relationship between sound and symbols (letters) as they watch parents puzzle over the spelling of *broccoli* for the shopping list. As they encounter favorite books again and again, they begin to relate key words to pictures and to notice the constancy of words.

6. *Children may recognize that texts are organized in consistent ways, that storybooks are presented differently from* books about real topics (expository texts). If children have had opportunities to experience both storybooks and informational books, they may begin to notice that storybooks have pictures that relate a story, whereas informational books seem to have more diagrams with labels. They expect one to begin something like "Once upon a time . . ." and the other "There are several kinds of . . ."

7. *As a result of being read aloud to from books, children will have much greater breadth of vicarious experiences,* beyond their own world into the world of other people, places, and times, as well as into the world of "might happen" and "could have been." With these new experiences, children are introduced to new vocabulary for talking about them. They will draw on these experiences and vocabulary as they become readers and writers (Ollila & Mayfield, 1992).

8. *When children are engaged in frequent and pleasurable reading experiences, they begin to anticipate becoming actively involved in meaning-making.* When children become engaged with a story, they construct mental pictures of the characters and events. With engagement comes increased anticipation; with increased anticipation comes increased comprehension and enjoyment; with increased comprehension and enjoyment come the desire and ability to attend, to listen. The active listener becomes the active reader.

Responding to Diverse Early Literacy Experiences

If children have had relatively few experiences with print, particularly with being read to, it is important for the teacher to provide opportunities to fill that void and to help children develop those crucial concepts and attitudes about print;

that is, teachers need to read to children and provide opportunities for others to read to them frequently both inside and outside the classroom. It is also important for the teacher to search out and acknowledge the understandings children do have about the form and function of print and to use those understandings as the building blocks for continued growth.

The classroom teacher must remember that all children, even those with seemingly deprived home literacy environments, come to school with some knowledge about the form and function of print. The experiences forming the base of this knowledge may not be those common to the classroom. For example, a child may recognize that the letter *B* is present in the logo for Burger King but may not be able to label it as the letter *B.* It is the teacher's responsibility to search out opportunities for the child to demonstrate what she or he knows and then to use what the child does know as bridges to "classroom literacy."

READING: A PROBLEM-SOLVING PROCESS

In the last decade, many educators have demonstrated a shift in their theoretical perceptions of the reading process, from viewing reading as an aggregation of component skills to viewing reading as a strategic process (Jones, 1989). Researchers and practitioners have increasingly emphasized the reader's cognitive processing and use of prior knowledge to construct meaning from text (Pearson & Valencia, 1987; Squire, 1987). Reading is a problem-solving process. It is both constructive and complex. The *strategic reader* attempts to make sense of print by *cross-checking* information from her or his background knowledge, from the text, and from the context of the reading event.

An emerging reader has developing understandings about print but is not yet able to read independently any unfamiliar connected text.

When attempting to make sense of unfamiliar print, an *emerging reader* uses the following:

- Developing understandings about how print works
- Intuitive feelings for how language should sound (syntax)
- Personal experiences and the language (semantics) used to talk about those experiences
- The expectation that familiar text will relate the same message each time it is encountered and her or his memory of that text
- The anticipation that unfamiliar text should make sense

The *proficient, independent reader* has developed more sophisticated understandings of the conventions of print and is able to use them in conjunction with an increased repertoire of life experiences and of previous experiences with literacy.

Although it happens so quickly as to seem simultaneous, strategic readers first *predict* (anticipate) the author's meaning by orchestrating many sources of information **(cues)** and coming up with possibilities for the word(s) to be read. They must then *compare* these possibilities with each available cue to confirm, reject, or modify the predictions. However, strategic readers may still not possess all the information necessary to identify successfully each unknown word.

🌿 TRY IT OUT   *Reading with Children*

As you read the following vignettes, try to identify the sources of information (cues) each reader uses to construct meaning with the text. Be aware of the ways the reader uses, neglects to use, or is unable to use knowledge of the world, knowledge of language, and knowledge of print conventions to *make and cross-check predictions.* When the reader is unable to construct the author's message successfully, try to identify the sources of information that were unavailable or unknown to the reader.

ಜ ಜ ಜ ಜ ಜ ಜ ಜ ಜ ಜ ಜ ಜ ಜ ಜ ಜ ಜ ಜ ಜ ಜ ಜ ಜ

SAM

Sam was looking through the journal in which he had recorded the changes he observed on the playground after a brief rainstorm the day before. He found his picture of the broken tree limbs. He knew what he had written. He proudly looked at his attempts to put his thoughts in print. He then looked at what the teacher had written to demonstrate how his message would look so that others could read his book too:

Text: The wind blew the limbs off the tree.

Sam: [pointing to each word as he read] The wind blew the limbs off of the . . . OOPS!

Noticing that he still had another word to say but none left on the page, he started over.

Sam: The wind blew the limbs off of the tree.

This time, he tapped twice on the word off!

Observations: Sam was developing the concept of *wordness*—that is, that one spoken word corresponds to one written word. He also *expected* to construct meaning with print. Consequently, when his memory for what he had written did not match exactly with the number of words in print, the meaning took precedence. He selected to assign greater value to meaning. He selected to assign two spoken words to one word in print in order to end up in the right place, thereby maintaining meaning and some sense of his understandings of the conventions of print.

Cues Used: *Wordness* (one-to-one correspondence), memory of the event (observing the

tree on the playground), memory for what he had written (*memory for text*), illustration, and his natural language pattern (*syntax*) to insert the word *of*.

Cues Neglected: Wordness and graphophonics. Sam was both using and neglecting wordness. He had not yet developed enough knowledge about *graphophonics* (knowledge of letter-sound correspondence) to cross-check his predictions of an unknown word with the print.

BERNARDO

While reading *Corduroy* (Freeman, 1968), in which the main character rides an escalator to another floor of a large department store, Bernardo got stuck on the word *escalator*. He examined the illustration for clues. His first prediction was *steps*, but when he cross-checked with the print, he knew this prediction did not fit the print. He was unable to suggest any other alternatives. Bernardo lived in a town that did not have two-story department stores.

Observations: Bernardo appropriately used the illustration to predict the unknown word. His absence of experience with escalators limited his predictions to the most familiar related concept, *steps*. The word *escalator* was simply not in his receptive vocabulary. He was able to use his limited knowledge of graphophonics to reject the word *steps* because the word in the text did not contain the anticipated letters in the expected positions. For example, Bernardo expected to see an *s* at the beginning of the word if it was *steps*.

Cues Used: Sight vocabulary, graphophonics (sound-symbol correspondences), illustrations, and his vocabulary (*semantics*)

Cues Neglected: Bernardo did not neglect any available cues. He even cross-checked sources of information by using what he did know. However, his limited vocabulary (semantics) and knowledge of graphophonics prevented him from successfully identifying the unknown word.

The ease with which readers can independently construct meaning with the text can be nurtured or hindered by the instructional context. Teachers can help children become independent problem solvers, to develop strategies for helping themselves notice and learn more about how print works. Likewise, teachers can create child dependence, rather than independence. Many teaching behaviors seem to imply that reading is a simple memorization process, rather than a strategic problem-solving process. As you read the following vignettes, try to identify teacher behaviors that nurture independence and problem solving versus those that nurture dependence on the teacher.

LAKESHIA

When reading *It Looked Like Spilt Milk* (Shaw, 1947), Lakeshia encountered the unknown word *mitten* in the sentence "Sometimes it looked like a mitten." She paused at the word, looked at the illustration, and suggested that the picture could be a mitten or a glove. The teacher confirmed that it could be either one. Lakeshia looked back at the text, noted that the word in question began with /m/, and confirmed aloud that the word was *mitten* and not *glove*. The teacher asked, "Why did you decide it was *mitten* and not *glove*?" "Because *glove* starts with a *g*, and this one starts with *m*," Lakeshia responded.

Observations: Lakeshia used the picture to generate predictions about the unknown

word. She was able to suggest two labels for the picture. She used her knowledge of graphophonics (the initial letter only) to reject one prediction and to confirm the other.

Cues Used: Illustration, her vocabulary (semantics), and graphophonics

Cues Neglected: None

HILLARY

Hillary was reading *Bikes* (Rockwell, 1987) to her teacher. This book has one sentence per page, accompanied by illustrations that support the text. Prior to reading the text aloud, Hillary had previewed the text with the teacher, chatting about the different kinds of bikes illustrated on each page and how the bikes were used for different purposes in different settings. The teacher primarily listened as Hillary talked, occasionally commenting about the types of bikes with which she was personally familiar. Although Hillary at one point referred to a bike by an inappropriate name, the teacher decided to say nothing. She knew Hillary had the ability to use her knowledge of graphophonics to modify her predictions of these unknown or unfamiliar words. She wanted Hillary to have the opportunity to do this independently.

> Text: Trail bikes have knobby tires that go on dirt and through mud puddles.
>
> Hillary: /Traaaail/Trail bikes have

Hillary paused and looked at the picture and then back to the print. Her eyes glanced ahead to the next few words of the sentence and returned to the beginning of the sentence.

> Hillary: Trail bikes have /kkknn/ . . .
>
> Teacher: The /k/ is silent.
>
> Hillary: Trail bikes have /nobby/ tires that go on dirt and

Hillary paused and looked at the picture, back to /through/, and then at the rest of the sentence. She mentally tried out words that would fit in that position in the sentence and made sense such as *in* and *over,* but she rejected both of these words because they did not fit the picture or look like the word in print. She then tried *through,* which matched both the picture and the print.

> Hillary: Trail bikes have knobby tires that go on dirt and through mud puddles.
>
> Text: This cycle has three big, fat tires.
>
> Hillary: This motorcycle has [pause]. This cycle has three big, fat tires.
>
> Teacher: Hillary, I noticed that when you were puzzled by the word *knobby* you tried a lot of things to figure it out. You looked at the picture, read the rest of the sentence, started the sentence over, and used letter sounds. That's what good readers do.

Observations (Hillary): By previewing the text with Hillary, the teacher demonstrated that she recognized the importance of encouraging Hillary to think actively about what she already knew about bikes prior to reading the text. As Hillary commented on the pictures, the teacher listened to the vocabulary Hillary used to share her experiences and knowledge. The teacher consciously compared Hillary's repertoire of strategies and information to the problems she anticipated the text might pose for Hillary to make appropriate instructional decisions. She chose not to intervene at the point of Hillary's puzzlement, but instead gave Hillary the *wait time* she needed to use her strategies to solve the problem. When it became obvious that Hillary did not know that the /k/ in /kn/ was silent, the teacher did not hesitate to supply the missing information, which then allowed Hillary to solve the problem for herself. The self-correction Hillary made of *cycle* for *motorcycle* is evidence

of the strategic habits of mind Hillary had developed. The teacher intentionally reinforced Hillary's strategic problem solving by recapping the process Hillary went through and by confirming the process as one that good readers use.

Cues Used: Sight vocabulary, illustration, graphophonics, and *context* (syntax and semantics)

Cues Neglected: None, but did need new information regarding the silent *k*

Teacher-Dependent Reader versus Independent Reader: The Decision Is Yours

Hillary's teacher was intentionally nurturing a strategic, independent learner. She did so by

- Modeling strategies for solving problems
- Making certain she gave Hillary time to use the strategies
- Reinforcing Hillary's success

These behaviors in and of themselves, however, were only part of the teacher's reasons for success. The teacher also

- Recognized and anticipated the possible interactions among the reader, the text, and the context (situation)
- Made it a point to know what Hillary could and could not do for herself
- Used this information to help Hillary develop as a strategic reader (see Figure 7.3)

Strategic teachers are aware that reading is a developmental process. They are aware of the importance of knowing what a child knows about literacy (stage of reading development and reading strategies) and of using this knowledge to mediate effectively and to design appropriate literacy opportunities.

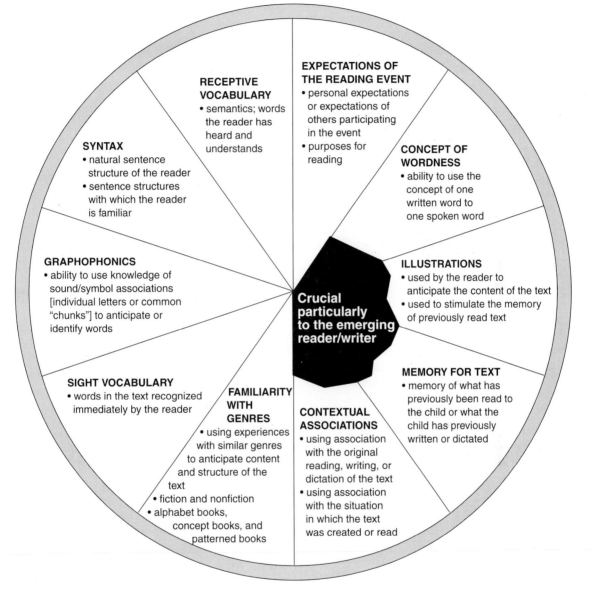

FIGURE 7.3 Cues used by a strategic reader

These examples clearly demonstrate the influence a teacher's instructional decisions have on the way children develop as readers. Teachers can choose to teach children to become passive, teacher-dependent readers who focus only on the print and seek accuracy sometimes to the neglect of meaning; teachers can choose to emphasize children's interpretation of a text to the neglect of accuracy; or teachers can choose to help children become independent, strategic readers who monitor for meaning and the author's intent as they read. Literate children become so by learning to be strategic readers, strategic writers, strategic thinkers—strategic learners (refer to Chapter 3).

Stages of Reading Development

Teachers can be overwhelmed by the wide range of literacy understandings that children in any one class may have. Helping children build new understandings based on what they already know (*schema theory*) can seem like a formidable task unless teachers have a framework for understanding the developmental continuum of learning to read.

The following continuum of reading development (see Figure 7.4) is presented in terms of stages. Children, as they experience uneven bursts of understanding, will sometimes demonstrate behaviors characteristic of more than one stage or may seemingly be between stages. Such discrepancies are also apparent as learners focus on using a new source of information and appear to ignore other sources they had used consistently in the past. Still, a broad continuum will be useful as a teacher develops skills for observing children.

The stages presented incorporate research and observations of several authors and researchers, primarily Teale (1982), Sulzby (1985), Hart-Hewins and Wells (1990), Clay (1991), and Jones and Crabtree (1994).

Stage 1: Immersion. Children at the first stage of reading development have had limited expe-

FIGURE 7.4 Stages of reading development

Stage 1:	Immersion
Stage 2:	Role-Playing "The Reader"
Stage 3:	Developing Inner Control
Stage 4:	Becoming Independent
Stage 5:	Independent Reader

riences with books. This may be related to age or the result of a lack of previous literacy experiences. Children at this stage may be two, five, or even eight years old and may not realize the relationship between the print on the page and the talk that comes from a reader's lips. At the beginning of this stage, children may still believe that the story is generated solely from the pictures. For children in this stage, frequent reading aloud to them in a one-to-one setting, as well as in group settings, is imperative. Once children are immersed in storybook reading experiences, they learn that the stories remain the same each time they are read. A positive sign that children are moving beyond this stage and developing critical attitudes and concepts about print is when children pretend read (emergent storybook reading), very familiar storybooks by using their memory of the story and the pictures. Concepts about reading that children are developing, such as that a book is read from front to back and that pages are turned from right to left, can be observed during these times.

Children at this stage of reading development may have little understanding of such conventions as **wordness** (there is one spoken word for every written word), **directionality** (print is read from left to right and top to bottom), or sound-symbol relationships (*graphophonics*). If asked to count the number of words on the page, children may indicate confusion by counting the letters. In fact, they may not yet understand the *instructional vocabulary* (terminology) of letter, sentence, or sound. These children must be immersed in print opportunities, demonstrations, and the language of literacy.

Although some children may not have had many experiences with storybook reading prior to entering the classroom, they may have had environmental experiences with print, such as reading cereal boxes, signs, and menus and observing parents reading letters, newspapers, magazines, messages from school, and directions on microwavable foods. Appropriate environmental print can be incorporated into daily classroom experiences (e.g., dramatic play centers, bulletin boards, writing center, instructional events) to provide the opportunity to observe what children might know and to help children see the relationship between the print with which they are familiar and the print in the classroom.

Creating reading materials from children's dictation about familiar and memorable experiences also serves this purpose **(dictated language experience [DLE])**. DLE materials consist of one to several sentences that a child or group of children dictates to an adult after discussion of an event. The adult serves as a scribe to record exactly what is said. *Because children are being supported in their attempts to make the connection between oral language and print, their exact words must be recorded.* The adult reads each word while writing it slowly and clearly. The adult then reads the entire message back, pointing to each word while reading. Children are then encouraged to reread and sometimes to illustrate their dictation. The picture then becomes a cue to support children's rereading of the dictation.

A dictated language experience can be a very powerful demonstration and source of initial reading materials. Directionality, wordness, familiarity with the look and conventions of written language, and the functions of print are concepts that children in this stage often grasp from repeated DLE opportunities. Because the print has been generated from the children's own experiences and in their own language, their memory will support their attempts to reread

what was written. As with all Stage 1 materials, children should be provided with opportunities to read and reread these dictations.

Children in the immersion stage are encouraged to experience what being a reader feels like through the technique of **shared reading** (Holdaway, 1979). The teacher first reads the book aloud to the children (making certain the pictures and print are clearly visible) so that they can enjoy the story, rhyme, and/or rhythm. The children are invited to participate during subsequent rereadings. Books selected for a shared reading require a pattern or predictability that children can easily chime in with and memorize. For examples, refer to *Getting the Most from Predictable Books* (Opitz, 1995).

If the book is to be shared with a group, an enlarged copy (*Big Book*) is required for children to be able to see the print and pictures clearly. The book may be reread several times in this way so that children become completely familiar with the story (develop memory for text). Once familiarity is established, the book is read again, slowly and clearly, yet fluently, while the teacher points to each word as it is read (demonstrating directionality and wordness). Children may spontaneously chime in during any of these rereadings or should be encouraged to do so by pausing at appropriate points (e.g., in Sue Williams's 1990 *I Went Walking*, "I went walking. What did I see? I saw a _____ _____ looking at me.").

During these rereadings, the teacher intentionally demonstrates how to use wordness, illustrations, and memory for text to reconstruct the story. Concepts about print are further developed and reinforced when frequent opportunities are provided for children to reread these books independently, to friends, or to an adult. Children should be encouraged to point to each word as they read to help them use their memory of the rhyme, pattern, or story to develop directionality and wordness. If a child is having difficulty grasping the concepts of directionality and/or wordness, the teacher can gently hold

TABLE 7.1 Materials for Stage 1: Immersion

Materials	Description	Examples
Concept Books	One word/short phrase per page One directly related picture	*One Rubber Duckie: A Sesame Street Counting Book* (Sesame Street, 1982)
Wordless Picture Books	Wordless: pictures relate story	*Good Dog, Carl* (Day, 1985) *Frog Goes to Dinner* (Mayer, 1974)
Nursery Rhymes, Songs, and Poems	Traditional and contemporary Printed on charts/individual books	*The Wheels on the Bus* (Raffi Songs to Read, 1988) *Five Little Monkeys* (Christelow, 1989)
Patterned, Predictable Books	Strong rhythms/linguistic patterns Supportive illustrations	*Mrs. Wishy Washy* (Cowley, 1980) *Brown Bear, Brown Bear* (Martin, 1983)
Dictations of Children's Own Language	Several sentences dictated by one or more children to adult	Relate an experience Tell a story Summarize new learning

the child's hand and help point appropriately. Print materials appropriate for shared readings and demonstrations in the immersion stage are listed in Table 7.1.

Oral Language Connections. It is important to remember that children at all stages of reading development can listen to, understand, and enjoy books that are at a higher level than those they can read. At the immersion stage particularly, children require many opportunities on a daily basis to listen to different kinds of books, both fictional and informational, to help develop crucial concepts and attitudes about stories, books, and print. Sharing a variety of quality literature, fiction and nonfiction, narrative and expository, is crucial to the continued development of oral language, syntax (grammar), and semantics (vocabulary). Children should be encouraged to ask questions and to discuss concepts and vocabulary reflected in the illustrations and text of the materials read. The teacher or more literate other reading the book should take the opportunities spontaneously provided in conjunction with storybook reading to build

and extend children's language base and to stimulate children's thinking. Regardless of children's previous experiences with books, reading aloud to them should be related to the learning that takes place during the day and should not be a single experience relegated to the last twenty minutes of the school day.

Writing Connections. Children at this stage of reading development are learning to differentiate between writing and drawing. As they are immersed in literacy opportunities, they will begin to use scribble writing, scribble strings, and letterlike marks, rather than drawings, when they attempt to experiment with, or communicate in, written form. Children nearing the end of this stage may use a random string of letters even though the selected letters may not reflect any knowledge of sound-symbol correspondence.

Even very young children must have opportunities to observe the process of writing, as well as to use writing in informal settings, for a variety of purposes. Encouraging and modeling for children ways to incorporate print into dramatic play centers serves this purpose particularly

TABLE 7.2 Materials for Stage 2: Role-Playing "The Reader"

Materials	Description	Examples
Language Predictable Books	Syntax patterns predictable by child Becoming more like "book talk"	*Dear Zoo* (Campbell, 1982) *If I Were You* (Wildsmith, 1987) *Where's the Halloween Treat?* (Ziefert, 1985) *Joshua James Loves Trucks* (Petrie, 1982)
Innovations of a Text	Newly created versions of patterned, predictable books with substituted words provided by children	*Polar Bear, Polar Bear* (Martin, 1991) *The Important Book* (Wise, 1949)

well. Teachers may demonstrate various ways in which children "write" (e.g., scribble strings, letterlike marks, random letters, invented spelling) to encourage children to use whatever written form they like. This strategy often frees children to explore with writing and has been shown to increase their attempts to write.

Mediation. For children to progress to the next stage of literacy development, they need opportunities to become aware of how literacy is related to their everyday lives. They also need a more literate other to stimulate their interest in the forms that print takes and to answer their questions about how print works. Children at this stage of reading development need to observe print being used for a variety of purposes, such as to organize the environment, to record experiences and information, to communicate information, and as a source of enjoyment. Literacy props should be incorporated into the dramatic play center and possible uses modeled and discussed. As children are provided with opportunities to dictate their experiences, to read and reread familiar stories and messages, to observe people writing, to use literacy in their play, and to write, they construct new understandings about literacy. The teacher uses these opportunities to observe what children know and to answer questions children have. The teacher nurtures independence and problem solving by encouraging children to use what they know to figure out the unknown.

Stage 2: Role-Playing "The Reader." Children at the second stage of reading development realize that print carries the meaning and can often be found pretend reading (**emergent storybook reading**) familiar books to a favorite stuffed animal or doll, to a friend, or simply to themselves. They rely heavily on previous experiences with that book, memorization of patterns within the text, such as repeated words or phrases, and the association of text sequences with particular illustrations. Children sometimes memorize the entire text if it is clearly supported by the pictures and their auditory memory is good. They may mimic the directionality and wordness of a parent or teacher even though their sense of wordness may still not be fully established. Although children may appear to have only memorized the text, they know not to "read" when the illustration is not accompanied by print. Print materials used with children at this role-playing "the reader" stage are not only to help them "feel" like readers but also to support them as they begin to notice some very basic features of print. These materials continue to include Stage 1 materials and are extended to include the materials listed in Table 7.2.

Shared reading materials now can be extended to books that are slightly less predictable. They still have a predictable nature to them but are not necessarily rhymes and may not contain patterns. These books, called **language predictable books,** usually have one phrase or sentence per page and are written in the natural language of the child (not literary language). The text is clearly supported by the picture. An example of a language predictable book is *Bump, Bump, Bump,* by Leslie Wood (1991): "Bump. Out fell a clock. Bump. Out fell a Hoover. Bump. Out fell a piano. Bump. Out fell two chairs, a violin, and a bucket." (The word *Hoover* may need to be introduced and explained to American children because it is a British label.) Language predictable books include many selections written by Byron Barton, Brian Wildsmith, and Harriett Ziefert.

Reading language predictable books requires children to "read" less familiar content and to identify less familiar words by using their knowledge of syntax and semantics. Children must generate words with similar meanings that might make sense in this particular part of the story, in this particular place in the sentence. Although children at this stage of reading development are not yet using print to narrow or confirm their hypotheses, this is a good time to demonstrate how print can help in this process while encouraging children to stretch their vocabularies at the same time. For example, when a child "reads" *flower* instead of *rose,* the teacher can take this opportunity to show the child what the word *flower* looks like and to help the child compare it with the author's word *rose.* The teacher may also take this opportunity to focus the child's attention on the initial consonants and tell the child the sounds *r* and *fl* represent. Children should not be expected to remember these generalizations about print. The process, not necessarily the specifics, is being modeled.

Children at this stage of reading development should be helped to create innovations of predictable books they have become familiar with. **Innovations of a text** are new versions of patterned, predictable books dictated by the children. Children are encouraged to substitute personally selected words for targeted words in the original text. For example, children might substitute "*Green frog,* green frog" for the ever-popular *Brown bear,* brown bear or "*Andrea* wore her *striped socks,*" in lieu of "*Mary* wore her *red dress*" (Peek, 1985) or "The important thing about *my sister* is that *she has curly hair*" instead of "The important thing about *snow* is that *it is cold.*" These innovations obviously maintain their pattern and predictability but now also possess the added intrigue and support of the children's own language. Innovations such as these can be written on chart paper to share with the whole class (Big Book style) or can be prepared as individual booklets. Both should remain accessible to children for rereading.

Interactive charts (Schlosser & Phillips, 1992) are excellent materials to help children construct relationships between oral and written language and to help guide their development of effective reading strategies. An *interactive chart* consists of a familiar poem, song, fingerplay, or chant written on a chart and/or sentence strips in such a way as to present the children with an opportunity to move around and manipulate the print physically in a concrete way.

The word/phrase/sentence that the children can manipulate (exchange for interchangeable words/phrases/sentences) is selected by the teacher on the basis of its meaningfulness to the text, the abilities of the children, and the objective of the chart. "By effectively guiding children in focusing on the print [of interactive charts], teachers can assist children in integrating semantic, syntactic, and grapho-phonic cuing systems" (Schlosser & Phillips, 1992, p. 11). Concepts such as directionality; differentiation among letters, words, and sentences; wordness; punctuation; letter recognition; graphophonics; and rhyming words can be easily developed through the use of interactive charts. An example of an appropriate poem to use as an interactive chart is *Pickles* (Schlosser & Phillips, 1992, p. 55):

PICKLES

My mother gave me a nickel

To buy a pickle.

But I didn't buy a pickle.

I bought some _____.

Interactive component: Food word cards are created for use in the final blank of the chart. Cards may include an appropriate picture as necessary. (For further information about interactive charts, see Schlosser & Phillips, 1992.)

Aural Language Connections. A large body of research indicates that phonemic awareness bears an important relationship to achievement in reading (Snider, 1995). **Phonemic awareness,** or phonological awareness, is the conscious awareness that words are made up of phonemes, or sounds, and the ability to segment spoken words into those sounds. Phonological awareness develops along a continuum ranging from the ability to recognize rhymes and alliteration to the ability to segment words into syllables, rimes, onsets, and finally into phonemic units (Swank & Catts, 1994). An inability to isolate the phonemes and the subsequent inability to relate them to the printed word appears to be a common problem of many children who experience difficulty learning to read, particularly if the teacher begins reading instruction at a level that assumes children have already developed this skill.

Some children do not develop phonemic awareness naturally, perhaps because they lack the types of experiences, both informal and structured, that facilitate the development of phonemic awareness. Phonemic awareness typically develops as children playfully participate in poems, songs, and stories filled with

Children have the opportunity to problem-solve with print and to construct new information about how written language works when they manipulate interactive charts.

rhymes and alliteration (Griffith & Olson, 1992; Yopp, 1992). Some children may require more directed experiences, such as stretching words slowly, making and breaking words, or activities using rimes and onsets (Castle, Riach, & Nicholson, 1994; Clay, 1993, Cunningham, 1995; Gastins, Ehri, Crass, O'Hara, & Donelly, 1997). A small percentage of children may require even more intensive interventions to develop phonemic awareness. If a child continues to experience problems with phonemic awareness, the teacher should collaborate with the special education teacher or language specialist for ideas to increase the child's phonemic awareness.

Oral Language Connections. (Note: Oral language connections for each stage are cumulative. Connections from all previous stages apply to each future stage.) Asking children to dictate innovations of a text encourages them to listen for patterns and rhymes with more intent and focus than shared reading. Creating innovations of a text also encourages children to play with language. They must often not only search, but stretch, their language repertoire to find just the right word to fit the pattern in terms of both syntax and semantics. Some children will "work hard" to find words for their innovation that will make the reader laugh. They literally begin to play with words.

Writing Connections. The *alphabetic knowledge* (ability to discriminate between and identify individual letters) of children at this stage of reading development is still developing, as is their *phonemic awareness* (ability to hear discrete sounds or sound units in words even though they may not be able to identify the letters that represent them). Early in this stage, children often use a random string of letters that reflect no sound-symbol correspondence. Gradually, they begin to represent the sounds they hear (ones that sound dominant to them) with the letter(s) they associate with these

sounds **(sound, temporary, or invented spelling).** The number of sounds children are able to hear within a word and to represent appropriately depends on their knowledge of graphophonics and how discriminating their ears have become. Children at this stage of reading development tend to be at the early phonemic stage of spelling and may use one or more letters to represent words or syllables; for example, *TRUCK* might look like *T* or *TK*. These children still may not demonstrate control of the concept of wordness in their writing or reading.

Mediation. At this stage of reading development, children continue to be encouraged to memorize predictable texts to help them anticipate meaning as they begin to incorporate print cues (voice-print match, length of word, sight words, some initial consonants) into their repertoire of reading strategies (memory, the use of illustrations). Teachers begin to ask children to look more closely at print. They bring to children's attention that the words they predict may or may not be exactly what they or the author wrote (*I spent the night at my cousin's* vs. *I spent the night at my cousin's house*) or (*Planes fly in the air* vs. *Planes fly in the sky*) and that they can confirm or challenge their predictions by looking at and cross-checking with the print.

Many times during this process, teachers informally provide children with information about sound-symbol correspondences (as they need or request it), which they may or may not internalize at the time. As this type of mediation occurs over time with a variety of texts (and in mediated writing experiences), children begin to make connections that lead to generalizations. Once children begin to notice that a certain letter tends to represent a certain sound or that a certain sequence of letters tends to represent a word, as with David in the example below, they begin to search for even more connections independently. They make hypotheses about connections and initiate the search for confirmations.

INITIATING SEARCHING BEHAVIORS

One evening, as David (age four) was playing with vinyl letters in the bathtub, he stuck the letters *MRQ* up on the side of the tub and announced, "This says 'rabbit'." Mom said, "There is an *R* in *rabbit*. It goes first. Listen, 'Rrrrrrrraaaaaaabbbbbbbiiiiiiiiiiiiiittttttttt.' " As she stretched out the word, she leaned down and put the *R* in front of the other two letters. "Each letter makes a different sound, like the *D* in your name makes a /d/ sound for `David.' *R* says /r/ and we hear /r/ at the beginning of *rabbit*."

David rapidly began retrieving letters from the tub, asking, "What sound does the *F* make? What sound does the *N* make? What sound does this one make?" David had made a connection and had begun the search.

Stage 3: Developing Inner Control. Children at the third stage of reading development are beginning to construct inner control over print (Clay, 1991). They have developed the concept of wordness (one written word for each spoken word although not necessarily the "correct" word) and use a reading-like voice to "read" their version of the text. They can point to print accurately across the page as they read (*tracking print*) and often do so to keep their place. **Self-monitoring behaviors** appear as children begin to read a familiar story or dictation, pointing to each word as they read (tracking) and then running out of print before the story is finished. On their own, they may start the process over to solve the mismatch problem, which initiates further analysis of the print.

Children developing inner control can use tracking to find individual words on a page; that is, they use their memory of the text and wordness to locate specific words. As they track and identify specific words, they continue to develop and refine their knowledge of graphophonics (sound-symbol relationships) and begin to develop a small sight word vocabulary as they notice that the print representing a particular spoken word looks the same every time **(constancy of words).** They begin to use picture cues, memory of the story, anticipation of the story line, and possibly some specific print cues to help identify unknown words.

Materials that can be used to support children (see Table 7.3) as they become independent strategic readers include Stage 1 and Stage 2 materials. Books from these stages, however, may be read independently or through **supported reading,** in which the teacher reads only

TABLE 7.3 Materials for Stage 3: Developing inner control

Materials	Description	Examples
Stretching Books	Concepts are familiar, but vocabulary is extended	*Goodnight Moon* (Brown, 1991)
	Less direct support from illustrations	*Hooray for Snail* (Stadler, 1984)
	Story and syntax more complex	*Building a House* (Barton, 1981)
	Predictable language patterns	*Airport* (Barton, 1982)
	One or two lines of print per page	

enough to help the child begin to anticipate the language or pattern of the book, instead of **shared reading,** in which the teacher totally familiarizes the child with the book by reading it completely.

Children at this stage of reading development can begin to develop personal word banks. A **personal word bank** consists of words from familiar materials (including DLE) and words that are personally significant. These words may be familiar and/or significant within the context of a DLE, a memorable portion of a favorite book, or a significant personal life experience. As a child reads and rereads her or his bank of words and refers to the words when writing, the words gradually become part of the child's sight vocabulary and/or writing vocabulary. These words then become the "known," which can be used as bridges to new literacy learnings. (For information on key words, refer to *Teacher* by Sylvia Ashton-Warner, 1963.)

Oral Language Connections. Reading aloud to children from storybooks and informational books containing less familiar concepts, rich vocabulary, more complex sentence structures, and illustrative literary elements is particularly important at this time. "Picture reading" these *stretching books* together before children attempt to read them independently is also important. Both situations provide opportunities for engaging children in stimulating (language and thought) conversations and contribute to their aural and oral language development.

These conversations also provide the teacher with an opportunity to listen to children's syntax, to determine their sense of story, to note their expressive and receptive vocabulary, and to extend their understanding of the concepts presented and the related vocabulary. This is accomplished by listening carefully as children relate stories and books in their own language and by skillfully and unobtrusively interjecting new information and new vocabulary into responses

to children's questions. This strategy increases children's ability to read *stretching books* with increasing success.

Writing Connections. When children at this stage of reading development write, they spell primarily on the basis of what they hear. They gradually develop the understanding that certain letter combinations make certain sounds. *TRUCK* may now be spelled *TRK,* rather than *TK,* as their ear for sounds (phonemic awareness) has become more refined and as they have internalized more sound-symbol correspondences. They may demonstrate an understanding of wordness in their writing by leaving spaces between words or by clearly pointing to words as they read. Children at this stage may also be developing a **writing vocabulary** (words they can write, read, and spell correctly; Clay, 1979) of personal words. They also reexamine already familiar environmental print from a new, more analytic perspective. They seem to enjoy searching for and copying specific words from familiar books, wall charts, and environmental print. In this process, they confirm or reject hypotheses about print and construct new hypotheses as they search for new connections.

Mediation. The goal of literacy mediation at this stage of reading development is to help children become strategic readers able to use independently what they know to figure out and solve print problems. The teacher supports their reading only to the extent that it is needed (scaffolding) and continues to nurture independence and problem solving (Clay, 1991; Fountas & Pinnell, 1996). A combination of shared reading, supported reading, and independent reading is recommended, depending on the difficulty of the text for a particular reader. The teacher's observations and instructional decisions are especially crucial at this point because children are at the jumping-off point, ready to sail independently if provided with the appropriate materials, instruction, and mediation to make those next connections. When children come to a difficult word, for example, rather than tell them the word, the teacher may prompt them to use the available information. These prompts may include, "Look at the picture to see if that would help," "Think of what would make sense there," or "What would make sense and start with that first letter?"

Stage 4: Becoming Independent. The fourth stage of reading development is very exciting for everyone—parents, teachers, peers—and especially for the children, as reading seems to come together magically. All the previous literacy experiences seem to come together like pieces of a puzzle, and children seem to understand how the pieces work together to form the whole picture.

These children read for meaning and are able to use several sources of information strategically to identify unknown words. Although they still need the support of pictures, clearly printed text, and familiar concepts and vocabulary (see Table 7.4), they are now able to use print cues effectively as part of this problem-solving process. They are rapidly expanding their sight vocabulary, their ability to recognize and use patterns in words, their knowledge of graphophonics, and their vocabulary concepts. They begin to integrate this knowledge independent of teacher prompts as they attempt to identify unfamiliar words. As children are provided with time to read new books and to reread old favorites independently, the automaticity and fluency with which they are able to use these sources of information effectively continues to increase while new knowledge is simultaneously constructed. The readers continue to develop control over the print (Clay, 1991) and become increasingly independent.

Oral Language Connections. (Reminder: All the oral language connections discussed in the previous stages are still applicable.) During this stage of reading development, the read alouds (both fiction and informational) shared with children should become longer, with varied themes, more complex text structures, and increasingly challenging concepts and vocabulary. Fiction books should be filled with literary embellishments. Teachers should continue with the prereading predictions and conversations and with discussion during and after the reading to stimulate thinking about the content of the material.

Writing Connections. Children at this stage of reading development consistently use spaces between words and have begun to use vowels (correct or incorrect), along with the more dominant consonant sounds. More and more conventional spelling creeps into their writing as they use visual memory of words and patterns with words they have seen in books and in their environment. *TRUCK* may therefore be spelled *TRAK, TRACK, TRUK* or *TRUCK.* Children in

TABLE 7.4 Materials for Stage 4: Becoming independent

Materials	Description	Examples
Stretching Books	Concepts are familiar, but vocabulary is extended	*George Shrinks* (Joyce, 1987)
	Less direct support from illustrations	Byron Barton books
	Story and syntax more complex	Harriet Ziefert books
	Predictable language patterns	
	One or two lines of print per page	

the becoming independent stage should be provided with opportunities to explore different genres of writing and to begin to tackle longer pieces. Children should be encouraged to begin revising and editing selected pieces before publishing them. Teachers should provide self-help tools such as checklists to help children in revising and editing their work. These help children become independent and internalize conventions of punctuation and grammar.

Mediation. Children at this stage of reading development begin to take on more responsibility for their reading habits. They need guidance in selecting books on the basis of their personal interests and capabilities. Monitoring the repertoire of strategies that children use as they read is the responsibility of both the individual child and the teacher. Teachers need to plan periodic opportunities to hear children orally read both familiar and new texts. As each child reads, the teacher should record the numbers and types of deviations from print (miscues). This information can be used to determine whether the child is self-correcting for meaning, overrelying on one source of information, or using a variety of cues appropriately (cross-checking). Children need to be reminded of what strategic readers do when they read, as well as of their personal strategies for reading

(*metacognition*). This allows teacher and children to continue to work as a team to nurture children's reading development.

Stage 5: Independent Reader. Readers at the fifth stage of reading development depend more on themselves than on others when reading. They have learned to employ a repertoire of problem-solving strategies to make sense of whatever they are reading. Their preference has shifted from the more public arena of oral reading to the more personal monitoring of silent reading. The problem-solving process has become internalized and automatic. Readers use various sources of information to anticipate a word and do not have to correct as many inappropriate spontaneous responses after the fact. Consequently, the reading process becomes more efficient and fluent. Reading has become less "work" and more pleasure. Children at this stage now have more energy for, and derive more pleasure from, reading longer, more substantive stories and books. They are eager to share with others the vicarious experiences they are having through books.

Oral Language Connections. During this stage of reading development, teachers should continue to include read alouds, as well as appropriate materials for independent reading from all genres (see Table 7.5). They should se-

TABLE 7.5 Materials for Stage 5: Independent reader

Materials	Description	Examples
Challenging Picture Books	Illustrations may not tell the whole story	*The Mitten* (Brett, 1989)
	Storybooks and informational books	*The Magic School Bus at the Waterworks* (Cole, 1986)
First Novels	Simple chapter books	*Amelia Bedelia* (Parrish, 1963)
		Frog and Toad Are Friends (Lobel, 1970)
		Henry and Mudge (Rylant, 1987)

lect stories that reflect diverse social and cultural contexts, as well as situations or problems to "stretch" children. Such variety will provide models and vicarious experiences and help children expand their knowledge of the pragmatics of language. Selections should be made with the intent to build upon and expand children's informational and conceptual knowledge base.

Writing Connections. When independent readers write, they usually use conventional spelling except when tackling long words. For these words, they use their knowledge of graphophonics and of similar words (patterns in words) to attempt to spell the word, or they substitute shorter words to avoid the conflict of spelling words "incorrectly." A teacher's (or parent's) response to incorrectly spelled words will affect which decision the child makes. Instruction and guidance in the writing process (Graves, 1983), familiarity with a wide variety of literature to provide models of writing forms and styles, and the use of peers and self-help tools to assist with revision and editing will alleviate stress and facilitate children's writing and spelling development while maintaining standards for conventions.

Mediation. Children at the independent reader stage assume greater responsibility for their reading development and for their reading habits. To guide and support their efforts, teachers need to plan for opportunities to (1) monitor the reading strategies each child uses with familiar and unfamiliar text, (2) evaluate the reading and conceptual levels of the books each child selects, (3) observe whether each child is appropriately challenged but not frustrated by the material she or he consistently selects, (4) help each child monitor both the quantity and quality of her or his reading, (5) observe and guide each child's understanding of the author's message, and (6) consider and further stimulate each child's critical thinking, which is being stimulated by the text.

WRITING: A CONSTRUCTIVE PROCESS

Becoming Aware of Written Language

Very young children learning to differentiate between animals may call all four-legged creatures "doggies" until they have had enough experiences with other animals to assign distinguishing features to each. The more and varied the experiences, both vicarious and real, they have with different animals, the more refined their discriminations and categorizations become. This refining of concepts through the subconscious processes of assimilation and accommodation progresses from gross to fine and is called **perceptual learning** (Bruner, 1976; Temple, Nathan, Burris, & Temple, 1988).

Children learn about written language and how to write in much the same way—globally; that is, "they experiment and approximate, gradually becoming aware of the specific features of written language and the relationships between symbols, sounds, and meaning. They form their models of how written language works as they encounter it in specific settings" (Genishi & Dyson, 1984, p. 30) and compare it with encounters they have had in other settings.

Lavine (1972) observed that young preschool children just learning to discriminate between drawing and writing identify specific features to distinguish between marks they consider to be writing and those they do not. These features are described in Figure 7.5.

Stages of Writing Development

When children first begin to differentiate between writing and drawing, they experiment with writing by producing uncontrolled scribbling. Between three and six years of age, children begin to gain control over their scribbling, which gradually develops into symbolic representations they can identify. Once they begin to incorporate letterlike marks or letters into their

FIGURE 7.5 Learning about writing through its features

Nonpictoriality	Writing cannot be a picture.
Linearity	The marks must be horizontal, in a straight line.
Multiplicity	Writing consists of more than one mark.
Variety	Writing cannot be just repetition of one mark; the marks have to vary one from another.

Older preschool children appear to ignore such features as linearity and variety if the figures are letterlike marks (individual marks resembling letters) or actual letters.

writing, they may still view letters as representing actual people or things. They may "still believe that writing, like drawing, only encodes or reflects specific objects, not 'filler' words such as articles or adjectives" (Morrow, 1997, p. 264). Only later do they recognize the alphabetic nature of written language and realize that writing represents language and is a means for encoding speech (Dyson, 1985; Ferreiro, 1978; Ferreiro & Teberosky, 1982; Morrow, 1997). Even before they replace "marks" with letters or letterlike forms, children's attempts will acquire such features of writing as linearity, variety, and multiplicity.

Researchers agree that children generally follow a similar path of development as they construct and apply new information about how written language works. The stages described in Table 7.6 have been identified by Elizabeth Sulzby (1986) as representing broad phases.

Understanding Function Precedes Attention to Form

Children naturally incorporate into their play the functions of print they have observed in their environment. At home, they may be seen writing out and issuing make-believe citations for traffic violations or making tickets to allow entrance into a zoo of stuffed animals. At school, they may initiate leaving a note for the janitor to prevent him from throwing away a rotting pumpkin the class has been observing. Initially, children are unconcerned about the end product of their labors, focusing solely on its purpose and on the act of accomplishing it. Researchers have noted that children become aware of what writing can be used for and attempt to use it long before they can produce it in conventional form (Morrow, 1989; Taylor, 1983; Teale, 1986).

Children who demonstrate understandings described in the first four stages of writing are at the immersion stage (1) and role-playing the "reader" stage (2) of reading development and are still exploring the various functions print can serve, the roles print plays in their everyday lives, and the various forms it can take. Writing children's names and messages on pictures and helping them notice the significance of labels, signs, directions, letters, notes, and so forth facilitate these understandings and provide children with opportunities to discover the consistent features of written language. Bringing to class examples of environmental print to stimulate discussions and sociodramatic play guides children to recognize the presence and power of literacy in their own culture and helps bridge possible gaps between home literacy and the literacy of school.

TABLE 7.6 Stages of Writing Development

Form	Characteristics
No message: Random scribble	Children do not appear to be differentiating between writing and drawing.
Writing via drawing	Illustrations convey, and are symbolic of, a story.
Writing via scribbling	It is intended as writing and therefore symbolic. The "act" looks like the child is writing (left-right). The child's motion imitates that of the adult writer. The pencil makes writinglike sounds and provides feedback to the child that she or he is "writing." The "writing" is linear, repetitious, uniform in size, and often wavelike (shape of writing).
Writing via letterlike forms	Shapes are creations that resemble letters. They are not poor attempts at letter formation.
Writing via imitating conventional print	Writing is random strings of letters and sometimes numbers. Letter sequences are learned from familiar sources, such as own name, family names, or copied print. Children sometimes change the order of the letters, writing the same ones many different ways. No sound-symbol relationships are evident.

Source: Adapted from "Kindergartners as Readers and Writers," by E. Sulzby, *Advances in Writing Research: Vol. 1. Children's Early Writing Development,* M. Farr, Ed. Copyright 1986 by Ablex Publishing Corp. Reprinted by permission.

The design of the learning environment has a marked effect on whether children will perceive themselves as writers. Children should see their own writing prominently displayed and should see print used to organize the classroom (e.g., labeling, instructions, helping charts, daily schedule) and to communicate with others (e.g., message boards, planning charts, newsletters). Children should have easy access to writing materials, which can be housed in a writing center so that children know where they can find, use, or return them.

Materials available in a writing center may include markers, pencils, erasers, crayons, pens, lined and unlined paper, correction fluid, glue, blank booklets, staplers, art supplies to construct and decorate their books, tape, and scissors. Similar materials should also be strategically placed in other areas of the classroom (e.g., sociodramatic play, science, mathematics/manipulatives) to spark the inclusion of writing into the play or study in progress.

Interdependence of Reading and Writing

Children should have daily opportunities to see print and to observe the processes of reading and writing demonstrated by more literate others. A dictated language experience story, a morning message, a shared reading from an enlarged text, and a class schedule can help children understand that the print holds the message. Opportunities to reread these familiar texts help young children understand that print remains constant and encourages children to search for familiar features or conventions and make discoveries.

The more frequent and more personally significant the opportunities children have with print, the more likely their writing will come to resemble conventional print. Teachers must provide even very young children of four and five years

Children can locate familiar print within a dictated language experience. DLE provides an opportunity for children to see and hear how written language is produced.

old with opportunities to try out writing and to see their personal attempts as authentic and valuable.

When children begin to understand that writing is a means of encoding speech and to incorporate letters into their writing, they have made a remarkable breakthrough. Teachers should celebrate children's attempts to use letters to represent their talk—even if their use of graphophonics is nonexistent, fledgling, and not yet conventional (Clay, 1979).

Roles of Demonstration

Dictated language experience (DLE) is a powerful and personal medium with which to model for children the process of writing. It can be used to demonstrate general or specific concepts. Dictation can be constructed as a group, such as with *The Daily News,* which is used to announce any plans or special notices for the day, a summary of an experience such as a trip to the aquarium, a thank-you note to a visitor, innovations of a favorite text, or a summing up of new information gleaned from a theme exploration. Children can also dictate brief individual messages to accompany their drawings, to communicate information to others (e.g., "Don't use this side of the sink. It gets you wet!"), or to add individual contributions to a group book. Dictation allows teachers of children in the later stages of writing development an opportunity to think aloud various, more sophisticated aspects of the writing process, such as the use of introductory sentences, descriptors, punctuation, and capitalization, as well as to demonstrate the relationship between writing and reading.

Teachers of emerging readers and writers can model sounding out a word by saying the word slowly and pretending to stretch it out like a rubber band (using two index fingers to indicate the stretching motion) to listen for its sound units (Calkins, 1986). Teachers can also model the process of stretching out a word as children write. Children may recognize different sound units in a word. For example, in the word *cat,* a child may hear /c-at/ or /ca-t/ or /c-a-t/. Many children may be able to segment sound units yet cannot identify which letters should represent the units. At this point, the teacher may provide the print for the sound unit or may provide the appropriate letter tiles to make the sound unit. This strategy helps the child begin to make appropriate graphophonic (sound-symbol) associations.

Development of Spelling

Figure 7.6 shows the stages of spelling development.

FIGURE 7.6 Stages of spelling development

Prephonemic:

Children at this stage are typically preschoolers, kindergartners and first-graders who are still emerging readers and writers and who have not yet developed the concept of wordness. They do not grasp the concept that words are comprised of sound units (phonemes) represented by letters. They frequently use a random string of letters and numbers to represent a complete thought or thoughts. Sometimes, however, they include symbols to represent people or objects they are writing about. Their writing can't be "read" by adults because there is too little information on the page for them to interpret. Children may or may not be able to reread their writing, depending on its meaningfulness and whether it is accompanied by an illustration or other contextual association.

Early Phonemic:

At this stage, children spell words on the basis of the dominant sounds they are able to isolate and identify. At the beginning of this stage, children may use only one letter to represent a word and not attempt to sound through the entire word. They often stop after identifying a letter they believe represents the most dominant sound within the word—usually, the initial consonant. As teachers, other children, and parents help them or model for them how to stretch a word to hear its additional phonemes, and as their auditory discrimination becomes more developed, they begin to add other letters. Typically, these are the final and then medial consonants. Again, these are the dominant sounds a child hears. Children at this stage still may not have the concept of wordness and may not use spaces between words although they may use spaces to differentiate between thoughts or sentences.

Phonemic:

Sik
(sick)

At this stage, children still base their spelling on what they hear versus any visual memory of the word. They include a letter for every phoneme (sound unit) contained in the word, and all sound features are represented. Endings such as -ed begin to appear, and wordness is in evidence. Vowels begin to appear in this stage, but they may not be the correct ones. Children at this stage may benefit from being introduced to word families, spelling patterns, and word structures (Gentry, 1982).

Transitional:

you hired

sumtime

Children in this stage tend to blend their visual memory of words with their knowledge of sound-symbol relationships. Sometimes their memory for words overrides their graphophonic awareness. Vowels appear in every syllable, and many words are correctly spelled. Knowledge of the silent e rule and inflectional endings is evident.

Conventional:

Sam likes me.

Children in this stage demonstrate a basic knowledge of their native system of spelling and its rules. They have an extensive knowledge of word structures (affixes, contractions, compound words) and are growing in their accurate use of silent consonants, doubling consonants, and irregular words. They have a large written vocabulary (number of words they can write and reread accurately). Children at this stage often sense when words don't look right.

Source: The stages presented are an adaptation and elaboration of observations of several authors and researchers, primarily Gentry & Henderson (1980); Gillette & Temple (1986); Hagerty & DiStefano (1985); and Henderson & Beers (1980).

Supporting Emerging Writers

FIGURE 7.7 "Closed" sign by Brennan, an emerging writer

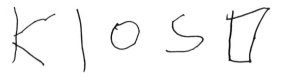

the word with him, he wrote all the sounds he heard (see Figure 7.7).

BRENNAN

Brennan, five-and-one-half years old, did not want to write on his own. He knew the letters and most of their sounds, but he had also reached "the age of convention"; that is, he recognized that words retain the same spelling in different contexts (constancy of word), and he was afraid he would not spell the words correctly. He also did not like the appearance of his still awkward handwriting and insisted that his thoughts or messages be dictated to an adult. This stance continued until one evening when his mother could not make the time to sit down and write out a letter to a television station in response to a contest it was promoting. She urged Brennan to try to write it himself, writing the letters for the sounds he heard as they stretched out the words together.

Brennan recognized the impasse of his mother's unwillingness to write it completely for him, but the need was urgent, so he began to write. As Brennan and his mother slowly said each word together, he carefully wrote down the sounds he heard. He wrote two lines, putting down the first letter of each word. After he had said all he wanted to say, he read his letter back several times. He also read it to his father when he came home. Brennan seemed surprised and delighted that he had produced such an important message all by himself.

Brennan wrote the next day and the next. He found reasons every day to copy lists, to write messages to friends and relatives, or to write a note to remind his mom not to forget an errand. His preschool teacher unknowingly reinforced his new identity as a writer by suggesting that someone write a closed sign for the climbing structure. Brennan quickly volunteered, and as his teacher stretched out

Children are sometimes afraid to attempt writing on their own. Various strategies can help reluctant writers begin to take a risk. Teachers thinking aloud and modeling the process of invented (temporary) spelling often help children to understand the composing process and to accept their approximations as developmental. Access to personal word banks, acknowledging shorter as well as longer pieces, and prewriting activities such as semantic webbing, drawing, and talking about the accompanying picture can also encourage children to write.

The more opportunities children like Brennan have to experiment independently with writing, the more they will understand about the conventions of written language, the more confident they will feel as writers and as problem solvers with literacy, and the more knowledge about print they will take to a reading event.

In addition to independent writing time, children need guided opportunities in which the writing task is divided into manageable steps and an adult mediates the process. Young children still developing understandings about sound-symbol relationships, wordness, and other concepts and conventions of print need to develop a comfort level in expressing ideas and thoughts in writing. Steps of the writing process (Graves, 1983) to consider with these young children are prewriting, writing, revising, sharing, and publishing. Expectations of conventional form should come later as children develop further understandings about print and are able to split their focus between composing and editing. Older children profit from guided opportunities in which they can choose to take certain pieces of their writing through the entire writing process that also includes revising and editing (Ollila & Mayfield, 1992).

SUMMARY

As you reflect on what you have read in this chapter, reexamine your beliefs about the value of literacy and about the nature of teaching and learning literacy. Consider how your beliefs influence the numerous decisions you must make when planning an environment that will nurture and support children's language and literacy development. Whatever your beliefs and understandings may be now, remember that becoming a teacher who is capable of helping children learn to use language and literacy effectively for a variety of purposes in a variety of contexts is a continuous process.

REFERENCES

Adams, M. (1990). *Beginning to read: Thinking and learning about print.* Cambridge: MIT Press.

Allington, P., & Cunningham, R. (1994). *Classrooms that work: They can all read and write.* New York: HarperCollins.

Ashton-Warner, S. (1963). *Teacher.* New York: Simon & Schuster.

Bloom, L. (1972). *Language development: Form and function in emerging grammars.* Cambridge: MIT Press.

Bodrova, E., & Leong, D. (1996). *Tools of the mind: The Vygotskian approach to early childhood education.* Upper Saddle River, NJ: Merrill/Prentice Hall.

Brown, R. (1973). *A first language: The early stages.* Cambridge, MA: Harvard University Press.

Brown, R., & Bellugi, W. (1964). Three processes in the child's acquisition of syntax. *Harvard Education Review, 34,* 133–151.

Bruner, J. (1976). On perceptual readiness. In J. Anglin (Ed.), *Beyond the information given.* New York: Norton.

Bus, A., vanIJzendoorn, M., & Pellegrini, A. (1995). Joint book reading makes for success in learning to read: A meta-analysis on intergenerational transmission of literacy. *Review of Educational Research, 65*(1), 1–21.

Calkins, L. (1986). *The art of teaching writing.* Portsmouth, NH: Heinemann.

Castle, J., Riach, J., & Nicholson, T. (1994). Getting off to a better start in reading and spelling: The effects of phonemic awareness instruction within a whole language program. *Journal of Educational Psychology, 86,* 350–359.

Cazden, C. (1972). *Child language and education.* New York: Holt, Rinehart & Winston.

Chomsky, C. (1965). *Aspects of a theory of syntax.* Cambridge: MIT Press.

Chomsky, C. (1968). *Language and mind.* New York: Harcourt, Brace & World.

Clay, M. (1979). *The early detection of reading difficulties* (3rd ed.). Portsmouth, NH: Heinemann.

Clay, M. (1991). *Becoming literate: The construction of inner control.* Portsmouth, NH: Heinemann.

Cunningham, P. (1995). *Phonics they use* (2nd ed.). New York: HarperCollins.

Durkin, D. (1966). *Children who read early.* New York: Teachers College Press.

Dyson, A. (1985). Individual differences in emerging writing. In M. Farr (Ed.), *Advances in writing research: Vol. 1. Children's early writing development* (pp. 59–126). Norwood, NJ: Ablex.

Ferreiro, E. (1978). What is written in a written sentence? *Journal of Education, 160,* 24–39.

Ferreiro, E., & Teberosky, A. (1982). *Literacy before schooling.* Portsmouth, NH: Heinemann.

Fountas, I., & Pinnell, G. (1996). *Guided reading: Good first teaching for all children.* Portsmouth, NH: Heinemann.

Gastins, I., Ehri, L., Crass, C., O'Hara, C., & Donelly, K. (1997). Procedures for word learning: Making discoveries about words. *Reading Teacher, 50,* 312–327.

Genishi, C., & Dyson, A. H. (1984). *Language assessment in the early years.* Norwood, NJ: Ablex.

Gentry, J., & Henderson, E. (1980). Three steps to teaching beginning readers to spell. In E. Henderson & J. Beers (Eds.), *Developmental and cognitive aspects of learning to spell.* Newark, DE: International Reading Association.

Gentry, J. R. (1982). An analysis of developmental spelling in GYNS AT WRK. *Reading Teacher, 36,* 192–200.

Gillette, J., & Temple, C. (1986). *Understanding reading problems: Assessment and instruction.* Boston: Little, Brown.

Graves, D. (1983). *Writing teachers and children at work.* Portsmouth, NH: Heinemann.

Griffith, P., & Olson, M. (1992). Phonemic awareness helps beginning readers break the code. *Reading Teacher, 45,* 516–522.

Hagerty, P., & DiStefano, P. (1985). Teaching spelling at the elementary level: A realistic perspective. *Reading Teacher, 38*(5), 373–377.

Halliday, M. (1975). *Learning how to mean: Exploration in the development of language.* London: Edward Arnold.

Hart-Hewins, L., & Wells, J. (1990). *Read books for reading: Learning to read with children's literature.* Portsmouth, NH: Heinemann.

Heath, S. (1982). Questioning at home and at school: A comparative study. In G. Spindler (Ed.), *Doing the ethnography of schooling* (pp. 102–131). New York: Holt, Rinehart & Winston.

Henderson, E., & Beers, F. (Eds.). (1980). *Developmental and cognitive aspects of learning to spell.* Newark, DE: International Reading Association.

Holdaway, D. (1979). *The foundations of literacy.* Portsmouth, NH: Heinemann.

Jones, M. (1989). *The emergent reading and writing evaluation: A reliability and content validity study.* Unpublished doctoral dissertation, University of Northern Colorado, Greeley.

Jones, M., & Crabtree, K. (1994). Guide for observing emerging readers and writers. In K. Crabtree, *Accelerated reading: Early prevention for emerging readers and writers at risk.* Unpublished manuscript, University of Northern Colorado, Greeley.

Lavine, L. (1972). *The development of perception of writing in prereading children: A cross-cultural study.* Unpublished doctoral dissertation, Cornell University, Ithaca, NY. (Xerox University overstay Microfilms, 73-6657)

Lennenberg, E. (1967). *Biological foundation of language.* New York: Wiley.

McNeil, D. (1970). *The acquisition of language: The study of developmental psycholinguistics.* New York: Harper & Row.

Menyuk, P. (1977). *Language and maturation.* Cambridge: MIT Press.

Morrow, L. (1985). *Promoting voluntary reading in school and home.* Bloomington, IN: Phi Delta Kappa Educational Foundation.

Morrow, L. (1989). *Literacy development in the early years: Helping children read and write.* Upper Saddle River, NJ: Prentice Hall.

Morrow, L. (1997). *Literacy development in the early years: Helping children read and write* (3rd ed.). Boston: Allyn & Bacon.

National Assessment of Education Progress (NAEP). (1994). *Reading assessment report.* Princeton, NJ: Educational Testing Service.

NCITE: National Center to Improve the Tools of Educators. (1996). *Learning to read; Reading to learn.* Washington, DC: U.S. Department of Education, Office of Special Education and Rehabilitative Services, Office of Special Education Programs.

Ollila, L., & Mayfield, M. (Eds.). (1992). *Emerging literacy: Preschool, kindergarten, and primary grades.* Boston: Allyn & Bacon.

Opitz, M. (1995). *Getting the most from predictable books.* New York: Scholastic.

Patton, M., & Mercer, J. (1996, Fall). "Hey, where's the toys?": Play and literacy in first grade. *Childhood Education,* 10–16.

Pearson, P., & Valencia, S. (1987). Reading assessment: Time for a change. *Reading Teacher, 40,* 726–732.

Preece, A. (1992). Oral language competence and the young child. In L. Ollila & M. Mayfield (Eds.), *Emergent literacy: Preschool, kindergarten, and primary grades* (pp. 42–70). Boston: Allyn & Bacon.

Schlosser, K., & Phillips, V. (1992). *Building literacy with interaction charts.* New York: Scholastic.

Snider, V. (1995). A primer on phonemic awareness: What it is, why it's important, and how to teach it. *School Psychology Review, 24,* 443–455.

Squire, J. (1987). Introduction: A special issue on the state of assessment in reading. *Reading Teacher, 40,* 724–725.

Sulzby, E. (1985). Children's emergent reading of favorite storybooks: A developmental study. *Reading Research Quarterly, 20,* 458–481.

Sulzby, E. (1986). Kindergartners as writers and readers. In M. Farr (Ed.), *Advances in writing research: Vol. 1. Children's early writing development* (pp. 127–199). Norwood, NJ: Ablex.

Swank, L., & Catts, H. (1994). Phonological awareness and written word decoding. *Language, Speech, and Hearing Services in Schools, 25,* 9–14.

Taylor, D. (1983). *Family literacy.* Portsmouth, NH: Heinemann.

Teale, W. (1982). Toward a theory of how children learn to read and write naturally. *Language Arts, 59,* 555–570.

Teale, W. (1986). The beginning of reading and writing: Written language development during preschool and kindergarten years. In M. Sampson (Ed.), *The pursuit of literacy: Early reading and writing.* Dubuque, IA: Kendall/Hunt.

Temple, C., Nathan, R., Burris, N., & Temple, F. (1988). *The beginnings of writing* (2nd ed.). Boston: Allyn & Bacon.

Wells, G. (1986). *The meaning makers: Children learning language and using language to learn.* Portsmouth, NH: Heinemann.

Yellin, D., & Blake, M. (1994). *Integrating the language arts: A holistic approach.* New York: HarperCollins.

Yopp, H. (1992). Developing phonemic awareness in young children. *Reading Teacher, 45,* 696–703.

Children's Books

Barton, B. (1981). *Building a house.* New York: Mulberry Books.

Barton, B. (1982). *Airport.* New York: Harper & Row.

Brett, J. (1989). *The mitten.* New York: Putnam.

Brown, M. (1991). *Goodnight, Moon.* New York: HarperCollins.

Campbell, R. (1982). *Dear zoo.* New York: Penguin.

Christelow, E. (1989). *Five little monkeys.* New York: Clarion.

Cole, J. (1986). *The magic school bus at the waterworks.* New York: Scholastic.

Cowley, J. (1980). *Mrs. Wishy Washy.* Auckland, New Zealand: Shortland.

Day, A. (1985). *Good dog, Carl.* Green Tiger.

Freeman, D. (1968). *Corduroy.* New York: Viking.

Joyce, W. (1987). *George shrinks.* New York: Harper & Row.

Lobel, A. (1970). *Frog and Toad are friends.* New York: Harper & Row.

Martin, B. (1983). *Brown bear, brown bear: What do you see?* New York: Holt, Rinehart & Winston.

Martin, B. (1991). *Polar bear, polar bear: What do you see?* New York: Holt, Rinehart & Winston.

Mayer, M. (1974). *Frog goes to dinner.* New York: Dial.

Parrish, P. (1963). *Amelia Bedelia.* New York: Harper & Row.

Peek, M. (1985). *Mary wore her red dress, and Henry wore his green sneakers.* New York: Clarion.

Petrie, C. (1982). *Joshua James loves trucks.* Danbury, CT: Childrens Press.

Raffi Songs to Read. (1988). *Wheels on the bus.* New York: Crown.

Rockwell, A. (1987). *Bikes.* New York: Dutton.

Rylant, C. (1987). *Henry and Mudge: The first book of their adventures.* New York: Bradbury.

Sesame Street. (1982). *One rubber duckie: A Sesame Street counting book.* New York: Children's Television Workshop.

Shaw, C. (1947). *It looked like spilt milk.* New York: Harper & Row.

Stadler, J. (1984). *Hooray for snail!* New York: Harper & Row.

Wildsmith, B. (1987). *If I were you.* New York: Oxford University Press.

Williams, S. (1990). *I went walking.* Orlando, FL: Harcourt Brace.

Wise, M. (1949). *The important book.* New York: Harper & Row.

Wood, L. (1991). *Bump, bump, bump.* Oxford, UK: Oxford University Press.

Ziefert, H. (1985). *Where's the Halloween treat?* New York: Penguin.

A major aim of education is to improve the learners' understanding of the world around them and to strengthen their dispositions to go on learning. When educational practices succeed in doing so, learners find their experiences enjoyable.

(Katz & Chard, 1989, p. 5)

8

Supporting Literacy Development Across the Curriculum

CONSIDER YOUR BELIEFS

- What is integrated literacy development? Why is integration important?
- What literacy materials, information, experiences, events, and interactions should you provide?
- How can you adjust instruction for the diversity of literacy understandings and ways of learning that children will demonstrate?
- How will you evaluate the impact of your instructional decisions?
- How will you document children's literacy growth?

THE TEACHER AS DECISION MAKER

Whether you are aware of it or not, you make decisions about every aspect of the school day on the basis of your beliefs about the nature of teaching and of learning—about how teachers and children learn from one another and about how children learn from each other as they interact throughout the day. You design the classroom environment, make choices about the curriculum, and make decisions about **literacy events** on the basis of your beliefs about the following:

- How important it is that a child become literate

- What it means for a child to be literate
- How a child becomes literate
- The roles of more literate others (parents, teachers, and other children) in this process

Decisions about the content of this chapter have been based on the *authors' beliefs* that a country's ability to meet the demands of a highly competitive, technological society is directly related to the extent to which its citizens become literate. Many academics, politicians, and business leaders believe that this country's high schools are graduating far too few students who can demonstrate a level of literacy that will permit them to become successful, contributing members of society. The authors of this text believe that **emergent literacy** forms the basis from which all subsequent literacy evolves and that failing to nurture and develop expressive and receptive language, attitudes, and skills early in a child's life imparts a heavy price on the child, on the child's family, and on society (Mitchell, 1989).

The authors believe that, to nurture the development of oral and written language effectively in school-age children, literacy should be integrated throughout the curriculum. Furthermore, the authors believe it is imperative that the teacher be a well-informed, reflective professional, rather than merely a manager of time and activities. As you interact with this chapter, you will begin to clarify your beliefs about language learning and teaching and you will become cognizant of how your beliefs can influence the literacy development of the children you teach.

LITERACY IN EFFECTIVE PRIMARY CLASSROOMS: DISTINGUISHING CHARACTERISTICS

Nurturing Literacy in the Classroom

Nurturing literacy in the classroom should mirror the nurturing environments found in the homes of children who have informally learned to read and/or who have had opportunities to play with and develop understandings about print before they come to school (Durkin, 1966; Taylor, 1983). Children in literacy-rich homes and classrooms have the following:

1. *A variety and quantity of reading and writing materials.* During a study of insects ("Creepy Crawlies"), the teacher of four- and five-year-olds, Mrs. Collinson, collected and purposefully placed in the Science Area selected issues of *Ranger Rick, Geographic World, National Geographic,* and *Our Big Back Yard.* She also placed a variety of fiction and non-fiction trade books in the Science Area. She intentionally selected books to represent a range of concept levels, as well as reading levels—from picture books to reference texts. Appropriately labeled diagrams and pictures of insects were displayed at children's eye level. Paper was available for children to draw their favorite insects, check the reference books, and label the drawings for themselves. A chart was used to keep track of the number of days the Painted Lady butterfly took to emerge from its chrysalis. Also displayed in the Science Area was a language experience story the children had dictated describing a visit from a parent who used insects in organic gardening.

2. *A physical and affective setting supportive of literacy events.* Mrs. Collinson made certain that all books, magazines, and writing materials were easily accessible to the children. The containers and shelving space for the materials were clearly identified with an icon and corresponding label. Mrs. Collinson demonstrated the appropriate use and storage of materials during group time in order to facilitate the children's independent use of the materials. For example, during group time she demonstrated how to use the tape recorder to play the taped books. The buttons on the tape recorder were color-coded to ensure the children's ability to use the recorder independently.

3. *Parents and teachers who read aloud frequently to children, who read and write for themselves, and who include children in reading and writing for a variety of purposes.* During a study of insects, Mrs. Collinson read aloud many fiction and non-fiction books to the children. The children wrote: thank-you notes to their visitors, a science journal reflecting their observations of the metamorphosis of the Painted Lady butterfly, personal stories patterned after *The Very Hungry Caterpillar* (Carle, 1987b), and labels for the plants in their organic garden. The

teacher used developmentally appropriate informational books to help the children find answers to the questions they had (e.g., "Why do lightening bugs light?"). After learning to sing the song, the children "read" the words to "The Ladybug Picnic" from the chart Mrs. Collinson had made and displayed. The children read and reread, independently and to each other, the group language experience story they had written about the collection of cocoons and chrysalises they had recently viewed at the Butterfly Pavilion.

4. *Parents and teachers who respond to children's questions about print.* While Mrs. Collinson was observing in the Science Area, Caitlin brought an opened informational book to her and asked, "Where does it say 'honeybee'?" Mrs. Collinson framed the word with her fingers. Caitlin proceeded to copy the word onto her drawing of a honeybee.

5. *Daily literacy routines.* Each day when the children arrived, they clustered around the morning message that Mrs. Collinson had written on the chalkboard. They collaboratively read the message to discover the plans and schedule for the day. At group time, children volunteered to read a part of the morning message. After the morning recess each day, the children looked forward to journal writing time as a means to reflect on the morning's work. Three days a week

Emergent storybook reading is an important literacy routine to incorporate into a young child's day.

the children broke up into pairs to share an emergent storybook reading with a classmate. Before going home, Mrs. Collinson read aloud from an informational book related to the current theme.

6. *Uninterrupted opportunities to read and write independently (to try out the understandings they have about written language and to develop ownership of the process).* Consistent learning areas in Mrs. Collinson's room include a Library Area and a Writing Area. These areas provide specific opportunities for the children to use their reading and writing understandings independently. The Library Area includes books related to the current area of study, familiar books from previous themes, books written and published by the children, language experience stories and charts dictated by the group, and other quality children's literature. The Writing Area includes a variety of paper and writing tools, a computer, a picture dictionary, a picture thesaurus, and charted word webs related to areas of interest and developed collaboratively by the children and Mrs. Collinson.

7. *Opportunities to engage in collaborative reading and writing events with others (authors' share, sharing books, informally sharing literacy understandings).* Austin, Ellis, and Kelli are in the Music Area, bedecked with headsets and listening to a tape recording of *The Itsy Bitsy Spider.* Austin is using a pointer to lead the choral singing of the song chart posted on the wall. They listen to the tape several times, taking turns as the leader.

8. *Parents and teachers who feel responsible for helping children learn and who believe that children are capable readers and writers.* When Maddie approached Mrs. Collinson and said that she was concerned about people walking in their newly planted garden. Mrs. Collinson suggested that she make a sign to remind people to not walk in the garden. Maddie quickly returned with a sign that said, "DMEAIMMDE."

Mrs. Collinson asked Maddie to read aloud what she had written, "Please do not walk in our garden." While complimenting Maddie on the message she had constructed, Mrs. Collinson printed Maddie's intended message clearly under her script so Maddie (and trespassers) could see it in conventional writing.

9. *Parents and teachers who are sensitive to children's development and who recognize, acknowledge, and support children's attempts to read and write as their attempts emerge toward conventional forms.* Jeffrey walked down the hall to the library with Mrs. Collinson. As they passed the rest room door labeled BOYS, Jeffrey turned to Mrs. Collinson and spelled, "B O Y S, that says bathroom." Mrs. Collinson responded, "You're right. This *is* the boys' bathroom," and she swept her hand under the word BOYS, "but this says, 'Boys.' "*

Providing Authentic Literacy Experiences

For all children, the introduction to literacy in the classroom should convey the message that reading, writing, listening, speaking, and thinking are sources of pleasure and power (Ollila & Mayfield, 1992). This message is naturally conveyed in classrooms that provide many varied, rich, and meaningful (authentic) opportunities for children to experience and use language.

Many educators cringe when they hear the nebulous terms *meaningful* or *authentic* used to describe classroom experiences. The terms seem to have many interpretations and misinterpretations. Hall (1987, p. 13) clarified this concept when he stated, "Most language that children experience is imbedded in the pursuit

---

*Source: Adapted from *Literacy's Beginnings: Supporting Young Readers and Writers* by L. McGee & D. Richgels, p. 109. Copyright 1990 by Allyn & Bacon. Reprinted by permission of Allyn & Bacon.

of other ends. Language is not the focus of these interactions; it is a medium for fulfilling objectives." Maddie's use of literacy to construct the sign to keep people from walking on the newly planted garden was the means to an end. Her sense of ownership of the situation encouraged her to use what she knew about print to construct the sign. This is quite different from assigning children to fill in and color a blank sign (e.g., stop sign, the "golden arches") of their choice during center time. In the sign assignment, writing the words on the sign is an end in itself. The sign serves no purpose. Given authentic opportunities to read and write for both personal and social purposes and supported by appropriate interactions with a more literate other, children will actively attempt to use their internal language acquisition mechanisms to construct new understandings about, and to master the use of, written language. Another example of an authentic language opportunity is provided in Figure 8.1.

INTEGRATING LANGUAGE AND LITERACY THROUGHOUT THE EXPLORATION OF A THEME*

The teacher who maintains these beliefs about literacy learning prepares a classroom environment that invites children to engage in authentic learning experiences, of which listening, speaking, reading, writing, and thinking are natural components—the means to the end. Contextual language and literacy opportunities are planned as integral to the learning experiences that occur. Language and literacy are integrated throughout the day—throughout the curriculum.

Theme explorations provide a natural context within which many purposeful opportunities to use language can be facilitated. The sociodramatic play center easily lends itself to many and varied opportunities for children to engage in authentic literacy experiences in which they see the role of literacy within their environment and can extend their understandings about the form of print. A restaurant setting

---

*In this chapter, the term *theme* is used to mean the topic or focus of a class exploration. (See Chapter 4, "A Cohesive Integrated Curriculum.")

FIGURE 8.1 An authentic language opportunity

Looking in on Mrs. Spalding's five-six class, we see children using reading, writing, listening, and speaking as they pursue their interests related to bugs. Noah, Paula, and Taylor are in the writing center, drafting a letter to a company to order new ants for the ant farm. They collaboratively decide what they want to say. To format their letter, they refer to a sample letter posted by Mrs. Spalding to be used for this purpose. As they write their letter, they retrieve some words from the sample letter (*Dear, Thank you, please, sincerely*) and collaboratively attempt to assign letters to the dominant sounds they hear as they stretch out the words they are spelling.

After the draft is finished, they read what they have written to make certain they are satisfied with the content. The paraprofessional, Mr. Kowalski, listens as the children read their letter to him. As the children read the letter a second time, Mr. Kowalski records the letter in conventional print. He acknowledges the understandings the children have demonstrated and points out new ones that are within their grasp. After the letter is completed, Mr. Kowalski staples the two letters together and helps the children address an envelope. The children take the letter to the school secretary to post in the morning mail.

Children are more likely to construct and extend understandings about written language when they have opportunities to use literacy within meaningful contexts. Brandon's letter read, "Dear Book Club, Me and another Kid in my class ordered a book that said there was free tattos and they were'nt there. I'd like 'em. It's a Disney chapter book and it's called "Doug's Hoop Nightmare". Please send ..."

can include menus, pads of paper, pencils, placemats, and signs. The waitress or waiter can write down a patron's carefully selected order and then read it to the cook. A veterinarian or family health clinic setting can include appointment books, prescription pads, magazines, and posters, which encourage children to notice the importance of print, as well as to manipulate print in ways that help them confirm or refine their understandings in a nonthreatening, familiar, contextual situation.

Children are more likely to experiment with print within themes that are personally familiar and less likely to do so within unfamiliar themes. For example, children who have not been in a veterinarian's office first search to discover the roles that literacy plays within this context before they begin to incorporate it into their sociodramatic play activities. Teachers can help familiarize children with the possible uses of literacy within a particular theme or context through field trips, discussions, role playing, videos, pictures, classroom visitors, and books. Both famil-

iar and unfamiliar contexts and themes must be provided to give children opportunities to both use and extend what they know—to extend the purposes for which, and the contexts within which, they are able to use language and literacy effectively.

As a class explores the habits of the woolly caterpillar several children brought in from the playground, the teacher may share both informational and related fiction books during read aloud time. The teacher can then place some of these books in the library corner and/or in the science area, where children are observing and recording the metamorphosis of a Painted Lady butterfly in narrative, expository, or graphic form. Other related books, including enticing picture books and books with tapes, can be made available for independent and collaborative exploration. **Literacy events** (planned contextual opportunities for children to read, write, listen, and speak) must be embedded (integrated) within the curriculum to be truly meaningful; *children must use literacy within such* *meaningful contexts to construct new understandings about literacy.* Using literacy and becoming literate are interactive, interconnected, inseparable processes.

Planning Literacy Events

What literacy events, materials, experiences, information, and interactions should be provided to support and nurture effectively children's literacy development? As stated, literacy events must be designed to be open-ended and purposeful for children. Literacy events must also be purposeful for the teacher; that is, they must provide opportunities for the teacher to observe and mediate as children use language and interact with print. During these events, teachers can observe how children are constructing understandings about listening, speaking, reading, writing, and thinking; what their current understandings are; and how they are applying them. Teachers use these observations to make spontaneous decisions about mediation and future decisions about instruction, such as the specific demonstrations that may be needed (e.g., wordness, making predictions, using reading strategies). Some of these events will take place with the teacher; others will occur independent of the teacher (alone and/or with other children). The literacy events generated within this environment include opportunities for teachers to

- Demonstrate helpful strategies
- Mediate/Scaffold (help children make connections between the known and the unknown) in both planned and spontaneous instruction
- Respond to children's attempts to use reading and writing
- Observe children's understandings about reading and writing
- Determine how children construct new understandings about reading and writing

- Model conventional reading and writing

Teachers plan opportunities for children to

- Explore reading and writing independently
- Interact with the teacher during reading and writing
- Construct new understandings about reading and writing
- Be actively involved in learning with peers
- Be actively involved with literacy materials
- Converse with peers and adults

Components of the Integrated Literacy Curriculum

To ensure that both children and teachers are afforded these opportunities on a regular basis, planning for each of the following literacy components to be naturally embedded (integrated) within the context of theme exploration is important. Each component is essential and interdependent. These components (see Figure 8.2) provide opportunities for children to use language, as well as for teachers to stimulate and mediate language development. No sequence or hierarchy is implied by the number assigned to each.

Theme explorations provide excellent vehicles for planning and organizing appropriate learning experiences for children. They especially provide a rich medium for planning the types of language events and opportunities discussed in this chapter. The theme of the seashore has been selected to demonstrate how the components of the integrated literacy curriculum can be embedded and used to support children's literacy development as they explore a topic of interest.

A Walk through the Planning Process

Step 1. Select a Broad Theme. Review the goals you, the parents, and the district or school have established for children. Brainstorm with colleagues and parents to generate a list of themes

FIGURE 8.2 Components of the integrated literacy curriculum

---

1. Experiences to expand background knowledge and vocabulary

2. Oral/Aural language opportunities

3. Reading aloud by the teacher

4. A variety of literacy contexts (themes and purposes for using literacy)

5. A variety of literacy materials available

6. Teacher observation time without mediation or intrusion

7. Time for children to converse and share reading, writing, and learning with each other and with adults

8. Independent reading time

9. Independent writing time

10. Individual and small-group mediated reading (shared reading, supported reading)

11. Individual and small-group mediated writing (interactive writing)

Note: For specific examples of literacy events appropriate for each component, see Table 8.1.

that could be used to plan a rich array of opportunities for children to progress toward these goals in meaningful ways. Goals from across content areas may naturally cluster around a theme. The themes generated should also reflect those areas of interest commonly expressed by children within the targeted age ranges. Select one theme to develop further. Consider student input.

Step 2. Identify General Topics within the Theme and the Critical Knowledge Related to Each Topic. With the children, identify several general topics and areas of interest within the theme (see Figure 8.3: Occupations, Recreational Activities, Issues, Geographical Characteristics, and Sea Life). Consider basic information, concepts, processes, and understandings you want

children to develop as they explore the topics. This **critical knowledge** is information all children will be expected to understand or learn. Immerse children in opportunities to explore these general topics, to begin to construct the new concepts and understandings (e.g., many people depend on the sea to make a living), to acquire new information (e.g., what causes the tides), and to develop new processes (e.g., skimming the index of an informational book to determine whether it might help answer a specific question). Ways to immerse children in the theme include guest speakers, videos, field trips, reading of related books aloud to the children, and the children's independent reading.

Step 3. Help Children Identify Specific Areas to Explore In-depth. After the immersion period, discuss with the class any areas of particular interest. These areas may or may not have been specifically addressed during the immersion period. Help children identify specific aspects or questions they would like to explore further. Some children may decide to explore selected questions together; some may choose to explore independently (see Figure 8.3: endangered species, tides, parasailing, shrimpers, and invertebrates).

Step 4. Generate Lists of Books, Projects, and Literacy Events That Could Be Used to Explore These Specific Areas of Interest. Include books (fiction and nonfiction) and other print (e.g., newspapers, magazines, maps, charts) and nonprint materials (e.g., CD-ROMs, Web sites, videos) appropriate to each stage of reading development, as well as books to meet children's aural/oral language needs (books appropriate for read alouds by the teacher). Encourage children and parents to contribute materials to be used. Literacy events may include letters to arrange visitations, independent or collaborative research, learning logs, and independent reading. Projects may include experiments, models, and demon-

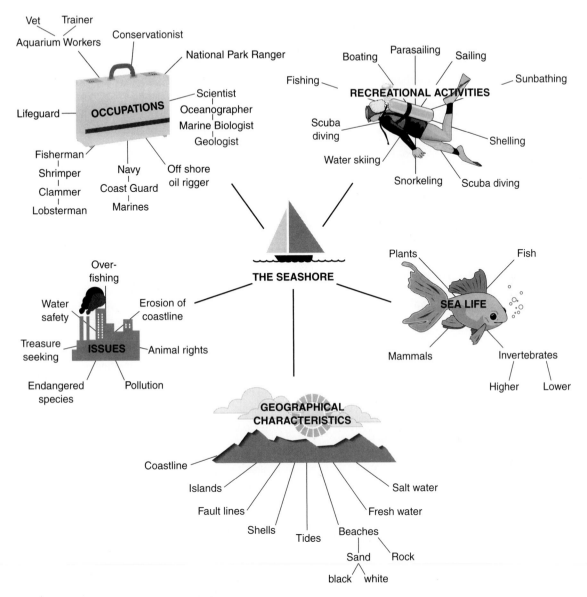

FIGURE 8.3 The seashore: A web of ideas

strations that will facilitate children's understanding of the topic(s).

Step 5. Plan Ways to Use Each Literacy Component. Use of each literacy component will provide opportunities for children to explore their selected areas of interest. Carefully consider the unique purposes and possible contributions of each component to children's literacy development (see Figure 8.2 and Table 8.1).

TABLE 8.1 Integrating literacy throughout a theme: Components

Components	Appropriate Literacy Events	Thematic Examples
Expand Background Knowledge/Vocabulary	Field trips and guest speakers	Aquarium; tropical fish store; fish market; museum Environmentalists; scuba diver; lobsterman; Coast Guard
	Artifacts	Shell, sand, and seaweed collections; hermit crab; anemone
	Videos/Pictures/Slides	*Free Willie* (movie); National Geographic series; Great Barrier Reef
	Reading aloud by teacher	*House for Hermit Crab* (Carle, 1987a); *Island of the Blue Dolphins* (O'Dell, 1960); *Night of Ghosts and Hermits* (Stolz, 1985); *Jacob's Little Giant* (Smucker, 1987)
	Independent reading	*Hungry, Hungry Sharks* (Cole, 1986); *How to Hide an Octopus* (Heller, 1985); *Boats* (Rockwell, 1982)
Oral/Aural Language Opportunities	Sociodramatic Play	Fishing boat; submarine
	Storytelling	Sharing oral traditions of islands; sea shanties
	Oral games	I am going to the seashore and I will bring . . . (A-Z)
	Author's share	Sea poems; share independent research; creative stories
	Listening center	Taped books; songs of the sea
	Conversations/Discussions	Endangered species; treasure hunting; Greenpeace
	Small-group projects	Research: visuals of different seashores, mapping sand table
	Large-group activities	Whale adoption project; guest speaker
Reading Aloud by Teacher	Songs and poetry	*The Homemade Boat* (Silverstein, 1974)
	Predictable books	*Grandpa, Grandpa* (Cowley, 1990); *Boats* (Rockwell, 1982)
	Picture books	*Farewell to Shady Glade* (Peet, 1966); *Time of Wonder* (McCloskey, 1977); *One Morning in Maine* (McCloskey, 1952)
	Chapter books	*Island of the Blue Dolphins* (O'Dell, 1960); *The Cay* (Taylor, 1969); *The Fantastic Mr. Fox* (Dahl, 1970)
	Informational books	*What's for Lunch: The Eating Habits of Seashore Creatures* (Epstein, 1985)
	Biography	*Jacques Cousteau, Man of the Oceans* (Greene, 1990)
Variety of Literacy Contexts/Materials	Science journal	Oil spill experiment—record observations
	Charts	Navigational oceanic charts
	Maps	Treasure map, location of oceans, latitude/longitude
	Classifying/Identifying	Labeling seashell collection

Components	Appropriate Literacy Events	Thematic Examples
Variety of Literacy Contexts/Materials *(continued)*	Letter writing	For information, whale adoption project, guest speakers
	Following directions	Cooking (bouillabaisse); tying knots
	Report writing/Research	Exploring independent topics
	Debate	Pollution, conservation, and endangered species issues
	Occupational studies	Oceanographer, marine biologist, environmentalist, fishermen
	Bookmaking	Pop-up books, innovations, information, fiction, poetry
Mediated Reading	Shared reading	Patterned, predictable books (*Grandpa, Grandpa* [Cowley, 1990])
	Supported reading	Language predictable books (*Boats* [Rockwell, 1982])
	Structured reading	Becoming independent and independent stages (*Hungry, Hungry Sharks* [Cole, 1986]), *Time of Wonder* [McCloskey, 1977], *One Morning in Maine* [McCloskey, 1952])
	Dictated language experience	Related to a field trip to an aquarium or beach; summarizing information gleaned from guest speaker or teacher's presentation or read aloud
	Daily News	Dictated message/summary of the day; may be generated by the teacher
	Reading conferences	May include modeling, giving new necessary information, and mediation to stimulate strategic reading and critical thinking; may include conversation to explore and extend comprehension
Mediated Writing	Dictated language experience	Children dictate the content and participate in the process although the teacher does the majority or all of the writing
	Innovations of a text *Daily News*	With the teacher's mediation, children may contribute to the spelling of words and the punctuation of messages
	Writing conferences	May include conversations that stimulate revision of content, style, and structure or editing for conventions
	Structured writing	May include modeling and mediated practice of writing techniques, such as writing a summary, writing an introduction, using a particularly literary element, developing character, or writing a technical report

Step 6. Design Projects to Share New Learning. With individual or groups of children, identify ways they can share the information they have gleaned from their explorations and investigations. Consider combining several of the following: visual aides, oral reports, simulations, videotapes, models, charts, research reports. Through discussions with children, determine the important content and/or critical knowledge that should be reflected in the project. Through similar discussions, establish expectations for the quality of the project. Develop an evaluation rubric based on these discussions that will serve as a guide to children as they develop their projects. Provide children with appropriate time lines for exploration and preparation of their projects. Plan time specifically for sharing and for evaluation (child and teacher).

Step 7. Evaluate the Process. As each investigation or exploration draws to a close, it is important that the children and the teacher reflect on the process. Children's responses to items such as those listed in Chapter 4 (section on evaluation) provide valuable information for the teacher when considering future investigations. Additional questions for older children may include the following:

- What did you learn about yourself as a researcher (investigator) as you explored your topic (questions)?
- You said that the most difficult part of this investigation was _____. How can I help make that part easier for you next time?

OBSERVATIONS, EVALUATIONS, AND REFLECTIONS

Purposes of Literacy Assessment

Teachers use observations, evaluations, and reflections for two primary purposes. The first is to evaluate how each child is progressing toward achievement of the goals, outcomes, or standards established for the individual child, for the class as a whole, and for the school or district. The second purpose is to evaluate the effectiveness of instructional decisions and to garner the information necessary to modify instruction. Teachers use this information to ensure that each child is progressing efficiently and effectively toward the desired goals.

What teachers decide to observe and evaluate and *how* teachers decide to do so will depend on the beliefs teachers hold about literacy and about how children become literate. Teachers should plan to observe and evaluate the following:

- Each child's current understandings of literacy
- How each child has come to construct those understandings
- How each child is able to use current understandings independently to (1) function effectively in a variety of contexts, (2) solve literacy problems encountered in each context, and (3) construct new understandings about literacy
- The impact of the physical and affective aspects of the literacy environment on the literacy development of each child
- The effectiveness of instructional interactions

Effective teachers reflect on this information in modifying their instructional environment and instructional interactions to ensure the maximum literacy development of each child.

Authentic Assessments

The goal of literacy instruction should be to help each student learn to use literacy effectively in an ever-increasing variety of contexts. Because assessment and instruction are based on the beliefs of the teacher, teachers will design assessment strategies and tools that are consistent with those beliefs and that directly

Frequent, planned assessment is crucial to effective instruction.

reflect instructional practices. For example, a teacher who views reading as a problem-solving process will observe how (the process) a child strategically uses various sources of information when attempting to construct meaning (the product) from a text. An assessment designed to evaluate a child's knowledge of isolated reading skills may be viewed as one piece of useful information, but not as sufficient information with which to evaluate the child's literacy development or to inform instructional decisions (see Chapter 5).

Types of **authentic assessment** strategies and tools that teachers may choose to use include the following:

- *Performance sampling:* observing children as they use literacy in real reading and writing situations
- *Reading conferences:* meeting with individual children to observe their use of reading strategies, to discuss the books they are reading, and to discover and document the reading strengths and weaknesses each child may have

- *Writing conferences:* meeting with individual children to discuss progress and intent and to assess various writing needs
- *Literacy portfolios:* a collection of dated samples of each child's writing, reading, and learning
- *Anecdotal records:* informal notes taken by the teacher to record observations and reflections during performance sampling and conferences
- *Oral reading records and miscue analysis:* coding and analysis of oral reading behaviors to determine the information the reader is using to identify words and to construct meaning from print
- *Checklists:* lists designed or selected by the teacher to record observations of each child's understandings and uses of literacy
- *Self-assessment by the learner:* learning logs, surveys, interviews, and **checklists** designed to chronicle a learner's awareness of personal literacy strengths and weaknesses and/or documentation of

anecdotal records of conversations with the literacy learner regarding personal literacy development

- *Parental input:* reading/writing logs, surveys, interviews, and checklists to record parents' perceptions of their children's literacy development

Teachers select and/or design strategies and tools to reflect *markers* (indicators of growth) within a continuum of development toward the established literacy outcomes or standards, information regarding how a child approaches a literacy task, and the information needed to make effective instructional decisions. Examples of observation and evaluation tools teachers may use are provided in the following sections.

Literacy events (e.g., pretend storybook reading, independent reading, DLE, shared reading, writing, rereading of familiar material, use of print in play activities, interactive charts, environmental print opportunities) provide opportunities for teachers to observe how readers and writers approach and interact with print in various contexts. Each literacy event provides an authentic opportunity to observe children's reading, writing, listening, speaking, or thinking behaviors. Literacy events in which the teacher participates with children provide the opportunity for teachers to observe how children respond to specific types of mediation or instruction. Examples are provided in Table 8.2.

Teachers need a framework for organizing and documenting the information they glean about individual children's literacy understandings from planned and unplanned observation opportunities. These observations should be made across time, on a regular basis, and within

TABLE 8.2 Opportunities to observe literacy development

Literacy Event	*Observe the Child's:*
When a child converses about stories/books	Comprehension Expressive oral language
When the child reads	Concept of reading Directionality Problem solving to construct meaning Self-monitoring Stage of reading development
When the child writes	Concept of writing Directionality and orientation Problem-solving behaviors Knowledge of graphophonics Stage of writing development Stage of spelling development
When the teacher mediates literacy events	Teacher dependence/independence Engagement/disengagement Response to wait time
When the child selects a text to read	Characteristics of text considered Topics of interest/topics disliked

Source: Selected from "Guide for Observing Emerging Readers and Writers," by M. Jones and K. Crabtree, 1994, *Accelerated Reading: Early Prevention for Emerging Readers and Writers At Risk,* by K. Crabtree. Reprinted by permission of the authors.

a variety of contexts. These observations should be made when the children are working with familiar, as well as unfamiliar, materials. Teachers must consider the specific aspects of each child's literacy development they want to know about and select or design literacy events and assessment tools for these purposes.

Observing Emerging Readers and Writers

Teachers of emerging readers and writers must create opportunities to

- Observe the children's understandings about the form of written language
- Observe the children's understandings about the process of reading
- Observe the children's understandings about the process of writing
- Learn about the children's home experiences related to literacy

Children's understandings about the form of written language can be observed during a shared reading, when a child attempts to read a book independently, and when a child attempts to write. The teacher can plan to observe these literacy events during informal play or center time or during more structured opportunities. Examples of assessment tools that a teacher can use to guide observations and documentations in these areas are provided in Figures 8.4, 8.5, 8.6, 8.7, and 8.8.

FIGURE 8.4 The print concepts checklist

Name: _____ Date: _____

Directions: Using a book the child has never seen before, test the following concepts.

	Yes	No	Sometimes
1. Identifies front/back of book	☐	☐	☐
2. Can indicate title	☐	☐	☐
3. Identifies print as "what is read"	☐	☐	☐
4. Can indicate picture	☐	☐	☐
5. Knows where to start reading	☐	☐	☐
6. Shows correct direction of print display	☐	☐	☐
7. Indicates beginning of story on a page	☐	☐	☐
8. Can show return sweep for a line of print	☐	☐	☐
9. Indicates end of story	☐	☐	☐
10. Identifies bottom of page	☐	☐	☐
11. Identifies top of page	☐	☐	☐
12. Can locate a word (by cupping, etc.)	☐	☐	☐
13. Can locate two words that appear together	☐	☐	☐
14. Can locate the space between words	☐	☐	☐
15. Can locate a letter	☐	☐	☐
16. Can locate two consecutive letters	☐	☐	☐
17. Can indicate a period	☐	☐	☐
18. Can indicate a comma, question mark	☐	☐	☐

Source: From *Assessment and Instruction of Reading and Writing Disability: An Interactive Approach,* 2nd Edition by Marjorie Y. Lipson and Karen K. Wixson. Copyright © 1997 by Addison-Wesley Educational Publishers Inc. Reprinted by permission.

FIGURE 8.5 Dictated story record form

Name:_____ Date: _____

Directions: Present topic, object, or experience for student to discuss or experience directly. Ask them to tell you something about it.

Dictated Story:

Assessment:

Language Development
- Does the child speak in sentences, in single words, or word clusters?
- Does the child use descriptive names for objects and events or many ambiguous terms like "it," "that," "this thing"?
- Does the child provide adequate information to reconstruct the experience?
- Does the child use appropriate grammatical structure?
- How does the child use language appropriate to the task?
- How easily and fluently does the child dictate?

Literacy Development
- Does the child speak clearly and pace the dictation to allow the teacher to record?
- What does the child do as the story is transcribed?
- Does the dictation have clarity and organization (does it make sense)?
- Does the child provide a title that reflects the major ideas or themes of the dictation?
- How does the child (attempt) to read back his or her dictation?

At the conclusion of a dictated story activity, it is helpful to reflect on the following:

- What evidence is there that the child understands the concepts of word, sentence, paragraph, and story?
- What aspects of the speech-to-print relationship does the child understand?
- In what ways does the child use memory for text as an aid to reading?
- What sight vocabulary does the child appear to have mastered?
- How does the child use graphophonic information to read?

Comments:

Source: From *Assessment and Instruction of Reading and Writing Disability: An Interactive Approach,* 2nd Edition by Marjorie Y. Lipson and Karen K. Wixson. Copyright © 1997 by Addison-Wesley Educational Publishers Inc. Reprinted by permission.

FIGURE 8.6 When a child reads

What I Observed . . . (date each entry)

Concept of Reading

Does the child

- turn pages from front to back
- recognize where to start reading on a page
- recognize where to stop reading on a page
- follow line of print from top to bottom
- follow line of print from left to right
- indicate awareness of line directionality with return sweep

Problem Solving to Construct Meaning

When attempting to read, does the child

- label pictures
- describe the action on each page (no story line)
- use the pictures to tell the story
- use memory
- use picture cues
- track words
- use sight words
- use syntax
- use semantics
- use graphophonics
  - beginning
  - middle
  - final
- self-correct to maintain meaning
- cross-check information
- reread
- skip and go on to get more information
- identify known parts of the word
- relate to words he or she can read or write
- try to maintain meaning

Self-Monitoring

When attempting to read, does the child

- use tracking to self-correct
- expect and construct meaning from text
- recognize when text does not make sense
- attempt to self-correct when text does not make sense
- recognize when meaningful substitutions differ from the printed word
- attempt to self-correct when meaningful substitutions differ from the printed word:
  - at the sentence level only
  - at the story level
- reread to regain and/or construct meaning or flow

Source: Reprinted from "Guide for Observing Emerging Readers and Writers: Accelerated Reading," by M. Jones and K. Crabtree, 1994, *Accelerated Reading: Early Prevention for Emerging Readers and Writers at Risk,* by K. Crabtree, p. 53. Reprinted by permission of the authors.

FIGURE 8.7 Writing

In the space that follows, write down what the child reads or pretends to read for her or his writing:

Concentration/Interest in Writing

_____ little
_____ moderate
_____ a great deal

Fluency of Writing

_____ did not write
_____ wrote with a lot of prompting
_____ wrote with a little prompting
_____ wrote with no prompting

Revision Process

_____ did not write
_____ neither reread nor revised while writing
_____ reread while writing
_____ revised handwriting or spelling during writing
_____ revised content during writing

Directionality

_____ indicated lack of knowledge of directionality
_____ consistently wrote top to bottom *or* left to right
_____ consistently wrote top to bottom *and* left to right

Message Representation

_____ mostly random scribbles or "cursivelike" scribbles
_____ mostly letterlike formations
_____ mostly limited or repeated use of letters, numbers, and/or random known or copied words
_____ generally used a variety of letters and numbers
_____ generally used functional/invented spelling

Use of Graphophonics

_____ no apparent sound/letter relationships
_____ represented the sounds heard at the beginning of words
_____ represented the sounds heard at the beginning and end of words only
_____ represented a few of the sounds heard within words (more than just the beginning and ending of words)
_____ represented the majority of sounds heard in words (you can read most of what the child writes without asking the child to read it to you)

Syntax

_____ did not write (no evidence of syntax)
_____ labeled picture items (no evidence of syntax)
_____ wrote connected text but did not use syntactic markers such as word boundaries and punctuation
_____ occasionally denoted word boundaries by using white space, dashes, periods, or some other mark between words
_____ occasionally denoted thought boundaries by using periods, commas, or some other punctuation

Message Meaning and Organization

_____ indicated no message intent
_____ conveyed ideas (even if they weren't written down), but ideas were not related to drawing
_____ conveyed ideas (even if they weren't written down), and ideas were related to drawing
_____ organized ideas (even if they weren't written down) into a pattern that made the message clear
_____ written text made sense standing alone (you can read the invented spelling, the ideas are organized, and it made sense without referring to the drawing)

Reading the Message

_____ refused to read or to pretend read
_____ pretended to read with no focus on print
_____ pretended to read while focusing on print
_____ read own writing with difficulty
_____ read own writing with relative ease
Other observations, comments, and notes:

Source: Reprinted from *The Emergent Reading and Writing Evaluation: A Reliability and Content Validity Study,* by M. Jones, 1989, Unpublished Doctoral Dissertation. This assessment tool is reprinted by permission of the author. Contributing authors to this assessment tool include L.K. Rhodes and consultants and teachers in the Denver Public Schools.

FIGURE 8.8 My child as a reader

Name _____ Date _____

Teacher _____ Grade _____

My Child as a Reader
(An Observational Guide for Parents)

With a vertical slash on the line indicate where you see your child's interest and participation in the reading process. Make comments or give examples of behaviors observed.

Never	Seldom	Sometimes	Often
(shows little interest)		(shows enthusiasm and attention)	

1. My child likes me to read to him or her. (e.g., brings books from school library to share; likes regular bedtime stories)

2. My child reads stories to me. (e.g., shares stories he or she has read at school; reads or attempts to read his or her own books and library books)

3. My child attempts to read in everyday situations. (e.g., street signs; store signs; cereal boxes, etc.)

4. My child can retell a story so that I can understand it. (e.g., retells a story heard at school; retells a story to a brother, sister, or friend)

5. My child figures out new words he or she sees. (e.g., uses letter sounds and meaning clues to read a store or street sign; perseveres in figuring out unknown words in a story)

6. When my child reads he or she "guesses" at words, but they usually make sense in the story. (e.g., the story might say "John was racing home" but child reads, "John was running home.")

Comments: _____
_____

Source: Reprinted from "My Child as a Reader" by Dawn Jamieson. In *Literacy Assessment: A Handbook of Instruments* edited by Lynn K. Rhodes (Heinemann, A division of Greenwood Publishing Group, Portsmouth, NH, 1993).

Observing Independent Readers and Writers

To observe which sources of information independent readers use to identify unknown words and construct meaning from print, teachers can record and analyze the reading strategies employed (Figure 8.9) and the **miscues** (deviations from print) readers make when reading. Miscues can be recorded during a structured observation by using an informal reading inventory (several published inventories are available) or a *Reading Miscue Inventory* (Goodman, Watson, & Burke, 1987) or by taping an oral reading record during a reading conference. Several formats and processes are available to help teachers in analyzing miscues. Each is accompanied by specific instructional suggestions based on the results of the analysis. One such format is provided in Figure 8.10. After selecting a procedure for miscue analysis, it is imperative that teachers thoughtfully read accompanying information

FIGURE 8.9 Reading strategies checklist

Name _____

#1 Book Title _____ Date _____

#2 Book Title _____ Date _____

#3 Book Title _____ Date _____

	#1	#2	#3

Miscues Observed:

- Substitutes but keeps intended meaning (cat/kitten)
- Substitutes similar parts of speech (syntax: ran/jumped)
- Substitutes graphophonically similar words (cat/can)
- Substitutes nonsense words (caten)
- Skips words
- Inserts words
- Self-corrects miscues

Flow: (e.g., choppy, word by word, fluent, struggling)

Reading Strategies the Child Uses:

- Anticipates content
- Uses picture cues
- Starts over and rereads whole sentence
- Uses graphophonics (beginning/middle/end)
- Cross-checks information

Does the Child Monitor Her or His Own Comprehension?

- Recognizes when text does not make sense
- Attempts to self-correct when text doesn't make sense
- Recognizes when meaningful substitution differs from text
- Rereads to regain/construct meaning or flow

When the Teacher Mediates, Does the Child:

- Ask for help
- Wait for help
- Look for confirmation
- Resist help
- Use teacher cues to initiate problem solving
- Disengage with increased mediation
- Increase effort with increased wait time
- Require significant amount of wait time to process information
- Use general/specific cues to make connections

Characteristics of Text That Support or Hinder Problem Solving:

FIGURE 8.10 Analysis of oral reading miscues

Text	Reader	Self-Correction	Semantics	Syntax	Graphophonics
1.					
2.					
3.					
4.					
5.					
6.					
7.					
8.					
9.					
10.					
		%	%	%	%

Cues Used:

Cues Neglected:

Evidence of Cross-checking:

Instructional Implications:

FIGURE 8.11 My strategies for spelling

My Strategies for Spelling	Often	Sometimes	Almost Never	Never
Name _____ Date _____				
Teacher _____ Grade _____				

Name _____ Date _____

Teacher _____ Grade _____

My Strategies for Spelling

	Often	Sometimes	Almost Never	Never
During drafting . . .				
I write down the sounds I hear and keep going.	4	3	2	1
I write down what I think the word looks like and keep going.	4	3	2	1
I mark any word that doesn't look right and keep going.	4	3	2	1
I look around the room to see if the word is on a sign, bulletin board, chart, or somewhere else.	4	3	2	1
I look for the word in a book other than a dictionary.	4	3	2	1
I think about the parts of the word.	4	3	2	1
I think of other words I know how to spell that may be similar to the word I want to spell.	4	3	2	1
I think about the spelling rules I know.	4	3	2	1
During editing . . .				
I try to spell the word several different ways and pick the one that looks right.	4	3	2	1
I look in the dictionary.	4	3	2	1
I ask someone.	4	3	2	1
I know I'll use the word again so I put it on my personal spelling list.	4	3	2	1

Other strategies I use for spelling are:

_____

_____

Source: "My Strategies for Spelling" by Nancy L. Shanklin reprinted by permission. In *Literacy Assessment: A Handbook of Instruments* edited by Lynn K. Rhodes (Heinemann, a division of Greenwood Publishing Group, Portsmouth, NH, 1993).

about the analysis process and subsequent instructional suggestions.

Teachers should not relegate this type of observation to instructional assistants or parent volunteers. Teachers are responsible for curriculum and instruction. They must have firsthand knowledge of each child's understandings. Others can assist in the process only if they are properly trained and well prepared. They must understand not only what they are to observe and the protocol they are to use but also the reading and writing processes and children's literacy development.

Teachers also need to gather information about what independent readers and writers understand about spelling and the writing process. Examples of assessment tools that teachers can use to gather information and guide observations and documentations of spelling and the writing process are found in Figures 8.11, 8.12, and 8.13.

Name _____ Date _____

Spelling Strategies

1. Circle what denotes the writing student is doing:

   drafting   revising   editing

2. What spelling strategies does the student appear to be using?

   _____

   _____

3. What spelling strategies need to be worked on?

   _____

   _____

   _____

Cut here- -

Name _____ Date _____

Spelling

1. Circle what denotes the writing student is doing:

   drafting   revising   editing

2. What words is the student misspelling?

   _____

   _____

3. What are some possible reasons the misspellings are occurring?

   _____

   _____

FIGURE 8.12 Spelling strategies

Source: "Spelling Strategies" reprinted by permission of Lynn K. Rhodes: *Literacy Assessment: A Handbook of Instruments* (Heinemann, a division of Greenwood Publishing Group, Portsmouth, NH, 1993).

Meeting the Needs of Diverse Learners

Some children, including those with learning disabilities, may have difficulty learning from implicit literacy experiences. These children must have more explicitly planned and mediated experiences designed to help them develop the skills and strategies needed by all children to become literate. No secret or magical instructional methods will assist all children with special or specific needs. The use of authentic assessment is especially crucial to making appropriate instructional decisions for children with special needs. Young emerging readers and writers should be observed as they demonstrate their understandings

FIGURE 8.13 Questions teachers ask in writing conferences

As students begin to write:

What are you going to write about?

How did you choose (or narrow) your topic?

What prewriting activities are you doing?

How are you gathering ideas for writing?

How will you organize your writing?

How will you start writing your rough draft?

What form will your writing take?

Who will be your audience?

What problems do you think you might have?

What do you plan to do next?

As students are drafting:

How is your writing going?

Are you having any problems?

What do you plan to do next?

As students revise their writing:

What questions do you have for your writing group?

What help do you want from your writing group?

What compliments did your writing group give you?

What suggestions did your writing group give you?

How do you plan to revise your writing?

What kinds of revisions did you make?

What do you plan to do next?

As students edit their writing:

What kinds of mechanical errors have you located?

How has your editor helped you proof-read?

How can I help you identify (or correct) mechanical errors?

What do you plan to do next?

Are you ready to make your final copy?

After students have completed their compositions:

What audience will you share your writing with?

What did your audience say about your writing?

What do you like best about your writing?

If you were writing the composition again, what changes would you make?

How did you use the writing process in writing this composition?

Source: *Teaching Writing Balance Process and Product* by Tompkins, Gail, © 1994. Reprinted by permission of Prentice-Hall, Inc., Upper Saddle River, NJ.

of the form and function of print in their play (Linder, 1990), as well as with more structured **performance sampling.** The teacher must create the opportunity to observe these children in the process of reading and writing to determine each child's individual understandings, needs, and ways of knowing. Diverse learners need thoughtful, intentional, explicit, implicit instruction planned by a knowledgeable, observant teacher. Some children must further be supported with abundant and appropriate mediation as they interact with print. This instruc-

tion and mediation will help them develop the strategic processes and construct the critical knowledge and concepts required to become literate.

Evaluating the Literacy Environment

Most teachers evaluate children's literacy development in some way. Little attention is given, however, to the evaluation of other aspects of the literacy environment. It is crucial that teachers evaluate the physical (see Figure 8.14) and affective (see

FIGURE 8.14 Evaluating the literacy environment: Physical

Appropriate items for an observation checklist may include:

1. There is abundant, well-displayed, familiar children's literature. For emerging and beginning readers, a good portion of it should have a rhythmic or predictable quality to the language.
2. Dictated language experience stories, children's published writing, group-generated word charts or word walls, familiar songs and rhymes are posted etc.
3. Books represent a range of cultures, and characters in a range of roles.
4. Books represent a range of genres, conceptual levels, experiences, and syntax patterns.
5. Writing and art materials are readily available in all areas of the room.
6. The classroom provides a caring, safe environment.
7. Children do not spend inordinate amounts of time sitting at desks unless by their choice.
8. The room is arranged to maximize independence of children.
9. Areas are provided for individual, small, and group activities.
10. Areas are provided for quiet activities and for less quiet activities and conversations.

Source: Adapted from *Knowing Literacy: Constructive Literacy Assessment,* by Peter Johnston, p. 141. Copyright © 1997 by Peter Johnston. Reprinted by permission of Stenhouse Publishers.

A rich, inviting literacy environment is crucial to the literacy development of children in the primary years.

FIGURE 8.15 Reflecting on the literacy environment: Affective

Appropriate items for an observation checklist may include:

1. Emerging readers are invited, not forced, to participate in shared reading of books, often enlarged ones.
2. The classroom organization is noncompetitive, and literacy is not presented as a linear scale of sequentially more difficult skills or books to be mastered.
3. The classroom focus is on involvement, not on ability.
4. Exploration and experimentation are encouraged.
5. Risk taking and experimentation are encouraged and celebrated.
6. The teacher encourages diversity in response to books, kinds of writing, and interests.
7. Children talk with each other and the teacher a lot.
8. Opportunities for children to engage in oral language and conversations are highly valued, planned for, and encouraged throughout each and every day.
9. The teacher listens to the children—each of them—and faces them at their own level.
10. The teacher values each child's contribution to the curriculum and encourages each child to share his or her unique background knowledge and experiences with the class.
11. Children are encouraged to treat themselves and each other as authors, readers, and illustrators.
12. Children are encouraged to help one another and to seek help as they need it, but to be independent when possible.
13. Feedback to children about their activity is focused on how something was done and is framed positively.
14. Children are encouraged to evaluate their personal progress in reading and writing.
15. A caring, cooperative, collaborative community of learners has been created in the classroom.

Source: Adapted from *Knowing Literacy: Constructive Literacy Assessment,* by Peter Johnston, p. 141. Copyright © 1977 by Peter Johnston. Reprinted by permission of Stenhouse Publishers.

Figure 8.15) aspects of the environment in an effort to ensure that the environment, in general, encourages the literacy development of children.

Evaluating Instructional Interactions

Teachers should intentionally focus attention on the instructional environment (see Figure 8.16) to determine whether it is effective. Many times, a child's difficulties in becoming literate are directly related to ineffective and unresponsive instruction. (For additional information on literacy assessment, see Rhodes, 1993; Rhodes & Shanklin, 1993; and Johnston, 1997.)

FIGURE 8.16 Reflecting on the effectiveness of instructional interactions and on the instructional environment

Appropriate items for a checklist may include:

1. Children are read to often.
2. More literate others deliberately interact and think aloud as they read aloud to children. Questions are encouraged. Vocabulary and concepts are discussed.
3. Storytelling, singing, and role play are encouraged, along with reading and writing.
4. Children are given information and taught strategies and skills as they need them to become more literate.
5. The teacher carefully observes each child while the child is engaged in literacy events in order to become cognizant of what the child knows and how the child knows it; the teacher becomes aware of the connections the child is beginning to make; the teacher builds on the known and the developing connections.
6. Language is used playfully in the classroom.
7. Language development is a major focus of instruction, interactions, and mediations.
8. Invented spelling is encouraged when children are drafting or writing independently and the focus is on getting the thoughts down.
9. Invented reading (reading from illustrations and memory, and possible some use of print) is encouraged for emerging and beginning readers.
10. Children are encouraged to cross-check sources of information when reading (memory, illustrations, wordness, semantics, syntax, and graphophonics).
11. The teacher recognizes and builds on the contextual nature of the young child's learning, especially as related to reading and writing.
12. Classroom activities, events, mediation, and instruction are effective, efficient, and engaging.
13. Groups are formed for various and explicit purposes and always flexible and fluid.
14. If children are grouped, it is rarely on the basis of "ability."
15. Children are encouraged to read and write about their explorations and experimentations.
16. Errors are seen as interesting events from which one can learn.
17. Some (quality instructional and mediational) teacher time is spent with individual children and some with larger groups.
18. Within the first month of school, the teacher is able to describe the literate development of all individual children in the class in some detail.
19. The teacher is able to mediate literacy events effectively for individual children on the basis of his or her knowledge of the child's current literacy development.
20. Children are encouraged to be persistent and strategic in solving their problems.
21. Children are taught to be independent problem solvers, to think metacognitively, and to self-monitor their reading and writing for comprehension. The teacher gives wait time and encourages all children in the class to do the same.

Source: Adapted from *Knowing Literacy: Constructive Literacy Assessment,* by Peter Johnston, p. 141. Copyright © 1977 by Peter Johnston. Reprinted by permission of Stenhouse Publishers.

SUMMARY

As you reflect on what you have read in this chapter, reexamine your beliefs about the value of literacy and about the nature of teaching and learning literacy. Consider how your beliefs influence the numerous decisions you must make when planning an effective and nurturing literacy environment.

Whatever your beliefs may be now, remember that change is a constant. Just as literacy learning is a lifelong process, becoming an excellent literacy teacher is also a lifelong process. Excellent teachers continuously reflect, self-evaluate, and collaborate with colleagues to improve instruction. They seek out new understandings through participation in professional organizations and by reading professional literature. They have high expectations for children, for themselves, and for the educational community. They can make a positive difference in the lives of children.

REFERENCES

Durkin, D. (1966). *Children who read early.* New York: Teachers College Press.

Goodman, Y. M., Watson, D. J., & Burke, C. L. (1987). *Reading miscue inventory: Alternative procedures.* New York: Richard C. Owen.

Hall, N. (1987). *The emergence of literacy.* Portsmouth, NH: Heinemann.

Johnston, P. (1997). *Knowing literacy: Constructive literacy assessment.* York, ME: Stenhouse.

Jones, M. (1989). *The emergent reading and writing evaluation: A reliability and content validity study.* Unpublished doctoral dissertation, University of Northern Colorado, Greeley.

Jones, M., & Crabtree, K. (1994). Guide for observing emerging readers and writers. In K. Crabtree, *Accelerated reading: Early prevention for emerging readers and writers at risk.* Unpublished manuscript, Greeley, CO.

Linder, T. (1990). *Transdisciplinary play-based assessment: A functional approach to working with young children.* Baltimore: Brookes.

Lipson, M., & Wixson, K. (1997). *Assessment and instruction of reading and writing disability: An interactive approach.* White Plains, NY: Longman.

McGee, L., & Richgels, D. (1990). *Literacy's beginnings: Supporting young readers and writers.* Boston: Allyn & Bacon.

Mitchell, B. (1989). Emergent literacy and the transformation of schools, families, and communities: A policy agenda. In J. B. Allen & J. M. Mason (Eds.), *Risk makers, risk takers, risk breakers: Reducing the risks for young literacy learners* (pp. 295–313). Portsmouth, NH: Heinemann.

Ollila, L., & Mayfield, M. (Eds.). (1992). *Emerging literacy: Preschool, kindergarten, and primary grades.* Boston: Allyn & Bacon.

Rhodes, L. (Ed.). (1993). *Literacy assessment: A handbook of instruments.* Portsmouth, NH: Heinemann.

Rhodes, L., & Shanklin, N. (1993). *Windows into literacy: Assessing learners K–8.* Portsmouth, NH: Heinemann.

Taylor, D. (1983). *Family literacy.* Portsmouth, NH: Heinemann.

Tompkins, G. (1994). *Teaching writing: Balancing process and product* (2nd ed.). Upper Saddle River, NJ: Prentice Hall.

Children's Books

Carle, E. (1987a). *House for hermit crab.* Natick, MA: Picture Book Studio.

Carle, E. (1987b). *The very hungry caterpillar.* New York: Philomel.

Cole, J. (1986). *Hungry, hungry sharks: A step two book.* New York: Random House.

Cowley, J. (1990). *Grandpa, grandpa.* San Diego: Thomas C. Right.

Dahl, R. (1970). *The fantastic Mr. Fox.* New York: Knopf.

Greene, C. (1990). *Jacques Cousteau, man of the oceans.* Danbury, CT: Childrens Press.

Epstein, S. (1985). *What's for lunch: The eating habits of seashore creatures.* New York: Macmillan.

Heller, R. (1985). *How to hide an octopus.* New York: Grosset.

McCloskey, R. (1952). *One morning in Maine.* New York: Viking.

McCloskey, R. (1977). *Time of wonder.* New York: Puffin.

O'Dell, S. (1960). *Island of the blue dolphins.* Boston: Houghton Mifflin.

Peet, B. (1966). *Farewell to shady glade.* Boston: Houghton Mifflin.

Rockwell, A. (1982). *Boats.* New York: E. P. Dutton.

Silverstein, S. (1974). The homemade boat. In S. Silverstein, *Where the sidewalk ends.* New York: Harper & Row.

Smucker, B. (1987). *Jacob's little giant.* New York: Puffin.

Stolz, M. (1985). *Night of ghosts and hermits: Nocturnal life on the seashore.* Orlando, FL: Harcourt Brace.

Taylor, T. (1969). *The cay.* Garden City, NY: Doubleday.

APPENDIX

The premises underlying the integrated literacy program described in this chapter are consistent with the premises and recommendations for reading instruction prepared by the Early Childhood and Literacy Development Committee of the International Reading Association.

PREMISES UNDERLYING EFFECTIVE LITERACY PROGRAMS

Premises:

- Reading and writing at school should permit children to build upon their *already existing knowledge* of oral and written language.

- Learning should take place in a supportive environment where children can build a positive attitude toward themselves and toward language and literacy.

- For optimal learning, teachers should involve children actively in many meaningful, functional language experiences, including speaking, listening, writing and reading.

- Teachers of young children should be prepared in ways that acknowledge differences in language and cultural background, and should emphasize reading as an integral part of the language arts as well as of the total curriculum.

Recommendations

1. Build instruction on what the child already knows about oral language, reading and writing. Focus on meaningful experiences and meaningful language *rather than on isolated skill development.*

2. Respect the language the child brings to school, and use it *as a base* for language and literacy activities.

3. Ensure feelings of success of all children, helping them to see themselves as people who enjoy exploring both oral and written language.

4. Provide reading experiences as an integrated part of the communication process, which includes speaking, listening and writing, as well as art, math and music.

5. Encourage children's first attempts at writing, without concern for the proper formation of letters or correct conventional spelling.

6. Encourage risk taking in first attempts at reading and writing, and accept what appear to be errors as part of children's natural growth and development.

7. Use reading materials that are familiar or predictable, such as well-known stories, as the basis to provide children with a sense of control and confidence in their ability to learn.

8. Present a model for children to emulate. In the classroom, teachers should use language appropriately, listen and respond to children's talk, and engage in their own reading and writing.

9. Take time regularly to read to children from a wide variety of poetry, fiction and nonfiction.

10. Provide time regularly for children's independent reading and writing.

11. Foster children's affective and cognitive development by providing them with opportunities to communicate what they know, think and feel.

12. Use developmentally and culturally appropriate procedures for evaluation, ones that are based on the objectives of the program and that consider each child's total development.

13. Make parents aware of the reasons for a broader language program at school and provide them with ideas for activities to carry out at home.

14. Alert parents to the limitations of formal assessments and standardized test of prefirst graders' reading and writing skills.

15. Encourage children to be active participants in the learning process rather than passive recipients, by using activities that allow for experimentation with talking, listening, writing and reading.

Source: From *Literacy development and early childhood (Preschool through Grade 3)*. (1990). A Joint Statement of Concerns About Present Practices in Prefirst Grade Reading Instruction and Recommendations for Improvement. Newark, DE: International Reading Association.

The ability to think mathematically is not a lesson objective but a long-range goal, and natural learning doesn't happen on a schedule. It's essential that teachers give the time needed for children not only to work through activities that promote thinking, but also to reflect on that thinking whenever possible. Children's experiences in mathematics need to be exciting and fun, not in the sense of easy or trivial, but in the sense of engaging them fully and keeping them involved in the investigation.

(Burns, 1985, p. 49)

9

Mathematics in the Primary Years

CONSIDER YOUR BELIEFS

- What do you believe is the nature of mathematics and the process of mathematics meaning-making?
- What does being literate in mathematics mean?
- What do you believe should be the goal of mathematics in the primary years?
- What is meant by "mathematical power"?
- What do you understand about the nature of children in the primary years that might influence mathematics teaching and learning?
- What important criteria do you believe should be considered when thinking about including mathematics in the primary curriculum?
- What are the characteristics of a good mathematics program?
- What is the significance of problem solving in the primary mathematics curriculum?
- What do you believe is the role of the teacher in facilitating mathematics understandings?
- What do you want the primary child to understand about the discipline of mathematics?
- How do you encourage young children to have power in thinking mathematically?

This chapter addresses issues related to teaching and learning mathematics in the primary years. The crucial role of the teacher in facilitating children's understanding and appreciation of mathematics is emphasized, as is the significance of understanding the nature of the young learner. Throughout this chapter, the importance of perceiving mathematics as an integral part of every child's daily life is affirmed. By helping children acquire a deeper understanding about mathematics and become skilled at making meaning in mathematics, teachers empower them as successful problem solvers.

As you read this chapter, consider the countless ways children encounter opportunities to use and appreciate mathematics naturally, regularly, and meaningfully. This relevancy of mathematics in children's lives enables them to accord it an engaging respect and a comfortable familiarity. One major goal of this chapter is to help the reader become mindful of the importance of helping children discover the joy and wonder of mathematics and understand the many ways mathematics enriches their lives.

While riding in the car with her father one day in February, five-and-a-half-year-old Emily was wondering how much longer it would be before she would be able to attend the skating party sponsored by the parents of the children in her kindergarten class. "Is it the day after today?" Emily asked.

"No," replied her father. "It's the day after that."

"You're not listening to my words," exclaimed Emily. "Is it the day after today?"

"No, Darling," explained her father. "There's that day, then the next day after that."

At that point, Emily glanced out the car window and spotted a row of houses: "Okay, see those houses?" she asked. "It's like that brown house is 'today,' that white house beside it is the 'next day,' and that next white house is 'skating day,' right?"

"Yes," beamed her surprised father. "You're exactly right!"

CHILDREN THINK MATHEMATICALLY

Every day of their lives, in countless ways, children experience situations that provide them with opportunities to use mathematics and to think mathematically. How much juice should Jonathan pour into his sister Sandra's glass, his mother's glass, and his own glass so that they will each get the same amount? How much more money does Celia need to earn to pay for the minipack she wants? For how many more minutes may Lucas work on the computer before he must stop and get ready for bed? What size block does Manny need to fit across the archway of his playhouse? If Angela and Renea keep pedaling their bikes at their current rate, what time will it be by the time they get to the other side of the park? What are the other remaining shapes Kareem needs to complete his design? How many muffins can Gale, Lawrence, and Bootsie share and still leave three for Aaron? What combination of snacks can Tia and Wesley purchase with the amount of money they have between them? How quickly must Elisha choose a hiding place before Dayna finishes counting to twenty? Will she fit between the sofa and the end table?

The busy lives of active young children are filled with a rich variety of experiences that encourage them to ponder, question, reflect, and decide about possible outcomes that are not immediately clear to them. Many events of their lives invite children to investigate and think mathematically as a natural part of being a child. These **investigations** are most often spontaneous occurrences that arise out of healthy young children's ceaseless and unbounded interest in the world around them. The following vignettes help illustrate the seamless way mathematics can be found woven into the fabric of young children's daily lives:

When school was dismissed for the day, five-year-old Katlyn started running through the hallway toward the exit. As she ran, she started bobbing and weaving slalom-like, trying to match her strides to a zigzag pattern formed by the colored tiles on the floor. When the tile portion of the hallway met a carpeted area, Katlyn maintained the "pattern" of her stride and ended the "game" only after she burst through the doors that led outdoors.

Six-year-old Samantha had been contemplating what "a hundred years" meant. She remarked to her father, "Daddy, I know what a hundred years is; that's when we die. We don't die for a hundred years!"

Samantha's father smiled and responded, "Well, you and Ty might live longer, you're both so healthy."

Pondering her father's comment, Samantha replied, "You mean we might live like 5,888 years?"

In appropriate primary mathematics programs, the focus of the curriculum, according to Bredekamp and Copple (1997), should be on mathematics skills and problem solving. Children's competencies in these areas are fostered through learning experiences designed to help young children make connections with events in their daily lives, incorporating instructional strategies featuring spontaneous play and projects that are integrated with other disciplines, such as social studies, the arts, and science. Especially for children in the primary years, a variety of mathematics games and manipulative materials should be available for use in collaborative learning groups.

Investigating and thinking mathematically are more a function of the interest children show in things ordinarily and naturally, not things that take place only when children interrupt their childhoods, as it were, to take time to "study math." Young children's wonder about their world fuels their mathematical thinking and investigating. And the increasing understanding that flows from their active investigations more fully informs the ever-curious child about some

A variety of mathematics games and manipulative materials should be made available for children to use in collaborative investigations.

relationship that may be shared by some set of things in which the child has expressed a good deal of interest.

WHAT IS MATHEMATICS?

From the dictionary, one discovers that *mathematics* comes from the Old French *mathematique,* with the stem *math,* meaning "to learn." **Mathematics** involves the study of number, form, arrangement, and associated relationships, often using a highly formal system of symbols. More directly, mathematics, one of civilization's oldest and most fascinating pursuits, is a way of understanding the world. It consists of questioning, proposing, and trying out various strategies for arriving at conclusions and determining the accuracy of results. Mathematics involves searching and inquiring, and working in a way that invites reflection, action, verification, and communication with others.

Returning to the first vignette at the beginning of this chapter, we find ourselves at once bemused and sympathetic to Emily's plight of trying to determine (and to increase her temporal understanding of) the day of her class skating party. In her mathematics investigation, it wasn't the arithmetic that posed a quandary to her, it was the thinking about how to make sense of the situation that was the problem. For several reasons, this vignette is an excellent example of an event in a young child's life that required her to demonstrate skill in mathematical thinking:

- The question at hand, or the matter to be decided, was an issue that was "real" to the child—one that was relevant to her daily life, that originated with her, and that she chose to undertake with a good deal of interest.
- The procedures used by the child to help settle the issue to her satisfaction were

rooted in the depth of her intuition, experience, and natural way of thinking.

- After arriving at a solution, the child was eager to explain her own ideas. She communicated her thinking and shared the outcome of her efforts with another person: inviting (with her final "right?") verification and/or comment from her father.
- By his positive response, the father demonstrated his acceptance of his daughter's own way of thinking, rather than imposed on her a more formal, adultlike way of reasoning that may not have made sense to her.

Mathematics as a Search for Meaning and Understanding

In the example just discussed, Emily posed for herself a question for which no answer was immediately obvious to her. This activity—searching for relationships that aren't obvious—is a defining characteristic of mathematics. *Mathematics,* according to Robert Wirtz (1974), "is what happens when people look at a situation as others do, but wonder if there isn't something more than meets the eye. . . . It's the excitement of the search, the disappointment of false tries, and the thrill of discovery" (p. 3). At the heart of mathematics, according to Richardson and Salkeld (1995), is "the search for sense and meaning, patterns and relationships, order and predictability" (p. 23).

Let's consider a determining relationship among things that enable one to conclude that "this belongs but that does not belong"—the process of classifying. Children and characters on *Sesame Street* participate in a version of a classification game accompanied by the song that goes, "Which one of these isn't like the other? Which one of these doesn't belong?" The teacher holds up several objects, such as a baseball, an apple, an orange, and a banana, and asks, "Which one of these is not like the other?" The children might point to the baseball. "Why doesn't it belong with the others?" Their answers are often vivid proof that children are capable of inventive ways of expressing themselves when they need to. One child might point to the banana instead of the baseball; it all depends on how one looks at things.

Classifying—the notion of a determining relationship—is one of the most pervasive, unifying ideas of all mathematics. Which of these triangles are similar? Which numbers belong to this list . . . 2, 4, 6, 8, 9, 10, 12, 15 . . . and which don't? Which pairs of lines are parallel? Which numbers have an even number as a sum when added to 6? Which of these objects weighs more than the ball of Play-Doh? The following vignettes illustrate the natural circumstances by which young children develop a profound mathematical idea: skill at noticing distinguishing relationships among things.

Six-year-old My-Linh has five music boxes in her bedroom. Each night, her parents select one somewhat randomly to play as My-Linh drifts off to sleep. One night, My-Linh pointed to the music box with Peter Rabbit on it and said, "Play the long one, Mama, that one right up there."

Over a period of several months, My-Linh had discovered which music box played for the longest period of time simply by listening to them as her parents randomly selected them each night.

While getting ready for school one morning, Tony, a first grader, was approached by his father, who remarked, "Son, you aren't spending enough time on your teeth. You need to brush for about three minutes."

"Oh," replied Tony, "You mean I need to count to sixty three times!"

Tony was able to demonstrate his understanding of the relationship between seconds (counting to sixty) and minutes (brush for about three minutes) and to use this knowledge to determine how many total "counts" were required for brushing his teeth properly.

Mathematics as Different from Arithmetic

A brief discussion of arithmetic might be in order at this point. Very simply, there is much more to mathematics than arithmetic. *Arithmetic* includes adding, subtracting, multiplying, and dividing by using whole numbers, decimals, and percents. Arithmetic is merely a subset of mathematics, however. Moreover, when doing arithmetic, children have often come to learn, unfortunately, that a premium is placed on memorizing formulas and working as fast as possible to get the right answer. According to Marilyn Burns and Bonnie Tank (1988), when children do mathematics, "arithmetic is moved off the static pages of pencil-and-paper drill into lessons in which they estimate, invent algorithmic procedures, and use numbers in problem-solving situations" (p. 3).

In the Mathematics Their Way program, developed in 1976 by Mary Baratta-Lorton, arithmetic is presented as being oriented toward skill development and requires the teacher to act as a diagnostician. As noted before, computation skills such as addition and subtraction fall into the area of arithmetic. Mathematics, in contrast, is oriented toward concept development and allows the teacher to act as a guide and facilitator. Topics such as patterning and classifying fall into the area of mathematics. According to Wolfinger (1989), because mathematics develops the underlying concepts that will allow children to compute with understanding, mathematics should hold a position of profound importance in the quantitative program for young children.

Making Mathematical Sense

The past decade or so has seen a major shift from learning mathematics as accumulating facts and procedures to learning mathematics as an integrated set of intellectual tools for making sense of mathematical situations (Resnick, 1987). This view of learning is summarized in *Everybody Counts: A Report on the Future of Mathematics Education:*

> In reality, no one can teach mathematics. Effective teachers are those who can stimulate children to learn mathematics. Educational research offers compelling evidence that children learn mathematics well only when they construct their own mathematical understanding. To understand what they learn, they must enact for themselves verbs that permeate the mathematics curriculum: "examine," "represent," "transform," "solve," "apply," "prove," "communicate." This happens most readily when children work in groups, engage in discussion, make presentations, and in other ways take charge of their own learning.
>
> All children engage in a great deal of invention as they learn mathematics; they impose their own interpretation on what is presented to create a theory that makes sense to them. Children do not learn simply a subset of what they have been shown. Instead, they use new information to modify their prior beliefs. As a consequence, each child's knowledge of mathematics is uniquely personal. (Mathematical Sciences Education Board/National Research Council, 1989, pp. 58–59)

The following example illustrates the natural way young children think about things they experience in an attempt to make mathematical sense of them:

BERTA

As she was helping her mother bag up leaves one Saturday morning in October, four-and-one-half-year-old Berta became distracted by the honking of a large flock of Canada geese flying in formation overhead. Gazing transfixed at the geese as they swept across the sky in splendid symmetry, Berta asked her mother how many geese there were. "I don't know, Gum Drop, maybe about a hundred," replied her mother. Berta stared at the geese until they were out of sight. After a minute or two of silence, she turned to her mother and remarked, " 'One hundred' doesn't make you rich, Mama; only '101' makes you rich."

One can only guess how and why young Berta made the transition from the context of "how many geese" to that of "what makes you rich." For some reason, her mother's response with the number "one hundred" provoked in Berta thoughts about a bigger number (and perhaps for Berta, a *much* bigger number—101; and a number, moreover, that transported her conceptually from geese to wealth. Clearly, she had established for herself a numerical equivalence for the concept of rich. For her (for now), the number 101 works—that is, makes sense as a numerical referent for richness. Most interestingly, Berta wasn't taught this relationship between 101 and rich; she constructed this understanding—this sense-making event—on her own.

Children will experience greater success making sense of mathematics when they understand how mathematics relates to their lives. Teachers can help children think mathematically by helping them see how mathematics connects to everyday thinking and communicating. All children bring to school a rich understanding of mathematics; however, they quickly lose confidence in their own understanding if mathematics is communicated primarily as a way to "crunch numbers."

GOAL OF MATHEMATICS IN THE PRIMARY YEARS

The goal of facilitating young children's mathematics understanding is to help all children develop mathematical power (National Council of Teachers of Mathematics [NCTM], 1989; Rowan & Bourne, 1994). The National Council of Teachers of Mathematics (NCTM) explains that **mathematical power** denotes an individual's abilities to explore, conjecture, and reason logically, as well as to use a variety of mathematical methods effectively to solve nonroutine problems. This notion is based on recognition of mathematics as more than a collection of concepts and skills to be mastered; it includes methods of investigating and reasoning, means of communication, and notions of context.

Helping Children Acquire Mathematical Power

Helping children acquire mathematical power involves helping instill in them the desire to be transactors in learning, even as teachers help them master the tools of making transactions (observing, inquiring, organizing information, reasoning, reflecting, and communicating). In addition, for each individual, "mathematical power involves the development of personal self-confidence" (NCTM, 1989, p. iii). Consider the following example:

Shortly after putting Monique to bed one evening, her father went into the kitchen and started cracking walnuts for a late snack. The nutcracker produced a loud "Craaaaccck!" each time a nut was cracked.

Monique: Who's doing that?!

Mother: It's Daddy cracking nuts.

Monique: Well, will someone tell him to be quiet doing it?

Father: Sorry. I'll just do three more. [Craaaaccck! Craaaaccck!]

Monique: Just one more!

Father: [Craaaaccck!]

Monique: OK, that's all!

In this example, Monique demonstrated considerable mathematical power. Not only was she able to compute in her head how many nuts remained to be cracked, but she was also able to apply her ability to subtract and to effectively communicate her knowledge, her feelings, and her confidence to others. The following vignette illustrates mathematical power a bit differently:

As her older sister, Rebecca, sat listening nearby, five-year-old Heidi was reciting some beginning addition facts:

Heidi: One plus one equals two. Two plus two equals four. Four plus four equals six . . .

Rebecca: No, Heidi, four plus four equals eight.

Heidi: [Looking scornfully at her sister] Well, I can make it whatever I want!

The willfulness in asserting her right to make her mathematics "whatever I want," which young Heidi displays in this vignette, is something teachers should take care to respect as they devote themselves to helping all the Heidis in their classrooms gain more accurate understanding of mathematics in their lives.

The NCTM (1989) perceives the concept of mathematical power as embracing five general outcomes for all children: (1) to value mathematics, (2) to become confident in their ability to do mathematics, (3) to become mathematical problem solvers, (4) to learn to communicate mathematically, and (5) to learn to reason mathematically. Moreover, included in the NCTM school mathematics curriculum and evaluation standards is the assertion that "schools should ensure that all children have an opportunity to become mathematically literate, are capable of extending their learning, have an equal opportunity to learn, and become informed citizens capable of understanding issues in a technological society" (1989, p. 5).

According to the NCTM (1990), success in mathematics through the development of mathematical power includes

> the ability to explore, conjecture, and reason logically; to solve nonroutine problems; to communicate about and through mathematics; and to connect ideas within mathematics and between mathematics and other intellectual activity. Mathematical power also involves the development of personal self-confidence and a disposition to seek, evaluate, and use quantitative and spatial information in solving problems and in making decisions. Children's flexibility, perseverance, interest, curiosity, and inventiveness also affect the realization of mathematical power. (p. 1)

In the view of Richardson and Salkeld (1995), "mathematical power develops in children who learn that mathematics makes sense and who learn to trust their own abilities to make sense of mathematics" (p. 23).

Mathematics Begins with Children's Interests

Teachers' understanding of the goal of facilitating young children's mathematical power is ex-

tended by the position advanced by the National Association for the Education of Young Children (NAEYC). A mathematics program for primary-age children that is developmentally appropriate "enables children to use math through exploration, discovery, and solving meaningful problems. Math activities are integrated with other relevant projects, such as science and social studies. Math skills are acquired through spontaneous play, projects, and situations of daily living" (NAEYC, 1989, p. 12). According to the NAEYC, in a developmentally appropriate math program for children in the primary years, teachers use the teacher's edition of the mathematics textbook as a guide to structuring learning situations and to stimulating ideas about interesting math projects. In such a program, many manipulative materials, as well as child-oriented board and card games and paper-and-pencil games, are provided and used. Consider the following example:

MRS. SANTOMASO'S CLASS

In Mrs. Santomaso's class of 7- and 8-year olds, a field trip to the museum of natural history stimulated a lively discussion about the different types of dwellings that people of different cultures lived in. Over the next several days, Mrs. Santomaso helped extend the children's understanding of the topic by providing books, magazines, and computerized encyclopedias for them to review. On one occasion, Mrs. Santomaso invited a fifth-grader to share a model of an Anasazi (Pueblo) cliff dwelling she had made. On another occasion, an architect who worked for a local building contractor shared with the class some ideas that people consider when designing a new home.

The following week, Mrs. Santomaso organized the class into cooperative groups to design and build a dwelling the group members believed would be appropriate for a geographic region and climate of their own choosing. One group decided to design and build a house to accommodate a family living near Antarctica. In their design, the group decided that the roof should be curved "like an igloo" and that it should have lots of glass "so the sun could help keep it warm." Mrs. Santomaso encouraged the children to maintain a daily journal in which they described their progress through drawings and reflective reports.

For more than a week, the group worked on the Antarctic house, following the scaled drawing they began with. Using found materials (e.g., cardboard, paper, fabric, scraps of wood, cellophane), they constructed the walls and roof of the house; built interior walls; designed, cut out, and constructed furniture, appliances, and utility fixtures scaled to accommodate a doll family they acquired; and even planned for an active solar system backed up by a collection of "storage batteries." At one point, the roof collapsed, necessitating a redesign and construction of a new roof.

Even such decisions as painting the house posed some problems. They decided to paint the house "olive brown" and had to experiment with several color combinations before deciding on the right mixture of yellow, blue, and red ("Do we need any green?"). Once they started painting, they discovered they hadn't prepared enough paint. They had to remix the paint and experienced the frustration of producing several mismatches to the brown they had started with before finally getting an acceptable match.

On completion of their projects, the groups shared their accomplishments with the class. Their structures and the accompanying journals were displayed in the school cafeteria so that the entire student body, staff, and visiting parents could enjoy their achievements.

The project just described illustrates how a teacher can capitalize on a theme in which children have expressed interest to provide a rich and stimulating context in which a host of mathematical investigations can occur.

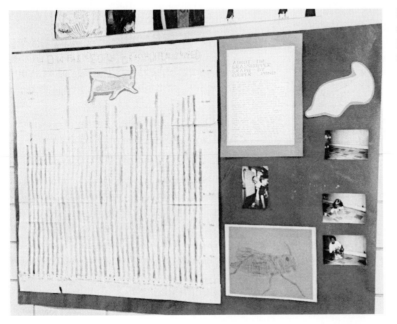

Integrated, project-based activities provide children with a rich context for investigating mathematics.

Engaging Children in Mathematics

As Mrs. Santomaso's children met in their groups over a period of several weeks to discuss, design, collect materials for, construct, record data about, and describe their projects, they were actively engaged in a wide range of mathematical processes: questioning; predicting; estimating; measuring; inventing; exploring spatial relationships; collecting; applying logical reasoning; problem solving; examining geometric angles, shapes, and linear relationships; performing arithmetic operations; and communicating. As they worked together, the children also experienced the importance of sharing ideas with others, dealing with differences of opinions, and organizing and agreeing on the delegation of tasks.

In the aforementioned project, the engaging in mathematics with a view toward its usefulness, rather than the doing of arithmetic, receives primary attention. Moreover, in this richly integrative body of activities, the children were actively engaged in stimulating literacy, science, art, and social studies processes as well. Through such exciting learning experiences, one of the fundamental goals of education may be realized: to help children develop an appreciation for carrying out and enjoying independent and cooperative investigations at increasing levels of complexity.

CRITERIA FOR INCLUDING MATHEMATICS IN THE CURRICULUM

It is instructive to consider different perspectives when examining criteria for including mathematics in the curriculum for the primary years: the NCTM's *Curriculum and Evaluation Standards for School Mathematics* (1989) relating to teaching strategies and curriculum content, and the nature of the young learner and of mathematical knowledge. These perspectives have implications for including mathematics in the curriculum and for implementing appropriate learning strategies and providing appropriate learning materials. In this section, these criteria are examined.

Assumptions Underlying Mathematics Standards

The NCTM researched, developed, sought feedback on, and refined a set of curriculum and evaluation standards for school mathematics over a ten-year period. The resulting mathematics standards, released in 1989, became the benchmark for other standard-setting projects—especially the NCTM's process for soliciting feedback from the profession and its ultimate focus on critical thinking and the application of knowledge to real problems.

Four assumptions underlie the NCTM standards:

1. Mathematics is dynamic; it's something one *does.*
2. Mathematics comprises a broad range of content covering many fields.
3. Mathematics learning and teaching are improved through appropriate evaluation of child understanding, of teacher strategies, of materials, of texts, and so on.
4. Successful mathematics programs mean mathematical power for all children.

In learning environments where these assumptions are shown respect and responsiveness, mathematics facts would not be learned meaninglessly. Arithmetic would be seen as relating to problem solving as phonics is related to literacy—as a repertoire of tools that may be of assistance in developing skill in much more compelling areas of human endeavor, such as critical thinking and decision making and problem solving. Against the backdrop of these four assumptions, a set of fundamental goals for children is emphasized:

- Children should learn to value mathematics.
- Children should learn to reason mathematically as a way to make sense of the world.
- Children should be able to present and interpret mathematics information.
- Children should learn to communicate mathematically.
- Children should be confident in their mathematics ability, confident that mathematics is something that makes sense to them.
- Children should become mathematics problem solvers.

The NCTM standards articulate a commitment to the belief that all children can gain power in mathematics by achieving some success in the processes of mathematics. All children can learn to "make" math; they can learn to be math creators. One way children can learn to become "math makers" is to create and write mathematics stories. According to Brown (1997), when children write about mathematics, they learn to communicate discoveries about school mathematics and connections to real life. With guided practice, children can learn to imagine, create, tell, write, edit, and share mathematics stories. A "mathematician's chair" (like an author's chair) might be a feature of the learning environment, and on a regular basis children would take turns sharing their mathematics stories with their peers. When children write about mathematics, they get excited about mathematical thinking, they produce a written record of their growth and understanding, and they engage in an integrated process in learning to write (Kroll & Halaby, 1997).

NCTM Curriculum Standards

The NCTM identifies thirteen curriculum standards for children ages four through eight. A list of these standards appears in the appendix at the end of this chapter.

In their discussion related to transforming mathematics curriculum, Richardson and Salkeld (1995) provide a keenly insightful perspective on these standards:

> [L]earning mathematics is an active endeavor. Children need to experience mathematics as problem solving: investigating, seeing what happens if . . ., and using mathematics to find out things for themselves that they do not already know. . . . Children need to understand that mathematics is about reasoning: making conjectures about why something is the way it is and then checking out those conjectures; thinking for oneself rather than trying to figure out what the teacher wants. . . . Mathematics is about communication: clarifying one's thinking by talking to friends, by listening to what they have to say, by finding ways to write down one's experiences and thinking with words, with diagrams and pictures, and with mathematical symbols. . . . Mathematics is about connections: seeing the relationships between mathematical ideas, seeing mathematics everywhere one looks. (p. 24)

It is no longer sufficient to interpret mathematics as comprising a set of skills to be mastered. Mathematics should be regarded as comprising large understandings or big ideas over which teachers want children to exercise mathematical power. As teachers work with children over time, "these 'essential understandings' are developed, elaborated, deepened, and made more complete. They can be explored in meaningful ways by the five-year-old as well as the thirteen-year-old" (California State Department of Education, 1987, pp. 13, 15).

NATURE OF THE CHILD AND MATHEMATICAL KNOWLEDGE

The work of Piaget has revealed to educators many surprising ways in which children think. In one of his classic experimental tasks, young children were shown two clumps of equal amounts of clay being rolled into two balls. Once agreeing that the two balls "had the same amount," the children watched as one ball was rolled into the shape of a cylinder. At that point, many of the young children believed that the cylinder-shaped object had more clay because, as explained by one six-year-old, "you can get lots of more pieces from it." A seven-year-old reasoned similarly when she replied, "There's more here (in the elongated object) because it goes from here to here (demonstrating with her outstretched arms), and the ball is just there." From this experiment, it was shown that when actions modify the shape of a clay ball, the young child is most likely to view the quantity as changing along with the shape or arrangement.

Children Construct Mathematical Understanding

From this kind of study and from many others, Piaget (Piaget & Szeminska, 1965) illustrated that no matter what the domain, young children think in quantitatively different ways from older children and adults. Piaget's work also demonstrated that children's "incorrect" ideas about the world reflect a unique subjective experience. When five-year-old Lucia exclaims, "The largest number in the world is eighty-eight hundred eight eight," for example, she is responding on the basis of a unique and personal perspective. The perspective of Chase, who replied when asked by his first-grade teacher what he thought "a few" meant, "Well, it's a little lot, and a little some," is similarly unique and personal.

No one told the children that quantity or identity changes as appearance or arrangement changes. Likewise, no one told Lucia that "eighty-eight hundred eight eight" is the largest number in the world nor told Chase his meaning for the concept of "a few." These ideas, therefore, must have come from the child—from his or her own effort to make sense out of experience. This is what

Piaget meant when he said that children construct knowledge. Moreover, according to Piaget (Piaget & Szeminska, 1965), children develop by constructing one level after another of being "wrong." Consider the following example, in which a teacher has just informed her class of six-year-olds that they will have a special guest:

Jan: How much longer 'til she gets here?

Ms. Vigil: She'll be here in about thirty minutes.

Jan: Are minutes "elephants"; like "one elephant, two elephant, three"?

Ms. Vigil: No, Sweet. Those are seconds; a minute would be like sixty "elephants."

On his last visit to the dentist, the dental hygienist gave seven-year-old RaJon a three-minute timer that measured the passage of time by sand passing from one glass funnel into another, just as time is measured in an hourglass. RaJon was instructed to use the timepiece each time he brushed his teeth so that he would be sure to brush for at least three minutes. As RaJon was brushing his teeth that evening, his mother noticed him trying to speed up the rate at which the sand was flowing by tapping the top of the timer:

Mother: What are you doing, RaJon?

RaJon: Three minutes is sure a long time, isn't it!?

Mother: Yes, RaJon, it sure is sometimes.

Jan will consider her teacher's response to her question about the length of minutes and compare it with her emerging conceptions about units of time. For now, her ability to establish a relationship between elephants and seconds serves her fairly well. In time, she will resolve any lingering discrepancies by adjusting her understanding on the basis of additional information (and skill at estimating) and then modifying her original conceptions.

In RaJon's case, his self-discipline and patience are both being tested as he begins to appreciate that time can seem to almost stand still when one is anxious to finish something. This real-life experience is important for RaJon. From the vignette, one cannot be sure whether RaJon believes that by increasing the rate at which the sand flows, the three minutes will be shorter. The anxiety he seems to feel over the length of three minutes, however, represents an insightful (if primitive) lesson in relativity. As he is afforded additional opportunities to connect real time to real-life experiences, his understandings about measuring time will continue to improve.

Young learners construct knowledge by creating linkages between new information and their existing conceptual frameworks. Young children's learning becomes more refined with each "course correction" that occurs with insight gained from discrepancies they encounter between their emerging conceptions and the conceptions they acquire from new experiences. Thus, a major point of constructivism is that each child has to develop by experiencing one level after another of being wrong.

In a mathematical context, children who have not learned number concepts will not learn them by filling out worksheets that typically require children to "write 5 next to a picture of five stars." According to Kamii (1985), number is something children construct by thinking in their heads about experiences they've had, not by simply completing worksheets. Rather than always doing math because the teacher says to do it, children should be encouraged to think about number when they feel a need and interest (How many candles are here? Who has the most blocks? You rolled a six, you have to go back!).

Cycle of Learning

One useful way of understanding children's learning is to see the process as a "recurring cycle that begins in awareness and moves to exploration, to inquiry, and finally to utilization" (NAEYC & NAECS/SDE, 1992, p. 16). To learn something new, according to Bredekamp and Rosegrant (1995),

> Children must become aware, be able to explore and inquire, and then use and apply what they have learned. This process occurs over time and reflects movement from learning that is informal, concrete-referenced, and governed by the child's own rules, to learning that is more formal, refined, more removed in time and space from concrete referents, and more reflective of conventional rule systems. (pp. 19–20)

This cycle of learning is constantly recurring because new knowledge or more accurate conceptions are created as the young learner applies existing understandings in a wide and complex range of ongoing experiences. This example of how the cycle of learning might relate to a specific mathematical context is provided by Bredekamp and Rosegrant (1995):

> In the understanding of a highly complex mathematical concept such as fractions, the learning cycle occurs over an extended period of time. In the early grades, children become aware of and explore the concept of fractions by solving real problems, such as dividing pies in halves or quarters, or building with unit blocks. Using symbols for fractions is not expected until later in the primary grades, after children have had many experiences exploring the meaning of fractions. (p. 21)

Logico-Mathematical Realm

In the illustration just cited from Bredekamp and Rosegrant, an allusion was made to children using unit blocks or concrete representations of pies. Children's interactions with manipulative materials contribute to their understanding of mathematical ideas by providing experiences with two types of knowledge identified by Piaget (1967): *physical knowledge* and *logico-mathematical knowledge.* The following example helps in understanding the difference between these two types of knowledge:

Sitting at opposite ends of the room, Ravi and Doreen were taking turns pushing small toy vehicles toward the funnel made by their spread legs. They interrupted their activity after a while and decided to divide the vehicles between them. They had eleven vehicles altogether, and they agreed that Doreen should get six of them because Ravi had first pick of the color and style he wanted.

In the process of holding and pushing their vehicles, Ravi and Doreen were building *physical knowledge*—knowledge of objects that can be observed. One acquires physical knowledge by manipulating an object; it is composed of physical properties that are in the object—for example, the weight or hardness of an object. The color and shape are also examples of physical knowledge.

In the process of determining that Ravi's largest vehicle, a green convertible, was larger than, but similar in weight to, Doreen's largest vehicle, an orange van, Ravi and Doreen were creating **logico-mathematical knowledge**—knowledge of objects generated by making a relationship between objects. The relationships longer than, different in color, two, and similar in weight are not observable in the objects and, according to Williams and Kamii (1986), can be created only by each child in his or her own mind: "The manipulation of objects is desirable in the logico-mathematical realm because young children think better when they physically act on the ob-

jects" (p. 25). As children grow older, they become able to group, order, or divide objects in their heads.

DISTINGUISHING CHARACTERISTICS OF A GOOD MATHEMATICS PROGRAM

When thinking about the characteristics that distinguish a good mathematics program, consider the notion of a classroom culture that is "mathematics friendly." In this section, different elements associated with such a classroom culture are examined.

Characteristics of Effective Learners

One major goal of education should be to help children learn to become successful lifelong learners. Learning experiences that children engage in at school should foster the appropriation of knowledge—an interest in taking possession of, celebrating, and preserving the wondrous things worth knowing about the world. The learning habits they acquire at school and at home will serve them all of their lives. Casey and Tucker (1994) propose that an *effective learner* is a creative problem solver able to harness that creativity through organizational and planning skills. In Figures 9.1 and 9.2, Casey and Tucker identify the characteristics of creative problem solvers and effective planners, respectively.

Good mathematics programs focus on problem solving—the principal reason for studying mathematics—and promote within a problem-solving context the skills identified in Figures 9.1 and 9.2. In addition to the elements related to an enriching, exciting, and meaningful mathematics program emphasizing problem solving discussed earlier in this chapter, effective learners share two additional traits:

1. *Effective learners are able to "talk" mathematics.* They exchange ideas, learn from

FIGURE 9.1 Characteristics of creative problem solvers

1. Problem-solving students are constantly curious and questioning.
2. Students enjoy figuring things out.
3. Students seek out challenges.
4. Students are persistent, often working for long hours on projects.
5. Students are resourceful and flexible in the way they approach tasks.
6. Students are independent learners, seldom relying on an adult.
7. Students feel confident about themselves as learners and are risk takers.

Source: "Problem-Centered Classrooms: Creating Lifelong Learners," by M. Casey and E. Tucker, 1994, *Phi Delta Kappan,* 76(2), p. 140.

FIGURE 9.2 Characteristics of effective planners

1. Effective planners think things through; they figure things out before they act.
2. Students organize their materials in a systematic way, gathering what they need in order to work on their project; and they find appropriate worksites.
3. Students are systematic in the way they approach different parts of the task.

Source: "Problem-Centered Classrooms: Creating Lifelong Learners," by M. Casey and E. Tucker, 1994, *Phi Delta Kappan,* 76(2), p. 140.

help children understand and interpret their world and solve problems in it. As in the example below, the more children can see themselves in everyday situations that involve mathematics (e.g., their ages, the number of trading cards they have), the more likely they are to be successful.

At school about midway through the school year, six-year-old Joanie proudly showed Tabby the tooth she had lost earlier in the day. When she got home, Tabby revealed to her mother: "I wish I could lose eight teeth—no, five teeth right now. Two in the back, two in the front, and—how many did I say? Oh—and one back here on the other side. Then I'd shout to the neighbors that I lost five teeth!"

According to Duckworth (1979), teachers can support children's struggles to make sense of data by introducing problem-solving activities that enable children to investigate actively the causes and effects of their actions on the people and objects in their environment. Almost any textbook activity can be made more personal by using data from the children's own world. Snacks, movies, softball

one another, and become mathematically literate. They learn to identify problems, even to create hypothetical problems, and then they learn how to solve them, often in several different ways. Effective learners are also able to explain their thinking and how they arrived at a solution. They are able to support their methods and ideas through thoughtful questioning.

2. *Effective learners are risk takers.* They are willing to fail and have learned that the road to success is often paved with failures. An effective mathematics program supports open, honest questioning by children. In this kind of program, children view errors, not as unfortunate mishaps, but as opportunities for learning. The classroom must be a safe place so that new and creative ideas can be tried out.

Personalizing Mathematics for Children

One of the NCTM's recommendations is to personalize the mathematics program as a way to uniforms, before-bedtime rituals, pets, and allowances are examples of subjects that reflect important aspects of their lives, and consequently, "through their writing, children will show a unique understanding of the process of solving problems related to their experiences" (Starkey, 1995, p. 195). *Personalizing learning experiences* refers to the fact that an ongoing relationship is evolving around children, the community, and the world of mathematics.

Using problems that occur naturally in children's play is another effective way of personalizing mathematics and helping children develop problem-solving skill. Why won't these pegs fit here? How many small blocks do I need to match the two large ones? What materials from the scrap box can we use to build the space station? Play is real life for young children, and problems encountered in play situations represent real problems in their lives and therefore are meaningful to them. Children who are encouraged to find and "play" with their problems (trying out various solutions) are more apt to learn generalizable skills and to be better equipped to cope with real-life problems than children who are presented with teacher-made problems and then taught one specific right solution (Tegano, Sawyers, & Moran, 1989).

Another excellent way to personalize problem solving for children is to provide them with opportunities to formulate problems themselves. As indicated in the earlier discussion about children as math makers, children can write variations for problems previously explored, problems that correspond to a number sentence, or perhaps a question that can be answered by investigating data on a menu, in an advertisement, on a calendar, or from a favorite book (NCTM, 1989).

Cooperative Interactions

When children explore new possibilities jointly, their thinking is not constrained by an expert who "knows better"; but rather is limited only by

Problems that children face spontaneously in play are a natural way for children to develop problem-solving skills.

the boundaries of their mutual imaginations. (Damon, 1984, p. 334)

Primary-age children can engage in interactive conversations with adults, as well as with other children, and can use the power of verbal communication, including jokes and teasing. The importance of providing primary-age children with opportunities "to work in small groups on projects that 'provide rich content for conversation' and that teachers facilitate discussion among children by making comments and soliciting children's opinions and ideas is one of the NAEYC relevant principles of practice" (NAEYC, 1987, p. 62). Thus, children working cooperatively in small groups is one important characteristic of a good mathematics program.

According to Burns and Tank (1988), a classroom in which social interaction and cooperative learning are valued and promoted provides children with support that is an essential ingredient for learning. When a learning environment is organized for cooperative learning, children are encouraged to work together and to explain their ideas, to listen to and question one another, and to agree on solutions. In this kind of environment, classrooms become more like communities of mathematical learners, rather than collections of individual learners.

Opportunities for becoming less egocentric are much more common when children discuss things with one another; they must acknowledge the fact that not everyone has the same perspective on situations. This exchange of perspectives allows children to learn how to take different points of view into account. Piaget (1959) argued that this was much more likely to be accomplished during the give-and-take of peer interaction than when a child was dealing with an adult. The sharing of differing points of view while attempting to achieve a common goal results in cognitive advance, and it makes cooperative problem solving a highly valuable aspect of the early childhood mathematics curriculum (Tudge & Caruso, 1988).

Use of Manipulative Materials

In the view of David Elkind (1988), **manipulative materials** are the most effective way to teach mathematics to young children. Primary-age children are not capable of thinking and problem solving in the same way as adults, and for this reason they still need real things to think about. Thus, although many children can use symbols such as words and numbers to represent objects and relations, "they still need concrete reference points. Therefore, a principle of

practice for primary-age children is that the curriculum provide many developmentally appropriate materials for children to explore and think about" (NAEYC, 1987, p. 64).

The rationale for providing a wide variety of manipulative materials and games to accommodate children's different mathematical competencies, according to Jarrell (1995), includes three important elements: (1) They allow children to handle concrete objects as part of their knowledge construction, (2) they pose questions that can only be answered with mathematical thinking (e.g., more and less, heavier and lighter, shorter and longer), and (3) they foster social interaction among children as they discuss their understanding of the mathematics processes.

When his mother picked him up from kindergarten, Liam proudly showed her several pages of construction paper on which he had created various geometric shapes by using glue and toothpicks.

> *Mother:* How nice. Did you do those in art?
>
> *Liam:* No, in pattern math.
>
> *Mother:* Oh! Mr. Cummings likes to teach math. Did he tell you that?
>
> *Liam:* No! Pattern math!
>
> *Mother:* Yes, that's math too.
>
> *Liam:* No, it's when you get to get out of your seat and get toothpicks—that's what I did.

Manipulative materials help children think and reflect about mathematical ideas. They help children develop understanding and provide tactile and visual opportunities for seeing mathematical relationships. Without manipulative materials, according to Burns and Tank (1988), "children are too often lost in a world of abstract

FIGURE 9.3 A sample listing of mathematics manipulative materials

Common Materials

toothpicks	raisins	beans
popcorn	macaroni	marbles
nuts	craft sticks	dice
washers	shells	rocks
paper clips	scraps of paper	boxes of various sizes
coins	straws	match sticks

Commercially Produced Materials

Cuisenaire rods	plastic counters	color tiles
Unifix cubes	base ten blocks	tangrams
geometric shapes	Hexaco blocks	
puzzle blocks	pattern blocks	

symbols for which they have no concrete connection or comprehension" (p. 5). Figure 9.3 is a list of some manipulative materials either available around the home or commercially produced that can be used to enhance mathematics learning.

It is important to provide children with time to explore freely any materials introduced in the classroom. The value of manipulative materials lies in the opportunities they provide for inquiry, exploration, problem solving, discovering relationships, and reflection, not in any intrinsic benefit they provide in and of themselves.

Integration Throughout the Curriculum

Children acquire broader notions about the interconnectedness of mathematics and its relationship to other fields when teachers relate one mathematical idea to others and to other areas of the curriculum. Teachers can help children make connections between how the knowledge they already have fits a particular problem by integrating subjects within broad sociocultural contexts.

The Project Approach. One effective way of integrating mathematics throughout the curriculum is incorporating a project or theme approach. The **project approach** involves an in-depth investigation of a particular topic that integrates the curriculum (language arts, mathematics, social studies, science, and the arts) and extends over a period of days or weeks (Katz & Chard, 1989). Rather than fragment the day into subject time blocks, the teacher can interweave the various subject areas around the topic of study. The project approach is child centered, and projects may be introduced by an individual child or group of children.

Describing the early childhood program at Reggio Emilia, Italy, which focuses on the use of projects to explore a topic over time and from many perspectives, Trepanier-Street (1993) mentioned a teacher who invited the children to collect and place into a box any items that interested them during their summer vacation. In one child's box were shells that led, not to an enriching project about the seashore, but to an equally promising one about what the child remembered most—the crowd. In their project investigations,

Manipulative materials provide tactile and visual opportunities for discovering mathematical relationships and help children in their thinking about mathematical ideas.

teachers using the **Reggio Emilia approach** encourage children to create albums filled with notes, observations, drawings, photographs, and anecdotal records. These albums provide evidence to children of their importance and the importance of this period of life.

When the *project approach* is implemented, children have the necessary time and multiple, active, concrete experiences to become absorbed and engaged in learning (Katz & Chard, 1989). They are involved in the selection of meaningful, relevant projects, in project development, and in ongoing evaluation. As summarized by Trepanier-Street (1993), through projects, "children develop cognitively by learning new concepts and by learning new problem-solving strategies or applying old strategies to new problems. They have multiple opportunities to represent, to elaborate and to refine their

thinking. They view themselves as problem-solvers and transformers of reality and develop a positive attitude toward learning" (p. 28).

GENDER EQUITY

Shortly after supper one evening, six-year-old Yenta remained in the kitchen to keep her mother company. Yenta's mother, a teacher, was preparing some geometry problems for her ten-year-old students to work on the following day with plastic Geoboards and rubber bands. Pointing to what looked like a very complex Geoboard puzzle, Yenta exclaimed, "Wow, that's a tough one; you better give that one to a boy!"

After finishing her homework, Emily joined her mother on the sofa and began playing Nintendo. After several minutes of concentrated playing, the seven-year-old paused to tell her mother how well she was doing:

Emily: But I've never gotten to Level III. Not even Becca has; it's too hard!

Mother: [Holding out her hand teasingly] Here, you need a professional to reach that level.

Emily: Or a boy. A boy could do it. They're lots better; they're so into cool stuff.

Mother: What are girls into?

Emily: [Pausing to think] Pretty things.

Mother: Do you think that's the way it's supposed to be?

Emily: Yes.

Young girls start out on a par with young boys in mathematical and problem-solving ability, but many of them lose confidence in this sometime during the school years. An important characteristic of good mathematics programs for young children is that they build every child's interest in mathematics and every child's confidence in his or her ability. Greenberg (1994) advances strategies that, if followed, can help teachers become more sensitive and responsive to issues of gender equity:

- Set a good example. Let children see that we notice and use math in our daily life with them. Show children that we have fun with math.

- Structure math learning activities so that each child will be able to achieve success.

- Give as many turns to girls as to boys—turns of equal length. Practice is critically important in creating comfort and confidence.

- Compliment each child on his or her accomplishment. Keep track; give equal attention and encouragement to girls.

- Encourage cooperation within the mixed-sex small groups you work with. Encourage children to help each other—especially girls to help boys. Avoid letting any child dominate the group.

- Place in the mathematics center a variety of books containing pictures of both women and men mathematicians, scientists, and engineers. Avoid using *he* more than *she* when talking about mathematicians and scientists. It's as important to counter in boys society's stereotypes regarding mathematics as a masculine, not feminine, subject, as it is to counter it in girls.

- Be sure to alert parents to stereotypes about "math as masculine." Encourage parents to make math seem as "OK" and as accessible for girls as for boys.

SUGGESTIONS FOR TEACHING PRIMARY MATHEMATICS

To support the development of understanding of mathematical ideas, teachers must create an environment in which children are actively engaged in thinking about mathematics. According to Bredekamp and Rosegrant (1995), teachers must be interested in what children are thinking and understanding. Teachers are constantly constructing the curriculum (making decisions about curriculum), and in the process, they need to know what concepts they want children to become aware of, explore, interact with, and think about. A teacher's task is to provide opportunities for children to learn by purposefully setting up the environment so that they are supported in the development of selected ideas.

Encouraging Children's Reflections

Often, children resolve a problem without understanding, or without knowing how to explain how the outcome was achieved. According to Goffin and Tull (1985), teachers' questions can challenge students to reflect on the thinking process they used to encourage the reorganization of their ideas into more adequate frameworks. Reflection can be encouraged by asking students to justify an answer, explain an outcome, or predict the consequences of an action. Teachers should be available as resources, facilitators, and probers, but not as authorities. Because good mathematics learning experiences provide opportunities for multiple successful approaches and solutions, support and encouragement are preferred over corrective comments and actions.

Role of the Teacher

By encouraging children to explain the purpose of what they are doing, teachers are better able to understand children's logic while affording children an opportunity to organize and communicate their thoughts. Moreover, children benefit from verifying their thinking for themselves, rather than depending on an outside authority. In addition to setting up appropriate learning situations and listening to and observing children, teachers should build upon children's efforts to think logically about a problem by guided questioning: Why does that make sense? What do you think of that? Can you explain how you worked through that? Does anyone have a different way to think about the problem? Does anyone have another explanation he or she would like to share?

Teachers promote mathematics learning by providing an environment rich in potential for exploration and by encouraging children to reflect on their actions. Observations should focus on what children do understand, as well as the understandings they still need to construct (Gelman, 1979; Goffin & Tull, 1985). When children hold

FIGURE 9.4 Major roles of teachers teaching mathematics

- Creating a classroom environment to support teaching and learning mathematics
- Setting goals and selecting or creating mathematical tasks to help students achieve these goals
- Stimulating and managing classroom discourse so that students and the teacher are clearer about what is being learned
- Analyzing student learning, the mathematical tasks, and the environment in order to make ongoing instructional decisions

Source: *Professional Standards for Teaching Mathematics* (p. 4), by National Council of Teachers of Mathematics. (NCTM), 1990 Reston, VA: Author

misconceptions, "the teacher can often help them come to new insights by providing additional experience that allows children to look again from another point of view. The teacher provides opportunities for children to consider, notice, and draw conclusions" (Bredekamp & Rosegrant, 1995, p. 29).

For a teacher to teach mathematics as envisioned in the NCTM's *Curriculum and Evaluation Standards for School Mathematics,* a vision of what a teacher must know and be able to do was developed. This framework emphasizing the teacher's major roles is shown in Figure 9.4.

In summarizing the variety of roles the teacher assumes as he or she engages with children in dialogues that advance their learning, Moll and Whitmore (1993) proposed a list of responsibilities very much consistent with the list developed by the NCTM in which the teacher serves as

- A guide and supporter who helps children organize their questions and ideas, translate them into manageable activities, and take risks in tackling new tasks within their zone of proximal development, thereby ensuring that each child experiences academic success.

- An active participant in learning who explores, experiments, and collaborates with children.
- A facilitator who consciously plans the environment and the curriculum and selects materials that foster children's purposeful uses of language and learning strategies.
- An evaluator who monitors children's individual and collective development, calling on this information to create and reformulate learning experiences to fit children's continuously changing needs. (p. 24)

Classroom Discourse

Like a theater production, classroom discourse has themes that pull together to create a whole that has meaning. The teacher has a central role in facilitating the discourse in ways that contribute to children's understanding of mathematics. The NCTM's *Professional Standards for Teaching Mathematics* (1990, p. 37) identifies some ways the teacher of mathematics should facilitate discourse by

- Posing questions and tasks that provoke and challenge children's thinking
- Asking children to clarify and justify their ideas
- Deciding what to pursue in-depth from among the ideas that children bring up during a discussion
- Deciding when to provide information, when to clarify an issue, when to lead, and when to let children struggle with a difficulty
- Monitoring children's participation in discussions and deciding when and how to encourage each child to participate

Figure 9.5 lists general principles that can serve as a guide for teachers attempting to facilitate classroom discourse from a Vygotskian the-

FIGURE 9.5 Vygotsky-based principles to guide teacher-child discourse

- Be sensitive to the knowledge, abilities, interests, attitudes, and cultural values and practices that children bring to learning situations.
- Arrange center-based activities that promote interactive problem solving.
- Promote and accept different solutions and strategies.
- Encourage children to tackle tasks within their zone of proximal development—that challenge and stretch their current skills.
- Offer many opportunities for modeling and engaging in higher-order thinking.
- Enrich communication: explain to children the purposes of classroom activities and experiences, and have children explain and justify their thinking.
- Use ongoing assessments of children's zones of proximal development to plan and monitor instruction.

Source: From "Vygotsky Revisited: Nurturing Young Children's Understanding of Number," by G. Jones and C. Thornton, 1993, *Focus on Learning Problems in Mathematics, 15*(2–3), p. 27.

oretical perspective. Note how similar these tenets are to the ones outlined earlier.

Extending Children's Mathematical Understandings

In an effort to find a way to deepen young children's mathematical understanding, Cobb, Wood, and Yackel (1993) designed a second-grade inquiry math program. At the onset of the program, teachers developed classroom learning environments that promoted joint inquiry: Listening to one another's ideas, expressing one's own thoughts clearly, cooperating with one another in problem solving, persisting at challenging problems, and attempting to achieve consensus about an answer. These processes were intended to encourage the idea of "negotiation of meaning," whereby the view that mathematics is an interactive as well as individual constructive activity is conveyed. In this program, according to Berk and Winsler (1995), children were provided with opportunities to build mathematical knowledge in collaboration with others; teachers and children form a social organization in which they mutually construct shared mathematical knowledge. The teacher's role in this kind of program is multifaceted, complex, and robust. It includes

> highlighting conflicts between alternative interpretations or solutions, helping children develop productive small-group cooperative relationships, facilitating mathematical dialogues between children, implicitly legitimizing selected aspects of contributions to a discussion in light of their potential fruitfulness for further mathematical constructions, redescribing children's explanations in more sophisticated terms that are nonetheless comprehensible to children, and guiding the development of shared representational systems. (Cobb et al., 1991, p. 7)

The learning environment just noted, with its emphasis on active, collaborative learning groups supported by a teacher who is ever-alert to capitalize on rich, unanticipated learning events to extend children's understanding, is echoed in the Reggio Emilia philosophy mentioned earlier. As in the inquiry math program, Reggio teachers, according to Abramson, Robinson, and Ankeman (1995), pay careful attention to all aspects of the environment, looking for ways to increase children's educational, aesthetic, and social opportunities.

According to Malaguzzi (1993), teachers in Reggio Emilia facilitate interactions within the context of small learning groups because such arrangements provide a social context that fosters meaningful dialogue, collaborative problem solving, and productive cognitive conflict. Children often collaborate on large-scale projects such as developing a poster campaign promoting conservation or designing and creating a classroom terrarium. Again, teachers are both facilitators and partners in learning as they work together with the children, not to cover a topic, but to "uncover" it. Teachers select topics on the basis of child interests and experiences and then help extend understandings through thoughtful questioning, by fostering collaborative inquiry, by encouraging an open sharing of ideas (promoting a conjecturing kind of classroom), and by allowing curriculum content to emerge from children's evolving understandings.

REFLECTIONS ON DIVERSITY

Children with diverse learning needs may demonstrate developmental delays in acquiring and applying various mathematical concepts and skills. These difficulties affect both computational proficiency and problem-solving abilities (Rivera, 1996). Teachers should adapt and modify their presentations of mathematical concepts to enable children to gain a clearer understanding of process, rather than mechanical and often incorrect skills. Also, the positive atmosphere of the classroom emphasizing concept development with appropriate adaptations for the learner will encourage risk taking in problem solving so that the understanding of concepts will be strengthened (Lock, 1996). According to Miller and Mercer (1997), individualization is needed if activities are to address adequately the needs of children with disabilities.

As an example of how the presentation of mathematical concepts might be modified to respond to individual learner needs, consider that children with disabilities will often benefit from extended experiences using concrete manipulatives and pictures before being able to transfer to the abstract level of problem solving (Miller & Mercer, 1993). They also may need mediation in finding the important aspects of the problem as they work with the manipulatives. According to Lambert (1996), careful planning must be used in developing learning activities to help move the child gradually toward internalization and integration of abstract concepts.

Children with learning disabilities and special needs can do well in an integrated, child-sensitive program when supports such as teacher mediation and peer support are provided. These supports are most effective as they apply to skills and understandings in varying contexts and in curriculum formats that are interesting, relevant, and engaging (Kataoka & Patton, 1996).

SUMMARY

Dear Mrs. Long

I like sckool and you to. I like math becoes its fun, callnging and sumthing you rumemdr all yore life.

Terrence, Third Grade

Teachers of young children face the exciting challenge of creating long-lasting impressions of mathematics that will inspire the children to continue building their mathematical knowledge. One way this can be accomplished is by helping all young learners feel a personal success with solving problems and making sense of the world. As children experience success and acquire a clearer understanding of things in their lives, they feel better about what they have accomplished and, more important, about themselves.

When trying to facilitate children's mathematical understanding, teachers are most likely to respond appropriately when they understand that children do not gain mastery of, or insight into, the world around them by being subjected to finely measured doses of discrete, isolated, and segmented concepts and procedures. Children learn as they live, work, play, and converse with peers and trusted adults in an environment that is psychologically safe. As children exchange ideas, according to Greenberg (1994), they challenge each other "to think, to reconstruct their ideas because they have new information and viewpoints. Play, with lots of thoughtful conversation, is what math for young children should be about" (p. 88).

REFERENCES

Abramson, S., Robinson, R., & Ankeman, K. (1995). Project work with diverse students: Adapting curriculum based on the Reggio Emilia approach. *Childhood Education, 71*(4), 197–202.

Baratta-Lorton, M. (1976). *Mathematics their way.* Menlo Park, CA: Addison-Wesley.

Berk, L., & Winsler, A. (1995). *Scaffolding children's learning: Vygotsky and early childhood education.* Washington, DC: National Association for the Education of Young Children.

Bredekamp, S., & Copple, C. (1997). *Developmentally appropriate practice in early childhood programs.* Washington, DC: National Association for the Education of Young Children.

Bredekamp, S., & Rosegrant, T. (Eds.). (1995). *Reaching potentials: Transforming early childhood curriculum and assessment* (Vol. 2). Washington, DC: National Association for the Education of Young Children.

Brown, S. (1997). First graders write to discover mathematics' relevancy. *Young Children, 52*(4), 51–53.

Burns, M. (1985). Questioning and mathematics. *Education Digest, 51*(2), 47–49.

Burns, M., & Tank, B. (1988). *A collection of math lessons: From grades 1 through 3.* New Rochelle, NY: Math Solutions.

California State Department of Education. (1987). *Mathematics model curriculum guide: Kindergarten through grade eight.* Sacramento: Author.

Casey, M., & Tucker, E. (1994). Problem-centered classrooms: Creating lifelong learners. *Phi Delta Kappan, 76*(2), 139–143.

Cobb, P., Wood, T., & Yackel, E. (1993). Discourse, mathematical thinking, and classroom practice. In E. Forman, N. Minick, & C. Stone (Eds.), *Contexts for learning* (pp. 91–119). New York: Oxford University Press.

Cobb, P., Wood, T., Yackel, E., Nicholls, J., Wheatly, B., Trigatti, B., & Perlwitz, M. (1991). Assessment of a problem-centered second-grade mathematics project. *Journal for Research in Mathematics Education, 22,* 3–29.

Damon, W. (1984). Peer education: The untapped potential. *Journal of Applied Developmental Psychology, 5,* 331–343.

Duckworth, E. (1979). Either we're too early and they can't learn it, or we're too late and they know it already: The dilemma of applying Piaget. *Harvard Educational Review, 49*(3), 297–312.

Elkind, D. (1988). Manipulatives. *Young Children, 43*(3), 2.

Gelman, R. (1979). Preschool thought. *American Psychologist, 34*(10), 900–905.

Goffin, S., & Tull, C. (1985). Problem solving: Encouraging active learning. *Young Children, 40*(3), 28–32.

Greenberg, P. (1994). How and why to teach all aspects of preschool and kindergarten math naturally, democratically, and effectively. (For teachers who don't believe in academic programs, who do believe in educational excellence, and who find math boring to the max). *Young Children, 49*(2), 12–18, 88.

Jarrell, R. (1995). Mathematics games to leap over old paradigms. *Association for Childhood Education International Focus on Early Childhood, 7*(2), 1–4.

Jones, G., & Thornton, C. (1993). Vygotsky revisited: Nurturing young children's understanding of number. *Focus on Learning Problems in Mathematics, 15*(2–3), 18–28.

Kamii, C. (1985). Leading primary education toward excellence: Beyond worksheets and drill. *Young Children, 40*(6), 3–9.

Kataoka, J., & Patton, J. (1996). Integrated programming and mathematics: An attractive plan for generalization. *LD Forum, 21*(3), 16–20.

Katz, L., & Chard, S. (1989). *Engaging children's minds: The project approach.* Norwood, NJ: Ablex.

Kroll, L., & Halaby, M. (1997). Writing to learn mathematics in the primary school. *Young Children, 52*(4), 54–60.

Lambert, M. (1996). Mathematics textbooks, materials, and manipulatives. *LD Forum, 21*(2), 41–45.

Lock, R. (1996). Adapting mathematics instruction in the general education classroom for students with mathematics disabilities. *LD Forum, 21*(2), 19–23.

Malaguzzi, L. (1993). For an education based on relationships. *Young Children, 49*(1), 9–12.

Mathematical Sciences Education Board/National Research Council. (1989). *Everybody counts: A report on the future of mathematics education.* Washington, DC: National Academy Press.

Miller, S., & Mercer, C. (1993). Using data to learn about concrete-semiconcrete-abstract instruction for students with math disabilities. *Learning Disabilities Research and Practice, 8*(2), 89–96.

Miller, S., & Mercer, C. (1997). Educational aspects of mathematics disabilities. *Journal of Learning Disabilities, 30*(1), 47–56.

Moll, L., & Whitmore, K. (1993). Vygotsky in classroom practice: Moving from individual transmission to social transmission. In E. Forman, N. Minick, & C. Stone (Eds.), *Contexts for learning* (pp. 19–42). New York: Oxford University Press.

National Association for the Education of Young Children (NAEYC). (1987). *Developmentally appropriate practices in early childhood programs serving children from birth through age 8.* Washington, DC: Author.

National Association for the Education of Young Children (NAEYC). (1989). *Appropriate education in the primary grades: A position statement.* Washington, DC: Author.

National Association for the Education of Young Children (NAEYC), & National Association of Early Childhood Specialists in State Departments of Education (NAECS/SDE). (1992). Guidelines for appropriate curriculum content and assessment in programs serving children ages 3 through 8. In S. Bredekamp & T. Rosegrant (Eds.), *Reaching potentials: Vol. 1. Appropriate curriculum and assessment for young children* (pp. 9–27). Washington, DC: Author.

National Council of Teachers of Mathematics (NCTM). (1989). *Curriculum and evaluation standards for school mathematics.* Reston, VA: Author.

National Council of Teachers of Mathematics (NCTM). (1990). *Professional standards for teaching mathematics.* Reston, VA: Author.

Piaget, J. (1959). *The language and thought of the child* (3rd ed.). London: Routledge & Kegan Paul.

Piaget, J. (1967). *Biology and knowledge.* Chicago: University of Chicago Press.

Piaget, J., & Szeminska, A. (1965). *The child's conception of number* (Rev. ed.). New York: Norton.

Resnick, L. (1987). *Education and learning to think.* Washington, DC: National Academy Press.

Richardson, K., & Salkeld, L. (1995). Transforming mathematics curriculum. In S. Bredekamp & T. Rosegrant (Eds.), *Reaching potentials: Transforming early childhood curriculum and assessment.* Washington, DC: National Association for the Education of Young Children.

Rivera, D. (1996). Effective mathematics instruction for students with learning disabilities: Introduction to the two-part series. *LD Forum, 21*(2), 4–9.

Rowan, T., & Bourne, B. (1994). *Thinking like mathematicians: Putting the K–4 NCTM standards into practice.* Portsmouth, NH: Heinemann.

Starkey, M. (1995). Their world. *Teaching Children Mathematics, 2*(3), 192–195.

Tegano, D., Sawyers, J., & Moran, J. (1989). Problem-finding and solving in play: The teacher's role. *Childhood Education, 66*(2), 92–97.

Trepanier-Street, M. (1993). What's so new about the project approach? *Childhood Education, 70*(1), 25–28.

Tudge, J., & Caruso, D. (1988). Cooperative problem solving in the classroom: Enhancing young children's cognitive development. *Young Children, 44*(1), 46–52.

Williams, C., & Kamii, C. (1986). How do children learn by handling objects? *Young Children, 42*(1), 23–26.

Wirtz, R. (1974). *Mathematics for everyone.* Washington, DC: Curriculum Development Associates.

Wolfinger, D. (1989). Mathematics in the preschool-kindergarten. *Dimensions, 18*(1), 5–7.

APPENDIX:
The NCTM Curriculum Standards

1. *Mathematics as Problem Solving.* Problem solving should be the central focus of the mathematics curriculum. It is a process that should permeate the entire program. Students should learn several ways of representing problems and strategies for solving them. Students should learn to value the process of problem solving as much as they value the solutions. At the primary level, most problem situations should arise from everyday experiences. Students should be able to:

   - Use problem-solving approaches to investigate and understand mathematical content;

   - Formulate problems from everyday and mathematical situations;

   - Develop and apply strategies to solve a wide variety of problems;

   - Verify and interpret results with respect to the original problem; and

   - Acquire confidence in using mathematics meaningfully.

2. *Mathematics as Communication.* Communication plays an important role in helping children construct links between their informal, intuitive notions and the abstract language and symbolism of mathematics; it also plays a key role in helping children make important connections among physical, pictorial, graphic, symbolic, verbal, and mental representations of mathematical ideas. It is important for young children to learn to "talk mathematics" while interacting with classmates. Writing about mathematics and reading children's literature about mathematics also needs more emphasis with this age-group. An important way of communicating mathematical ideas is through representing—translating a problem or an idea into a new form. Students should be able to:

- Relate physical materials, pictures, and diagrams to mathematical ideas;
- Reflect on and clarify their thinking about mathematical ideas and situations;
- Relate their everyday language to mathematical language and symbols; and
- Realize that representing, discussing, reading, writing, and listening to mathematics are a vital part of learning and using mathematics.

3. *Mathematics as Reasoning.* Mathematics is reasoning. At this level, mathematical reasoning should involve the kind of informal thinking, conjecturing, and validating that helps children see that mathematics makes sense. Children should be encouraged to justify their solutions, thinking processes, and conjectures in a variety of ways. The ability to reason is a process that grows out of many experiences that convince children that mathematics makes sense. Students should be able to:

- Draw logical conclusions about mathematics;
- Use models, known facts, properties, and relationships to explain their thinking;
- Justify their answers and solution processes;
- Use patterns and relationships to analyze mathematical situations; and
- Believe that mathematics makes sense.

4. *Mathematical Connections.* Children need to see how mathematical ideas are related. It is important for them to connect ideas both among and within areas of mathematics. Mathematical ideas also need to be connected to everyday experiences. Chil-

dren need to create relationships among concrete and pictorial models of concepts and procedures and to determine how they can be represented with symbols. Students should be able to:

- Link conceptual and procedural knowledge;
- Relate various representations of concepts or procedures to one another;
- Recognize relationships among different topics in mathematics;
- Use mathematics in other curriculum areas; and
- Use mathematics in their daily lives.

5. *Estimation.* Terms such as *about, near, closer to, between,* and *a little less than* associated with estimating illustrate that mathematics involves more than exactness. Estimation skills and understanding enhance the abilities of children to deal with everyday quantitative situations. Children should develop an estimation mind-set so they can use good judgment and logical reasoning to make decisions in their daily lives. Students should be able to:

- Explore estimation strategies;
- Recognize when an estimate is appropriate;
- Determine the reasonableness of results; and
- Apply estimation in working with quantities, measurement, computation, and problem solving.

6. *Number Sense and Numeration.* Children need to use numbers to quantify, to identify location, to identify a specific object in a collection, to name, and to measure. An understanding of place value is crucial for later work with number and computation. Work with number symbols should be meaningfully linked to concrete materials.

Children's intuition about number relationships helps them in making judgments about the reasonableness of computational results and of proposed solutions to numerical problems. Students should be able to:

- Construct number meanings through real-world experiences and the use of physical materials;

- Understand our numeration system by relating counting, grouping, and place-value concepts;

- Develop number sense; and

- Interpret the multiple uses of numbers encountered in the real world.

7. *Concepts of Whole Number Operations.* Understanding the fundamental operations of addition, subtraction, multiplication, and division is central to knowing mathematics. One essential component of what understanding an operation means is recognizing conditions in real-world situations that indicate the operation would be useful. Other components include building an awareness of models and the properties of an operation, seeing relationships among operations, and acquiring insight into the effects of an operation on a pair of numbers. Understanding the meaning of operations focuses on concepts and relationships rather than on computation. Students should be able to:

- Develop meaning for the operations by modeling and discussing a rich variety of problem situations;

- Relate the mathematical language and symbolism of operations to problem situations and informal language;

- Recognize that a wide variety of problem structures can be represented by a single operation; and

- Develop operation sense.

8. *Whole Number Computation.* The purpose of computation is to solve problems. Children should learn a variety of ways to compute, including the usefulness of calculators. Expectations for proficiency with paper-and-pencil computation should be reasonable. A developmental approach to computation fosters a problem-solving atmosphere in which children are actively involved in using materials, discussing their work, validating solutions, and raising questions. Students should be able to:

- Model, explain, and develop reasonable proficiency with basic facts and algorithms;

- Use a variety of mental computation and estimation techniques;

- Use calculators in appropriate computational situations; and

- Select and use computation techniques appropriate to specific problems and determine whether the results are reasonable.

9. *Geometry and Spatial Sense.* Geometry helps children represent and describe their world in an orderly manner. Spatial understandings are necessary for interpreting, understanding, and appreciating our inherently geometric world. Children need to investigate, experiment, and explore with everyday objects and other physical materials. Children must have many experiences that focus on geometric relationships; the direction, orientation, and perspectives of objects in space; the relative shapes and sizes of figures and objects; and how a change in shape relates to a change in size. Students should be able to:

- Describe, model, draw, and classify shapes;

- Investigate and predict the results of combining, subdividing, and changing shapes;

- Develop spatial sense;

- Relate geometric ideas to number and measurement ideas; and

- Recognize and appreciate geometry in their world.

10. *Measurement.* Children should experience a variety of activities that focus on comparing objects directly, covering them with various units, and counting the units. Children need to understand the attribute to be measured (e.g., capacity, length, weight), as well as what measuring means. Estimation should be emphasized. Children's initial explorations should make use of nonstandard units. Students should be able to:

- Understand the attributes of length, capacity, weight, area, volume, time, temperature, and angle;

- Develop the process of measuring and concepts related to units of measurement;

- Make and use estimates of measurements; and

- Make and use measurements in problem and everyday situations.

11. *Statistics and Probability.* The study of statistics and probability highlights the importance of questioning, conjecturing, and searching for relationships when formulating and solving real-world problems. Collecting, organizing, describing, displaying, and interpreting data, as well as making decisions and predictions on the basis of that information, represent significant applications of mathematics to practical questions. Statistics and probability are important links to other content areas such as social studies and science. Students should be able to:

- Collect, organize, and describe data;

- Construct, read, and interpret displays of data;

- Formulate and solve problems that involve collecting and analyzing data; and

- Explore concepts of chance.

12. *Fractions and Decimals.* Learning experiences should help children understand fractions and decimals, explore their relationship, and build initial concepts about order and equivalence. Physical materials, diagrams, and real-world situations should be used in conjunction with ongoing efforts to relate learning experiences to oral language and symbols. Decimal instruction should include informal experience that relates fractions to decimals. Students should be able to:

- Develop concepts of fractions, mixed numbers, and decimals;

- Develop number sense for fractions and decimals;

- Use models to relate fractions to decimals and to find equivalent fractions;

- Use models to explore operations on fractions and decimals; and

- Apply fractions and decimals to problem situations.

13. *Patterns and Relationships.* Identifying and working with a wide variety of patterns help children develop the ability to classify and organize information. The curriculum should give children opportunities to focus on regularities in events, shapes, designs, and sets of numbers. Physical materials and pictorial displays should be used to help children recognize and create patterns and relationships.

Relating patterns in numbers, geometry, and measurement helps students understand connections among mathematical topics. Students should be able to:

- Recognize, describe, extend, and create a wide variety of patterns;
- Represent and describe mathematical relationships; and

Source: From *Curriculum and Evaluation Standards for School Mathematics,* by NCTM, 1989, Reston, VA: Author. Reprinted by permission of NCTM.

- Explore the use of variables and open sentences to express relationships.

Within the context of each of the thirteen standards, there is increased emphasis placed on:

- Word problems with a variety of structures
- Use of everyday problems
- Application to real-life situations
- Study of patterns and relationships
- Problem-solving strategies

The principal goal of (science) education is to create individuals who are capable of doing new things, not simply repeating what other generations have done—individuals who are creators, inventors, and discoverers. The second goal of (science) education is to form minds which can be critical, can verify, and do not accept everything they are offered. The great danger today is from slogans, collective opinions, ready-made trends of thought. We have to be able to resist individually, to criticize, to distinguish between what is proven and what is not. So we need pupils who are active, who learn early to find out by themselves, partly by their own spontaneous activity and partly through materials we set up for them; who learn early to tell what is verifiable and what is simply the first idea to come to them.

(Duckworth, 1970, p. 139)

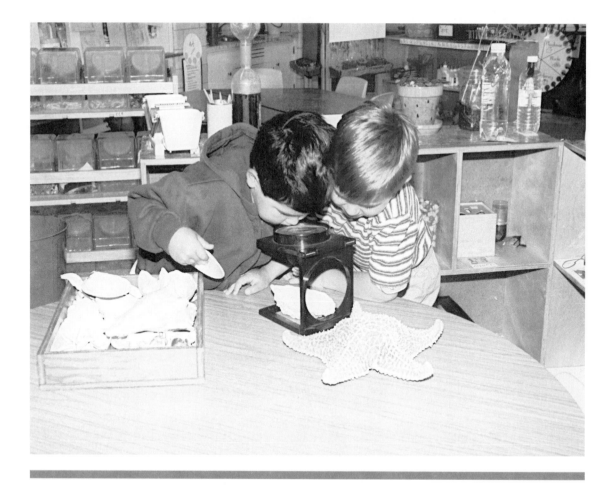

10

Science in the Primary Years

CONSIDER YOUR BELIEFS

- What do you believe is the nature of science and the process of sciencing?
- What does being literate in science mean?
- What do you understand about constructivist strategies for teaching or for learning?
- What is the role of teachers in facilitating science understandings?
- What are the characteristics of a good science program?
- What is meant by pedagogical content knowledge, and what are its essential elements?
- What is the nature of the young science learner?
- What do you want primary children to understand about the discipline of science?
- How do you encourage a child to think like a scientist?

This chapter addresses issues related to teaching and learning science in the primary years. Emphasis is on understanding the nature of the young learner, as well as on the crucial role played by the teacher in facilitating children's deeper understanding and appreciation of science. The focus throughout this chapter is on the acknowledgment that science is an indelible part of every child's daily life. To help children understand more clearly about science is to help them understand more about themselves and about their interactions with objects and with others.

As you read this chapter, consider how one might develop science learning experiences based on the interests of children and on the opportunities for developing science understandings that every child's busy life provides. Consider how science learning experiences might connect to children's lives, rather than center on isolated, disjointed topics "plucked out of the void" because it is the time in the week for science. Last, consider the wonderfully receptive state of young children—eyes and ears open, focused, amazed at all the world's wonders—and how one might continue to nurture this magical disposition to learn.

SCIENCE AND THE CHILD'S LIFE

As the little girl drifts off to sleep, her mother salvages from the wash the contents of her dress pocket—a wilted dandelion, a pigeon feather, some weathered twine that once held a scarecrow's vest secure, and a wing from a praying mantis. Smiling knowingly, the girl's mother carefully adds these treasures to the growing collection of memories residing in the shoe box on the dresser. These found objects join other discoveries in the box—a spider's egg sac, a piece of petrified wood, two keys, three child's teeth, and a small rock almost perfectly round—as concrete testimony to the wonders of science surrounding the young girl in the "laboratory" that is her backyard and the field just beyond. Before sleep finally overtook her at day's end, the five-year-old scientist discovered that night crawlers are slippery, that spoiled food smells bad, that spinning round and round makes her dizzy— and she almost discovered that bees sting.

For all healthy young children, each day is filled with opportunities to learn more about themselves and their world. One of the glories of childhood is that children are natural seekers, finders, observers, keepers, and collectors. Their waking hours are spent searching, examining, investigating, and wondering, awestruck by the richly diverse nature of things around them. Whether gazing in fascination at the commotion

provoked by a daub of spit on top of an anthill or tracking the course of "bark boats" swept through a street gutter by rain-wash, young children invest no small measure of each day happily and effortlessly engaged in learning as much as possible about their surroundings (Hagerott, 1997). In these boundless, absorbing pursuits of greater understanding played out daily in yards, streets, parks, fields, and forests all over the country, the fundamental processes of science learning (e.g., observing, experimenting, measuring, predicting, classifying, judging) so elemental to childhood are applied with singular objectivity, confidence, and naturalness. Thus, science can be seen as part of the child; it is not something a child does for just an hour now and then.

WHAT IS SCIENCE?

According to the dictionary, the word **science** comes from the Latin meaning "to know." It embraces all systematized knowledge of nature and the physical world derived from observation, study, and experimentation. The purpose of science is to make sense, to reveal what is in nature, from the largest objects in space to the smallest subatomic particles. Very simply, science is a way of looking at the world. It consists of asking questions, proposing answers, and testing them against the available evidence. Science, then, is also a way of working that requires verification of results and, according to Deborah Fort (1990), their communication to others. Studying science should lead not only to a better understanding of that subject but also to a better understanding of human problems.

Science is concerned with all of nature, medicine, and technology—concerns that are empirical, of course, but ethical and social as well. The responsibility of teachers and the function of science curricula are to prepare children for the decisions they must face as adults—decisions that daily become, according to the California *Science Framework* (Cal-

Children spend every day doing science: searching, examining, investigating, testing, and wondering.

ifornia State Board of Education, 1990), increasingly dependent on a clear understanding of science. Scientists reach conclusions based on evidence, and conclusions are always subject to modification based on new knowledge.

Children should be taught about evidence, developing questions, and how scientists reach conclusions. Teachers should show how the unique combination of reliability on existing evidence and tentativeness based on new information is the central characteristic and fundamental strength of science. Teachers should help children understand that nothing in science is decided just because someone important says it

is so or because it has always been done that way. In the free marketplace of ideas, the better new ideas supersede or absorb the previous ones. As pointed out in the *Science Framework,* this honest, open *competition of ideas* is a major part of the excitement of science.

As an important part of the primary curriculum, science, according to Bredekamp and Copple (1997), should build upon children's natural curiosity about the world. Science learning experiences for young children should foster development of thinking skills. Through investigative projects that involve children in active, collaborative explorations, these learning experiences should promote all children's active engagement in the *processes* of science.

As she was about to enter the preschool building with her father one wintry morning, three-and-a-half-year-old Kendra noticed a small pile of frozen bird droppings on the sidewalk. Running her fingers across the crusty surface of the droppings, Kendra asked, "What's that, Daddy?"

"Oh, that's bird doo-doo," replied her father.

On hearing her father's reply, Kendra examined her discovery a bit more closely and then declared, "No. It's not bird doo-doo! It's wood. It's wood, Dad."

Most children awaken to the wonders of the world in early childhood. Fueled by an innocent curiosity, they are touched by the mystery and magic of the universe while marveling at a flower blossom, caressing a caterpillar, or staring transfixed at the trail of a shooting star on a clear, dark night. There is wonder in all of this—simple, naive wonder at the why and how and if of the world. This wonderment, according to Holland (1991), is the subtle, driving engine that for centuries has pointed the curious toward science and the quest for knowing. The scientist revels in the questioning, the learning, and the knowing. That is why scientists do science. The learning. The knowing. The chance, in Holland's words, "to read an assembly manual for the universe" (p. 11).

SCIENTIFIC LITERACY: THE GOAL OF SCIENCE IN THE PRIMARY YEARS

The goal of teaching science is to help all children develop science power. Science must be perceived as a dynamic engagement in wonder-ing about and solving problems. Teachers must help children communicate science ideas clearly, to use a variety of concrete materials naturally and routinely in their learning, and to enjoy science and appreciate its power and beauty. Primary teachers must be committed to science power for all children in technological society. The experiences that teachers provide for children should reflect the notion that science is something individuals *do* (e.g., wonder, question, hypothesize, solve problems, observe, test, reason, communicate).

Project 2061, a massive program sponsored by the American Association for the Advancement of Science (AAAS, 1989), currently has six teams of elementary educators developing a plan to revise science education in the nation's primary schools. Members of Project 2061 make the following assumptions about the learning and teaching of science:

- The goal of teaching is to help all children develop scientific literacy.
- *What* children learn is fundamentally related to how they learn it.
- All children can learn *to think* scientifically.

As he watched his younger sister blowing bubbles in her milk with a straw, eight-year-old Ali looked at his father and asked, "Do you know why milk bubbles, and juice and water don't?"

"Tell me why," replied his father.

Ali explained, "It's because milk is thicker. It's got all of this stuff in it, and when you blow in it, the bubbles are thick. The bubbles are so thick, they won't break; they just keep going and keep going."

Empowering all primary children to think scientifically means they should understand the scientific thinking implicit in four fundamental questions: What do I know? How do I know it? Is it true? and What do I want to know? Ultimately, the scientifically literate person is one who is aware that science, mathematics, and technology are interdependent human enterprises with strengths and limitations; understands key concepts and principles of science; is familiar with the natural world and recognizes both its diversity and unity; and uses scientific knowledge and scientific ways of thinking for individual and social purposes. These perspectives, which are articulated most thoroughly by the American Association for the Advancement of Science (AAAS) in *Science for All Americans* (1989), are complemented by the five primary goals for science education in the early years advanced by Roger Bybee and his associates at the National Center for Improving Science Education (Bybee, Buchwald, & Crissman, 1989):

1. Develop children's natural curiosity.

2. Broaden children's procedural skills for investigating the world, solving problems, and making decisions.

3. Increase children's knowledge base.

4. Develop children's understanding of the nature of science and technology.

5. Ensure children's understanding of the limits and possibilities of science and technology in explaining the natural world and solving human problems.

DEVELOPING HABITS OF THE MIND

Perhaps it is most important that teachers help children in the primary years form the habits of mind that thinking like a scientist requires. Before teachers help children refine the intellectual tools for making intellectual transactions (reading, computing, questioning, writing), they must instill in children the desire to be transactors in the learning process. Children who develop appropriate **habits of mind** manifest an untiring willingness to try, to challenge, to question,

to explore, to test, and to examine. Children who have developed appropriate habits of mind demonstrate curriculum courage; they are willing, eager even, to take risks as they learn, and they are not afraid of frustration or even failure. Children who have developed appropriate habits of mind demonstrate a "passion" for learning.

How Learning Occurs

Learning is an active process that occurs within and is influenced by the learner at least as much as by the teacher and the school. Learning outcomes depend less on what the teacher presents than on the interactions among the information presented, how it is presented, and how the child processes it on the basis of perceived notions and existing personal knowledge. A crucial role of the teacher is to provide children with experiences that will help them extend themselves beyond current understandings to new insights—to help children make connections between what knowledge they now have and what knowledge they might desire or find meaningful.

In the primary years, children are building a basic mental picture of the world through such processes as observing, communicating, comparing, ordering, and categorizing. They are quite adept at identifying the characteristics of objects, determining similarities and differences among objects and events, grouping items together by some rationale, and communicating with others about what they have done. Children are natural observers, collectors, and categorizers. In the primary years, children should be collecting leaves, classifying animals, and observing the activity in a terrarium. Children in the primary years should be conducting "informal experiments" (putting a cup of ice outside on a warm day; mixing colors in a dish of water; combining different liquids; adding a teaspoon of syrup to a glass of lemonade; shaking a "smidgen" of baking soda into a small cup of vinegar)—experiments that ask, What would happen if . . . ?

SCIENCE AS PLAY

Four-year-old Billy idly picks up a ball-point pen from the kitchen table and begins tapping it on a cup while he keeps company with his mother. Almost absentmindedly, he taps a plate, then a dish. Before long, Billy is hurrying around the kitchen, noticing with great interest the different sounds produced as he continues his playful tapping on various objects—a chair, the tabletop, the cabinet, the refrigerator.

Educators have learned from the work of Piaget that the learning patterns of primary-age children are greatly affected by the gradual shift from preoperational to concrete operational thought. **Play** is the essential medium by which children progress along the developmental sequence from the sensorimotor stage through the preoperational and concrete operational stages exhibited by primary children.

A growing body of work affirms that children learn most effectively through a concrete, play-oriented approach (Hughes, 1991; Goldhaber, 1994). Through play-oriented experiences, children are actively engaged with objects and with others at a level of interaction that holds meaning for them. Much of the pace and direction of the activities is determined by the interests and emerging insights of the participants. In his little game with the ball-point pen, Billy's playful investigations led him to the discovery that different objects produce different sounds when struck. He also had fun in his investigations.

CHILDREN CONSTRUCT KNOWLEDGE

Children are "knowledge navigators," and although they may not always be learning the prescribed curriculum presented by the teacher, they are creating meaning for themselves all the time. From a constructivist perspective, children actively learn and constantly construct (and re-construct) their world. Young children build conceptual frameworks that are complex, highly organized, and strongly tied to specific subject matter. Learners construct knowledge by making connections between new information and their existing conceptual network—"navigating," as it were, the pathways between the naive conceptions they often bring to a learning situation and the conceptions they formulate on the basis of new experiences revealing some level of being "wrong." As a natural consequence of their attempts to gain insight from their experiences, children are constantly creating and re-creating theories that help them understand the world (Chaillé & Britain, 1997).

Cognitive psychologists and neo-Piagetian philosophers posit that young learners bring their idiosyncratic and personal experiences to most learning situations. These experiences have a profound effect on the learners' views of the world and a startling effect on their willingness and ability to accept other, more scientifically grounded explanations of how the world works (Watson & Konicek, 1990). Thus, when planning appropriate science learning experiences, the teacher must consider the learners' perceptions, interests, and passions. The teacher must "read" the learners, try to understand how they understand information, and then base mediation, guidance, and planning of experiences on his or her interpretation of the learners' understanding.

Seven-year-old Cindy stared as her father took several pills to relieve a headache. As her father swallowed the second pill, Cindy remarked: "What I don't understand is why you take the medicine in your throat and it goes to your stomach instead of putting it up here [pointing to her nose]."

A puzzled look appeared on Lucia's face as the first grader sat with her mother watching a highlight in black and white of a 1956 baseball game on television. After a moment or two of thought, Lucia asked her mother: "Was it really black and white back then?"

"Yes," answered her mother, "everything on television was black and white."

"I know," replied Lucia, "but I don't mean that. I mean in real life—like, was this sofa black and white, or this table?"

In both of these examples, children's natural wonderment about their world can clearly be seen. These moments of spontaneous curiosity emanate from children's everyday experiences and exemplify elemental "needs to know" in the purest form. Children's motivation and attention are highest in such instances, and teachers and parents alike are seldom afforded a more desirable or effective opportunity to share a learning experience with children. Capitalizing on such opportunities by offering a child enough information for even a little bit of reconstruction to occur (new meaning with keener insight) would represent a lesson well taught and well learned. The child's prior understandings (in some ways quite meaningful to the child, albeit not entirely accurate) are thereby modified—not so much "corrected," as "refined." As Chaillé and Britain (1997) might suggest, the new information the child acquires as a result of inquiry and investigation leads the child to develop new theories or to fine-tune existing ones he or she has built.

THE LEARNING CYCLE

Bybee and his research colleagues at the National Center for Improving Science Education have designed a teaching model that uses a constructivist learning perspective (see Chapter 1) within the context of a four-step **learning cycle:** invitation, exploration, proposing explanations and solutions, and taking action (see Figure 10.1).

According to Robert Yager (1991), many exemplary teachers instinctively use many procedures that illustrate the constructivist learning model. These include the following:

- Seeking out and using children's questions and ideas to guide lessons and whole instructional units
- Accepting and encouraging children's initiation of ideas
- Promoting children's leadership, collaboration, location of information, and taking actions as a result of the learning process
- Using children's thinking, experiences, and interests to drive lessons
- Encouraging the use of alternative sources of information from written materials, field trips, experts, video productions, and so forth
- Using open-ended questions and encouraging children to elaborate on their questions and responses
- Encouraging children to suggest causes for events and situations and to predict consequences
- Encouraging children to test their own ideas (answering their questions), their guesses as to causes, and their predictions of certain consequences
- Seeking out children's ideas before presenting the teacher's ideas or before studying ideas from textbooks or other sources
- Encouraging children to challenge each other's conceptualizations and ideas
- Using cooperative learning strategies that emphasize collaboration, respect individuality, and use division-of-labor tactics
- Encouraging adequate time for reflection and analysis: respecting and using all ideas that children generate

FIGURE 10.1 Constructivist strategies for learning

Invitation	Observe surroundings for points of curiosity.
	Ask questions.
	Consider possible responses to questions.
	Note unexpected phenomena.
	Identify situations where others' perceptions vary.
Exploration	Engage in focused play.
	Brainstorm possible alternatives.
	Look for information.
	Experiment with materials.
	Observe specific phenomena.
	Design a model.
	Collect and organize data.
	Employ problem-solving strategies.
	Select appropriate resources.
	Discuss solutions with others.
	Design and conduct experiments.
	Evaluate choices.
	Identify risks and consequences.
	Define parameters of an investigation.
	Analyze data.
Proposing Explanations and Solutions	Communicate information and ideas.
	Construct and explain a model.
	Construct a new explanation.
	Review and critique solutions.
	Use peer evaluation.
	Assemble multiple answers/solutions.
	Determine appropriate closure.
	Integrate solutions with existing knowledge and experiences.
Taking Action	Make decisions.
	Apply knowledge and skills.
	Transfer knowledge and skills.
	Share information and ideas.
	Ask new questions.
	Develop products and promote ideas.
	Use models and ideas to illicit discussion and acceptance by others.

Source: From *Science and Technology Education for the Elementary Years: Frameworks for Curriculum and Instruction,* by R. Bybee, S. Buchwald, and S. Crissman, 1989, Andover, MA: National Center for Improving Science Education. Reprinted by permission of NCISE.

- Encouraging self-analysis, collections of real evidence to support ideas, and reformulation of ideas in the light of new experiences and evidence

CONNECTING SCIENCE TO CHILDREN'S LIVES

A good science (and mathematics) program for young children, according to Kokoski and Downing-Leffler (1995), fosters the development of lifelong skills and attitudes. The most appropriate way to do this is to discover ways to make connections between learning experiences provided in classrooms and learning opportunities that children encounter regularly at home and in their communities. Moreover, *concepts*—the essential units of human thought—that do not have multiple links or connections with how a child thinks about the world are not likely to be remembered or useful. Expressed in another way, only that which is *connected to life* will be remembered for life. Concepts are learned best when they are encountered in a variety of contexts and expressed in a variety of ways; that ensures more opportunities for them to become embedded in a young learner's knowledge system (Rutherford & Ahlgren, 1990).

It is worth remembering that when a five-year-old explains, "There's wind because the branches on the tree are moving," or when a seven-year-old answers, "Because sometimes it's closer to us than other times," when asked why the moon sometimes looks very large and at other times very small, their answers are *authentic*; that is, their answers have meaning to them—make sense to them. If teachers consider these responses to be reflecting "alternative" or emerging or developing concepts, rather than simply consider them to be erroneous concepts, they respect the young learners' meaning-making attempts. From a diagnostic point of view, teachers also identify a point at which they might initiate a meaningful instructional experi-

ence or exchange that builds upon the concepts learners bring to that experience. The following vignette illustrates the point:

As Mrs. Weinberg greeted her seven-year-olds as they arrived at school through a downpour of rain, she overheard the following conversation among several of the children:

Janet: I hope it stops raining before recess.

Paco: Me too. Anyway, where does the rain come from?

Aretha: It's in the clouds; it falls from the clouds!

Paco: Yeah, but how did it get up there?

Janet: I know! The sun makes the clouds warm and gives them rain. The way they're shaped—the corners of the clouds—makes the rain come down.

Engaging Children in Science

Later that morning, Mrs. Weinberg encouraged the children to form small groups and discuss where they thought rain comes from. The children shared their ideas as Mrs. Weinberg wrote them on chart paper. In the succeeding days, she gathered materials and planned some activities she thought would help extend the children's thinking about where rain comes from. Her activities included the following:

- G.I. Joe's (the pet salamander) glass tank was set on the sunlit windowsill, and the children were asked to watch as Mrs. Weinberg covered it with a plate of glass. Throughout the day, the children were encouraged to observe changes in the tank and to discuss their observations with their peers.

- Early one morning, each child was provided with a clear plastic cup and was invited to go outside on the school lawn to cover a small patch of grass with the cup. About an hour later, the class returned to retrieve their cups and were asked to discuss in small groups what they noticed might be different about the cups.

- An unused fish tank was drafted for use as a terrarium. Everyone pitched in to add a variety of small potted plants, moss, and earthworms to a layer of moist potting soil. The terrarium was set on the windowsill, and several children volunteered to cover it with a sheet of clear plastic wrap. Again, the children were asked to observe the tank and to share the results of their periodic observations with each other.

As the seven-year-olds became engaged in these activities, Mrs. Weinberg guided some of their thinking: "What did you find on the lid of G.I. Joe's tank?" "How do you think it got there?" "What was different about your cups when you went back to get them?" "What have some of you seen around your home that reminds you of what we've been observing in these activities?" "Where do you think the water drops we've been noticing come from?" As she encouraged active discussion around these and other questions, Mrs. Weinberg encouraged the class to share any new thoughts about where rain comes from. She even mentioned such terms as *water cycle, evaporate,* and *condense,* describing them in terms she believed some of the children might understand.

These experiences were designed to engage children in observing, reflecting, discussing, and hypothesizing—processes by which their wonderment might be heightened and their understandings extended. For this group of children, the elements of the water cycle will be investigated much more formally some years later. For now, the wonderment stimulated in these seven-year-olds and the chance for them to share ideas with one another fully justified Mrs. Weinberg's responsiveness to the curiosity expressed by members of her class one rainy morning.

CRITERIA FOR INCLUDING CONTENT IN THE SCIENCE CURRICULUM

When the space shuttle *Challenger* exploded in 1986, some teachers wondered whether to encourage their children to discuss it. Most teachers seemed more easily receptive to discussing with their children the disclosure in 1997 that a sheep had been cloned. The same can be said of the report in 1996 of evidence of life on Mars found in a meteorite retrieved from Antarctica or of the Pathfinder exploration of the Martian surface in 1997 by the robotic rover Sojourner. These events, like countless others, illustrate the diverse and unpredictable nature of information that children encounter, and they help raise the issue of curriculum content. Too often, the classroom is regarded and conducted like a test tube or beaker in which only a few selected things are examined while most of life is excluded. Here, again, the notion of "authenticity" can be raised.

One measure of the authenticity of curriculum content is the extent to which the content is "real" to children (e.g., the extent to which children's lives or imaginations have been touched by an experience with an object or an event— the ability with which children can *make connections* to an experience). What could provoke greater child interest than the exploration of issues that affect their lives in so many ways? In many ways, the content of the science curriculum for the primary years is the investigations of the children's life experiences themselves.

SCIENCE LEARNING EMERGES FROM CHILDREN'S INTERESTS

According to the *Guidelines for Appropriate Curriculum Content and Assessment in Programs Serving Children Ages 3 Through 8,* developed by the National Association for the Education of

Young Children and the National Association of Early Childhood Specialists in State Departments of Education (NAEYC & NAECS/SDE, 1991), content for scientific inquiry is generated from children's interests and experiences with what is in their world and what is worth knowing about. For example, themes a teacher or children may draw from the natural world include rocks, sand, soil, plants, water, animals, sky, weather (wind, rain, snow), and seasons. Themes drawn from the human-made world include construction (building houses, offices, cities), transportation (air, land, water, space), communication (writing and pub-

lishing books, telephones, television, computers), cooking (from open fire to microwaves, exploring processes such as boiling, steaming, frying, baking, and freezing), and the human body.

The curriculum for three- through eight-year-olds provides opportunities for them to investigate natural and human-made phenomena. Children engage in the processes of predicting, gathering data, making observations, drawing conclusions, and making generalizations. The curriculum provides many hands-on, science-related learning experiences for children to raise questions and solve problems and to communi-

Content for scientific inquiry flows from children's interests and curiosities about what in their world (both natural and human-made) is worth investigating.

cate about the process and findings through a variety of representational forms (NAEYC, 1989).

Guidelines for Science Worth Knowing

Science for All Americans (AAAS, 1989) recommends a common core of learning (K–12) that focuses on the ideas and skills having what the AAAS regards as the greatest scientific and educational significance for scientific literacy. The AAAS favors including science curriculum content that has had great influence on what is worth knowing now and what will still be worth knowing decades hence. It identifies five criteria related to human life and the broad goals that justify universal public education in a free society:

1. *Utility.* Will the proposed content—knowledge or skills—significantly enhance the child's capacity for making personal decisions?

2. *Social Responsibility.* Is the proposed content likely to help citizens participate intelligently in making social and (ultimately) political decisions on matters involving science and technology?

3. *The Intrinsic Value of Knowledge.* Does the proposed content present aspects of science, mathematics, and technology that are so important in human history or so pervasive in the culture that a general education would be incomplete without them?

4. *Philosophical Value.* Does the proposed content contribute to the ability of children to ponder the enduring questions of human meaning, such as life and death, perception and reality, the individual good versus the collective welfare, and certainty and doubt?

5. *Childhood Enrichment.* Will the proposed content enhance childhood (a time of life that is important in its own right) and not solely for what it may lead to in later life?

Clearly, science curriculum content for the primary years selected on the basis of these criteria would hold promise for the development of learning experiences that reflect and enhance children's life experiences.

The National Center for Improving Science Education (Bybee et al., 1989) suggests six criteria for selecting and designing science curriculum themes and topics:

1. They build upon children's prior experiences and knowledge.

2. They capture children's interest.

3. They are interdisciplinary, so children see that reading, writing, social studies, mathematics, and other curricular areas are part of science and technology.

4. They integrate several science disciplines.

5. They are vehicles for teaching major organizing concepts, attitudes, and skills.

6. They allow a balance of science technological activities.

These six criteria emphasize the notion of "permeability." The learning of young children is "permeable" in the sense that they do not learn in the narrow categories often defined by adults, such as reading, mathematics, health, and science. As Elkind (1986) explains, the level at which young children learn has no sharp boundaries. Subject matter is not sorted out and packaged in neat, discriminate servings. Conceptual processing ebbs and flows effortlessly and naturally across subject matter boundaries, resulting in the generation of new concepts more holistically perceived:

> When young children make soup, for example, they learn the names of vegetables (language), how to measure ingredients (math), the effects of heat on the hardness and softness of the vegetables (science), and the cross-sectional shapes of the vegetables (geometry). It would be nonsense, however, to single out any one of these learnings as a separate lesson in one of the subjects listed in the parentheses. (p. 635)

DOING SCIENCE

Whether children come to view science an integrated whole rather than a fragmented collection of arbitrary topics and whether they ultimately come to value science will depend on how science is taught. Science is more than a collection of concepts and skills. For all children, it involves learning to think like a scientist—developing habits of mind from which flow a joy and excitement about engaging in "scientific" inquiry. Science involves methods of investigating and reasoning, ways of communicating science (e.g., writing, speaking, modeling, demonstrating, performing). It involves connections to all the subjects outside science in an active, constructive context.

Science experiences and teaching strategies designed to provide primary children with opportunities for conceptual clarification and change share one or more characteristics that complement the criteria for including specific content in the science curriculum just considered. In particular, these characteristics are associated with the extent to which a learning experience has *meaning* for the learner.

Science That Has Meaning for Children

Aspects of a learning experience closely associated with meaning include the following:

- *Physical Closeness.* Some things have meaning because they are physically close. They're hands-on, concrete. The manipulative nature of the experience often has meaning for primary-age children.
- *Psychological Interest.* One can hardly imagine three more abstract, complex things to think about than plant growth, dinosaurs, and the solar system. Yet, young girls and boys seem endlessly fascinated with these topics. In some topics, young children have a deep interest and motivation that can be built upon

even if the ideas are abstract and complex. If a teacher simply explores some topics with the children, they'll let the teacher know what things appeal to them.

- *Social Relevance.* Some things in the world of a young girl or boy are timely for her or him. Again, teachers need only consider what things might be socially relevant for children. What is in their society? What are they interested in, and does it really work for them?

Each of these aspects of learning experience closely associated with meaning can be seen in the weekend experience of two eight-year-olds whose teacher introduced to their class several activities promoting care of the environment. The two girls spent most of one Saturday busily drawing and labeling pictures related to protection of the environment. When asked what made them start doing that, one replied, "Our club. The name of the club is The Earth and Animal Savings Club. So, we just made these flyers and posters and reminded people to save the Earth!" The girls proudly displayed their work along the sidewalk: artwork promoting the importance of recycling; handwritten flyers with the message "'Save the Earth and animals please,' Kristen and Gizela"; even the words to a song they had made up:

BIO-DE-GRADABLE KIDS

We're Biodegradable kids, Yeah
We're, Biodegradable kids,
We're, Biodegradable kids,
You can look at us and sniff us,
And when you're through,
Just put us on the ground,
and we'll sink right through.
Yeah, we're biodegradable kids,
Yeah, we're BI-O-DE-GRAD-A-BLE kids!

The girls' enthusiasm for their work was unmistakable. They were cooperatively engaged, excited, and actively and thoroughly absorbed in their scientific purposes. And under the most natural of circumstances, they integrated several subject areas (writing, reading, music, science, and art) toward a common and compellingly personal (and scientific) focus.

Science as an Informal Process

Informality and geniality are two final criteria worth considering when determining the content of the primary science curriculum. What could be more genial (and natural) for a four- or five-year-old than playing at sand and water tables, rolling balls across floors, building with blocks, and exploring the different textures and patterns in a box of various fabric samples? In one worthwhile, if unintentional, science lesson, a four-year-old splashes with kitchen utensils at a water table full of soap bubbles, beating them until they become smaller and smaller. The teacher might comment, "I wonder why the bubbles got smaller?" Or the teacher may decide to simply encourage the child's pleasure in his experiment, confident that one day he'll ask why the bubbles got smaller, having already mastered the fundamental principle of cause and effect. With the right materials and the opportunity to explore, young children will discover things by themselves, and they'll be anxious to confirm their understandings by sharing their discoveries with peers or with an adult.

Six-, seven-, and eight-year-olds benefit from the same informality, suggests Chittenden, for the Educational Testing Service in Princeton, New Jersey (as cited in Begley, 1990). They could learn about natural change by feeding and observing caterpillars; by capturing the image of objects on a sheet of colored construction paper allowed to sit in direct sunlight for a few days; or by doing kitchen chemistry to learn about changes of state, such as from water to steam. They'll learn something about air pressure, nasal passages, and carbonation as a spray of soda pop escapes through their nose when they recall being forced to laugh after taking a large sip.

Children could observe the change that occurs to a glass of milk left uncovered for a few days. They could record change in the weather over a period of days or note changes in the position of the Big Dipper in the evening sky. These activities illustrate how curriculum can evolve organically out of the needs and interests of children as perceived by teachers and parents. These activities also reveal how teaching and learning often rely, according to Martin (1985), "on specific responses of teachers and children to each other, on mutual understanding and acceptance, on valuing children's gifts and creating possibilities for every child to contribute to the classroom community" (p. 24).

Consider how a pumpkin might be the object and source of meaningful scientific inquiry. A Halloween pumpkin might be allowed to rot so that children can observe natural changes in the world. For some such science activities, the teacher might decide simply to recognize the joys of discovery and to appreciate the pedagogical value of a moldy pumpkin. In many instances, the teacher might suggest that the children gather into small groups and describe their observations made over a period of days, sharing ideas about what is causing the pumpkin to change. A short time later, the teacher may encourage the children to reflect on their experience with the pumpkin as they observe over a period of several days the fate of a collection of colorful leaves brought in for display in the classroom.

DISTINGUISHING CHARACTERISTICS OF GOOD PRIMARY SCIENCE PROGRAMS

The National Science Foundation (NSF) maintains a list of contemporary science programs for elementary schools and exemplary science education programs and practices in the National Diffusion Network (NDN). A survey of the descriptions accompanying each program reveals several distinguishing characteristics:

Hands-On. The programs engage children as active participants in the learning process. Concrete, materials-based experiences are the most appropriate learning activities for children to develop more sophisticated schema and to acquire better understanding of science. Active manipulation of the environment is essential for children to construct knowledge. Children's actions on objects and their thinking about the consequences of their actions inevitably change their knowledge, reasoning, and understanding about their experiences. Indeed, materials-based, hands-on, process-oriented science programs foster superior process skill development, better attitudes toward science, and better achievement than do text-based programs (Shymansky, Kyle, & Alport, 1983).

Integrated. When science is integrated with other subjects, children learn both science and the other subjects more effectively. In these programs, the learning experiences draw on content and processes associated with other subject matter disciplines by planning, in many instances, around themes or big ideas (e.g., change, movement, endangered species). For example, children read, from the journals they have written, about a science experiment they have done involving predicting and measuring the changes in temperature of different objects left in sunlight. Once again, the boundaries between discrete subject matters give way before experiences that yield direct connections among language, writing, reading, computing, recording, and other skills.

Cooperative Learning. For such activities as problem solving, divergent thinking, and inquiry, which are emphasized in these programs, cooperative learning is most appropriate. Children's intellectual development is linked to their social development, which relies on reciprocity, mutual respect, and cooperation. As they engage in cooperative learning experiences, children learn to interact positively, share ideas and materials, support one another as they take risks, contribute to the group effort, and capitalize on the diversity of views among the members of the group.

Technology. Many of these programs emphasize science and technology. Technology has strongly influenced the course of history and the nature of human society. Technology is largely responsible for such large-scale changes as the increased urbanization of society and the growing economic interdependence of communities worldwide. It is appropriate, therefore, that new science programs for children introduce and develop science methods of inquiry hand-in-hand with technological strategies for problem solving. In particular, the programs should indicate that technology proposes solutions for problems of human adaptation to the environment.

Problem Solving. As in mathematics, problem solving is *why* one learns to do science. Problem solving exists only when the learner is unclear about what needs to be done to arrive at a solution. The teacher can pose tasks, but the learner determines whether the tasks are problems. The activities in most of these programs focus on problem solving through tasks that engage children in actively constructing new meaning between prior knowledge and newly acquired information. The activities help children become better problem solvers by providing them with opportunities to learn and use skills needed to solve problems: the ability to state questions, identify problems, hypothesize, predict, separate and control variables, infer, design experiments, formulate models, and interpret data.

Problem solving makes learning interesting, and it makes knowledge come alive. It helps children understand as well as remember, and it facilitates the mastery of all the processes teachers attempt to use in science. As the following two activities show, problem solving also affords teachers opportunities to bring subjects together—to integrate the content:

- Children determine the change in the height of a column of water in a container as they drop in marbles. Following their observations, they graph the results and speculate about what happened. Last, they share their views with each other and, if necessary, revise their conclusions.
- Children observe and record the distance traveled by toy cars rolling down an incline. Mathematics and science work together as the children discuss the functional relationship between the slope of the incline as it is changed and the distance traveled by the toy cars. The children predict, compile data, use concrete materials, measure, and interpret.

Children will have a better environment for constructing the reasoning processes needed to understand concepts presented in texts, according to Staver and Bay (1989), if they are provided with opportunities to observe, predict, infer, communicate, and in essence, *do* science. With their emphasis on the characteristics identified here, contemporary science programs are effective supplements (or alternatives) to textbook approaches to science at the very least; and when serving as the focal point of the primary science curriculum, they help children gain power in science, as well as in the other subject areas integrated with science.

SUGGESTIONS FOR TEACHING PRIMARY SCIENCE

If a child is to keep alive his inborn sense of wonder, he needs the companionship of at least one adult who can share it, rediscovering with him the joy, excitement and the mystery of the world we live in. [Rachel Carson, American Biologist, 1907–1964] (Carson, 1965, p. 42*)

To help children have power in doing science, teachers must demonstrate a love of science content and a loving spirit for doing science. They must establish an environment in which children see the excitement and usefulness of the science that is modeled and taught. Although children must work at learning science, learning science need not *seem* like work. Learning science can be made more pleasurable than worklike when the learning environment is one the children find relaxing, comfortable, and inviting.

Jessica Howard, a teacher in rural Vermont, has attempted to set up an environment such as that described. At the Prospect School in North Bennington, Vermont, Howard (1989) creates a setting that gives plenty of room and time "for the making of knowledge." As she helps children learn how their own perceptions position them in the larger world, Howard wants the children to feel that they are in the middle of "plenty of time and room." In her classroom, she devotes quite a bit of time to activities and media (e.g., sand, clay, paint, yarn) that invite children to explore. She believes that children's experiences with these media, under the watchful eye of a guiding mentor, often provide them with a richer ground for making knowledge than would a sole concentration on academic skills.

Role of the Teacher

One major responsibility of the primary teacher is to help children improve, extend, refine, develop, and deepen their understandings, constructions, or representations of their own worlds. This process begins with the teacher's desire to understand what children are thinking about. What do

---

*Copyright ©1956 by Rachel L. Carson. Copyright © renewed by Roger Christie. Reprinted by permission of HarperCollins Publishers, Inc.

children know? What do they think about? As teachers improve in their ability to "read" children's perceptions, emerging perceptions, and misconceptions, they become better able to help children transform their thinking and knowing. Helping children make transformations in science, in turn, requires the development of a sequential structure of experiences that builds upon and extends children's prior experiences and understandings.

The model of teaching developed by the National Center for Improving Science (described earlier in this chapter) is one example of a teaching model that can be used by primary teachers as a guide in the development of an instructional program responsive to a constructivist model of the learner and reflective of the generative nature of science: Questions and problems lead to tentative explanations and solutions and, in turn, generate new questions and problems. As explained earlier, this teaching model is based on four stages characteristic of the approach taken by practicing professionals in science and technology when they learn and apply new skills and information within their fields. In this examination of suggestions for teaching primary science, learning more about the four stages of the model as described by Bybee et al. (1989) is instructive:

1. *Invitation.* The beginning of any learning process in science and technology, the invitation originates with a question about the natural world or a problem in human adaptation. More specifically, an invitation may be quite spontaneous, such as a child discovering an empty eggshell, or it may be elicited by a demonstration of a discrepant event. In both cases, questions emerge immediately, children and teacher are observing together, and the stage is set for further investigation. Teachers should remember that invitations must *engage* the learner.

Invitations can be made to the entire class. For example, to encourage children to embark on a study of water organisms and environmen-

tal issues, the teacher may bring in a sample of pond water and ask, "What lives in a drop of pond water?" Because recognizing and accepting invitations involve choice, the teacher should return to this stage in the process often. Making choices based on new opportunities easily excites children and will quickly create a classroom of eager learners.

2. *Exploration, Discovery, Creativity.* This stage builds upon and expands the science learning initiated by an investigation. It is crucial at this point that children have access to materials and that they have ample opportunities to observe, collect data, organize information, and think of additional experiments they might try.

This stage is characterized by a strong element of constructive play or informal investigation in which children try one approach with the materials, share their findings with each other, and try another experiment. They may use analogies or visual imagery to help themselves think about newly encountered ideas. They begin to explore how new information gained from their investigations relates to previous experiences and their current level of understanding. The teacher is a co-learner and facilitator who designs the learning environment and chooses materials and activities that are likely to lead children to new discoveries and information. The teacher can also informally assess children's developing understanding of a concept: "Please tell me how you arrived at such a thoughtful explanation." "Can you explain how what you just described is like something we observed with the rolling objects a few days ago?" "Good thinking! Do you think you and Jonas can work together and discover what might happen when you mix the mystery solution with the plaster of paris?" The teacher can also pose questions that motivate children to investigate further and try to link the new findings to their current formulations of a concept.

3. Proposing Explanations and Solutions. Learners continue to refine their developing understanding of a concept. They construct a new view of the concept by integrating their current conception with new information. Learners then analyze data they began to organize in the preceding stage and consider alternative interpretations prepared by classmates and the teacher. Cooperative learning is an important part of the teaching and learning approach. Children, guided by the teacher, may decide to perform additional investigations that will help resolve conflicts the children may have between their previous understanding of a concept and a newly emerging view. Each learner brings new meaning to a concept.

4. Taking Action. Once children have constructed a new view of a concept, they are usually ready to act on that new level of understanding. They may defend a point of view before the class or write a letter to a local authority. Their new level of understanding may lead to new questions that provide the foundation for new explorations and subsequent refinement of conceptual understanding. The teacher's role is to encourage children to act through the constructivist strategies for learning listed in Figure 10.1 and to assist children to transfer their new knowledge to other fields of study. The teacher can also assess, informally and formally, each child's new levels of understanding and gauge the effectiveness of the science program. This practice will help the teacher in planning future activities appropriate to children.

In a classroom study on pond water, for example, children's new understanding of ecological diversity and the intricate relationships of a pond ecosystem may lead them to greater appreciation for, and understanding of, factors that affect a pond. Depending on their developmental level and interests, children may create and share stories about a favorite pond inhabitant; debate the merits of various methods for maintaining a pond's ecological balance; write to a local council to argue that sources of pollution should be stemmed; create and display posters that focus attention on the benefits of a clean and healthy pond to the community; or explore how proposed measures of controlling pollution might affect the local community beyond the immediate pond they are studying.

THE BSCS SCIENCE MODEL

The teaching model just described is compatible with the model of teaching and learning developed by the Biological Sciences Curriculum Study (BSCS, 1992). The BSCS five-stage instructional model (see Figure 10.2) is congruent with the constructivist learning theory that suggests children learn best when they are allowed to construct their understanding of concepts over time.

The BSCS model of teaching and learning is designed to introduce children to a knowledge base, scientific attitudes, and scientific thinking and problem-solving skills within the context of active conceptual development. The focus in this model is on "teaching for meaning and understanding, not teaching for the memorization of facts, principles, and the definitions of vocabulary words" (BSCS, 1992, p. 2.36).

Robert Yager offers points to characterize a science classroom in which the constructivist model can work best. According to Yager (1991), such classrooms are those that

1. Use child identification of problems with local interest and impact as organizers for the course

2. Use local resources (human and material) as original sources of information that can be used in problem resolution

3. Involve children in seeking information that can be applied in solving real-life problems

FIGURE 10.2 The BSCS instructional model

1. **Engagement.** Activities in this phase mentally engage the students with an event or question. Engagement activities help the students make connections between what they know and can do with new ideas.
   [**What the Teacher Does:** Creates interest; generates curiosity; raises questions; elicits responses that uncover what the students know or think about the concept/topic.]

2. **Exploration.** The students work with each other to explore ideas through hands-on activities. Over time, and under the guidance of the teacher, they clarify their own understanding of major concepts and skills.
   [**What the Teacher Does:** Encourages the students to work together without direct instruction from the teacher; observes and listens to the students as they interact; asks probing questions to redirect the students' investigations when necessary; provides time for children to puzzle through problems; acts as a consultant for students.]

3. **Explanation.** The students explain their understanding of the concepts and processes they are learning, and determine how their understanding fits with what they already know. The teacher clarifies the students' understanding and introduces new concepts and skills.
   [**What the Teacher Does:** Encourages students to explain concepts and definitions in their own terms; asks for justification and clarification from students; formally provides definitions, explanations, and new labels; uses students' previous experiences as the basis for explaining concepts.]

4. **Elaboration.** Activities in this phase challenge the students to apply what they have learned, to build on their understanding of concepts, and to extend their knowledge and skills.
   [**What the Teacher Does:** Expects students to use formal labels, definitions, and explanations provided previously; encourages students to apply or extend the concepts and skills in new situations; reminds students of alternative explanations; refers students to existing data and evidence and asks: "What do you already know?" "Why do you think . . .?" (Strategies from "Exploration" apply here also.)]

5. **Evaluation.** The students assess their knowledge, skills, and abilities. These activities also allow teachers to evaluate a student's progress.
   [**What the Teacher Does:** Observes students as they apply new concepts and skills; assesses students' knowledge and/or skills; looks for evidence that the students have changed their thinking or behaviors; allows students to assess their own learning and group-process skills; asks open-ended questions, such as: "Why do you think . . .?" "What evidence do you have?" "What do you know about . . .?" "How would you explain . . .?"]

Source: From "The 5 Es Instructional Model," by Biological Sciences Curriculum Study, 1992, *Science for Life and Living: Integrating Science, Technology, and Health,* D. Turnbull (Ed.), pp. 2.36–2.39. Copyright 1992 by Biological Sciences Curriculum Study. Reprinted by permission.

4. Extend learning beyond the class period, the classroom, and the school

5. Focus on the impact of science on each individual child

6. De-emphasize process skills as the "special" skills that should be mastered because they are used by practicing scientists

7. Emphasize career awareness—especially careers related to science and technology

8. Provide opportunities for children to perform in citizenship roles as they attempt to resolve issues they have identified

9. Demonstrate that science and technology are major factors that will affect the future

Children's scientific explorations extend beyond the classroom.

Yager's points illustrate quite accurately a learning environment that is child sensitive, dynamic, and connected to real-life experiences.

PEDAGOGICAL CONTENT KNOWLEDGE

Pedagogical content knowledge (PCK) is a construct that refers to the integration of content and one's methods of teaching. In our discussion of strategies for teaching primary science, an understanding of PCK provides insight to the process of teaching within the specific context of the subject area. According to Lee Shulman (1992), PCK includes, for the most regularly taught topics in one subject area,

> the most useful forms of representation of those ideas, the most powerful analogies, illustrations, examples, explanations and demonstrations. In a word, ways of representing and formulating the subject that makes it comprehensible to others.

Pedagogical Content Knowledge also includes an understanding of what makes the learning of a specific topic easy or difficult; and the conceptions and preconceptions that children of different ages and backgrounds bring with them to the learning of those most frequently taught topics and lessons. (p. 14)

In her analysis of PCK, Pamela Grossman (1990) identifies four components:

1. An overarching conception of what it means to teachers teaching the subject
2. Knowledge of instructional strategies and representations for teaching a particular topic
3. Knowledge of children's understanding and potential misunderstanding of the subject area
4. Knowledge of curriculum

Following is a closer examination of these four components of PCK and then an example to illustrate their relationship to a science lesson.

Overarching Conception of What It Means to Teachers Teaching the Subject. (Serves as a conceptual map for instructional decision making) An overarching conception serves as the basis for judgments about classroom objectives, appropriate learning experiences, curriculum materials, and evaluation of child learning. The standards of the National Science Teachers Association (NSTA) are an embodiment of PCK. An overarching conception represents a strong grounding in what it means to teach science, or mathematics, and so forth—a strong grounding in the vision of what it means to teach something. Strong PCK means command of an overarching understanding of what it means to teach the subject matter; it's like a road map for the teacher—something that shows the way toward fulfillment of objectives.

Knowledge of Instructional Strategies and Representations. (The idea of having powerful instructional tools for making subject matter comprehensible to children) The tool that has probably received the most attention is the idea of *instructional representation*—the model, example, or illustration a teacher uses to foster a child's understanding of a specific topic. That kind of instructional representation is seen when a beach ball, a softball, and a flashlight in a darkened room are used to illustrate a solar eclipse. It's not just the use of the balls and the flashlight that's important; it's also the problem that one chooses to investigate with the materials, the kinds of questions one asks, and the kinds of discourse one tries to generate among the children. All become part of the representational context. Strong PCK is characterized by an extensive repertoire of powerful representations and the ability to adapt those representations in multiple ways to best meet the specific goals for specific sets of learners—in other words, the ability to construct multiple representational contexts for a single representation. These are referred to as a teacher's *representational repertoire* and *adaptational repertoire* (Grossman, 1990).

Knowledge of Children's Understanding and Potential Misunderstanding of the Subject Area.

This component differs from general knowledge of learners in its focus on specific content. In science, the teacher's concern would focus on children's emerging conceptions, preconceptions, naive conceptions, alternative conceptions, and so forth. Children's preconception, for example, that the sound one hears when two objects collide is heard the *instant one sees* the collision, no matter how far one is from the event, is a wonderful point of departure when beginning a discussion or series of lessons about sound waves.

Knowledge of Curriculum.

Strong PCK in this area is characterized by in-depth knowledge of curriculum materials, how the curriculum is organized, and available materials pertinent to the subject area within a certain age-group, as well as across age ranges. In preparing for a unit about the solar system, for example, a teacher with thorough knowledge of the curriculum understands how this topic fits into the scope and sequence of science across multiple years of schooling, including the years immediately before and after the age-group for which the unit is being planned. By examining the scope and sequence for the school district's science studies, the teacher understands the lessons and materials to which children in his or her class have already been exposed. The teacher also understands the lessons, materials, and experiences his or her children are likely to receive later in school.

Next we look at a learning experience for seven-year-olds about things that sink or float. In the example, note both the teacher's thinking and deliberations about the lesson, as well as the nature of the lesson that is presented.

TEACHING ABOUT SINKING AND FLOATING

With respect to content of a project related to sinking and floating, the teacher first helped children think about their current ideas about sinking and floating by writing or illustrating them on a concept map (or a "webbing" of concepts): What sorts of objects are generally thought of as those that sink or float? What *form* of objects or materials might be illustrated? How might something that sinks be made to float, and vice versa? The teacher also included information in the web about common things in a child's world that sink or float (e.g., bark from a tree, toy boats, an ice cube, a plastic part from a child's toy). Regarding curriculum, the teacher considered state and school district objectives for science understandings and information about what most six- to eight-year-olds might be expected to know.

With respect to information about learners, the teacher also considered what seven- and eight-year-olds might have previously encountered about the idea of sinking and floating—in school and out. Drawing on her knowledge of the materials available in the school and of the district curriculum, the teacher concluded that children's experiences were limited to interactions they had with individual objects and assorted materials in nonscientific contexts. The teacher also considered what she has learned about children's ideas after listening to them in classroom discussions about related issues (e.g., rafting, fishing from a boat, swimming, playing with objects in the bathtub). By listening to the way children talk, she could draw some conclusions about their knowledge of sinking and floating.

From all the knowledge she had pulled together, the teacher came up with an appropriate representational context with which to introduce the unit on sinking and floating. The teacher might begin formal exploration of sinking and floating by presenting the class with the following problem:

> [Provide each pair or group of children with a golf ball and a plastic container that has a volume of about two quarts. Have the children fill their containers about half full with water from an available supply bucket. Let each group secure enough clay to form a ball as close as possible in size to that of the golf ball. Then ask the children to predict whether the golf ball and the clay ball will sink or float and to write a reason for their speculations. One would then encourage the children to share what questions they had and how they could go about confirming or rejecting their hypotheses. Then ask the children to place the golf ball and the clay ball into the container of water and to explain in writing the results and their conclusions.]

On the basis of what she knew about the prior experiences of her children, the teacher anticipated that the children's explanations about why the golf ball and the clay ball both sank would probably focus on their notion that the balls were "too heavy." After some discussion of their findings, the teacher then asked the children whether they could get the clay to float. As the class pondered this next problem and explored ways to investigate it, the teacher monitored the children's progress. If necessary at some point, she might pose additional questions to assist children in their explorations: "Can anyone get a speck of clay to float?" "A larger speck?" "What is the difference between the speck of clay and the ball of clay?" "Would the clay in the speck float if it were formed into a ball?"

TEACHERS EXTEND CHILDREN'S UNDERSTANDING

The teacher of the lesson described above anticipated that it would launch the class into an extended exploration of the concepts of sinking and floating. Throughout these explorations, the teacher sustained an important role in providing probes, prompts, and suggestions both individually and with groups. Her decisions about which representations to introduce and how to structure their use, as well as how to respond to (and shape) the representations of the children, remained at the heart of her deliberations about their work.

To teach science is to help children develop science understanding and ways of thinking. To do this, the teacher must select and construct models, examples, stories, illustrations, and problems that can foster children's science development. In the example above, not only do Grossman's (1990) four components of PCK come out, but one also sees how they are interrelated. An individual who is strong in PCK can interrelate and intertwine these four components and do so with a sense of confidence and an apparent effortlessness that comes with being comfortable and well grounded with respect to one's understanding of the learner, the curriculum, and teaching methodologies.

The major points made in this section are worth reviewing: Individuals strong in PCK have a clear, overarching conception of what it means to teach the subject matter (science), and they are able to use it systematically as a conceptual map for instructional decision making. They have a repertoire of instructional strategies that includes an abundance of powerful representations, as well as the ability to construct representational contexts, taking into account instructional objectives and the characteristics of learners. Teachers who can implement effective PCK have greater knowledge of what children in their classes know about particular topics and where children are likely to experience difficulty in learning about those topics. Moreover, they have more extensive knowledge about curriculum designed for children representing a one- or two-year age span or for children of mixed ages. Teachers also have more knowledge about the curriculum materials available to them.

The skills just outlined here are those of a competent master teacher. They represent an ideal to which inexperienced and emerging reflective practitioners may aspire. These abilities are mastered over time in a process of learning that becomes more refined with experience, with continuing professional development, and with the meaningful interactions that teachers nurture throughout their careers with their colleagues, their students, and their students' parents. Their *passion* for wanting to help children learn fuels the teachers determination to do their best. The journey toward professional excellence that teachers are inspired to undertake is the same one traveled by every fine teacher who came before. The first step from beginning teacher to master teacher is one all who choose this profession are privileged to contemplate.

REFLECTIONS ON DIVERSITY

One of the most important tenets regarding the education of children with physical or psychological problems involves facilitating communication and social relationships with teachers and age-mates. This would suggest that children with disabilities should be included in the everyday activities of the primary learning environment whenever possible (Berk & Winsler, 1995). According to Vygotsky (1993), mature intellectual functions originate in children's collaborative social interactions. Children whose opportunities to experience and benefit from supportive interactions with adults and other children are unrealized may experience a dysfunction in their social development at least as serious as their original developmental delay.

Curricular and educational opportunities for children with special needs should have goals very similar to those of other children. For some children, the processes and learning experiences designed to achieve these goals may need to be modified to respond to individual children's particular strengths. Children with physical and mental problems often develop a unique and complex arsenal of learning skills that must be considered when designing social environments that respond to what each child can do independently and with assistance.

Every child should be able to participate in some legitimate way in learning experiences through which they are afforded access to the wonders of their world. Child-sensitive teachers plan ways for all children to engage in scientific inquiry in some meaningful way. From a basic sensory level of exploration (seeing, smelling, hearing, tasting, feeling), through various other levels, finally extending to levels inviting careful reflection and abstract representation, the teacher can choose for different children the level of scientific investigation that seems most appropriate. In the primary science curriculum, *what* children are able to discover about their world is not nearly so important as the fact that they are *engaged in the processes* of investigation and discovery.

All children enjoy participating in meaningful ways in investigating the wonders of their world.

A MOMENT OF SCIENTIFIC WONDERMENT

As they were leaving their apartment to walk with their mother to school, Nita and her three-year-old brother, Devon, saw a dead bird lying on the sidewalk.

Nita: How did he die? Did he hit the window? The door? Did he freeze?

Devon: Oh dear bird. Can we eat him?

Nita: I wish he was only hurt . . . like if his wing was broken, and we fixed him.

Devon: Can I keep him?

Mother: [Carefully lifting the bird and placing it under a bush] We'll bury him after school.

Devon: We gave him a warm spot.

Nita: I could keep him for a play bird; but then he'd stink.

As the three started walking toward school, Nita broke the silence tearfully.

Nita: Oh, I just start shaking whenever this happens. Maybe he was blind and someone ran over him . . . no, then he'd be smooshed. Maybe a drop of oil got on him—or he swallowed a drop of oil.

From the moment of birth, children naturally interact with their environment and begin to learn about the world. Intuitively, they develop ideas, concepts, and theories to interpret that world. According to Cleminson (1990), those ideas, concepts, and theories are imaginative constructions brought to bear on the world of observation. They are *meanings* generated by the learner. In Cleminson's (1990) view,

> Everyday happenings provide a wealth of sensory input for children which lead children to form meanings and explanations for these phenomena. Such meanings are usually from a self-centered point of view and rely on an intuitive understanding of the natural world derived from their sensory input. Such meanings and understandings are invariably different from the accepted scientific explanations for the same phenomena but for the child are sensible and meaningful. The ideas in this "children's science" are usually strongly held . . ., and are invariably expressed in everyday use of language. Indeed one of the main reasons for the sometimes poor communication that occurs in science classrooms is the mismatch between the teacher's use of scientific meanings for words and the children's everyday-language understandings of those words. (p. 440)

SUMMARY

A major consideration associated with teaching science involves the teacher (a) giving a child the opportunity to express his or her intuitive ideas about the world and (b) respecting those ideas as having validity and meaning—authenticity—for that child. Once this step has been carried out, one can present alternative scientific explanations for the phenomena being investigated.

Devon and Nita will not soon forget their encounter with the dead bird. As Nita's sensitivity, Devon's innocence, and their different levels of understanding are revealed, it is clear that their struggles to understand their world are often col-

ored by passion and feelings. In children's lives, such is the *soul* of science—the *humanness* of it all. This passion teachers must help preserve in children's learning above all else.

REFERENCES

American Association for the Advancement of Science (AAAS). (1989). *Science for all Americans, Project 2061.* Washington, DC: Author.

Begley, S. (1990). Rx for learning. *Newsweek, 65*(15), 55–64.

Berk, L., & Winsler, A. (1995). *Scaffolding children's learning: Vygotsky and early childhood education.* Washington, DC: National Association for the Education of Young Children.

Biological Sciences Curriculum Study (BSCS). (1992). The 5 Es instructional model. In D. Turnbull (Ed.), *Science for life and living: Integrating science, technology, and health* (Teacher's edition; pp. 2.36–2.39). Dubuque, IA: Kendall/Hunt.

Bredekamp, S., & Copple, C. (1997). *Developmentally appropriate practice in early childhood programs* (Rev. ed.). Washington, DC: National Association for the Education of Young Children.

Bybee, R., Buchwald, S., & Crissman, S. (1989). *Science and technology education for the elementary years: Frameworks for curriculum and instruction.* Andover, MA: National Center for Improving Science Education.

California State Board of Education. (1990). *Science framework for California public schools kindergarten through grade twelve.* Sacramento: California Department of Education.

Carson, R. (1965). *The sense of wonder.* New York: Harper & Row.

Chaillé, C., & Britain, L. (1997). *The young child as scientist: A constructivist approach to early childhood science education* (2nd ed.). White Plains, NY: Longman.

Cleminson, A. (1990). Establishing an epistemological base for science teaching in the light of contemporary notions of the nature of science and of how children learn science. *Journal of Research in Science Teaching, 27*(5), 429–445.

Duckworth, E. (1970). *The having of wonderful ideas and other essays on teaching and learning.* New York: Teachers College Press.

Elkind, D. (1986). Formal education and early childhood education: An essential difference. *Phi Delta Kappan, 67*(9), 631–636.

Fort, D. (1990). From gifts to talents in science. *Phi Delta Kappan, 71*(9), 664–671.

Goldhaber, J. (1994). If we call it science, then can we let the children play? *Childhood Education, 71*(1), 24–27.

Grossman, P. (1990). *The making of a teacher: Teacher knowledge and teacher education.* New York: Teachers College Press.

Hagerott, S. (1997). Physics for first-graders. *Phi Delta Kappan, 78*(9), 717–720.

Holland, E. (1991). Wonder bred. *Quest, 13*(2), 10–11.

Howard, J. (1989). On teaching, knowledge, and "middle ground." *Harvard Educational Review, 59*(2), 226–239.

Hughes, F. (1991). *Children, play, and envelopment.* Boston: Allyn & Bacon.

Kokoski, T., & Downing-Leffler, N. (1995). Boosting your science and math programs in early childhood education: Making the home-school connection. *Young Children, 50*(5), 35–39.

Martin, A. (1985). Back to kindergarten basics. *Harvard Educational Review, 55*(3), 22–25.

National Association for the Education of Young Children (NAEYC). (1989). *Developmentally appropriate practice in the primary grades, serving 5- through 8-year-olds.* Washington, DC: Author.

National Association for the Education of Young Children (NAEYC), & National Association of Early Childhood Specialists in State Departments of Education (NAECS/SDE). (1991). Guidelines for appropriate curriculum content and assessment in programs serving children ages 3 through 8. *Young Children, 46*(3), 21–38.

Rutherford, J., & Ahlgren, A. (1990). *Science for all Americans.* New York: Oxford University Press.

Shulman, L. (1992). Merging content knowledge and pedagogy: An interview with Lee Shulman. *Journal of Staff Development, 13*(1), 14–16.

Shymansky, J., Kyle, W., & Alport, J. (1983). The effects of new science curricula on student performance. *Journal of Research in Science Teaching, 20*(5), 387–404.

Staver, J., & Bay, M. (1989). Analysis of the conceptual structure and reasoning demands of elementary science texts at the primary (K–3) level. *Journal of Research in Science Teaching, 26*(4), 329–349.

Vygotsky, L. (1993). The fundamentals of defectology. In R. Rieber & A. Carton (Eds.) and J. Knox & C. Stevens (Trans.), *The collected works of L. Vygotsky* (Vol. 2). New York: Plenum.

Watson, B., & Konicek, R. (1990). Teaching for conceptual change: Confronting children's experience. *Phi Delta Kappan, 71*(9), 680–685.

Yager, R. (1991). The constructivist learning model: Toward real reform in science education. *Science Teacher, 58*(6), 52–57.

Every classroom of young children contains future artists, writers, musicians, mathematicians, scientists, and athletes. Each young child has the potential to become a healthy, sensitive, caring, and fully contributing member of society. Even in most instances of young children with identified disabilities, given appropriate intervention and support, damage can be alleviated and greater potential can be achieved than is sometimes predicted.

(Bredekamp & Rosegrant, 1992, p. 6)

11

Social Studies in the Primary Years

CONSIDER YOUR BELIEFS

- What do you believe is the nature of social studies and the process of meaning-making in social studies?
- What do you believe should be the goals of social studies in the primary years?
- What does having "power" with respect to social studies skills and understandings mean?
- What do you understand about the nature of children in the primary years that might influence social studies teaching and learning?
- What important criteria do you believe should be considered when one thinks about including social studies in the primary curriculum?
- What does the concept of the "democratic classroom" mean?
- In what ways does the project approach relate to teaching and learning social studies?
- What are the characteristics of a good social studies program?
- What do you believe is the role of the teacher in facilitating social studies understandings?
- What do you believe it means to include "voice" for all children in the classroom?
- What do you want the primary-age child to understand about the discipline of social studies?
- How do you encourage young children to have power in thinking about, and acting on, their understandings about social studies?

The individual potentials that Bredekamp and Rosegrant mention are most likely to be maximized in classrooms that provide young children with many of the experiences of life in a democratic society. Life in a democratic society is reflected in classrooms when children perceive there is order and safety, when they become familiar with the physical aspects of their environment, when they share a sense of purpose with others, when they learn to take action that leads to greater understanding and appreciation, and when they interact with others in ways that advance their humane natures.

Preparing young children to become healthy and productive members of society is one principal goal of education in America. When today's children reach adulthood, they should be able to communicate well with others, value and work collaboratively with others, and interact effectively as productive and supportive members of a group (Resnick, 1996). According to Carol Seefeldt (1995), social studies is "uniquely suited to fostering the knowledge, attitudes, values, and skills believed necessary for citizens not just to participate in a democratic society, but to continually improve and perfect that society" (p. 109).

Teachers can help children become more intimate with, and appreciative of, democratic ideals by providing them with opportunities to contemplate the true nature of our democratic society. In our culturally diverse society, for every story of success, celebration, and brotherhood one might explore, there is a story of failure, despair, and inhumanity as profoundly important as any story worth sharing—but sadly, one less likely to be discussed. In a healthy classroom, as in a healthy society, the darker aspects of human nature and existence might be examined with as much openness as the brighter aspects.

This chapter addresses issues related to teaching and learning social studies in the primary grades. The importance of the teacher as a facilitator of children's understanding and apprecia-

tion of social studies is underscored, and the significance of understanding and responding to the nature of the young learner is reinforced. Throughout this chapter, the importance of creating developmentally appropriate learning experiences for young children is emphasized, as is the importance of perceiving social studies as an inextricable part of every child's daily life. By helping children acquire a deeper understanding of social studies and develop greater insight into the responsibilities they face as contributing members of society, teachers can help children realize their potentials mentioned in the opening quote.

SOCIAL STUDIES IN CHILDREN'S EVERYDAY LIVES

For her tenth birthday, Alma received a copy of Sylvia Branzei's book *Grossology: The Science of Really Gross Things!* (1995). At breakfast for the next several mornings, Alma shared items from the book with her five-year-old brother, Dillard. On one particular morning, the subject being discussed was "snot":

> *Dillard:* What is snot?
>
> *Alma:* It's mucus.
>
> *Dillard:* Is it brain mucus like you thought?
>
> *Alma:* It's just mucus; it didn't say where it was from.
>
> *Dillard:* Maybe it's from Germany.

As he patrolled the school playground hand-in-hand with one of his six-year-old students, Mr. Winters casually asked the girl what she wanted to be when she grew up:

> *Emma:* I don't know what I want to be when I grow up.

Mr. Winters: Do you want to be a classroom teacher?

Emma: No. I want to be a rock discoverer or an artist.

Mr. Winters: Both of them would be good.

Emma: Or I could be both. Maybe I could be a rock discoverer with my friends during the day, and an artist on my days off.

Mr. Winters: Would you like to be a singer? You have a great voice!

Emma: Oh, no way! I don't want to work real hard for a living!

As the preceding vignettes illustrate, young children's perceptions (and misperceptions) related to social studies issues are revealed on a daily basis. In the most natural (and often unexpected) ways, young children's understandings about social studies weave through their lives like the colorful threads of a rich tapestry. Why are those big kids fighting? When it's raining, does it rain in China too? When we moved here, was I just a baby? What country is Atlanta in, where the Olympics were? How can we settle where to go eat when everyone says someplace different? Is the moon just for us, or is it in Ohio, where Grandma is, too? Look, that man's poor, Mommy; can we help him? Such wonderments fill the minds of young children and provoke often poignantly personal searches for understanding, as illustrated in the following vignettes:

Four-year-old Thomas gazed at his mother as she and his grandmother prepared to leave the house one Sunday morning:

Thomas: Where are you going?

Mother: We're going to church, Sweetie; be a help to Daddy, OK?

Thomas: Will you buy me something?

Mother: I can't, Sweetie. You don't buy things at church.

Thomas: Oh, yeah. That's where you sing.

When her mother picked her up after kindergarten, Linda told her that the school nurse checked everyone's head for lice:

Mother: Did they check your head?

Linda: Yes, well, they found two boys with it.

Mother: Do you know what they were checking for?

Linda: Well, there's these little bugs, and they jump from one person's head to your head to make a new nest and lay eggs.

A few minutes later, Linda told her mother that she didn't want to grow up:

Mother: Why don't you want to grow up?

Linda: 'Cause I don't want to get hair on my bottom and get lice. I just have one teeny tiny hair on my bottom, and I'm going to clip it off!

As these vignettes vividly reveal, children have an insatiable appetite for discovering meaning about their fascinating lives and about the variety of experiences and opportunities for learning they encounter throughout every busy childhood day. Propelled by an unending sense of wonder and a boundless enthusiasm for making sense of the world around them, young children explore, reflect on, develop, and engage in relationships with others, plan, try things out, check what happened, compare outcomes of an experience with what they've observed before, try again, ponder—they're doing social studies, living it every day.

Young children have a boundless enthusiasm for discovering meaning in their lives and in relationships with others.

WHAT IS SOCIAL STUDIES?

As a leader among the complex, diverse, and often troubled nations of the world with whom it must learn to work cooperatively, America (and its democracy) is

constantly evolving and in continuous need of citizens who can adapt its enduring traditions and values to meet changing circumstances. Meeting that need is the mission of the social studies. In social studies, students develop a core of basic knowledge and ways of thinking drawn from many academic disciplines, learn to analyze their own and others' opinions on important issues, and become motivated to participate in civic and community life as active, informed citizens. (National Council for the Social Studies [NCSS], 1994, p. vii)

The National Council for the Social Studies (NCSS) has defined **social studies** as

the integrated study of the social sciences and humanities to promote civic competence. Within the school program, social studies provides coordinated, systematic study drawing upon such disciplines as anthropology, archaeology, economics, geography, history, law, philosophy, political science, psychology, religion, and sociology, as

well as appropriate content from the humanities, mathematics, and natural sciences. The primary purpose of social studies is to help young people develop the ability to make informed and reasoned decisions for the public good as citizens of a culturally diverse, democratic society in an interdependent world. (NCSS, 1994, p. vii)

NCSS Social Studies Standards

The national curriculum standards in the social studies developed by the NCSS specify what children should be learning in social studies programs from the age of four or five through adolescence. The standards define what children should know and when they should know it; and they are articulated within a framework of ten themes incorporating fields of study that correspond with one or more relevant disciplines (see Figure 11.1).

CONNECTING WITH OUR HUMANNESS

Perhaps the most compelling feature of social studies is the almost insistent way it invites one to connect with one's (and others') humanity. We take a greater interest in the features of a map

FIGURE 11.1 Framework of the social studies standards: The ten themes

I. Culture

The study of culture prepares students to answer questions such as: What are the common characteristics of different cultures? How do belief systems such as religion or political ideas influence other parts of the culture? How does the culture change to accommodate different ideas and beliefs? What does language tell us about the culture?

II. Time, Continuity, and Change

Human beings seek to understand their historical roots and to locate themselves in time. Knowing how to reconstruct the past allows one to develop a historical perspective and to answer questions such as: Who am I? What happened in the past? How am I connected to those in the past? How has the world changed and how might it change in the future? Why does our personal sense of relatedness to the past change?

III. People, Places, and Environments

The study of people, places, and human-environment interactions assists students as they create their spatial views and geographic perspectives of the world beyond understanding to answer questions such as: Where are things located? Why are they located where they are? What do we mean by "region"? How do land forms change? What implications do these changes have for people?

IV. Individual Development and Identity

Personal identity is shaped by one's culture, by groups, and by institutional influences. Students should consider such questions as: How do people learn? Why do people behave as they do? What influences how people learn, perceive, and grow? How do people meet their basic needs in a variety of contexts? How do individuals develop from youth to adulthood?

V. Individuals, Groups, and Institutions

Institutions such as schools, churches, families, government agencies, and the courts play an integral role in people's lives. It is important that students learn how institutions are formed, what controls and influences them, how they influence individuals and culture, and how they are maintained or changed. Students may address questions such as: What is the role of institutions in this and other societies? How am I influenced by institutions? How do institutions change? What is my role in institutional change?

VI. Power, Authority, and Governance

Understanding the historical development of structures of power, authority, and governance and their evolving functions in contemporary U.S. society and other parts of the world is essential for developing civic competence. In exploring this theme, students confront questions such as: What is power? What forms does it take? Who holds it? How is it gained, used, and justified? What is legitimate authority? How are governments created, structured, maintained, and changed? How can individual rights be protected within the context of majority rule?

VII. Production, Distribution, and Consumption

Because people have wants that often exceed the resources available to them, a variety of ways have evolved to answer such questions as: What is to be produced? How is production to be organized? How are goods and services to be distributed? What is the most effective allocation of the factors of production (land, labor, capital, and management)?

FIGURE 11.1 *continued*

VIII. Science, Technology, and Society

Modern life as we know it would be impossible without technology and the science that supports it. Technology brings with it many questions: Is new technology always better than old? What can we learn from the past about how new technologies result in broader social change, some of which is unanticipated? How can we cope with the ever-increasing pace of change? How can we manage technology so that the greatest number of people benefit from it? How can we preserve our fundamental values and beliefs in the midst of technological change?

IX. Global Connections

The realities of global interdependence require understanding the increasingly important and diverse global connections among world societies and the frequent tension between national interests and global priorities. Students will need to be able to address such international issues as health care, the environment, human rights, economic competition and interdependence, age-old ethnic enmities, and political and military alliances.

X. Civic Ideals and Practices

An understanding of civic ideals and practices of citizenship is critical to full participation in society and is a central purpose of the social studies. Students confront such questions as: What is civic participation and how can I be involved? How has the meaning of citizenship evolved? What is the balance between rights and responsibilities? What is the role of the citizen in the community and the nation, and as a member of the world community? How can I make a positive difference?

Source: From *Expectations of Excellence: Curriculum Standards for Social Studies,* by National Council for the Social Studies, 1994, pp. 65–66, Washington, DC: Author.

when we learn from it the location and characteristics of places we (or people we care about) inhabit or would like to visit. We learn to care in meaningful ways about the past as we identify with, and are influenced by, the ideas and deeds of those who preceded us. We are interested in the values and beliefs of others because we share the planet Earth—the human home—with them, and as we come to understand them, we are able to understand ourselves better. It is the people we care about most enduringly.

On reading Fritz's autobiography *Homesick: My Own Story* (1982), one is transfixed by her description of American history as it was commonly taught when she was a child:

> I skimmed through the pages, but I couldn't find any mention of people at all. There was talk about

dates and square miles and cultivation and population growth and immigration and the Western movement, but it was as if the forests had lain down and given way to farmland without anyone being brave or scared or tired or sad, without babies being born, without people dying. (p. 153)*

Children's interest in, and experience with, history becomes much more transforming when teachers help them put faces and personalities with it—lessons about challenges, problems, successes, and failures (large and small) confronting individuals who came before them who experienced childhood and led lives similar to, and yet

---

*Source: From *Homesick: My Own Story,* by J. Fritz, 1982, New York: Dell.

somewhat different from, their own. Consider the following discussion about a historical figure that took place over dinner between twelve-year-old Lynn and her six-year-old sister Nancy:

Lynn: Who was George Washington?

Nancy: Did he die of a heart attack?

Lynn: No. Who was he?

Nancy: Was he president?

Lynn: Yes! Which one?

Nancy: Second?

Lynn: No.

Nancy: Third?

Lynn: No, he was first. And he . . ." [Lynn pauses, reflecting on the "fact" that George Washington could never tell a lie] . . . What could he never do?

Nancy: [Pausing thoughtfully] He could never be second or third!

Lynn: Huh uh. He could never tell a lie. Can you remember that?

Nancy's linear and literal response to her sister's tutorship is both amusing and refreshing. Her reasoning, though not yet adorned with subtlety and factual accuracy, is charming in its directness and simplicity. Moreover, it is graced with a kind of embracing, straightforward meaningfulness that reveals much about Nancy's ability to respond to her inquisitor in a purposeful and contextually legitimate way.

Staying within the context of historical figures, the next vignette affords another opportunity to gain insight into young children's conceptual and reasoning abilities, similar to that provided by Lynn and Nancy:

Holding up a holiday ornament box portraying a picture of Uncle Sam, Rodney's father asked the seven-year-old who the person pictured on the box was. After staring intently at the colorful portrait on the box for a few seconds, Rodney replied, "Bill Clinton?"

Although Rodney's guess about the identity of the figure portrayed on the box was wrong, on careful examination one can detect in his reply several perspectives that accord it a distinct level of appropriateness. His answer was contextually sound: Bill Clinton (like Uncle Sam) is a historical political figure of some repute; thus, his reply is very much consistent, contextually speaking (much more so than it would be if he would have identified the person as John Elway, for example). Rodney reveals other levels of understanding in his reply as well: His sense of governmental officialdom is tied closely to regal stature, patriotic colors, and so on; his sense of governmental officialdom is rooted to contemporary political personalities; and he has an appropriate sense of how someone presidential should look.

For young children, learning history (and learning about historical people) is an ongoing process in which they construct historical meaning as they talk, read, write, draw, and reflect. As one can see from the discussion between Lynn and Nancy, through language, they propose and test historical ideas by predicting, confirming, and negotiating with others. Similarly, Rodney responds to his father on the basis of the somewhat narrow accumulation of historical/political information he has acquired up to this period of his life. According to Jorgensen (1993), young children weigh new ideas and information against what they already understand about the world, their own purposes, their understandings of relevant historical source materials, and the responses of other learners.

Concern about humankind largely influences the extent to which one acquires an interest in geography as well. As expressed in *Geography for Life: National Geography Standards* (National Council for Geographic Education [NCGE], 1994), geography "is not a collection of arcane information. Rather, it is the study of spatial aspects of human existence. People everywhere need to know about the nature of their world and their place in it" (p. 18): Where is the Mississippi River? Why is it there? How did it get there? What impact does the Mississippi River have on other things? In what ways does the Mississippi River interact with peoples' lives?

As she was traveling by car with her seven-year-old daughter, Stephanie, up the East Coast from Tennessee to Vermont, Gail Deevers pulled into a state park to check their progress and location on a map. As she folded the map and put it away, Gail wondered whether her daughter knew what a map was. Stephanie replied, "It's something that knows ways to places and you write . . . Okay, it's a piece of paper that shows people places they want to go; and you take a permanent marker and draw on it like a state or the world."

From this exchange between Stephanie and her mother, one could conclude, quite accurately, that Stephanie has a fairly sophisticated understanding of the purpose of a map, as well as some other geographical understandings that are comparatively less refined but probably no less meaningful to Stephanie. Later during the trip, or on reaching their destination, were her mother to share with Stephanie more information about the map she was using—pointing out where their trip began, tracing the route to places they had visited, describing details about sights they had seen, locating their destination—the experience would contribute in a personally meaningful way to an increase in Stephanie's geographical understanding.

THE DEMOCRATIC CLASSROOM: A PRIMARY GOAL OF SOCIAL STUDIES IN EARLY CHILDHOOD

The only way to prepare for democratic participation is to create a (classroom) community in which democracy is practiced each day. (Kriesberg, 1993, p. 29)

A major goal of social studies instruction for young children is citizenship education. According to Emma Holmes (1991), learning citizenship involves acquiring the knowledge, values, and behaviors characteristic of citizens in a democracy. Children are helped to understand concepts such as liberty and justice; they begin to comprehend democratic values by exploring the meaning of ideas such as rights, responsibilities, and respect for self and others. With teacher guidance, asserts Holmes, children learn to relate ideas to behaviors and can thereby practice democracy in their classrooms. Citizenship learning is a process of acquiring democratic values and behaviors that permeate the entire school day; it is not reserved for just those periods in a school week when time is taken to "teach" social studies.

On Election Day 1996, seven-year-old Dirk accompanied his father to the polling booth and participated in the voting process as part of the Kids Vote program sponsored by the local school district. At breakfast the next day, Dirk's father shared with him the outcome of the election:

Father: Well, Dirk, the person you voted for won: Bill Clinton.

Dirk: Oh, well. I thought that guy who sounds like a duck should win.

Father: Bob Dole?

Dirk: No.

Father: Perot?

Dirk: No. It's not one of those guys.

Father: Wayne Allard? (The winning candidate for U.S. Senator from Colorado)

Dirk: Yeah, that one! He sounds like a duck, so he should be president.

A few weeks prior to the 1996 national elections, six-and-a-half-year-old Alisa asked her mother about one of the candidates for the office of U.S. president:

Alisa: Mom, is a guy with white hair running for president?

Mother: Um—do you mean who is president now, or is running for president?

Alisa: I mean who's going to be president?

Mother: Why are you asking?

Alisa: 'Cause, I want you guys to vote for a guy with white hair . . . that looks like George Washington, 'cause I like white hair; it's cool.

Children as Decision Makers

An important feature of democratic classrooms involves passing on a democratic belief that people can be trusted to make sensible decisions concerning their own lives and the lives of others. Citizens of our country are empowered to decide matters for themselves. In classrooms in which democracy is practiced, young children are encouraged to choose among different options and to make decisions. As the following vignette illustrates, however, learning to make the most appropriate decisions can be challenging for a young child:

As her father was tucking her into bed for the night, six-year-old Guadalupe felt compelled to share with him some of her day's misadventures: "I took too long at the water fountain; I played in the bathroom; Allana and I played while we were crossing the street; I had to stay in time-out; and Nicholas got Halloween candy and I didn't."

Leaning down to kiss her, Guadalupe's father replied: "Well, Lupe, tomorrow is certain to be a much better day, don't you think? Sleep tight now."

With continuing guidance and support from her teacher, Guadalupe is certain to have better days, just as she is certain to have (like all actively curious young children) a few more misadventures before she slips the gentle embrace of childhood. As young children are empowered with greater opportunities to make choices and participate in decision making, they will become more skilled at managing their impulsiveness and make more appropriate decisions. In addition, they will become more adept at making decisions based on grounds more well reasoned than, for example, whether a person's name "sounds like a duck," whether a person has "cool hair," or on some other trivial basis.

As outlined by Joanne Hendrick (1992), empowering children to make decisions is a process that involves several steps:

1. *Making Decisions: The Power to Choose.* Every time teachers present children with true choices and honor their decisions about those choices, they foster the children's ability to take independent action. When teachers include self-select opportunities for children, it is a time when children can learn to take responsibility for making their own choices. This kind of empowerment builds self-confidence and trust in one's own judgment.

2. *Building Autonomy: The Power to Try.* Teachers of young children guide the drive toward autonomy into reasonable channels in countless practical ways. Each time teachers permit a group

When they have opportunities to make decisions and to take responsibility, children develop self-confidence and trust in themselves.

of five-year-olds to plan their own bulletin board or allow a seven-year-old the opportunity to share a project with children in another class, they are fostering the growth of autonomy: the ability of children to do things on their own.

Four-and-a-half-year-old Ann had been watching her older brother, Sam, getting ready for school—moving with assurance around the house, helping himself to the things he needed. After following her brother around the house for a few minutes, Ann sought her mother for some solace:

Ann: Mommy, I want to be like Sammy.

Mother: Why do you want to be like Sammy, Sweetheart?

Ann: 'Cause . . . so I can reach things . . . so I can get my own cup; so I can go into my own room by myself.

Ann's desire to be able to do things for herself is precisely the sort of yearning characteristic of

all healthy young children that Hendrick suggests should be nurtured in democratic classrooms.

3. *Fostering Competence: The Power to Do.* Competence is knowing how to do something, and it is a great builder of self-confidence. When teachers help children acquire skills, they help instill an inner sense of competence. Once a child possesses a skill, whether it be roller-blading, dealing with personal frustration, or negotiating conflicts, the child owns that skill and need not depend on someone else's assurance that she or he is competent.

Empowering children to choose, to experiment, to reflect, and to choose again helps them become thinkers and doers—active participants in a democratic classroom—precisely the sort of outcomes one seeks as a goal of the social studies curriculum. Thinkers and doers, young children actively involved in their own learning, experiencing and enjoying firsthand the challenges of making informed and reasoned decisions about things that are important to them—this is the essence of improved understanding.

THE CLASSROOM AS A MODEL OF DEMOCRACY

Teachers can help young learners begin to comprehend democratic values by creating democratic classrooms that reflect the ideals on which democratic societies are based: rights, responsibilities, and respect for self and others (Holmes, 1991). With teacher guidance, children learn to relate ideas in democratic classrooms to behaviors appropriate for citizens in a democracy. Most important, as indicated earlier, the process of acquiring democratic values and behaviors should characterize the entire school day, rather than being addressed simply during the times when social studies is formally taught.

According to Bredekamp and Copple (1997), in appropriate primary social studies classrooms, the learning environment becomes "a laboratory of social relations where children learn rules of social responsibility and respect for individual differences through structured experiences directed toward those goals" (p. 173). Through integrated learning opportunities, children engage in a variety of investigative projects that encourage them to plan and work together in cooperative learning groups.

Strategies for Establishing Democratic Classrooms

According to Holmes (1991), teachers can employ four major strategies to help young children reflect on the meaning of democratic values and behave in ways characteristic of citizens in a democracy: discussions, democratic decision making, modeling, and examining reasons for democratic behaviors. Elaboration of these four strategies can be found in Figure 11.2.

Understanding of democratic classrooms is enhanced by Greenberg's (1992) views about what she refers to as the *ingredients of democratic practice*. Asserting that teachers should take time, while children are young, to start "guiding each child toward ethical individuality and con-structive membership in groups," Greenberg advances a set of tenets that comprise ethical and moral character and practice—the foundations of democratic classrooms:

- A firm, positive sense of self as an effective person
- Freedom from excessive anger
- Respect for others regardless of whether we agree with or approve of their views and ways (providing they are not hurting anyone)
- Ability to see a situation from another person's point of view
- Ability and preference for negotiating disagreements and resolving conflicts nonviolently
- Willingness to spot problems and imaginativeness to see alternatives
- Desire and ability to plan, work, and make decisions cooperatively
- Empathy toward anyone who is hurting
- Motivation and capability to contribute responsibly to the well-being of others
- Ability to get along naturally and constructively with people who have disabilities, are of other races, or are richer or poorer
- Ability to think about the ethics of things (pp. 13–16)

In classrooms characterized by these "ingredients," young children are afforded opportunities throughout each day to participate in democratic processes; they are immersed in the ecology of democracy. In such classrooms for young children, democracy isn't simply taught or simply valued; rather, it is something experienced—something lived—by every child, all day, every day. The classroom becomes a democratic society in which children's rights are respected, children learn to conduct themselves responsibly, and children learn to value themselves and others. These learning environments are rich with opportunities to choose, to make

FIGURE 11.2 Major strategies for establishing democratic classrooms

---

Discussions

Teachers should initiate discussions in which children explore their rights and responsibilities and examine the meaning of respect for self and others at the start of the school year when the group is developing an identity. The teacher stimulates discussion by asking questions: Why is it good to go to school? Who pays for you to go to school? What are children supposed to do in school? Why should you be kind and help others? What does it mean to be happy? What can you do to feel pleased with yourselves? Discussions might be followed by children role-playing situations portraying democratic behaviors. Teachers can also help children summarize their discussions and listing points in the summary on a chart.

Democratic Decision Making

Teachers share decision making with children. Children participate in setting learning goals and establish rules for school behavior. They make choices in some aspects of school life. Children have opportunities to discuss how to make good choices and what their responsibilities are when they are given options.

Modeling

Teachers serve as models of responsible behavior. They care about and support all children. The teacher invites the children to reflect on the teacher's actions and to discuss how the teacher's actions relate to responsible democratic citizenship.

Examining Reasons for Democratic Behaviors

Teachers guide children to suggest reasons for democratic behaviors. They help children focus on the consequences of actions and they help children examine their own feelings in various situations and to try to imagine how others might feel in similar situations.

Source: From "Democracy in Elementary School Classes," by E. Holmes, 1991, *Social Education, 55*(30), pp. 176–178.

decisions, to learn the consequences of one's actions, and to celebrate working collaboratively with others toward common goals. In democratic classrooms, personal and group values are weighed and compared, negotiation and compromise are explored, tolerance and acceptance are promoted, and freedom to learn (rather than fear of failing) prevails.

According to Derman-Sparks (1989), as early as four years of age, "children have internalized stereotypic gender roles, racial bias, and fear of the differently-abled" (p. 2). In culture-, gender-, race-, and ability-mixed collaborative work and play groups; through books, posters, films, and stories made available for children to explore; and by the particular individuals and images se-

lected to illustrate important values and lessons, children can begin to develop attitudes and dispositions that help counter ignorance and discriminatory influences present in society.

COMPETENCIES CHILDREN SHOULD BE LEARNING

In her discussion of what children should be learning, Lillian Katz (1990) emphasizes the view that young children learn most effectively when they are engaged in active interactions with others, with materials, and with the world around them in ways that help them make sense of their environment and their experiences in it.

In democratic classrooms, children develop perspectives and values based on respect for individual and group differences.

Katz affirms the importance of children exploring aspects of their lives that are worthwhile (often through spontaneous play) and then documenting their discoveries and ideas through conversation and storytelling, drawings and paintings, and writing.

Relating to the goals of social studies for young children, four categories of learning posited by Katz seem especially relevant:

1. Knowledge. In early childhood, knowledge consists of facts, concepts, ideas vocabulary, and stories. A child acquires knowledge from someone else's answers to his or her questions, explanations, descriptions, and accounts of events, as well as through observation.

In the vignette that follows, five-and-one-half-year-old Abraham, responding to his teacher who asked him to explain what history meant, is clearly knowledgeable about this key social studies construct; one can only guess as to the source of the information he was ready to share so eagerly and competently:

Abraham: Was it like when there were cave men?

Teacher: Yes!

Abraham: And they discovered time with sun, shadows, and sticks, huh?

Teacher: Wow, you're right! Nice job!

2. Skills. Skills are small units of action that occur in a relatively short period of time and that are easily observed or inferred. Physical, social, verbal, counting, and drawing skills are among the almost endless number of skills learned in the early years. Skills can be learned from direct instruction and improved with practice and drill.

From the next vignette about six-year-old Serena chatting with her father in the kitchen of her home, both geographic and mathematical skills can be inferred:

Serena: Dad, what if the chair weighed thirty pounds and I weighed one hundred and ninety pounds, and I got up on it and fell through the floor?

Father: Well . . . where would you land?

Serena: [After thinking about it momentarily] I'd land on the stairs . . . or somewhere in the basement!

Just as we can draw inferences about Serena's mathematics and geography skills from the previous vignette, the following vignette involving seven-year-old Jefferson provides us with a basis for understanding some extent of his skill, insight, and recall regarding history and geography:

Jefferson was performing cartwheels on the sidewalk while accompanying his father, who was picking up trash around the neighborhood. As they approached a spot on the walk about thirty steps from their driveway, Jefferson interrupted his cartwheeling and exclaimed, "Oh, I can't touch that spot. Cassie (his dog) peed there one time!"

---

3. Feelings. Feelings are subjective emotional states, many of which are innate. Among those that are learned are feelings of competence, belonging, and security. Feelings about school, teachers, learning, and other children are also learned in the early years.

About one-third of the way through the school year, Mrs. Cornell sensed that the occasional episode of antagonism among several of her students had started to escalate. Ken seemed to have become increasingly ostracized because of his limited physical abilities. Steffen had become so upset over the attention that his friend Buster was paying Jim that his emotional outbursts were disrupting the class. At the same time, Mrs. Cornell noticed that Sheila had detached herself almost completely from social contacts and that the quality of her schoolwork had dropped significantly. When she mentioned this to Sheila's mother, Mrs. Cornell learned that the parents were in the process of getting a divorce.

In response to these events, and in an effort to support the positive emotional climate that usually prevailed in her classroom, Mrs. Cornell, with the assistance of a district guidance counselor, instituted voluntary Friendship Groups that would meet on a weekly basis. The purpose of the Friendship Groups was to provide opportunities for small groups of students to gather and share with each other whatever concerns they wanted to discuss. As time went on, students learned that the Friendship Groups offered them a safe and accepting environment in which to think through how best to deal with difficult emotional issues. Mrs. Cornell gently guided the discussions within the groups and tried to help reignite in the children the desire to participate once again in the classroom's culture of friendship.

4. Dispositions. Dispositions can be thought of as habits of mind or tendencies to respond to certain situations in certain ways. Curiosity, friendliness or unfriendliness, bossiness, and creativity are dispositions, rather than skills or pieces of knowledge. The dispositions that children need to acquire or to strengthen—curiosity, creativity, cooperation, friendliness—are learned primarily from being around people who exhibit them.

One disposition that Katz mentions (curiosity) is exemplified by Latisha. At almost five years of age, Latisha is curious about everything. Whether it's a mound of dog poop, the silver trail of an airplane, a layer of frost on the car windshield, the sad expression of a disappointed parent, or a fresh scrape on a friend's knee, Latisha will stop anything she's doing to investigate—poke it, smell it, feel it, or simply gaze at it. She'll even jump up from a meal to investigate an unusual sound—or an unusual silence. Adults describe Latisha as being easily distracted, but understanding teachers will celebrate her curiosity and discover ways to help her manage her disposition within a productive context for learning.

In social studies, at least as much as in any other discipline, learning experiences should be promoted that enable young children to grow in each of these four categories of learning. The facilitation of rich interactions that arise in the course of investigations in each of the categories provides the optimal context for meaningful social and cognitive learning.

Excellence in social studies is likely to be achieved through learning experiences in which children gain the knowledge, skills, feelings, and dispositions necessary to help them understand, respect, and practice the ways of the laborer, the artist, the leader, the healer, and the citizen in support of the common good. Thus, support of the common good (the general welfare of all individuals and groups within their community and the nation) stands as a major goal of social studies.

Unfortunately, in many communities across the country, disrespect, fear, and hatred based on differences of race, language, culture, socioeconomic status, sexual orientation, and religion prevail. Children exposed to these attitudes in their homes and neighborhoods may begin to adopt these same hateful dispositions unless values supporting individual decency and the common good are advanced in the schools. The preservation of children's nobler interpersonal instincts is a goal to which all teachers must be dedicated.

According to the NCSS (1994), teachers can help children learn to become citizens devoted to the common good of their community and the nation by

- Helping them construct, evaluate, and refine a personal perspective that enables them to make sound decisions about people and events in their lives

- Helping them construct a pluralist perspective based on respect for differences of opinion and preference; of race, religion, and gender; of class and ethnicity; and of culture in general

- Helping them connect knowledge, skills, feelings, and dispositions to civic action as they engage in social inquiry

CRITERIA FOR INCLUDING SOCIAL STUDIES IN THE PRIMARY CURRICULUM

Noting that concern for the common good and citizen participation in public life are essential to the health of our democratic system, the NCSS statement *Essentials of the Social Studies* (1990) identifies citizenship education as the primary purpose of social studies (pp. 9–11). In this position statement, the NCSS asserts that effective social studies programs

- Foster individual and cultural identity, along with understanding of the forces that hold society together or pull it apart

- Include observation of, and participation in, the school and community
- Address critical issues and the world as it is
- Prepare children to make decisions based on democratic principles
- Lead to citizen participation in public affairs

According to the NCSS, curriculum components include knowledge, democratic values and beliefs, thinking skills, and social and civic participation skills. The content focuses on the world—near and far, social and civic, past, present, and future. The appropriateness of establishing the basics for global understanding during a child's early years has been articulated by Seefeldt (1977):

> Young children, through activities involving relationships with others, cooperative group experiences, and many forms of firsthand experiences, can develop awareness of: (1) the interdependency of humans on one another, (2) the cultures of our world, and (3) the similarities between people everywhere. (p. 153)

The NCSS Social Studies Performance Expectations

As discussed earlier in this chapter, the NCSS developed a set of curriculum standards for social studies in 1994. Along with the ten themes that form the framework of the social studies standards, the NCSS also advanced a set of performance expectations for early grades, middle grades, and high school. The NCSS performance expectations accompanying the ten major curriculum themes for the early grades appear in Appendix A at the end of this chapter.

A Unifying Theme: Caring

An easily identifiable unifying theme that relates to practically all NCSS performance expectations is the concept of caring—an issue at the very core of human existence—caring for self, for intimate others, for strangers and the global community, for the natural world and its nonhuman creatures, for the human-made world, and for ideas (Noddings, 1995). Acquiring the disposition to care, developing a sense of charity with regard to all that one surveys, is one fundamental characteristic by which lives are ennobled.

In the movie *Toy Story*, an antagonist named Sid gained considerable pleasure bullying and threatening others and destroying the toys and playthings he found at his disposal. On the way home after viewing the movie with her father, five-year-old Debbie commented about Sid: "That boy . . . when he grows up he'll do drugs, huh!?"

While watching the evening news with her six-year-old daughter, Leesa, Mrs. Chien asked her whether she thought soldiers were bad or good.

Leesa: They're bad.

Mother: Why do you believe that?

Leesa: Because they fight.

Mother: Are all soldiers bad?

Leesa: Well . . . no.

Mother: How do you tell who the bad soldiers are?

Leesa: The bad ones are the ones that start the fight first.

Both vignettes indicate the insights young children have about aspects of the world around them that lack dignity or decency. In the first story, the bully Sid was perceived to be a person who did not care for others. Similarly, certain groups of soldiers were perceived to be persons who were not caring because "they started the

Helping children acquire the disposition to care is one of the fundamental principles of social studies for young children.

fight first." These two vignettes illustrate the concerns, feelings, and dispositions many young children have around the issue of caring.

More profoundly, children in many communities are all too familiar with the absence of caring. Their lives are ravaged by family and neighborhood violence. Too many of their role models sustain themselves on greed, selfishness, deceit, and avarice. How are children to come to know about generosity, charity, and concern for others?

When teachers help children learn about caring and to care, they help children develop genuine concern for others and for their surroundings. According to Noddings (1995), the issue of caring must be taken seriously as a major purpose of schools, and helping young people develop a strong capacity for caring should be a major objective of responsible education. Toward this end, Noddings submits that teachers should (1) introduce themes of care into the regular curriculum, (2) be prepared to respond spontaneously to unwelcome events that occur in school or in the community, (3) support children who are saddened or suffering, and (4) help create and maintain a school environment in which children are cared for and learn to care.

Considering the Nature of the Young Learner

Even a cursory review of the NCSS performance expectations identified earlier leads one to the self-evident conclusion that many of them are far removed from many young children's life events. Although many of the performance expectations can be easily accommodated within the life experiences of most children, others cannot. For many teachers, merely introducing some performance expectations that are judged to be on the periphery of their children's understanding will make sense. Other performance expectations will be judged to be so far removed from some children's realities that these will not be addressed during the early years at all. These decisions will be made largely on the basis of what the teacher determines is appropriate, given the abilities, interests, and understandings of his or her group of students.

What one hopes to help a child learn must be relevant to the child's current level of interest, knowledge, and conceptual ability. For some children, certain geographic, historical, or civic concepts will be so distant from them in experience, time, and mind as to be almost meaningless. In such instances, teachers can introduce children to other important social studies concepts at the level of awareness and exploration, knowing that these ideas may need to be revisited over time for deeper understandings to develop.

When Mrs. Sanchez asked her class of five- and six-year-olds whether they were happy to have the next day off because of the holiday, one girl, Consuela, responded: "Yes! We need to make cards and sing `Happy Birthday' for O.J.!"

Mrs. Sanchez replied, "Not O.J., Darling; Martin Luther King, Jr."

Following this exchange, Mrs. Sanchez told her students about Dr. King and how he worked to get respect and equal rights for all people. After she was through, Consuela raised her hand and asked: "If he was good, then why did those people squirt him with a hose?"

By her comments and questions, Consuela leaves no doubt about her interest in Dr. King's struggle for civil rights. She also leaves no doubt about her ability to learn more about these issues and about her potential for reaching deeper levels of understanding about them. Understanding children's interpretations about particular personalities, concepts, or events and observing how they change over time give teachers significant insights into how children come to know. Providing children with experiences in which they control their own learning, ask their own questions based on informed observations, and learn to appreciate their personal connections with the subjects "not only allows children to reconsider their developing understanding but provides teachers with knowledge about how misunderstanding is reconsidered in the process of learning" (Jorgensen, 1993, p. ix).

The "Voices" of Children

In the example just cited, Consuela spoke out in a way that made her interest in a subject clear. From their understanding of the Reggio Emilia approach to early childhood education that fosters children's intellectual development through a systematic focus on symbolic representation, teachers know that children may speak to them in different "voices" or "languages." In the Reggio Emilia approach, young children are encouraged "to explore their environment and express themselves through all of their natural languages, or **voices**—including stories, words, movement, drama, drawing, painting, building, sculpture, shadow play, collage, poetry, dramatic play, and music" (Edwards, Gandini, & Forman, 1993, p. 3). Each different means or form a child uses to express a thought or feeling represents another "voice" contributing to the understanding of self and others.

In democratic classrooms, contexts are provided in which all children are free to use their voices to affirm their "place" and to create new possibilities for themselves. Teachers can guide the expressive articulation of children's voices in a number of ways:

a. By providing opportunities for children to (communicate) from their lives with absolute acceptance;

b. By providing many varied opportunities for expressive (communication) that develops a voice reflecting social context;

c. By guiding children to explore the ideas of others who speak clearly about social context;

d. By helping children reflect upon their own ways of expressing themselves;

e. By helping children learn to respond to each other's voices in the form of questions that encourage others to expand their ideas and "say" more; and

f. By helping children celebrate (their growing expressiveness) by encouraging them to share their thoughts with one another under circumstances that are casual, nonthreatening, even festive (Quintero & Rummel, 1996)

When children are able to express themselves in honest, open, and heartfelt ways about their thoughts and feelings, they step closer to becoming creative thinkers, effective communicators, and imaginative learners. In this way, according to Phyllis Brady (1992), "new vistas become possible. It frees up new thinking; it allows for voices that have not been heard—including those of young children" (p. 13).

DISTINGUISHING CHARACTERISTICS OF A GOOD SOCIAL STUDIES PROGRAM

When thinking about distinguishing characteristics that underpin social studies programs of excellence, consider ideas that contribute to a classroom learning environment that becomes the "societal context" within which important concepts about social studies are examined. When the classroom becomes the society, children interact in social ways, in groupings of various sizes, to achieve common goals.

Principles of Teaching and Learning

In a position statement of the NCSS, a set of principles of teaching and learning are advanced that characterize social studies programs of excellence in which, in many ways, the learning

FIGURE 11.3 Principles of teaching and learning for all social studies programs of excellence

1. Social studies teaching and learning are powerful when they are meaningful. Students learn knowledge, skills, beliefs, and attitudes that they will find useful both in and outside of school.

2. Social studies teaching and learning are powerful when they are integrative. Social studies is integrative across the curriculum and in its treatment of topics.

3. Social studies teaching and learning are powerful when they are value-based. The ethical dimensions of topics are considered and controversial issues are addressed, providing an arena for reflective development of concern for the common good and application of social values.

4. Social studies teaching and learning are powerful when they are challenging. Teachers model seriousness of purpose and thoughtful inquiry; and they encourage well-reasoned, reflective responses.

5. Social studies teaching and learning are powerful when they are active. Authentic activities that call for real-life applications using the skills, processes, and content of the field are emphasized.

Source: From National Council for the Social Studies (NCSS). (1994). *Expectations of excellence: Curriculum standards for social studies.* Washington, DC: Author.

environment is the societal context. These principles are highlighted in Figure 11.3.

Learning Through Reciprocal Interactions

A hallmark of a learning environment in which the classroom becomes society is what Paulo Freire (1972) calls **reciprocal interactions,** whereby teachers and children share control. Freire's model advances the idea of teachers and children holding knowledge collectively and, through diverse modes of interaction, negotiating further knowledge. Within this model, according to Steffey and Hood (1994), is a sharing of knowledge, decision making, power, and voice. Key features of this model include adapting the curriculum to children and guiding children's learning through collaborative problem posing and problem solving.

According to Steffey and Hood (1994), adapting the curriculum to children implies planning and implementing learning experiences that foster relevant, meaning-centered inquiry. Learning occurs in active classrooms in which children are encouraged to take risks, to experiment, and to further knowledge by connecting what they already know with what they wonder about in the real world. An additional aspect of this curriculum adaptation process involves encouraging learning in collaboration with others.

In classrooms in which social studies investigations are moored to a curriculum model that accommodates and highlights reciprocal interactions, topics of study are primarily based on children's interests. Selected topics develop naturally in response to questions or problems posed by the children and the teacher, usually in connection with some interesting or memorable event experienced by one or more children. Farm life became a topic of extended investigation by a group of seven- and eight-year-olds, for example, after one child shared with her classmates a visit her family took to a dairy farm. Learning experiences emerged from a set of questions posed by children in response to the teacher's invitation to share what they knew about farm life and what more about farm life they wanted to learn. In Figure 11.4, some representative questions about farm life posed by the children suggest a host of meaningful and inventive learning experiences the group might possibly undertake as they work together to gain new insights.

Here is an example of pursuing new insights through an inquiry approach. The topics investi-

FIGURE 11.4 Things about farm life we want to know more about

1. What different kinds of farms are there?
2. How are farms important to us?
3. How is life on a farm different from life in the city?
4. What kind of work do farmers do?
5. What kinds of tools do farmers use to help them do their work?
6. What is a farmer's barn for? What is it like?
7. Do farms stink? If so, why?
8. What kinds of animals live on a farm?
9. How are farms today different from farms of a long time ago?

gated by children, and the learning experiences their teacher helps plan for them, flow from the search for answers to questions that matter to children.

IMPLEMENTING SOCIAL STUDIES IN THE PRIMARY YEARS: THE PROJECT APPROACH

A powerful way to encourage young children to undertake investigations that are personally meaningful, to plan and make decisions about events and experiences in their lives, and to document, reflect on, evaluate, and gather meaning from those experiences is a curriculum process called the **project approach.** The project approach capitalizes on familiar experiences of children; offers multiple ways of active interaction with people, objects, and the environment; and extends over a period of time (Diffily, 1996). According to Katz and Chard (1989), as child-directed (and child-sensitive) research studies, projects can take many forms and include many areas of study. Projects are comprised of a set of

Projects provide children with a variety of opportunities for investigating their understanding around a topic that is important to them.

learning experiences designed to help children integrate their learning around an important topic. They include activities from a variety of disciplines, giving children and teacher the opportunity to explore the central questions from a variety of perspectives (Freeman & Sokoloff, 1996). Projects can last a few days or extend into several weeks or more.

The Reggio Emilia Approach

In the **Reggio Emilia approach,** a major feature is extensive use of relatively long-term, multi-faceted projects and themes that offer a broad and integrative framework for interaction (Berk & Winsler, 1995). Howard Gardner (1993) captures the spirit and philosophy of the Reggio Emilia approach in this elegant description:

It is a collection of schools for young children in which each child's intellectual, emotional, social, and moral potentials are carefully cultivated and guided. The principal educational vehicle involves youngsters in long-term engrossing projects, which are carried out in a beautiful, healthy, love-filled setting. Dewey wrote about progressive education for decades but his school lasted a scant four years. In sharp contrast, it is the Reggio community, more so than the philosophy or method, that constitutes Malaguzzi's central achievement. Nowhere else in the world is there such a seamless and symbiotic relationship between a school's progressive philosophy and its practices. [Loris Malaguzzi, the inspiring leader of the Reggio approach, died in January 1994.] (p. x)

Themes or projects are based on these considerations:

- They must allow for both individual child contributions and collective purposes;

- They must have some external structure, in terms of general goals, while allowing children to decide on their own subgoals and rules;

- They should provoke much dialogue and discussion among participants; and

- They should lend themselves to a variety of modes of representation. (Berk & Winsler, 1995, p. 145)

Notably, the specifics of what takes place in the Reggio Emilia curriculum depend on joint teacher and child decision making during shared inquiry and explorations. Such collaboration and negotiation are the key features of a curriculum that is "emergent." Encouraging children to "revisit" their work is a hallmark of the Reggio Emilia approach. Revisiting one's work involves, first, reflecting on the experience that resulted in the work. Reflection on one's learning experiences is often as important as the learning experience itself. In Reggio Emilia classrooms, children are constantly thinking about how their work might be changed and improved (Ruenzel, 1996).

As suggested earlier, rather than fragment the school day into subject time blocks, projects help integrate the curriculum. With guidance from the teacher, language arts, social studies, mathematics, science, and the fine arts can be interwoven around the topic of study (Katz & Chard, 1989; Trepanier-Street, 1993).

A Sample Project

The description of a curriculum project for six- to eight-year-olds in Appendix B illustrates some important constructs that have been addressed in this chapter. The host of questions and activities reflects a diverse array of interconnected learning experiences representing most of the basic content areas, including acquiring and communicating knowledge through reading, writing, speaking, and graphic/visual representations.

The project approach described in Appendix B at the end of this chapter is integrative, interactive, inventive, and dynamic. With the use of journals and drawings, the creation of models and dramatic presentations, and representations through sociodramatic play, it incorporates a rich variety of representational modes—sometimes referred to as the different voices of children (as indicated earlier in this chapter): various expressive avenues by which children can demonstrate their understandings. Throughout the unit, children are thoroughly involved in collaborative pursuit of greater understanding about concepts and questions that matter to them.

Benefits of the Project Approach

As the representative learning experiences indicate, the project-based curriculum activities permit children to work in various ways to accomplish both individual and group academic goals they have a major hand in determining for themselves. Because of the rich diversity of experiences implemented throughout each day (and over an extended period of time), across numerous content areas, and shared with the entire school, each child is able to make meaningful connections with his or her current understandings and useful contributions to the understanding of others. In this project approach, children are able to attain levels of understanding seldom possible without the combination of teacher guidance and cooperative interaction with classmates that characterize these project-approach activities.

The project approach involving collaborative learning groups is ideally suited for collective construction and attainment of meaningful goals through dynamic classroom interactions that, according to Berk and Winsler (1995), promote higher-order, literate modes of communicating and thinking. Projects help children acquire new knowledge and skills while developing dispositions toward learning and creating feelings of competence (Katz & Chard, 1989). Through projects, children have a variety of opportunities to represent their understanding; they learn to view themselves as successful problem solvers and "transformers of reality."

Small-group interactions that focus on common group learning goals enable teachers "to fulfill their crucial role of assisting children in explaining their ideas, raising questions, overcoming fears of risk taking when new challenges arise, and working together despite possible differences in language, cultural background, and abilities" (Berk & Winsler, 1995, p. 118). Moreover, by working together on projects, children develop more sophisticated social skills, becoming in the process more competent socially.

The example of a project-based curriculum unit described in Appendix B focused on hospitals as a theme. In Figure 11.5, other possible themes appropriate for children four- to eight-years-old are listed.

Although these areas of inquiry are typical of the kinds in which primary-age children might be interested, the specific projects ultimately selected for in-depth exploration emerge, ideally, from the interests and passions voiced by the children themselves.

SUGGESTIONS FOR TEACHING PRIMARY SOCIAL STUDIES

The variety of roles the teacher assumes while engaging in cooperative interactions with children that advance their learning is summed up by Moll and Whitmore (1993):

1. The teacher serves as a guide and supporter who helps children organize their questions and ideas, translate them into manageable

Farm animals	Water	Dental
Plants	Family	Bears
Seasons	Nighttime	Clothing
Tracks	Insects	Rocks
Food and nutrition	Weather	Dinosaurs
Farms	Oceans	Colors
Polar regions	Nursery rhymes	Pets
Native Americans	Flight	Work
Birds	Human body	Reptiles
Zoo animals	Recreation	Patterns
Fairy tales	Deserts	Forests
Amphibians	Outer space	Bones
Endangered species	Humor	Vehicles
Neighborhoods	Health and safety	Heroes
Dwellings	Conservation	Change
Human differences	Toys and games	Friendships

FIGURE 11.5 Representative topics for project-based curriculum units appropriate for children four to eight years of age

activities, and take risks in tackling new tasks within their zone of proximal development, thereby ensuring that each child experiences academic success.

2. The teacher serves as an active participant in learning, who explores, experiments, and collaborates with children.

3. The teacher serves as a facilitator, who consciously plans the environment and the curriculum and selects materials that foster children's purposeful uses of language and learning strategies.

4. The teacher serves as an evaluator, who monitors children's individual and collective development, calling on this information to create and reformulate learning experiences to fit children's continuously changing needs. (pp. 36–40)

According to Berk and Winsler (1995), richly diverse learning opportunities offered under the insightful guidance of teachers are keenly "important for sparking the interest and curiosity necessary to energize learning" (p. 130). A series of broad principles that offer guidance for teachers challenged by these diverse roles is advanced by Jones and Thornton (1993):

- Be sensitive to the knowledge, abilities, interests, attitudes, and cultural values and practices that children bring to learning situations.

- Arrange center-based activities that promote interactive problem solving.

- Promote and accept different solutions and strategies.

- Encourage children to tackle tasks within their zones of proximal development—that challenge and stretch their current skills.

- Offer many opportunities for modeling and engaging in higher-order thinking.

- Enrich communication: Explain to children the purposes of classroom activities and experiences, and have children explain and justify their thinking.

- Use ongoing assessments of children's zones of proximal development to plan and monitor instruction. (p. 27)

In good social studies programs, projects are frequently initiated and developed in response to teachers' suggestions, questions, or materials. Teachers hold themselves accountable for children's learning. On completion of an activity, children and teacher collaboratively evaluate what they did and why, what they will do next, and how they will do it. Together, they decide what they have learned from their investigations (Trepanier-Street, 1993).

Role of the Teacher in Reggio Emilia Programs

In a Reggio Emilia program, teachers carefully collect and save children's work and, if necessary, transcribe children's comments and questions. Albums for each child (like the journals maintained by the children in Mrs. Vega's classroom described in Appendix B) are filled with notations, drawings, observations, photographs, and anecdotal accounts. Like children's journals in the example from the hospital project, these albums serve as a method of organizing information, communicating with others, documenting children's progress, and providing evidence to children of their importance and the importance of this period of life (Rinaldi & Gandini, 1991).

One of your principal roles as a teacher is to engage children in dialogue and encourage them to communicate with you and with each other in as many of their voices or representational modes as they feel comfortable with, whether it be drawing, sculpting, writing, playing, or dramatizing. One ultimate purpose of these interactions is to encourage children "to search out people and experiences that will give them further insight and understanding" (Blair, 1994, p. 16).

When interacting with children, teachers need to be aware of the extent to which they might be imposing themselves on the situation. The following guidelines will help teachers establish pathways for interacting with children that are child sensitive and intuitive, rather than intrusive:

- Be aware of children's zones of proximal development. Interact with them at the level at which they are currently succeeding and help stretch their understanding to a higher (but reachable) level by use of a thought-provoking question, an illuminating comment, or an unexpected metaphor or analogy. (When Mrs. Vega noticed that a six-year-old in her class found that the tape she was using to fasten the head of her puppet on its body would not hold, Mrs. Vega withheld her assistance and watched as the child tried another kind of tape and then, after that failed, some glue. After the glue failed as well, Mrs. Vega gently intervened:

Mrs. Vega: My, Vera, you're working so hard on your puppet! Are you satisfied with how it's coming along?

Vera: No, I can't get the head to stay on good.

Mrs. Vega: Would you like to use some of these other materials? They might work better for you.

Vera: OK, I'll try.

By observing patiently, Mrs. Vega allowed Vera several opportunities to solve her problem on her own. When Mrs. Vega finally offered some assistance, she did so in an encouraging and supportive fashion.

- Monitor each child's level of frustration. This will enable you to know whether to continue to challenge, to back off, or to change direction or strategy.
- Review your progress and your students' progress regularly. What went well? What

needs improvement? What can you do next? How do you feel? How do your students feel?

- Encourage children to seek gradual improvement in their performance. One way to do this is help them document and evaluate early and later efforts to represent their understanding.
- Interact with children regularly, inviting them to share with you and with others their impressions about each successive stage of their learning.

(At the entrance to the sociodramatic play area in her classroom, Mrs. Vega approached a group of children just as they were concluding their activities there.)

Mrs. Vega: What have you learned during your work?

Phillip: I learned that you need to move that metal thing to the "zero" on the scale before you weigh a baby!

Marcie: I learned a new word—*syringe*! And I learned that you need to clean your hands first before you put the bandages on.

This brief discussion enabled Mrs. Vega to document some of the progress Phillip and Marcie were making in their explorations, and it provided an opportunity for the two children to demonstrate with pride what they had learned.

- Encourage children to explain a problem they encountered in their work; or invite them to share with you changes they decided to make between the first and second drafts of a story they are creating. These interactions afford teachers with unique insight into how children are thinking about the challenges they face in their explorations.

REFLECTIONS ON DIVERSITY

In the primary years, all children should be actively involved in the social studies curriculum, just as they should be involved in all other aspects of the curriculum (Ferretti & Okolo, 1996). In the social studies curriculum in particular, no child's voice should go unheard; no child's feelings should go unheeded. In a democratic, child-sensitive learning environment, a climate of celebration of individual differences prevails.

When provisions are made for including all children in project investigations, one's expectations for each participant must be realistic. In any well-conceived, project-based, social studies learning experience, opportunities for authentic contributions to a group's effort can be found for any child. Finding useful ways that each member of a collaborative learning group might contribute to the group's goals is itself a valuable educational experience for young children. Everyone learns (and wins) when worthwhile opportunities are provided each day for all children to assert themselves and to feel empowered.

Teachers should exercise caution not to surrender this precious time of children's lives to examination of ideas and events that are not substantive, engaging, or enduring in importance. They should not be reluctant to address issues of compelling human significance (e.g., racism, bigotry, elitism, injustice). These are among the things that imperil the harmony within the human community; and in the face of these sad realities, curriculum should not blink.

SUMMARY

Perhaps teachers face no more important task than nourishing the positive and purposeful dispositions of the young children in their care. Toward this end, teachers must create learning environments in which democracy is alive as the defining characteristic and the most influential force. Teachers must encourage children's reflections on those aspects of shared learning from which they might come to appreciate the contributions of others. Teachers must engage children in learning experiences that provide opportunities for them to discuss issues openly, to express ideas freely, to disagree agreeably, and to respect each person's voice in the community of learners.

Classrooms should be places in which all children will be able to follow the calling of their individual passions, where opportunities for constructing meaning flow, first and foremost, from the children's experiences. And last, young children should discover through their journey toward learning that, in classrooms, every individual is valued; every voice resonates.

REFERENCES

Berk, L., & Winsler, A. (1995). *Scaffolding children's learning: Vygotsky and early childhood education.* Washington, DC: National Association for the Education of Young Children.

Blair, H. (1994). Voice for indigenous youth: Literature for adolescents. In S. Steffey & W. Hood (Eds.), *If this is social studies, why isn't it boring?* (pp. 13–22). York, ME: Stenhouse.

Brady, P. (1992). Columbus and the quincentennial myths: Another side of the story. *Young Children, 47*(6), 4–14.

Branzei, S. (1995). *Grossology: The science of really gross things!* Reading, MA: Planet Dexter.

Bredekamp, S., & Copple, C. (1997). *Developmentally appropriate practice in early childhood programs.* Washington, DC: National Association for the Education of Young Children.

Bredekamp, S., & Rosegrant, T. (Eds.). (1992). *Reaching potentials: Appropriate curriculum and assessment for young children* (Vol. 1). Washington, DC: National Association for the Education of Young Children.

Derman-Sparks, L. (1989). *Anti-bias curriculum: Tools for empowering young children.* Washington, DC: National Association for the Education of Young Children.

Diffily, D. (1996). The project approach: A museum exhibit created by kindergartners. *Young Children, 51*(2), 72–75.

Edwards, C., Gandini, L., & Forman, G. (1993). *The hundred languages of children: The Reggio Emilia approach to early childhood education.* Norwood, NJ: Ablex.

Ferretti, R., & Okolo, C. (1996). Authenticity in learning: Multimedia design projects in the social studies for students with disabilities. *Journal of Learning Disabilities, 29*(5), 450–460.

Freeman, C., & Sokoloff, H. (1996). Children learning to make a better world: Exploring themes. *Childhood Education, 73*(1), 17–21.

Freire, P. (1972). *Pedagogy of the oppressed.* New York: Herder & Herder.

Fritz, J. (1982). *Homesick: My own story.* New York: Dell.

Gardner, H. (1993). Complementary perspectives on Reggio Emilia. In C. Edwards, L. Gandini, & G. Forman (Eds.), *The hundred languages of children: The Reggio Emilia approach to early childhood education* (pp. ix–xiii). Norwood, NJ: Ablex.

Greenberg, P. (1992). How to institute some simple democratic practices pertaining to respect, rights, roots, and responsibilities in any classroom (without losing your leadership position). *Young Children, 47*(5), 10–17.

Hendrick, J. (1992). Where does it all begin? Teaching the principles of democracy in the early years. *Young Children, 47*(3), 51–53.

Holmes, E. (1991). Democracy in elementary school classes. *Social Education, 55*(30), 176–178.

Jones, G., & Thornton, C. (1993). Vygotsky revisited: Nurturing young children's understanding of number. *Focus on Learning Problems in Mathematics, 15*(2–3), 18–28.

Jorgensen, K. (1993). *History workshop: Reconstructing the past with elementary students.* Portsmouth, NH: Heinemann.

Katz, L. (1990). What should young children be learning? *Child Care Information Exchange, 76,* 12–14.

Katz, L., & Chard, S. (1989). *Engaging children's minds: The project approach.* Norwood, NJ: Ablex.

Kriesberg, S. (1993). The Constitution and democratic education: Practicing what we preach. *Democracy and Education, 1,* 25–30.

Moll, L., & Whitmore, K. (1993). Vygotsky in classroom practice: Moving from individual transmission to social transition. In E. Forman, N. Minick, & C. Stone (Eds.), *Contexts for learning* (pp. 19–42). New York: Oxford University Press.

National Council for Geographic Education (NCGE). (1994). *Geography for life: National geography standards.* Washington, DC: National Geographic Research & Exploration.

National Council for the Social Studies (NCSS). (1990). *Essentials of the social studies.* Washington, DC: Author.

National Council for the Social Studies (NCSS). (1994). *Expectations of excellence: Curriculum standards for social studies.* Washington, DC: Author.

Noddings, N. (1995). Teaching themes of care. *Phi Delta Kappan, 76*(9), 675–679.

Quintero, E., & Rummel, M. (1996). Something to say: Voice in the classroom. *Childhood Education, 72*(3), 146–151.

Resnick, L. (1996). Schooling and the workplace: What relationship? In *Preparing youth for the 21st century* (pp. 21–27). Washington, DC: Aspen Institute.

Rinaldi, C., & Gandini, L. (1991, September). *Beginning theme project work with children.* Paper presented at the Hundred Languages of Children Conference, Detroit, MI.

Ruenzel, D. (1996, May/June). Paradise lost. *Teacher Magazine, 7*(8), 26–34.

Seefeldt, C. (1977). *Social studies for the preschool child.* Upper Saddle River, NJ: Merrill/Prentice Hall.

Seefeldt, C. (1995). Transforming curriculum in social studies. In S. Bredekamp & T. Rosegrant (Eds.), *Reaching potentials: Transforming early childhood curriculum and assessment* (Vol. 2, pp. 109–124). Washington, DC: National Association for the Education of Young Children.

Steffey, S., & Hood, W. (Eds.). (1994). *If this is social studies, why isn't it boring?* York, ME: Stenhouse.

Trepanier-Street, M. (1993). What's so new about the project approach? *Childhood Education, 70*(1), 25–28.

APPENDIX A:
THE NCSS SOCIAL STUDIES PERFORMANCE EXPECTATIONS

THEME 1—CULTURE

Social studies programs should include experiences that provide for the study of culture and cultural diversity, so that the learner can:

a. Explore and describe similarities and differences in the ways groups, societies, and cultures address similar human needs and concerns;

b. Give examples of how experiences may be interpreted differently by people from diverse cultural perspectives and frames of reference;

c. Describe ways in which language, stories, folktales, music, and artistic creations serve as expressions of culture and influence behavior of people living in a particular culture;

d. Compare ways in which people from different cultures think about and deal with their physical environment and social conditions;

e. Give examples and describe the importance of cultural unity and diversity within and across groups.

THEME 2—TIME, CONTINUITY, & CHANGE

Social studies programs should include experiences that provide for the study of the ways human beings view themselves in and over time, so that the learner can:

a. Demonstrate an understanding that different people may describe the same event or situation in diverse ways, citing reasons for the differences in views;

b. Demonstrate an ability to use correctly vocabulary associated with time such as *past, present, future,* and *long ago;* read and construct simple time lines; identify examples of change; and recognize examples of cause and effect relationships;

c. Compare and contrast different stories or accounts about past events, people, places, or situations, identifying how they contribute to our understanding of the past;

d. Identify and use various sources for reconstructing the past, such as documents, letters, diaries, maps, textbooks, photos, and others;

e. Demonstrate an understanding that people in different times and places view the world differently;

f. Use knowledge of facts and concepts drawn from history, along with elements of historical inquiry, to inform decision-making about and action-taking on public issues.

THEME 3—PEOPLE, PLACES, & ENVIRONMENTS

Social studies programs should include experiences that provide for the study of people, places, and environments, so that the learner can:

a. Construct and use mental maps of locales, regions, and the world that demonstrate understanding of relative location, direction, size, and shape;

b. Interpret, use, and distinguish various representations of the earth, such as maps, globes, and photographs;

c. Use appropriate resources, data sources, and geographic tools such as atlases, data bases, grid systems, charts, graphs, and maps to generate, manipulate, and interpret information;

d. Estimate distance and calculate scale;

e. Locate and distinguish among varying land forms and geographic features, such as mountains, plateaus, islands, and oceans;

f. Describe and speculate about physical system changes, such as seasons, climate and weather, and the water cycle;

g. Describe how people create places that reflect ideas, personality, culture, and wants and needs as they design homes, playgrounds, classrooms, and the like;

h. Examine the interaction of human beings and their physical environment, the use of land, building of cities, and ecosystem changes in selected locales and regions;

i. Explore ways that the earth's physical features have changed over time in the local region and beyond and how these changes may be connected to one another;

j. Observe and speculate about social and economic effects of environmental changes and crises resulting from phenomena such as floods, storms, and drought;

k. Consider existing uses and propose and evaluate alternative uses of resources and land in home, school, community, the region, and beyond.

THEME 4—INDIVIDUAL DEVELOPMENT & IDENTITY

Social studies programs should include experiences that provide for the study of individual development and identity, so that the learner can:

a. Describe personal changes over time, such as those related to physical development and personal interests;

b. Describe personal connections to place—especially place as associated with immediate surroundings;

c. Describe the unique features of one's nuclear and extended families;

d. Show how learning and physical development affect behavior;

e. Identify and describe ways family, groups, and community influence the individual's daily life and personal choices;

f. Explore factors that contribute to one's personal identity such as interests, capabilities, and perceptions;

g. Analyze a particular event to identify reasons individuals might respond to it in different ways;

h. Work independently and cooperatively to accomplish goals.

THEME 5—INDIVIDUALS, GROUPS, & INSTITUTIONS

Social studies programs should include experiences that provide for the study of interactions among individuals, groups, and institutions, so that the learner can:

a. Identify roles as learned behavior patterns in group situations such as student, family member, peer play group member, or club member;

b. Give examples of and explain group and institutional influences such as religious beliefs, laws, and peer pressure, on people, events, and elements of culture;

c. Identify examples of institutions and describe the interactions of people with institutions;

d. Identify and describe examples of tensions between and among individuals, groups, or institutions, and how belonging to more than one group can cause internal conflicts;

e. Identify and describe examples of tension between an individual's beliefs and government policies and laws;

f. Give examples of the role of institutions in furthering both continuity and change;

g. Show how groups and institutions work to meet individual needs and promote the common good, and identify examples of where they fail to do so.

THEME 6—POWER, AUTHORITY, & GOVERNANCE

Social studies programs should include experiences that provide for the study of how people create and change structures of power, authority, and governance, so that the learner can:

a. Examine the rights and responsibilities of the individual in relation to his or her social group, such as family, peer group, and school class;

b. Explain the purpose of government;

c. Give examples of how government does or does not provide for needs and wants of people, establish order and security, and manage conflict;

d. Recognize how groups and organizations encourage unity and deal with diversity to maintain order and security;

e. Distinguish among local, state, and national government and identify representative leaders at these levels such as mayor, governor, and president;

f. Identify and describe factors that contribute to cooperation and cause disputes within and among groups and nations;

g. Explore the role of technology in communications, transportation, information-processing, weapons development, or other areas as it contributes to or helps resolve conflicts;

h. Recognize and give examples of the tensions between the wants and needs of individuals and groups, and concepts such as fairness, equity, and justice.

THEME 7—PRODUCTION, DISTRIBUTION, & CONSUMPTION

Social studies programs should include experiences that provide for the study of how people organize for the production, distribution, and consumption of goods and services, so that the learner can:

a. Give examples that show how scarcity and choice govern our economic decisions;

b. Distinguish between needs and wants;

c. Identify examples of private and public goods and services;

d. Give examples of the various institutions that make up economic systems such as families, workers, banks, labor unions, government agencies, small businesses, and large corporations;

e. Describe how we depend upon workers with specialized jobs and the ways in which they contribute to the productions and exchange of goods and services;

f. Describe the influence of incentives, values, traditions, and habits on economic decisions;

g. Explain and demonstrate the role of money in everyday life;

h. Describe the relationship of price to supply and demand;

i. Use economic concepts such as supply, demand, and price to help explain events in the community and nation;

j. Apply knowledge of economic concepts in developing a response to a current local economic issue, such as how to reduce the flow of trash into a rapidly filling landfill.

THEME 8—SCIENCE, TECHNOLOGY, & SOCIETY

Social studies programs should include experiences that provide for the study of relationships among science, technology, and society, so that the learner can:

a. Identify and describe examples in which science and technology have changed the lives of people, such as in homemaking, childcare, work, transportation, and communication;

b. Identify and describe examples in which science and technology have led to changes in the physical environment, such as the building of dams and levees, offshore oil drilling, medicine from rain forests, and loss of rain forests due to extraction of resources or alternative uses;

c. Describe instances in which changes in values, beliefs, and attitudes have resulted from new scientific and technological knowledge, such as conservation of resources and awareness of chemicals harmful to life and the environment;

d. Identify examples of laws and policies that govern scientific and technological applications, such as the Endangered Species Act and environmental protection policies;

e. Suggest ways to monitor science and technology in order to protect the physical environment, individual rights, and the common good.

THEME 9—GLOBAL CONNECTIONS

Social studies programs should include experiences that provide for the study of global connections and interdependence, so that the learner can:

a. Explore ways that language, art, music, belief systems, and other cultural elements may facilitate global understanding or lead to misunderstanding;

b. Give examples of conflict, cooperation, and interdependence among individuals, groups, and nations;

c. Examine the effects of changing technologies on the global community;

d. Explore causes, consequences, and possible solutions to persistent, contemporary, and emerging global issues, such as pollution and endangered species;

e. Examine the relationships and tensions between personal wants and needs and various global concerns, such as use of imported oil, land use, and environmental protection;

f. Investigate concerns, issues, standards, and conflicts related to universal human rights, such as the treatment of children, religious groups, and effects of war.

THEME 10—CIVIC IDEALS & PRACTICES

Social studies programs should include experiences that provide for the study of the ideals, principles, and practices of citizenship in a democratic republic, so that the learner can:

a. Identify key ideals of the United States' democratic republican form of government, such as individual human dignity, liberty, justice, equality, and the rule of law, and discuss their application in specific situations;

b. Identify examples of rights and responsibilities of citizens;

c. Locate, access, organize, and apply information about an issue of public concern from multiple points of view;

d. Identify and practice selected forms of civic discussion and participation consistent with the ideals of citizens in a democratic republic;

e. Explain actions citizens can take to influence public policy decisions;

f. Recognize that a variety of formal and informal actors influence and shape public policy;

g. Examine the influence of public opinion on personal decision-making and government policy on public issues;

h. Explain how public policies and citizen behaviors may or may not reflect the stated ideals of a democratic republican form of government;

i. Describe how public policies are used to address issues of public concern;

j. Recognize and interpret how the "common good" can be strengthened through various forms of citizen action.

Source: From *Expectations of Excellence: Curriculum Standards for Social Studies,* by National Council for the Social Studies (NCSS), 1994, Washington, DC: Author. Copyright 1994 by the National Council for the Social Studies.

APPENDIX B: "WHAT HAPPENS AT THE HOSPITAL": A CURRICULUM PROJECT FOR SIX- TO EIGHT-YEAR-OLDS

During his spring vacation, seven-year-old Paolo had spent several days in the hospital, recovering from an appendectomy. When he returned to school, Paolo's teacher, Mrs. Vega, invited him to share his hospital experience with the class. Paolo's colorful description of his hospital experience stimulated a great deal of interest among his classmates, as well as the desire of many of his friends to talk about their own hospital experiences. Although some children mentioned having stayed in the hospital before, many could not remember ever being in a hospital, and others could remember being there simply to visit a sick relative or family friend. Noting the high level of interest in hospitals expressed by her students, Mrs. Vega asked them whether they would be interested in learning more about what goes on in hospitals. From their excited reactions to her question, it was clear that the class would welcome the opportunity to participate in a curriculum project focusing on the topic of hospitals.

THE HOSPITAL WEB

To stimulate the children's thinking about the topic and to gain some insight about the level of the children's understanding about hospitals, Mrs. Vega followed up the discussion accompanying Paolo's personal account by engaging them in the development of a curriculum web around the topic of hospitals. The development of a web, or webbing, is a simple and useful planning approach that invites children to brainstorm about a particular topic. As children generate ideas, these are incorporated into an expanded web that becomes a visual illustration of what may be included in a project approach to curriculum planning. Webbing is a playful and open-ended process designed to generate concepts, ideas, and questions related to a topic or theme. Webbing produces a picture of the way ideas may connect with one another. No idea or question is rejected as the web is being generated.

As the children expressed thoughts about hospitals, Mrs. Vega wrote these on a large sheet of paper for all to see. Some children wrote ideas on the chart themselves. After the children seemed to have exhausted all their thoughts about hospitals, Mrs. Vega extended their thinking with some questions: "Are all the people working at a hospital doctors or nurses?" "How do people get to hospitals?" The children's responses to these questions were added to the web, and the continuing discussion led to additional thoughts from class members. Lannie wondered, for example, whether everyone who goes to the hospital gets well. Davis wanted to know how much it cost to stay in the hospital. Tori was interested in what happens to animals that get sick. These thoughts were added to the web, along with all the other ideas and questions. As the web evolved, Mrs. Vega guided the class toward acknowledging those things about hospitals they knew, those things about hospitals they weren't certain they knew, and those things about hospitals they were certain they did not know. On the web, Mrs. Vega used a code to indicate these various levels of "knowing" indicated by the class.

Although webbing doesn't commit the class to investigating all the ideas it contains, many topics and questions generated will become areas of focus during succeeding in-depth exploration. The class may decide to investigate areas of concern lying along any of the web's pathways, depending on what interests them. Curriculum developed through webbing is one way the interests of class members are taken into account. It is one way in which curriculum (e.g., what happens in a learning environment) flows, or emerges, from the dynamic social milieu that is the classroom. Figure 11B.1 shows the web developed by Mrs. Vega's class of six- to eight-year-olds. The questions and issues of concern raised by the class were grouped on the web according to five or six subcategories of interest. These issues and questions formed the basis for Mrs. Vega's plans regarding her children's subsequent investigations into hospitals.

[Another relatively straightforward process for generating ideas to consider as part of a project for study is a procedure called K-W-L [see Chapter 4], or "Know" (What do we already *know* about the topic?"); "What" (What more about the topic do we *want* to know?"); and "Learned" ("What did we *learn* about the topic?"). In the K-W-L procedure, two lists are created as children express what they already know about a topic and what more they would like to know. This second list ("What more do we want to know?") serves as the point of departure for children's further investigations and is used as a basis for determining the kinds of learning experiences the children engage in. Serially throughout the unit and at the end of the unit, the teacher uses one or more assessment strategies to determine what the children actually learned. Teachers may experiment with both the webbing process and the K-W-L procedure and see which of the procedures best suits them.]

IMPLEMENTING THE PROJECT

After the web was completed, Mrs. Vega organized her class into collaborative working groups of four to five children. Each group was composed of at least one representative from each age level in the classroom. Once they were organized, the members of each group discussed the topics on the web chart and selected for in-depth investigation several topics that interested them.

After she observed which topics were selected, Mrs. Vega discussed with the class possible sources of information about hospitals, as well as possible activities the class might do to learn more about hospitals. From this discussion, it was discovered that the mother of a boy in class (Levi) was a nurse. Bianca, a girl in class, had an uncle studying at the state university to be a veterinarian. Mrs. Vega revealed that her family physician, Dr. McCall, worked one day each week at the local hospital. As they continued to brainstorm about possible sources of information about hospitals and about activities they thought would be exciting, the class generated a Resources and Activities list (see Figure 11B.2).

FIGURE 11B.1 Illustration of hospital web

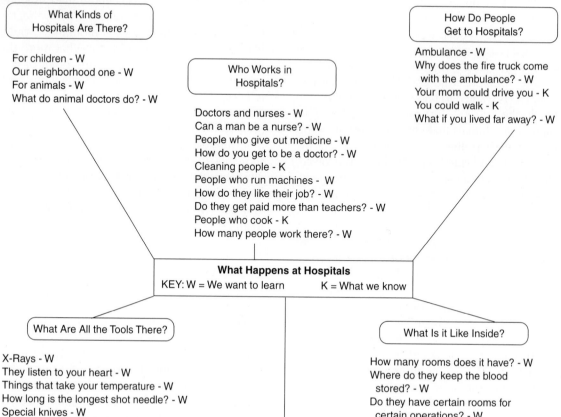

What Kinds of Hospitals Are There?

For children - W
Our neighborhood one - W
For animals - W
What do animal doctors do? - W

Who Works in Hospitals?

Doctors and nurses - W
Can a man be a nurse? - W
People who give out medicine - W
How do you get to be a doctor? - W
Cleaning people - K
People who run machines - W
How do they like their job? - W
Do they get paid more than teachers? - W
People who cook - K
How many people work there? - W

How Do People Get to Hospitals?

Ambulance - W
Why does the fire truck come
  with the ambulance? - W
Your mom could drive you - K
You could walk - K
What if you lived far away? - W

What Happens at Hospitals
KEY: W = We want to learn   K = What we know

What Are All the Tools There?

X-Rays - W
They listen to your heart - W
Things that take your temperature - W
How long is the longest shot needle? - W
Special knives - W
A thing that counts your heart pounding - W
How do they get blood into someone's body? - W
How many staples do they put in people's heads? - W
How much money does it cost for an operation? - W
What are those things that stop bleeding? - W

What Is it Like Inside?

How many rooms does it have? - W
Where do they keep the blood
  stored? - W
Do they have certain rooms for
  certain operations? - W
How much blood do they have in the
  blood room? - W
Where do you keep all the tissues? - W
In the blood place—How do they
  match up people's blood? - W

Why Do We Go to Hospitals?

You have trouble with your body - K
People who have something growing in
  them and they have to get it out - W
How do you do that plastic surgery—Like
  rearrange their face? - W
People who have "amnea" and forget who
  they are - W
How do they make casts when an arm is bent? - W
When you're hurt - K

People who have a hernia - W
When your leg is broken - W
To get stiches - W
To visit someone - K
To have a baby - W
When you're sick - K
Brain damage - W
You can't take care of yourself - K
Having your "abdominus" out - W

FIGURE 11B.2 Representative resources and activities list

1. Visit school and local library for books, tapes, and computer programs about hospitals.
2. Contact "experts" and invite them to speak to the class:
   - Dr. McCall
   - Levi's mother
   - Bianca's uncle
   - A local ambulance driver
   - The school nurse
3. Take a field trip to the local hospital and to the county health clinic.
4. Write and request catalogs from the regional medical supply office.
5. Work with parents to request health and medical brochures from individual family physicians.

Throughout the next several weeks, Mrs. Vega and her class were actively engaged in a host of intensive, richly diverse, challenging, and personally meaningful set of learning experiences related to interests they had previously expressed about what takes place in hospitals. The following learning experiences were included among the activities during a six-week period:

A visit to the school and local libraries yielded more than thirty books in which hospitals and the role of various medical personnel were discussed. These books formed the basis for extending the children's initial understandings about hospitals and medical care. The children read the books and recorded in their journals information about their topics obtained from the books. Information from the books also led to the development of a list of questions each group set out to address during the unit.

For each of several field trips the class took, a different group of children volunteered to plan the outing. To identify individuals willing to provide transportation, the children wrote and sent letters to parents. Schedules for the dates and times of the trips were made, arrangements for snacks while on the trip were made, and charts indicating how many vehicles were available and how many children each vehicle could accommodate were developed for each trip. The charts also indicated which children would be assigned to which driver.

In notebooks brought along on the field trips, each child wrote down things he or she found interesting and wanted to learn more about. The children wrote down questions for further investigation and drew sketches of things they saw at the hospital and the health clinic. Each group developed a map of the different rooms and floors for the locations they visited and indicated on them who worked there and the kind of work done at each site. The children also recorded in their notebooks the kinds of equipment and medical instruments they were able to observe on their visits. On returning to the classroom, the children reviewed their notes and sketches and refined them as they had opportunities over time to reflect and gather new insights.

Each collaborative learning group developed a journal in which group members kept a descriptive account of all they were learning about hospitals and medical care—documenting their learning experiences in terms that made sense to them. Contained in these journals were each group member's field notes, sketches and drawings, information gathered from books and discussions with guests, and sample brochures from the medical personnel and establishments they and their parents had visited. In addition, each child maintained a personal notebook in which to record individual reflections about what he or she experienced throughout the project and how he or she felt about those experiences. On a weekly basis, Mrs. Vega reviewed these journals and noted the children's new understandings, their misunderstandings, and their feelings about the project. She used these weekly reviews as a basis for modifying her project plans and for focusing learning experiences on areas of inquiry in which the children demonstrated continuing interest or misunderstanding.

The children returned from their field trips determined to create an exhibit of medical equipment they learned about. On tables set up around the room and in the school hallway, they displayed medical brochures they received from written inquiries to local physicians and the hospital and health clinic. From their notebook sketches, they drew pictures and made models of medical instruments. From several family physicians, they received donated surplus supplies, such as gauze, surgical tape, latex gloves, tongue depressors, and materials for making tourniquets. On clear acetate, they drew X-ray images; and on discarded animal X-rays they received from a local veterinarian, they labeled different animal bones and body parts. On one memorable day, Bianca's uncle (the student of veterinary medicine) used the animal X-rays to point out different animal body parts and challenged the class to decide in their groups (1) what animal body part was represented and (2) the function of the part.

Prior to a visit from the school nurse, Mrs. Vega encouraged the class to develop a set of questions they wanted her to address. Following the school nurse's visit, during which she responded to their questions and talked with them about first-aid and the dangers of medications, the children decided to sponsor a schoolwide poster contest to publicize these two issues. The children developed guidelines for the contest, publicized the event throughout the school, supervised the display of the posters, established parameters for judging the posters, and determined the contest winners for each of several age categories.

Once again relying on their field notes and sketches, the different groups worked together to develop a mural and scale model of their local community on large sheets of chart paper taped to a hallway floor. Various construction materials were gathered and used to create buildings, houses, trees, hills, bodies of water, and so forth. Included on the model were the locations and names of important community landmarks, including the school, each child's home, and of course, the hospital. Roadways and intersections were also sketched in and labeled. Again, as time went on, the children had ample opportunity to add to and refine their representations. After first estimating and predicting their answers, the children used the scale model over the course of several days to determine how far each child lived from the hospital, which child lived closest to the hospital, and which child lived farthest. On another occasion, the children took turns giving each other a series of directions beginning with a location on the model to see whether their friends could identify the "target" location.

Each collaborative group collected birth announcements from the local newspaper. Information from the announcements was used to create graphs to report information about weights of babies, time of day the babies were born, names of babies, and gender of each new baby.

A favorite activity was the development of a sociodramatic play area focusing on the hospital and medical care themes. Again, information the class had collected on their field trips (notebook sketches and notes), from books, and from discussions with guests provided the basis of the design and function of the play area. The children equipped this area with surplus items they received from community medical personnel and from home, with props they designed and created themselves (e.g., X-ray machine made from a large, discarded appliance box), and with uniforms found at various secondhand shops or created by the class from scraps of material with the help of their parents. On one occasion, the children brought in favorite dolls and stuffed animals and, using a scale supplied by the county health clinic, measured and recorded the weight of each "patient" after first estimating it. Another day, the children used this information to develop mathematics problems focusing on differences in weights of the dolls and stuffed animals.

Several weeks into the project, Mrs. Vega provided the children with an opportunity to write and send "get well" letters to some patients at the hospital. Using patients' names that Mrs. Vega had received from the Head Nurse at the hospital, the children wrote notes and created cheerful stories and pictures and sent them to selected patients experiencing prolonged hospitalization.

The children recorded the scale model of the community they created, as well as the dramatic play area, on videotape. In addition, each group created a script for a hospital story to be dramatized with puppets they created from paper mâché and cloth. The children also created, from assorted arts and crafts materials, hospital sets on which their puppets would perform. In collaborative learning groups, the children visited other classes in the school and presented their puppet drama, shared the videotape, and discussed the information they had gathered in their journals and notebooks. At the end of the six-week period, these same materials were shared with family members during a special evening presentation in appreciation for the families' participation in the project.

Throughout the period devoted to the evolution of this project, the teacher encouraged the children to continually revisit their products, reflective notes, journals, artwork, and other representations to refine their accounts and the details of their work. The purpose of this refinement was to acquire greater clarity and accuracy of understanding as new experiences may yield deeper meanings as well as new discoveries. At the conclusion of the project, Mrs. Vega was able to use the children's journals, their reflections on their experiences, the videotape, and other products to assess the growth made by the children.

Education is the fostering of growth, but apart from physical maturation, growth is only made apparent in expression—audible or visual signs and symbols. Education may therefore be defined as the cultivation of modes of expression.

(Read, 1956, p. 11)

12

Self-Expression in the Primary Years

CONSIDER YOUR BELIEFS

- What do you understand about the term *self-expression?*
- What do you understand is the distinction between "art" and self-expression?
- What is meant by the concept of numerous voices of children as it relates to children being self-expressive?
- What do you think should be the goals of a program for helping young children learn to be self-expressive?
- What does the term *enchantment* mean as applied to childhood?
- What are the characteristics of a developmentally appropriate self-expressive program in the primary curriculum?
- What do you believe is the role of the teacher in facilitating children's ability to be self-expressive?
- What do you believe is the importance of play for primary children? What do you think teachers can do to help facilitate children's play?

As much as anything else, education is a process of self-discovery, self-acceptance, and self-explanation. It involves a search for understanding about one's place in the world and, more important, a search for understanding about that world and about those with whom one shares life on the planet. In the complex, changing, pluralistic world in which we live, it is often difficult, according to Curry and Johnson (1990), "for children to construct and maintain valued identities" (p. 8).

In large measure, the world that children experience and their perceptions of it depend on the extent to which they have opportunities to gaze at it through the filter of their individual imaginations. Through their imaginations—their personal representations of their experience—young children are able to make (and reveal to others) some sense of all they encounter. It is not so much the experiencing of love, sorrow, anger, or accomplishment that informs the child, as it is the child's reflections on, and subsequent *representations* of, those experiences.

This chapter examines issues related to children's developing self-expression. What appropriate outcomes might one hope for when reality collides with young children's inventiveness and richness of expression? Throughout this chapter, the value of creating developmentally appropriate environments in which children's self-expression is nurtured is underscored. The importance of the teacher as a source of guidance and support for children's self-expression is also emphasized. By encouraging and helping children develop and give voice to their imaginations, teachers can help them learn to connect more intimately and more passionately with the world they inhabit and with the people who make up their families, their classrooms, and their communities.

WHAT DOES SELF-EXPRESSION MEAN?

Shortly after supper one September evening, Linda Rowe decided she would pick some zinnias while there was still enough daylight. As she strolled toward the back of her side yard, Linda's eyes caught sight of an unusual scene on the ground; she stopped to examine it more carefully. Nestled in the grass was a large semicircle of small pebbles that Linda's six-year-old daughter, Christy, had retrieved from a neighbor's gravel driveway. "Oh my," thought Linda to herself, "this is where Christy has been playing all day . . . until I called her to supper!" Linda could see at once that Christy had been very busy that day. The

pebbles formed the boundaries of a small village, and within the village "walls," more pebbles had been placed in a circle to form what appeared to be a village fire site. Christy had used sticks to construct family shelters, and cedar chips from beneath the small aspen grove to make roofs and pathways. Dried raspberries and a few corn kernels were piled together near one of the shelters. Near another shelter, a "water pond" was located, made from the plastic top from a margarine tub. Most interestingly, Christy had wrapped a collection of smooth, round pebbles in strips of dried corn husk. She had twisted and then tied these grassy sleeves around the pebbles with slender threads from a garden vine, creating by this process seven village "inhabitants." Cradling one of the creations in her hands, Linda smiled and whispered to herself, "Yes, how precious! These must be the people who live here!"

Precious indeed. To her surprise, Linda had stumbled on "Christy's World"—a playscape perceived and constructed out of her six-year-old daughter's inventiveness. In this magical village, Christy had spent one wondrous fall afternoon, abandoning it only on her mother's call to supper. From a stick shelter post to a family of cloaked figures, every aspect of this fantasy flowed from a young child's imaginative spirit. Christy hadn't simply occupied the side yard that day, she had transformed it. In that place, on that day, "people" had worked, slept, loved, played, ate, worried, laughed, got sick, got well, fought, and made up. What transpired in the lives of the village inhabitants was limited only by the boundaries of a young girl's imagination.

The playscape—a rich, authentic "archeological find"—reveals that it was most probably a site of spectacular self-expression, although one can only speculate as to the wondrous nature of it all. The pebbles, grass, dirt, and sticks remain as silent witnesses to all that Christy felt compelled to "say" that afternoon. Her corn-husk-clad friends give only an inkling of the nature of her adventures, and they'll divulge little of Christy's thoughts and feelings. Her heartfelt little girl secrets are safe with them—as they should be.

Self-expression refers to those things one does to "say" something—to convey a personal message about something or someone. When one is self-expressive, one "remarks" on one's experience; that is, one comments on it, criticizes it, or praises it. A child who twirls to the sounds of a spirited tune is expressing herself, demonstrating how the music makes her feel. A child who writes a poem about his grandmother is demonstrating how he feels about her or what he is thinking about her. The girl's dance and the boy's poem, like Christy's playscape, are other examples of ways by which children can be self-expressive.

To be self-expressive means to indicate how one feels or thinks about something or someone. If we could have been present to observe Christy's play, we might have been privileged to learn something about what Christy was thinking or feeling as she held reign over the domain she created. We could simply ask her, of course, but then we would risk getting a response that might not be as straightforward and unadorned as the messages that are conveyed when we observe her at play. When our interest is fixed on the domain of childhood self-expression, it is not so much insight regarding children's intellectual ability, as it is children's emotions and passions that are the objects of our concern and interest.

During group share time, six-year-old Zoe retrieved from her backpack a new pen she had received for her birthday. The pen could write in several colors, but what fascinated Zoe the most were the gizmos at the top of the pen: Dangling from a spring at the top of the pen was a clear plastic bulb containing sever-

al small wooden marbles. In skilled young hands, the contraption could be made to reproduce any number of different sounds.

"Hey, you guys, this is my impression of 'scared'!" said Zoe. [By plucking the top of the bulb and releasing it to spring back and forth, a sound was emitted similar to that of chattering teeth.] "Neat, huh? See, I'll make it sound like my teeth crunching together!" [By putting the bulb in her mouth and plucking the protruding pen-end, Zoe was able to produce a wobble-waggle-wobble sound.] "Isn't it just amazing what you can do with one pen!?" she exclaimed.

What intellectual illumination regarding her pen Zoe provides her peers in this illustration pales in comparison to the richness of her spirited and animated imaginative discourse. Capturing images of "scared" and "teeth crunching" through manipulation of her remarkable pen, Zoe transcends the academic significance of the moment, and through humor and creative impulse, she achieves the noble heights of passionate human interaction. This example of one moment in one day of a group of children's formal education, transformed by a child's imagination, is the sort of human experience that humanizes classroom discourse—a moment "civilized" by one child's self-expression. What Zoe shared with her friends wasn't anything earth-shattering, just something personal and kind of quirky—something *human.* In many classrooms, that's sometimes not half bad.

The following vignettes give some idea of the creative range children are capable of when they give free rein to their imaginations:

As Mr. Hooker was leading his seven-year-olds from the school cafeteria to the playground after lunch, Lori rushed up to him and exclaimed: "Mr. Hooker, did you hear me?! I did the Can-Can in burps! See, like this [starts singing]: 'Can-Can, can you do the Can-Can, can you do the Can-Can?' "

On an unseasonably warm Sunday in February, four-year-old Alexis found a beetle beneath a garden rock. Depositing it in an old peanut butter jar along with some grass and a slice of apple, she brought it inside the house, where it provided her company. The following Saturday, as she cradled "Sleepy" in her hand, Alexis pondered what to do with her new buddy:

Alexis: Should I keep him or garage-sell him?

Mother: Let's not decide right now, it's winter.

Alexis: Let's find a friend for him and sell them together so they won't be lonely.

Mother: We'll see.

Alexis: [Bringing Sleepy up to her face] Here, let's give him a little kiss so he'll know we're not going to get rid of him right now. [She gives Sleepy a kiss.]

Early in September, shortly after the beginning of school, Mrs. Burnstein, invited each of her kindergarten children to share what they thought anyone in their family might be good at. Rusty's response was one that took her completely by surprise:

Teacher: Rusty, I know that your father is a professor. What do you think he is good at?

Rusty: Cooking potato soup.

Teacher: OK. Is he good at anything else?

Rusty: Yes, stinking up the bathroom! Ha, ha, ha, ha!

From humor to compassion, young children astonish us with their spontaneous outbursts of intense playfulness on the one hand, and drama on the other. In these three examples, children's *humanity* escaped the bonds of the expected and the commonplace and jolted the observer out of the rut of ordinary thinking. If teachers respect and remain close to children, the children will help the teachers remain intimate with the wonder that is the nature of childhood. If teachers watch carefully, children will show them how inventiveness can overshadow plainness; how creative impulses can bring order to chaos; and how stylish daring can restore enlightenment to dulled senses.

Relationship of the Arts to Self-Expression

> The Arts are for the people, for everyday life, and they give that ordinary life civility and beauty. Nothing can be a work of art which is not useful, . . . which does not amuse, soothe, or elevate. (Morris, 1914, p. 17)

Learning experiences that fall into the popularly understood domain of the visual and performing arts (e.g., drawing, painting, sculpting, collage and other mixed media creations, drama, music, dance) all represent forms or modes by which children may choose to express themselves. These are the so-called **fine arts,** which, like play, poetry, block construction, and storytelling, are processes by which children express themselves aesthetically and physically. Simply, then, art is a form of expression—a kind of language. Indeed, in the Reggio Emilia approach, art, along with many other forms of self-expression, is considered a language, another way to communicate what one thinks or how one feels (Commune of Reggio Emilia, 1987).

As a means of representing ideas and feelings, the fine arts in developmentally appropriate primary classrooms are sometimes the specific focus of children's study, whereas at other

The visual and performing arts are forms of "languages" that children use to express themselves.

times, they are integrated into other areas of the curriculum (Bredekamp & Copple, 1997). Once children complete an art project, it speaks to others, just as language does. The power of art to communicate to others is explained by Carol Seefeldt (1995): "What were once personal thoughts, feelings, or experiences belonging to one person are now shared visually with others" (p. 40).

In reference to Seefeldt's quote, one might add all forms of expressive representations (e.g., music, poetry, movement, drama). For the sake of helping children become as competently self-expressive as possible, it is desirable to nurture children's creative dispositions in all the fine arts, just as it is desirable to help children become more imaginative players and storytellers.

Fostering children's creative expression in the fine arts includes helping children explore and experiment with various visual and performance media, as well as nurturing children's appreciation for the arts.

Interrupting her piano practice, seven-year-old Tiffany turned to another page and started playing for her father a piece she had not been introduced to yet:

Tiffany: I like playing this one, but I'm not supposed to play it.

Father: Why not? It sounds good.

Tiffany: 'Cause I'm just supposed to practice what I learn.

(Turning to the back of the book, Tiffany discovers a very complicated piece of music.)

Ohhhh! Look at all those dots [musical notes]! Hey, I bet that's what that guy we saw on TV plays! Oh boy, I get to learn to play like that!

One can tell from this vignette that Tiffany has a lot going for her in terms of creative motivation.

Teachers must nurture this kind of fondness for the arts that children demonstrate so early in their lives. One way of doing this is to allow them to "turn to the back of the book" if they wish and to indulge themselves at times in the pure fancy of courageous, creative exploration. In this way, they are likely to enjoy artistic investigations, as well as the various artistic forms they are likely to encounter in the process. The more children learn to appreciate the arts and to use various art media as "tools" for spontaneous (as well as guided) self-expressive representations, the more likely it is that they may become lifelong advocates of the arts as ennobling cultural influences.

The foundations for art history and art appreciation can be laid early. Children enjoy hearing stories about family heirlooms displayed around the house, just as they get excited about browsing through family treasures tucked away in captivating containers and nearly forgotten. A teacher can nurture children's pride in their history and culture by encouraging them to discover these family treasures and share them (and the stories behind them) in class.

The pride that children experience in learning about treasured family artifacts is matched by the almost instinctive reverence they have for beautiful objects. Provide children with opportunities to touch and hold delicate and gorgeous objects, and observe how wondrously focused they become. In the "be careful, don't touch" climate too often surrounding children, an opportunity to examine closely something classically and uncommonly engaging can be unforgettably transporting. Yes, even the young can be entranced.

ENCHANTMENT: THE SELF-EXPRESSIVE NATURE OF THE PRIMARY CHILD

If I had influence . . . I should ask [the good fairy] that her gift to each child in the world be a sense of wonder so indestructible that it would last throughout life, as an unfailing antidote against

the boredom and disenchantments of later years, the sterile preoccupation with things that are artificial, the alienation from the sources of our strength. (Carson, 1965, p. 42)*

When Kafele announces to his mother, "You know what I like, Mommy? I like it when people have a scab and I want to pick at it and crumble it up into pieces," he is expressing a child's sense of wonder. It is wonder that thrill's Deanna when she first learns to make her cheek "pop" by thrusting her finger out of her closed mouth. It's also wonder, colored by a touch of innocence, that inspires a child to name her new doll baby House-Key, as it is when a little girls chooses "long hair" when asked whether she'd rather have long hair or a million dollars. These examples of wonder illustrate the wondrous nature of young children.

A life filled with wonder about things is an *enchanted* life, a life possessed by innocence and overwhelmed by the charm and beauty of the world. **Enchantment,** according to Thomas Moore (1996), is "an ascendancy of the soul, a condition that allows us to connect, for the most part lovingly and intimately, with the world we inhabit and the people who make up our families and communities" (p. xi). In the following vignette, enchantment in her heart compels four-year-old Audrey to share with her mother the concern she is feeling for others dwelling in her house:

Audrey: Mama, I don't want you to set those mousetraps anymore!

Mother: Why not, Darling?

Audrey: 'Cause I like those mouses; they're sweet!

In addition to the many wonders that envelope childhood, the enchanting nature of the young child is sustained by the power of play—an unrelenting determination to conceive (and dream) of the most noble and civilized conditions possible for human existence. In her charming book *The Boy Who Would Be a Helicopter,* in which she celebrates children's creative imaginations, Vivian Gussin Paley (1990) refers to children as individuals who possess so much daring that they would "reinvent mythology." With vivid prose, Paley describes children's play as a journey of discovery in which children come to understand as much about themselves as they do about the world around them.

It is enchantment when a small boy's curiosity about his world is so acute that he feels compelled to sniff his shoes on removing them. More profoundly, it is also enchantment when a young girl's deep sorrow over the death of Cup Cake, her pet hamster, leads her to honor and memorialize it in the only thoughtful ways she can imagine—with her tears and a heartfelt drawing (see Figure 12.1). The experiences of both children speak of the singular nature of childhood: small bodies filled to overflowing with curiosity, daring,

FIGURE 12.1 Good-bye Cup Cake

compassion, and meaningfulness of purpose. How can primary teachers not be charmed?

Teachers demonstrate respect for children when they try to understand and accept children's special expressive natures. Teachers honor children when they show the children that what they *feel* is at least as important to the teachers as what they *know*. Children will know that teachers respect and honor them when they discover that in classrooms they can express themselves fully and freely.

"VOICES" OF CHILDREN: REPRESENTATIONS AND PASSIONS

As her family sat down to enjoy supper, Heather's mother announced that the seven-year-old had prepared the beans by using a recipe she created herself:

Heather: Yeah, it's Weird Beans; that's what I call it 'cause of what's all in there.

Mother: You might want to tell everyone what all you put in them.

Heather: Well, there's salt, spices, some beans, of course, garlic, because garlic's good for you, barbecue sauce. Guess what? I even put mustard in there . . . there's mustard. Oh, and some of that stuff you put in oatmeal, you know?

Mother: Brown sugar?

Heather: Uh huh, brown sugar. Then cook 'em; and that's what you do for Weird Beans. Neat, huh?

Before she had a chance to begin the school day with some group sharing activities with her kindergartners, Mrs. Nomo called on Juan Carlos, who had raised his hand to speak:

Juan Carlos: Mrs. Nomo, you don't go together today.

Mrs. Nomo: [Laughing] I don't? Why not?

Juan Carlos: Because that red [pointing to his teacher's sweater] doesn't match that red [pointing to her slacks].

One can see from Heather's creative recipe for beans and Juan Carlos's "reds that match" fashion statement that children's expressive sensibilities are fairly keen in the primary years. Variations on the broad theme of expression are demonstrated by Heather's original, if daring, bean creation on one hand, and Juan Carlos's aesthetic sensitivity on the other. In their different voices, both children share with others something about themselves—a personal preference, an attitude, an opinion—revealing in the process an intimacy they have with some aspects of aesthetic self-expression (e.g., creativity, coordination of color, balance and harmony among colors and flavors, or simply "what I like").

Children express themselves in countless ways: through drawings, play, music, mask making, poetry, movement, humor, weaving, dramatics, block building, snow sculpting, jewelry designing. In a richly diverse host of ways, children provide a window into their minds and their hearts as surely as they reveal to themselves, through their expressive products and experiences, a clearer understanding about their world.

A vivid example of a thoughtful and imaginative self-expressive project that a group of young children are capable of creating is the *Great America Afternoon News* project. This project was developed as a result of a series of investigations about their community undertaken by a class of seven- and eight-year-olds.

The **Great America Afternoon News** *Project*

The *Great America Afternoon News* project was planned, researched, and developed by a small group of seven- and eight-year-olds as part of a series of investigations in social studies. The group's teacher, Mrs. Fisher, had been guiding the class through an investigation of their community. One of the many questions in which the class expressed interest was, How do people find out what's going on in their community? As Mrs. Fisher led them through a discussion of this question, the class identified ways by which members of a community become informed (e.g., radio, television, newspapers, posters and flyers, group meetings, word of mouth).

Following the discussion, Mrs. Fisher encouraged those who were interested in this question to create projects that would help them address the issue. A group of four classmates thought finding out more about newspapers would be interesting. Over a period of almost three weeks, the friends discovered all they could about such questions as How are newspapers made? What kinds of information appear in newspapers? Who decides what appears in the newspaper? Where does the information in a newspaper come from? How does a newspaper make money? Why do people read the newspaper?

As the group's investigations evolved, they agreed that one thing they should include in their project presentation was a newspaper they would develop themselves; thus, the *Great America Afternoon News* newspaper was born. Members of the group met daily at school and visited regularly by telephone after school to discuss what their newspaper would look like, the kind of information to include, and who in their group would take responsibility for which parts of the paper. One member of the group, Shirley, volunteered to write the paper and draw pictures based on the ideas the group came up with. After the group developed, evaluated, and refined a few drafts of the paper, they were ready to share the first edition of the *Great America Afternoon News* with their classmates (see Figure 12.2).

The *Great America Afternoon News* is a creative tour de force. It is an inventive, self-expressive undertaking that reflects the insightful, sometimes humorous, and sometimes poignant imaginative representations of a group of young children. Through this project, the group members reveal to us their interest in, and the compassion they feel for, working with people with disabilities, helping women who are poor, and protecting the environment. Their humorously dramatic reflections on the weather, sports, and a violent criminal round out the "news of the day."

The *Great America Afternoon News* project is a remarkable example of the creativity young children are capable of when they are encouraged to engage in self-expressive projects that interest them. The teacher facilitated their efforts by providing guidelines that encouraged risk taking and free exploration of ideas; she also allowed ample time for planning, research and investigation, and refinement. The teacher also made herself available to pose questions, offer comments, and suggest possible sources of information to pursue.

In the vignette that follows, *dramatic play* serves as the medium for rich self-expression:

For an hour twice a week, eight-year-old Raesa visits one of the kindergartens in her school to work with the five-year-olds as a student volunteer. In the dress-up center, several boys and girls were engaged in a play theme related to working at the zoo. Raesa pretended she was a secretary at an animal clinic. During the play episode, Raesa announced that her clinic was starting a new service: animal braces! She then located some paper and markers and created this advertisement:

Animal Braces

THE NEW IMPROVED ANIMAL BRACES

The DELTA T animal clinic has animal braces. If your pet is having trouble with it's teeth bring it in right a-way our

FIGURE 12.2 *Great America Afternoon News*

Great America afternoon

News

coupons for mothers without much money

Recipies

Sports

in the world series loonie Smith on the Braves team hit a homerl over the wall two Braves Playe on the other side Started turnen Simon on hollerring

On the 21 Of Nov the Broco played the raiders the scors were Bronxos 0 Raiders 24 Not close Not!

Then Elway enjoy ha ha ha ha 20 peaple enjod in each sport all in hespitol to Dad

Weather

on fri and thers we are expecting a blizzard with 11,000 feet in snow

tempeture 100 below 0 brrrrrr

Sugg Jestion Stay in side very cold turn up heater

Handycaps

More and more people with disabiliteis are learning other kids are helping get groops started to help people with disabil teis

Specals

One hospital in greely has new Birthing rooms and mothers are haveingbabys like crazy no afence

radio

songs on the radio will be cut down because ot new for snow

recycling is

recycling is inpotant to our earth to clean the ocean and don't litter

More Weather

I conecicitt there was 70 inches ot snow all schools closed

calitonia oct 10 inches

in georga 10 inches of snow fell they were Suprised

but Antartica go 90,000,000 feet of snow

Blah Blah Blah Blah Blah Blah Blah Blah Blah Blah Blah Blah Blah Blah Blah Blah Blah Blah Blah Blah

1 most wanted

I don't pull the triger math?

Killed 3 people in the last 1 day

Ht 6 feet Weight 100 pounds?

Age 48

braces are gauunted to work and if they don't you get you money back but don't worry they work.

Dr. Raesa

This unexpected turn of events in the direction of the play inspired new and interesting possibilities for role play and for thematic elaboration within the group. The easy availability of writing tools helped Raesa move seamlessly into this mode of self-expression once her imagination conceived of a clinic advertisement as a natural representational extension of the dramatic play. From simple gestures and face making to more sophisticated forms of representation such as elaborate play themes or storytelling, children use a multitude of self-expressive modes to gain (and convey) greater understanding. Equally important, perhaps, all of these diverse modes of self-expression serve as different means by which children themselves might be more intimately understood by others.

Multiple Intelligences

Teachers' understanding of the different voices or forms by which children demonstrate self-expressive representations is further informed by the work done in the area of multiple intelligences. Since the early 1960s, the views about human intelligence that have most influenced the popular professional educational and psychological cultures have been those of Piaget and Vygotsky. In more recent years, however, the view of intelligence has expanded, thanks largely to the work of Howard Gardner and his theory of **multiple intelligences.** In 1983, Gardner proposed that a number of distinctive ways of thinking exist and that each way of thinking warrants acknowledgment as a unique type of intelligence (Gardner, 1993). As shown in Figure 12.3, seven types of intelligences were proposed in Gardner's theory.

FIGURE 12.3 Gardner's seven types of intelligences

1. *Verbal/Linguistic.* Intelligence with words and language, such as the skill possessed by a writer or a person who can speak several languages fluently.

2. *Logical/Mathematical.* Intelligence with sequential thinking and numerical reasoning ability, such as the abilities possessed by a mathematician or scientist.

3. *Bodily/Kinesthetic.* Wisdom about one's own body and its movements, such as the intelligence possessed by a figure skater or a wide receiver in football.

4. *Visual/Spatial.* Intelligence in using "the mind's eye" to work with images and see their relationships, such as the intelligence needed by an architect.

5. *Musical/Rhythmic.* Intelligence having to do with sound patterns, mastery of musical notation, and musical talent, such as the skills of a composer/performer.

6. *Interpersonal.* Intelligence in dealing with human interaction and perceptivity about how to resolve social problems, such as the abilities of a skilled counselor or therapist.

7. *Intrapersonal.* Wisdom about the self that leads to self-knowledge and personal growth, such as the intelligence of a person with "detailed, accurate self-knowledge."

Source: From "Multiple Intelligences Go to School," by H. Gardner and T. Hatch, 1989, *Educational Researcher, 18*(8), p. 6.

In recent years, Gardner (1995) has contemplated the inclusion of an eighth intelligence—the intelligence of the naturalist—to his theory of multiple intelligences. "Nature" intelligence might apply to a person who is easily capable of making and acting on knowledge about important distinctions in the natural world (e.g., plants, animals) and about the biological sciences.

Historically, verbal/linguistic and logical/mathematical have been the two forms of intelligence nurtured—some would say *stressed*—in a sustained and systematic manner in American schools. The remaining forms of intelligence (if recognized at all as important for classroom learning) have been addressed in only incidental fashion. Everyone has all seven intelligences and probably uses more than one intelligence to do any task. In terms of which intelligences they favor and which ones they excel in, children differ from one another. Teachers can help children develop each intelligence so that it is useful.

In primary learning environments in which programs promote self-expression as an important feature of the curriculum, development of the "whole" child is a guiding principle. This guiding principle would be reflected in classroom practices that promote children's skills and understanding across all seven types of intelligences. The sample project for seven-year-olds on pets (see Appendix A at the end of this chapter) developed by Isenberg and Jalongo (1997) provides a glimpse of a curriculum theme that addresses Gardner's seven types of intelligences.

Through the work of Gardner and other learning theorists (Forman, 1994; Katz, 1995; Malaguzzi, 1993), a clearer understanding exists regarding the ways by which individuals seek meaning in the world around them. Children not only exhibit different ways of learning and understanding but also demonstrate different ways of representing what they know (Bredekamp & Copple, 1997). The diverse approaches that children use suggest that teachers should (1) provide ample opportunities for children to use their "preferred" learning modalities and (2) plan experiences for children to exercise the types of intelligences or modalities of learning with which they may not be as proficient.

Art and the Child

Going all the way back to humankind's first attempts to represent an idea through a series of scratches on a cave wall, art in one form or another has been acknowledged (and used) through-

out history as a way to express feelings, experiences, ideas, or thoughts. When six-year-old Michael sets out with paints to produce the orangest, fattest, happiest jack-o'-lantern in the history of Martin Luther King Elementary School, he is connected in an almost spiritual way to our ancient cave-dwelling ancestors who felt compelled by some similar representational urge to make a statement (e.g., "running animal"; "a good hunt") and to express it in a form that might permit it to be seen by others. Both Michael and his Stone Age predecessor gazed at a blank surface and, surrendering to their imaginative impulses, transformed the cold surface into something warm and uniquely human. What links Michael and his cave-dwelling ancestral graffiti artist is the *intent* each had to use an "art medium" (e.g., a painting and a stone-scratched drawing) to express something each was feeling or thinking. Thus, the power of art to serve an effective communicative function similar to that of language can be seen.

One of the most compelling rationales for including the arts in a child-sensitive curriculum is to maximize children's creative self-expression in all its forms (Dixon & Chalmers, 1990). Among many young learners for whom words and written symbols may have insufficient connection with their personal expression of ideas and feelings, experience in music, art, and other expressive art forms can provide an avenue by which they can participate and contribute among the community of learners.

In a briefing paper prepared for the National Art Education Association, Colbert and Taunton (1992) addressed curriculum goals related to the visual arts for children. Colbert and Taunton emphasized the importance of nurturing children's ability to

- Use a wide variety of art media and artistic processes in a productive manner
- Observe works of art critically and interpret their meaning
- Use the visual arts to effectively communicate thoughts and dispositions

- Incorporate visual art forms to express oneself creatively

These visual arts curriculum goals for young children refer to technical, as well as creative, aspects of the discipline. Teachers can help children become familiar and skillful with the technical aspects of the visual arts by providing them with many opportunities to experiment with different art materials and media. The primary goal is to help children acquire an appreciation for the wide variety of art forms. Another goal is to help children become comfortable in their interactions with, and use of, a diverse array of art materials and processes. Children are most likely to develop increased proficiency in the technical aspects of art when their visual arts learning experiences flow naturally from personal interests they convey, when the environment is stress free, and when expectations are broad and open ended.

The creative aspect of art is the dimension most closely linked with a child's impulses, intuitions, and self-possessed perspectives about how things are and what they might become. Creative expression relies heavily on each child's personal inclinations and unique ways of perceiving. Children's creative expressions spring from the power of their imaginations and the freedom they feel to impose themselves on reality. In the process of imposing themselves on reality, child artists alter it—enliven it, color it, and subdue it.

Role of the Teacher

One goal of a child-sensitive primary expressive arts curriculum is to help children make the connection between an inspiration and its expression in some sort of self-reflective art form (Szekely, 1990). Besides helping children develop skill with the materials and processes of art, teachers can awaken the artistry in all children by

- Sharing with children numerous interesting and diverse examples of how people have used various art forms to express themselves creatively, including examples of artistic representations that portray (and that have been produced by) the richness of human diversity in our world

- Modeling for children examples of their own creative self-expression, as well as the appreciation they have for all forms of creative self-expression

- Planning and implementing learning experiences in which art is integrated as much as possible with the other curriculum domains

- Encouraging children to explore the countless ways they might represent an idea, a concept, a thought, or a feeling

- Providing numerous opportunities for children to *do* art

- Encouraging children to reflect on their artistic representations over an extended period of time, returning to them from time to time to modify, refine, or improve on them

- Praising children for all their attempts to be original and personally revealing in their work

- Working closely with every child to help each one discover her or his particular inner "voices"

- Encouraging all children in the community of learners to be accepting and appreciative of the attempts of their peers to be artistically self-expressive

- Providing a learning environment that is physically safe and psychologically comforting and in which every child feels welcome, secure, and valued

Technology as a Vehicle for Self-Expression

Although most of children's learning occurs through real-life experiences and active physical

Technologies offer children exciting ways to represent their ideas.

manipulation of things, educational technology—most notably, computer programs—can be used in primary classrooms to help children consolidate the understandings they have acquired from concrete activities. Computer technology can be integrated throughout the total curriculum to support and extend children's learning and development. Good computer programs are interactive and give immediate feedback. They also respond to children's individual learning needs and motivate children to attempt higher-level skills and accomplishments, thus extending their understandings (Beaty & Tucker, 1987). An example of how children can use technology as a medium for self-expression can be found in Appendix B at the end of this chapter.

One beauty of technology as a form of expressive representation is that it is an account of children's individual journeys. It is *their* presentation; it's what *they* make and what *they* say

that is important. It is an opportunity for children to express personal statements, and because of this, it helps reluctant learners blossom and gifted learners take flight. On the one hand, poor readers or writers, for example, may find their voice by using graphic representations to express their ideas. Gifted students, on the other hand, may overlay several layers of complicated animation effects on their presentations. Everyone can find some meaningful ways to represent her or his thoughts and passions successfully and effectively.

Whether teachers use HyperStudio (Wagner, 1995) or another computer program for helping children develop multimedia projects, computers can be an exciting, self-expressive medium with which teachers should help children become familiar. The future is almost certain to be more inviting to those with technological competence than to those who are not technologically competent. In addition, learning experiences that involve the sorts of multimedia, computer-based investigations as described in Appendix B encourage creativity, and children find them to be enjoyable, exciting, and highly motivating.

GOALS OF PROGRAMS FOR HELPING CHILDREN BECOME SELF-EXPRESSIVE

According to a position paper prepared for the National Art Education Association (Colbert & Taunton, 1992), at least three major guiding themes should be evident relative to the fine arts curriculum domain in developmentally appropriate primary classrooms: (1) Teachers should provide children with numerous opportunities to create art; (2) teachers should provide children with numerous opportunities to observe and discuss art; and (3) teachers should help children become mindful and appreciative of art in their daily lives. The attention and emphasis given to expressive arts, as with other areas of the primary curriculum, should emerge from the interests expressed by the children. In addition, children's artistically expressive projects should be primarily initiated by the children (Schiller, 1995).

In the following vignette, a young child points out what she sees as one of the difficulties about playing the piano. This account points out how it is sometimes necessary to interrupt a learning experience in which one is engaged to respond to some fairly immediate personal needs.

Seven-year-old Jodi had just finished practicing the piano, and her mother was complimenting her for doing so well on some difficult pieces. Jodi swelled with pride and remarked: "The hardest thing about playing the piano like at plays or in front of people is not to scratch yourself, but sometimes you can scratch yourself in the middle of beats, like right here" [pointing to a passage on a sheet of music].

Oh, to scratch! Is this the regal flaw that proves Jodi to be human? There is something warmly humane about this account. In pointing out sections in a musical piece that someone might exploit for the purpose of stealing a scratch (without missing a beat), Jodi reveals a nice bit of childhood inventiveness. At the age of seven, she's still innocent enough to share her "secret" about being able to scratch while playing an instrument. Most important, we are reminded that we are not working with wood, metal, or plastic, but rather with the bright minds, stirring imaginations, and gentle hearts of the young children of the world. Robots, after all, do not need to scratch.

The young piano player in the previous vignette reveals more than just a taste of childhood inventiveness. When Jodi comes up with a way to scratch while playing the piano, she is demonstrating in a small but important way that she can take control of a little part of her universe. She is showing that she can overcome an uncomfortable (if minor) constraint to which she is subjected when playing the piano. She shows that, with a little imagination, she can impose herself on the situation and modify it (to tame it) to suit her needs.

One major goal of a creative, self-expressive primary curriculum is to help children acquire the will and the means (the most appropriate media) by which they can impose themselves on their world. Teachers should help children understand that fulfillment in life involves more than simply experiencing the world as a passive occupant and consumer. Every time children impose themselves on their world by expressive words or acts of beauty, kindness, courage, charity, or humor, a small part of that world is illuminated and transformed. By helping children become more actively and creatively self-expressive, teachers are helping empower them with the means and desire to transform their lives and to touch the lives of others.

A second major goal of a self-expressive curriculum is to help children understand the power of self-expressive representations. The power in self-expressive creations lies in the *message* one hopes to convey. What are creative expression and the arts good *for*? This is the important question. This concern should overpower the question, What is good art? that seems to preoccupy so many people. What do children want to *say* through their self-expressive creations? Love? Unhappiness? Concern? Delight? Children are young message makers and communicators. One major concern of educators should involve helping children express their ideas, thoughts, and feelings to others in the most effective way possible.

A third major goal of primary curriculum that values the ability of children to express themselves through creative representations is to provide many opportunities for children to experience aesthetic enjoyment. Teachers should encourage children to interrupt their actively playful lives to observe, experience, represent, and preserve all the things surrounding them that are lyrical, harmonious, fascinating, decent, and noble. By helping children experience life's aesthetic pleasures (and by helping them create some of their own), teachers can help fill their hearts and imaginations with the best representations that nature and all of humankind can produce.

CHARACTERISTICS OF A GOOD SELF-EXPRESSIVE PROGRAM

When considering the characteristics of a good self-expressive primary program, the notion that should come to mind first is that of an atmosphere of acceptance and tolerance. The classroom climate is one in which all children are encouraged to express themselves openly and freely. It is a learning environment in which a sense of community spiritedness prevails, a place where the only unacceptable ideas and actions are those that are harmful to others.

In primary classrooms in which students and teachers alike are receptive to a wide range of ideas and viewpoints, learners feel encouraged to take chances. In these kinds of classrooms, a liberating of minds and attitudes takes place that allows for exploration and discussion of richly diverse expressive experiences, both in terms of substance and content and in terms of form and style. Thus, not only do learners feel free to express different or unpopular viewpoints, but they are also at liberty to choose from among countless expressive forms (e.g., poems, songs, paintings, dramatics, play, dance, sculpture, storytelling) a medium of expression they feel is most suitable to fit their needs.

In a developmentally appropriate self-expressive classroom, children are introduced to a wide variety of media with which they may de-velop representational ideas. Young children, especially, benefit from experiences that encourage to investigate different materials and to become comfortable "messing around" with them. In child-sensitive classrooms, teachers encourage children to explore the expressive possibilities of different media without requiring them to use a specific one as a means for expressing themselves. Some children prefer not to use such media as finger paints, plaster of paris mixes, or paper mâché that they may find messy or difficult to manage. Some children like to sing but not dance. A child who may enjoy designing and creating a puppet may be reluctant to perform with it.

In addition to introducing children to different *media* with which to develop expressive creations, the teacher should familiarize children with different expressive *styles*. Some messages that children may like to convey are most effectively represented in a fashion that is concise and to the point—information about fire safety, for example. On other occasions, the expression of humor can be very effective—an investigation about why people get so excited about the high school basketball team, for example. By modeling with examples from their personal lives or in their teaching, teachers should provide children with numerous examples of how different expressive styles (e.g., excited, angry, somber, humorous) can be effective.

With insightful comments and guiding questions, the teacher continually encourages children to "return" to their representations and constructions to consider what improvements they might wish to make: "This poster looks grand! Does it accomplish all that you had hoped when you first began?" "What might you do with some of our paints to liven up your puppet?" "Would any of these tools help you get the sort of shape in your sculpture that you're thinking about?" "The house you built certainly looks sturdy enough! What thoughts do you have about making it more cozy?" The teacher may also encourage children to keep a chronological record of their designs and notes throughout the evolution of their projects in order to see the changes that were made over time. To this record may be added photographs of each child's (or group of children's) project serially throughout the various planning and creation stages of the project.

An important feature of classrooms with good self-expressive programs is that the ideas and productive efforts of the children are celebrated. Children are provided with numerous opportunities to discuss their thoughts about a project and to share their ideas with others. The teacher may use a video camera to record the children working on their projects and then share the video with other classes and with parents. After the children's expressive representations are completed, these could be displayed around the school, along with the children's written descriptions of them.

A Perspective on Diverse Cultures

Creative, self-expressive art is the universal language. Every culture has some form of artistic self-expression and communication as part of its identity and celebrations. It is imperative that children have access to all forms of creative self-expression so that their lives may be enriched just as the lives of humankind throughout the ages have been enriched.

Children and teachers alike represent a wide variety of cultures, experiences, and backgrounds. Moreover, they bring with them diverse ways of expressing their feelings and ideas. Because children interact most effectively with others when they are not bound by inappropriate assumptions about their neighbors, teachers must provide them with many opportunities to explore and read about different cultures (Derman-Sparks, 1994; McMahon, Saunders, & Bardwell, 1997). Awareness and appreciation of other people's points of view begin with the realization that everyone is influenced by cultural experiences. By encouraging children to respect

every person's individuality and to broaden their view of valued modes of self-expression, teachers can help children learn to engage more purposefully with, and to reveal, their individual ways of understanding.

As children learn to be more artistically self-expressive, they acquire more "languages." More languages implies more (and more diverse) ways of looking at the world. Fostering appreciation for the variety of "languages" that children acquire is an element of a child-sensitive, self-expressive program that is cherished with the same unyielding passion as the appreciation fostered on behalf of richness of multiple cultural perspectives. One major purpose of a developmentally appropriate self-expressive program is to emphasize children's cultural strengths and to provide opportunities for children to reflect on, as well as preserve, personal memories they hold dear.

Healthy Minds and Healthy Bodies

In our society today, too many children are forced to confront home and community realities that seriously threaten their well-being. In an atmosphere of threats, stress, and depression, even the most stalwart of children can lose the grace of childhood. Family dysfunction and family and community violence are commonplace occurrences in the lives of tens of thousands of children; for many of them, school is their only sanctuary. For children who face physical and emotional torment on a regular basis and for children who are reminded every day of their inadequacy and insignificance, that step across the doorway into a classroom is a momentous stride that takes them from places of despair into a place of hope.

From about the age of three, the most fantastic thoughts spring from children's imaginations. Children's imaginations are the wellsprings of all that might be; through the powers of the imagination, anything is possible. As a result, children are both liberated and imprisoned by their fantasies. One moment a child can be a soaring eagle; in the next moment, the child is threatened by a terrible monster. Children's imaginations can visit upon them the loveliest dream, as well as the darkest nightmare. The following account of a young boy's anxiety around bedtime shows the influence his imagination has over him:

Eight-year-old Drake confided in his mother this brief acknowledgment of the demons he faced at bedtime when he was younger: "I used to be scared when I went to bed 'cause I thought something might happen to me. So I'd get out of bed and go to your guys' room and get you to rock me, remember? So you'd rock me 'til I went to sleep 'cause I'd be with you. The next day I'd wake up and go, 'Wow, I did it!' I'd feel like that almost every night. You know, if you think of something, it might happen; so you have to be careful what you think."

Children learn best in an environment in which they feel secure and in which they are made to feel valued. In a climate in which their psychological needs are being met, children not only grow and learn better but also are more creative in how they express their understanding. One key to children's emotional well-being is the establishment and nurturance of consistently positive supportive relationships with the teacher and other children. Through these relationships, children not only receive and benefit from the positive regard expressed by others but also experience the satisfaction of conveying the esteem they have for others.

Teachers can help establish a positive emotional climate by modeling positive dispositions in the classroom and by sharing with children examples of positive relationships from literature, film, news reports, and other sources. Another way the teacher can foster the creation and maintenance of supportive relationships is to incorporate lots of opportunities for cooperative learning experiences, as well as to establish "friendship groups" designed to help children discuss and resolve interpersonal difficulties. Although these important supportive relationships begin in the home, in psychologically healthy learning environments they grow to include school friends and, over time, members of the greater community.

The relationship of children's physical well-being to their successful development and learning is as significant as that of their psychological well-being. Healthy habits that children learn to follow early in their lives remain with them throughout their lives. On the one hand, children who eat and exercise properly and get adequate rest are able to apply themselves energetically and alertly to learning opportunities afforded them. On the other hand, children who are continually weakened and overwhelmed by disease, injury, poor hygiene, inadequate dental care, and poor nutrition are not ready and able to learn.

Child-sensitive primary programs include learning experiences that help foster children's development of healthy lifestyles. Children identified as suffering from ill health or practicing unhealthy lifestyles should be recommended to receive medical and dental health services. All children should be assured of receiving nutritious meals at school, as well as encouragement to develop healthy personal habits such as eating healthful meals and snacks, getting plenty of exercise and rest, and avoiding overindulgences. Teachers should be models of healthy lifestyles; they should plan and implement interesting and engaging lessons that address the importance of sound personal health practices. Children in the primary years have opportunities every day to make choices affecting their health; teachers

Children are more creatively expressive when they feel safe and comfortable.

should help them make the right choices for good health.

The personal safety of children should be a primary concern in all schools. Habits and concepts related to all forms of personal safety (e.g., water safety, fire safety, traffic safety, playground safety, safety issues regarding strangers) should be the focus of classroom discussions and activities throughout the school year. Having children act out and discuss scenarios related to common causes of accidents and what one can do to avoid them helps children learn how accidents can be prevented. Activities involving games in which children are asked to explain, "What would you do if . . .?" help children think about what to do or say when something unex-

pected happens. It is not a cliché to say that what children learn about safety could save their lives; it's true.

Children who develop safe and healthy personal habits set the stage for a lifetime of physical and emotional fulfillment. When teachers help them learn to make good choices regarding their health and well-being, every aspect of their lives is positively affected. Young children who practice lifestyles that help foster good psychological and physical health not only feel better but also *feel better about themselves.* For helping young children become more actively self-expressive, what better foundation than this can teachers try to provide them?

SELF-EXPRESSION THROUGH PLAY

Because of the fundamental role it has in children's development, play is recognized as an important (many would even say necessary) element in the lives of children of all ages (Bredekamp & Copple, 1997; Elkind, 1990; Isenberg & Quisenberry, 1988; Stone, 1995; Wolfgang & Wolfgang, 1992). **Play** represents a natural, spontaneous, goal-free process children engage in, almost instinctively, as they confront the marvelous (and sometimes inglorious) challenges that unfold throughout childhood. Imagination and fantasy, two fundamental elements of play, constitute the grand psychological liberators and artistic self-expressive assets of early childhood (Isenberg & Jalongo, 1997). Including play as an important part of the primary curriculum is one way of demonstrating that one's approaches to teaching and learning are child sensitive (Perlmutter & Burrell, 1995).

Perhaps more than any other human activity, play is the ultimate expression of humanity. Through the self-expressive medium of play, all children can find inspiration, excitement, insight, and healing, and in the process, they can "stand a head taller." Because the content and form of play emanate from the children themselves, it is an expressive form that respects (and frequently *reflects*) children's unique differences and diverse interests. As an essentially anxiety-free process with boundaries and rules determined by the children themselves, play has been referred to as children's best defense against stress (Elkind, 1988), and its place in the educative process of young children is crucial.

In a half-day kindergarten program for five-year-olds, a child in the afternoon program lay down on the oval rug and pulled a carpet flap over himself. The child then remarked to another child, "Hey, move those Legos; I'm going to roll up into a burrito!"

While playing in the sandbox during recess, Crystal and Brittany began imagining different uses to which they could put the various sandbox tools:

Crystal: [Holding a wooden spoon between her legs] Hey, Britt, look! Now I have a penis! Ha, ha, ha, ha!

Brittany: Wheeeeeeeeeeee! [Brittany then seizes two small plastic cups and, after filling them with sand, holds the cups behind her. Crouching a bit, Brittany pours the sand down between her legs onto the ground.] But look at this, Crys; pee-pee and poo-poo!

Crystal: Ha, ha, ha, ha! Hey, Goofy, you got some on you!

Brittany: Shhhhhsh; not so loud!

Although every level of play provides distinct benefits for children, the dynamic, complex, and spontaneous play interactions involving symbolic creations enable children to pursue avenues of communication that are richly self-expressive.

In the two examples above, natural, instinctive, colorful, and effortlessly conceived symbolic interactions are vividly illustrated. In both vignettes, reality (in the form of a carpet, a wooden spoon, plastic cups, and sand) is transformed, and a "new world" is created—one in which a boy becomes a burrito, a little girl "experiences" what being a boy may be like, and so on. Comfortable yet often spirited excursions into fantasy at levels such as these help children develop an ever more imaginative capability that will lead them eventually into the wonderland of play at the highest level. The highest level of play (**sociodramatic play**) is described in Appendix C at the end of this chapter.

Family roles are dominant in dramatic play, but children constantly try out a wide variety of character and functional roles as well (e.g., fire-fighter, princess, doctor, evil magician, school teacher). Dramatic play props that are not overly structured or rigidly suggestive of specific purpose are most likely to stimulate children's creative thinking processes. The specific functions of dramatic play are idiosyncratic and subject to the ever-changing whims of the player. They are limited only by the ability of children to determine the direction and intensity in which they want a theme to proceed. Common forms of play include simple imitation of adults, interpretation and elaboration of real-life roles, extensions of domestic relationships, reversal of roles, and expression of pressing needs and forbidden impulses (Hughes, 1995).

In sociodramatic play, children explore the ultimate in self-expressive accomplishment—transformation of oneself into a new self-identity, one that frees them to be as strong or bright or beautiful or brave as they might desire. Throughout those magic moments of fantasy, "living" for them becomes more exciting or more joyous or more peaceful or more tolerable. For that brief, glorious time, children are unhindered by the uncertainty, the anger, the awkwardness, the sadness, and the insecurity that may sometimes be visited upon them in reality.

Role of Adults in Enriching Children's Play

During breakfast, four-year-old Julia was watching intently as her father carved a face from a piece of banana. After he had finished, he "walked" the "banana man" across Julia's plate, from which spot Banana Man announced: "Hi, I'm Banana Man. What's your name?"

Julia smiled and answered, "Julia." Julia then seized the banana peel and created the following exchange between herself and the banana peel:

Julia: Are you Cinderella?

Peel: Yes, I am!

Julia: [Laying the peel on her plate] Oh, you forgot your pillow!

Peel: [Lying on the plate] Yes, I did! Good night.

(Julia then breaks off a piece of her banana and starts hopping it through the air.)

Hey, I'm Santa Claus! Ho, ho, ho, ho! Merry Christmas!

In the vignette above, Julia responded enthusiastically and seamlessly to her father's playful overtures. The ease with which Julia was able to slip into symbolic fantasy is readily apparent. If time had permitted, Julia's playful father could have easily *scaffolded* her play by engaging further in the play himself, by posing provocative questions focusing on "Cinderella," and by commenting on the scenarios initiated by Julia. By observing children's play and capitalizing from time to time on opportunities to scaffold the play episodes, adults can help extend the thematic possibilities, the rich opportunities for language stimulation, and the symbolic complexity. All of this results in children's increased understanding, as well as increased enjoyment.

One way that adults can encourage children to learn to play imaginatively is by modeling symbolic use of objects, just as Julia's father modeled symbolic use of the banana for her. Listed below are other things teachers and parents of young children may do to encourage children's imaginative play:

- In a dramatic play center, provide a rich assortment of real-life and make-believe props and dress-up clothes (hats and helmets; boots; belts; scarves; old furs; uniforms; purses; telephones; dolls and doll clothes; dishes and kitchen utensils; medical supplies and instruments; restaurant supplies, pads, and menus; maps and travel posters; typewriter; calculator; jewelry; wigs; writing materials).

- Provide time every day for children to play (both dramatic play and games with rules).

- Stimulate possible dramatic play themes by providing children with many ideas, stories, and concepts through books, films and videos, discussions, guest speakers, field trips, and so on.

- Join in the play of reluctant or nonproductive players; play alongside them and guide their play by introducing them to the play potential of different materials and by modeling play excursions for them; ease yourself out of the play as they assume more and more control over the materials and themselves.

- Encourage children to engage in many kinds of play opportunities throughout the week (dress-up; miniature-life play with cars, small animals, dolls; building with construction materials such as blocks, interlocking materials, and sand).

- Stimulate children's consideration of more in-depth play by offering timely comments, suggestions, and queries: "Your friend may need some medical attention. What do you think?" "Maybe the horses need a strong shelter. It looks like a storm's coming," "Should we make some signs describing what you're selling?".

- Ease out of children's play episodes as they demonstrate the ability and willingness to create, manage, and sustain productive play independently.

- Provide a wide assortment of materials and plenty of opportunities for large- and small-scale construction (appliance boxes for post offices, restaurants, fortresses; tabletop building materials for doll homes, animal shelters; large sheets of newsprint paper placed on the floor with materials for drawing and constructing a village, a jungle, a farm, a vacation site).

- Help organize children into cooperative play groups whereby productive players teamed with less productive players are able to model and assist.

- Show children that you value play by praising their play experiences, their efforts, and the fruits of their labor while engaged in play.

- Provide opportunities and encouragement for children to discuss the content of their play and to share some of their play adventures with their school friends.

- Allow time and opportunity for children to revisit their play-related constructions and to continue adding to and refining them over an extended period of time. Often as their constructions become more refined, the level of play increases.

- Recognize that even solitary players may be playing productively.

- Value the content of play as something a child self-determines, and therefore it becomes significant for the function it serves in helping the child be self-expressive in some personally meaningful way.

Appropriate adult encouragement, intervention, and modeling in children's play can increase the level of productive play, as well as stimulate social and intellectual competence (Ward, 1996). Through interested, supportive, and thoughtful adult involvement in children's play, positive and mutually respectful adult-child relationships are fostered as well. Effective adult intervention in children's play can result in more sustained and elaborate play episodes; by virtue of their supportive efforts, adults can convey the important message that play is a worthwhile and highly valued enterprise.

In their fantasy world, young children can try out resolutions to difficulties and, in the process, become better prepared to confront them with greater insight when play is finished. Through play, children can be refreshingly incautious,

The numerous benefits available to children through play are limited only by the power of their imaginations.

free to take chances and risks, because they understand that failing is not for keeps. Through play, children can experience fame, bravery, power, fortune, and "They lived happily ever after" endings in their mind-dreams. From those experiences, children can learn a little something about what is worth celebrating among the promises of each day.

As pointed out earlier, through play, children's journeys, experiences, and destinies are restricted only by the limits of their imaginations. Through what other experiences are children able to command such power over their existence? Play, so much more so than any other childhood endeavor, *liberates* the child and, in doing so, vividly illustrates the power of the human imagination.

REFLECTIONS ON DIVERSITY

As she was sharing books with her group of five-year-olds, Mrs. Ferrari observed that Gilley seemed more interested in *her* than in the books that morning. She couldn't help but notice that Gilley was staring at her face, rather than gazing at the pictures in the books. After the group finished discussing the stories and returned to work at the various centers, Gilley, who had remained at Mrs. Ferrari's side, looked up at her and finally spoke:

Gilley: Mrs. Ferrari, do you wish you weren't handicapped?

Mrs. Ferrari: Why, Gilley, I'm *not* handicapped. Do you think I am?

Gilley: Uh huh. You have a scar on your chin like I do on my knee, and that means you're handicapped.

Mrs. Ferrari: Well, Gillster, we both *do* have scars, but a scar doesn't make us handicapped. Being handicapped means a person needs to find ways of doing things that are different from the ways most people do them. Having a scar doesn't do that.

Gilley's concern about being handicapped presented Mrs. Ferrari with a perfect opportunity to refine her young student's understanding of this aspect of diversity. Observing the nature of Gilley's understanding of what being handicapped means, Mrs. Ferrari might follow up this episode with a more in-depth discussion about diversity involving the entire class. Mrs. Ferrari's response to Gilley brought out the fact that because someone has a handicap, it doesn't mean she or he can't do things; the person just accomplishes them in a different way. Young children have little difficulty understanding this concept, especially when they have opportunities to observe it in inclusive classroom settings.

In developmentally appropriate inclusive classrooms, the abilities of all children are valued, their limitations are understood, and opportunities are provided for all to develop self-esteem and respect for others. In inclusive classrooms, "students work toward the same educational outcomes; what differs is the level at which these outcomes are achieved and the degree to which emphasis is placed on them" (Schrage & Burnette, 1994, p. 1).

The concept of inclusion is one of the most polarizing issues in education. The various positions on the issue are often debated by the different constituent groups under an intensely emotional cloud. One reason why the issue of inclusion is so divisive is so many examples exist of poorly instituted inclusionary practices. If inclusion is ever to become widely adopted and supported in public schools, the way it is put into practice must be feasible, positive, and educationally defensible.

McLeskey and Waldron (1996) suggest that four criteria be used to judge the viability of inclusive programs. These four criteria are listed in Figure 12.4.

A fundamental tenet of an **inclusion** model holds that all children will be able to succeed academically and socially. At the heart of this principle is the acknowledgment that children may be learning different things at different rates and in different ways. When a child plays, works, and learns in a fashion that is appropriate, *that*

FIGURE 12.4 Four criteria of good inclusion programs

1. A good inclusion program is one in which students with disabilities make at least as much academic and social progress as they would in a separate classroom.

2. A good inclusion program is one in which there is academic and social progress for typical students that is at least as great as these students would make in noninclusive classrooms.

3. A good inclusion program ensures that teachers are supported as they make the necessary classroom adaptations to meet student needs and that they are actively involved in determining the form of this support.

4. A good inclusion program reflects the concept of normalization; that is, the rhythm of the day for students with disabilities is as similar as possible to the rhythm of the day for typical students.

Source: From "Responses to Questions Teachers and Administrators Ask About Inclusive School Programs," by J. McLeskey and N. Waldron, 1996, *Phi Delta Kappan, 78*(2), p. 155.

child will succeed. As teachers provide similarly appropriate experiences for every other child, *all* children will experience success.

When a teacher welcomes a child with a disability into the classroom, the rest of the children will observe how the teacher conducts him- or herself around that child. By treating the child with a disability the same as any other child, the teacher demonstrates to the other children that the child with a disability is as important to the community of learners as every other child. All the things a teacher does to show children that he or she values them (e.g., play with them, talk with them, praise them, assign them classroom responsibilities, joke with them) should be done in equal measure with children with disabilities.

In a developmentally appropriate inclusive primary classroom, children with disabilities may require educational accommodations to achieve learning expectations within the same content area as their nondisabled peers. For example, for children with disabilities, teachers might engage them in learning different social studies concepts, mathematics problems, or self-expressive projects. Giangreco (1996) suggests other adaptations or alternative teaching methods one might effectively implement on behalf of children with disabilities:

- Peer tutoring
- Computer-assisted learning experiences
- Reorganization of chairs and tables to allow for closer proximity to peers and competent modeling
- Different ways for the students to respond if they have difficulty speaking or writing
- Use of tactile and auditory cues for students with visual impairments; and
- Materials that are easier to manipulate for children with physical disabilities (p. 59)

"Josh takes a lot of teasing . . . 'Short bus! Short bus!' Short on intelligence, you know? And Josh is even smarter than most of them; he's just really emotionally high-strung. Poor thing."

A Primary Teacher

It's always unfortunate when children are subjected to ridicule and taunting. One important teacher responsibility is to create a learning environment in which all children are valued and the self-esteem of every child is nurtured. Children sometimes seize on an observed difference between themselves and another person and use that difference as a reason for demeaning that other person. In a community of learners in which (1) differences among individuals are honored and (2) everyone's personal strengths are recognized and nurtured, there is a greater likelihood that caring dispositions can be fostered and a climate of mutual respect will prevail. One major goal of inclusion is that children will learn to better understand each other by working and playing together; from that understanding, respect and acceptance will follow.

SUMMARY

Too often, primary learning experiences that promote creative self-expression are included in the curriculum as a cosmetic frill, a fancy fringe decorating the outer edges of "real" education. One important challenge facing educators is to retrieve the arts in all their forms from the outlying (and isolated) regions of the curriculum and install them as a vital and permanent fixture of curriculum that is developmentally appropriate.

Teachers can nurture self-expression in children by encouraging them to venture sometimes beyond the facts and to gaze with wonder at the stars or discover not simply how many legs a caterpillar has but also how it *feels* to have one crawling up the length of one's arm. When children learn to be artistically self-expressive, they learn to contemplate the appeal of the nonsensical over the necessary; with them, faith remains strong in the possibility of creating a world that is calm and beautiful, rather than savage and garish. Just imagine.

REFERENCES

Beaty, J., & Tucker, W. (1987). *The computer as a paintbrush: Creative uses for the personal computer in the preschool classroom.* Upper Saddle River, NJ: Merrill/Prentice Hall.

Bredekamp, S., & Copple, C. (1997). *Developmentally appropriate practice in early childhood programs* (Rev. ed.). Washington, DC: National Association for the Education of Young Children.

Carson, R. (1965). *The sense of wonder.* New York: Harper & Row.

Colbert, C., & Taunton, M. (1992). *Developmentally appropriate practices for the visual arts education of young children.* NAEA Briefing Paper. Reston, VA: National Art Education Association.

Commune of Reggio Emilia. (1987). *The hundred languages of children.* Reggio Emilia, Italy: Author.

Curry, N., & Johnson, C. (1990). *Beyond self-esteem: Developing a genuine sense of human value.* Washington, DC: National Association for the Education of Young Children.

Derman-Sparks, L. (1994). Empowering children to create a caring culture in a world of differences. *Childhood Education, 70*(2), 66–71.

Dixon, G., & Chalmers, G. (1990). The expressive arts in education. *Childhood Education, 67*(1), 12–17.

Elkind, D. (1988). From our president: Play. *Young Children, 43*(5), 2.

Elkind, D. (1990). Academic pressure–too much, too soon: The demise of play. In E. Klugman & S. Smilansky (Eds.), *Children's play and learning: Perspectives and policy implications* (pp. 3–17). New York: Teacher's College Press.

Forman, G. (1994). Different media, different languages. In L. Katz & B. Cesarone (Eds.), *Reflec-*

tions on the Reggio Emilia approach (pp. 37–46). Urbana, IL: ERIC Clearinghouse on EECE.

Gardner, H. (1993). *Frames of mind: The theory of multiple intelligences* (10th Anniv. ed.). New York: Basic Books.

Gardner, H. (1995). Reflections on multiple intelligences: Myths and messages. *Phi Delta Kappan, 77*(3), 200–209.

Gardner, H., & Hatch, T. (1989). Multiple intelligences go to school. *Educational Researcher, 18*(8), 4–10.

Giangreco, M. (1996). What do I do now? A teacher's guide to including students with disabilities. *Educational Leadership, 53*(5), 56–59.

Hughes, F. (1995). *Children, play, and development.* Boston: Allyn & Bacon.

Isenberg, J., & Jalongo, M. (1997). *Creative expression and play in early childhood* (2nd ed.). Upper Saddle River, NJ: Merrill/Prentice Hall.

Isenberg, J., & Quisenberry, N. (1988). Play: A necessity for all children. *Childhood Education, 64*(3), 138–145.

Katz, L. (1995). *Talks with teachers of young children: A collection.* Norwood, NJ: Ablex.

Malaguzzi, L. (1993). History, ideas, and basic philosophy. In C. Edwards, L. Gandini, & G. Forman, (Eds.), *The hundred languages of children: The Reggio Emilia approach to early childhood education* (pp. 41–89). Norwood, NJ: Ablex.

McLeskey, J., & Waldron, N. (1996). Responses to questions teachers and administrators ask about inclusive school programs. *Phi Delta Kappan, 78*(2), 150–156.

McMahon, R., Saunders, D., & Bardwell, T. (1997). Increasing young children's cultural awareness with American Indian literature. *Childhood Education, 73*(2), 105–108.

Moore, T. (1996). *The re-enchantment of everyday life.* New York: HarperCollins.

Morris, W. (1914). The lesser arts. In *The collected works of William Morris* (Vol. 22). London: Longman's Green.

Paley, V. (1990). *The boy who would be a helicopter.* Cambridge, MA: Harvard University Press.

Perlmutter, J., & Burrell, L. (1995). Learning through "play" as well as "work" in the primary grades. *Young Children, 50*(5), 14–21.

Read, H. (1956). *Education through art.* New York: Pantheon.

Schiller, M. (1995). An emergent art curriculum that fosters understanding. *Young Children, 50*(3), 33–38.

Schrage, J., & Burnette, J. (1994). Inclusive schools. *Research Roundup, 10*(2), 105–108.

Seefeldt, C. (1995). Art: A serious work. *Young Children, 50*(3), 39–45.

Smilansky, A. (1968). *The effects of sociodramatic play on disadvantaged preschool children.* New York: Wiley.

Smilansky, S., & Shefatya, L. (1990). *Facilitating play: A medium for promoting cognitive, socio-emotional, and academic development in young children.* Gaithersburg, MD: Psychosocial & Educational Publications.

Stone, S. (1995). Wanted: Advocates for play in the primary grades. *Young Children, 50*(6), 45–54.

Szekely, G. (1990). An introduction to art: Children's books. *Childhood Education, 66*(3), 132–138.

Wagner, R. (1995). *HyperStudio: Reference and tutorial.* El Cajon, CA: Author.

Ward, C. (1996). Adult intervention: Appropriate strategies for enriching the quality of children's play. *Young Children, 51*(3), 20–25.

Wolfgang, C., & Wolfgang, M. (1992). *School for young children: Developmentally appropriate practices.* Boston: Allyn & Bacon.

APPENDIX A: APPLYING THE THEORY OF MULTIPLE INTELLIGENCES

1. *Verbal/Linguistic.* Imitating or identifying animal sounds, discussing storybooks about pets, maintaining an observational log about a classroom pet, creating group booklets about favorite pets, tape-recording reports about a particular type of pet

2. *Logical/Mathematical.* Counting the number of pets owned by everyone in the class, creating a simple bar graph of the favorite pets of children in the class, listing the common features of domesticated animals, rank-ordering pets from most to least popular, identifying the most unusual pet owned by anyone in the group, matching various pets to their preferred food choices, analyzing the consequences of neglecting pets' care

3. *Bodily/Kinesthetic.* Moving like different pets (e.g., a turtle, a puppy, a bird), comparing the relative sizes of pets to one another and oneself, inventing a dance that characterizes a particular animal

4. *Visual/Spatial.* Making sculptures of various pets, examining a pet closely and creating life-size drawings, identifying animal tracks and arranging them from largest to smallest, designing a poster to encourage responsible pet ownership

5. *Musical/Rhythmic.* Finding or inventing an instrumental selection that captures the feelings associated with various pets, singing songs about animals, choosing a rhythm that matches the characteristic movement of a pet

6. *Interpersonal.* Participating in a class project designed to safeguard the welfare of pets in the community, interviewing a pet shop owner, arranging a classroom visit with an expert on animal care

7. *Intrapersonal.* Maintaining a journal of activities enjoyed with a pet, describing reasons for choosing a particular pet as a favorite, preparing a statement of beliefs about animal rights.

Source: From *Creative Expression and Play in Early Childhood* (2nd ed.) (p. 13), by J. Isenberg and M. Jalongo, 1997, Upper Saddle River, NJ: Merrill/Prentice Hall.

APPENDIX B:
TECHNOLOGY AS A VEHICLE
FOR SELF-EXPRESSION

Not only can computers be used to help children learn, but they can also help children become excited about learning. In the following vignette, the seven-year-old's enthusiasm over using the computer as a learning tool is quite apparent:

Driving home after school with her mother, Gayla could hardly contain herself as she described what she was learning on her class's regular visits to the computer lab in her school:

Gayla: You know what, Mom? I learned about HyperStudio . . . and I can get animals! I can use ClarisWorks and find animals out of it! And today, you know what? I made a dog and I made its tail move!

Mother: It sounds like you had a great time! What else are you learning about the computer?

Gayla: You draw things with tools, you can write, you can make movies on it—little short movies. You can do Ghost Writer . . . and . . . I don't know how to do it. Next time we go to computers, we're going to do something about countries. I'm thinking about doing Atlanta, that place we visited.

The computer program that Gayla found so exciting is HyperStudio, a computer software program developed by Roger Wagner (1995).

HyperStudio is a multimedia educational computer tool that lets children produce self-expressive representational "environments" (e.g., children can use drawing tools to create their own illustrations; they can input pictures about a topic; they can input video clips; they can add their own voices or other sounds; they can enter words and sentences; and as Gayla pointed out, they can add animation—make a dog's tail wag or create a car driving across a landscape or map). The representations that children create are interactive, and in their development, children learn to combine information and facts in text form with graphics, movies, and sound into exciting projects.

Very briefly, HyperStudio presentations are developed by children who engage in a process of designing and creating a "stack" comprised of a small number of "cards" containing information about a particular topic. For example, if the project theme for a group of seven- and eight-year-olds were "My Favorite Things," each child or group of children would develop a stack of cards around such topics as favorite foods, favorite television programs, a favorite sport, a favorite season, a favorite hobby, or a favorite holiday. Each card the children created would contain (1) different information the children discovered about the topic, (2) different expressive forms the children chose for representing the information, and (3) "buttons" created by the children that help the user navigate through the stack.

A set of cards for a HyperStudio stack (presentation) about summer as a favorite season may include such representations as:

Text: "Summer is my favorite season. It is the warmest time of the year."

Visual: A multicolored computer drawing of several children riding their bicycles on a bright, sunny day.

Text: "People like to get outside and do a lot of things in the summer."
Visual: An assortment of pictures illustrating different kinds of things people like to do in the summer scanned onto the card.

Text: "This is me with my family on vacation last summer."
Visual: A picture of the child's family visiting a national park drawn with markers and scanned onto the card.

Text: "Last summer, I went fishing with my family and caught this big fish!"
Visual: A photograph of the child proudly holding the fish she caught last summer.

Text: "Our team won four games last summer. In one game, I had a hit every time up!"
Visual: Crayon drawing of the child in her softball uniform, holding her arms up in celebration.
Audio: Child's voice hollering "Yeaaaaaaaah!"

Text: "In the middle of every week, we would roast marshmallows at night and tell ghost stories."
Visual: A picture drawn with markers of the child's family around a campfire, with ghosts swirling above their heads.
Audio: A howling sound as a ghost might make produced by the child, followed by the statement: "I wish summer would last longer."

FACILITATING INVOLVEMENT IN COMPUTER-BASED REPRESENTATIONS

The teacher's role in facilitating children's use of computer technology to develop self-expressive presentations begins by discussing with the children possible topics they wish to explore. These discussions would also involve brainstorming ideas regarding what different segments of a presentation on a particular topic might look like. After children decide on the topics they wish to explore, the teacher familiarizes them with the procedures for using the computer program selected. If HyperStudio is used, the class may create a stack together as a collaborative, guided lesson.

Once the class has worked through a few cards together, the children should be ready to begin planning possible concepts and ideas they want to address and sketching or listing their ideas on index cards. At this point, the teacher undertakes a chronology of guidance and support procedures that proceed throughout the two or three weeks devoted to the project. The teacher

- Plans and implements learning activities related to the broad topic the students are investigating and that complement their individual investigations

- Provides resources (e.g., books, magazines, newspapers, videos, posters, maps) containing information the children might use and ideas about how they might design their presentations

- Monitors students' progress in implementing the guidelines and procedures accompanying the computer program

- Reminds students and guides their work with procedures to follow to create the expressive representations they desire

- Points out to students the location of pictures, graphics, and other devices they wish to incorporate into their projects, as well as what they need to do to retrieve the information and resources

- Encourages children to reflect on their projects and offers suggestions and poses questions to stimulate and focus their reflections

- Provides children with reminders, brief checklists, and visual cues that help them recall the steps they need to follow at various stages of their projects as practiced in their earlier guided lesson with the entire class
- Observes children's progress, praises their ongoing efforts, and offers suggestions related to editing, spelling, and grammar

- Encourages children to review their progress continually, with an eye toward modifying and refining their work as they acquire new information
- Provides opportunities for children to share their completed projects with other members of the class, with others in the school, and with parents

APPENDIX C: SOCIODRAMATIC PLAY

Beginning in the preschool years, children's fluid use of symbolization in their play evolves in continuously elaborate fashion, attaining, after several years, competency at the level of richest self-expression—sociodramatic play. The parameters of sociodramatic play have been defined by Smilansky and Shefatya (Smilansky, 1968; Smilansky & Shefatya, 1990) on the basis of six components:

1. *Imitative Role Play.* The child undertakes a make-believe role and expresses it in imitative action and/or verbalization. [Roger slips on a dress and high heels and places an old pair of spectacles on his nose. Turning to two other children, he announces: "All right students, it's time to get out your readers. Bonita, you read first."]

2. *Make-Believe with Objects.* Toys, unstructured materials, movements, and verbal declarations are substituted for real objects. [Elvin wraps strips of paper towel around Binh's "wounded" leg. Picking up the cardboard tube remaining from an empty roll of toilet tissue, Elvin gazes into Binh's mouth: "Say 'ah, ah.' Wow, that thing back there moves too much; I might have to take it out. Lay down."]

3. *Make-Believe with Actions and Situations.* Verbal descriptions are substituted for actions and situations. This procedure consists largely of make-believe with situations in which the child says, for example, "OK, you better not move, you're hurt. I'll take care of you just like I did for Fluffy, so don't worry. Here, take some of this." Verbal descriptions at times accompany make-believe actions such as pretending to give a patient an injection.

4. *Persistence in Role Play.* The child stays with a single role or related roles for an extended period of time—from a five- to fifteen-minute time period throughout which the child remains essentially "in role."

5. *Interaction.* At least two players interact within the framework of a sociodramatic play episode. [Miranda assumes the role of mother, while Ritchie assumes the role of father. Along with dolls that are assigned roles as their children and housekeeping and workplace-related props, Miranda and Ritchie engage in imaginative scenarios related to the theme of parenthood. The actions and verbalizations they create are tightly connected to the theme they share—their behaviors and dialogue remaining in character and directly

related to the cues each provides the other.]

6. *Verbal Communication.* Some verbal interaction is related to a sociodramatic play episode. [In the role of a space shuttle commander named Captain Starlighter, Darlene directs the training of Cometman, a new recruit in the astronaut program played by Nate. Early in the play episode, Captain Starlighter asks Cometman to explain why he would be a good astronaut. A bit later, Captain Starlighter poses various space-flight-related problems and challenges Cometman to try to figure out and tell or show her what one should do in a given situation. The discussion between the two is true to their characters and is rich, colorful, and fluid.]

Sociodramatic play experiences afford children opportunities to escape the bounds of reality and, through fantasy, to generate a new reality, one in which they hold power over all that takes place. The outcomes of fantasy play are the outcomes the children search for and dictate. The content and themes of fantasy play are those they summon from their own imaginations.

Glossary

accommodation   a Piagetian concept that refers to the process by which a child creates a new mental structure or modifies old ones on the basis of new information.

adaptation   a Piagetian concept that refers to how a child's knowledge is created and changed over time through the processes of assimilation and accommodation; as the demands of the environment change, so does the child's ability to deal with them.

anecdotal records   factual narratives or notes written by the teacher to document an observation of a child's behavior as the child engages in learning.

assessment   the process of collecting information and gathering evidence about what children know and/or are able to do.

assessment portfolio   a collection of a child's work samples over a period of time, including planning documents, drafts, and final products selected by the child and the teacher to document the child's learning and progress.

assimilation   a Piagetian concept that refers to the process by which a child "takes in" information from the environment and incorporates it into an existing knowledge structure.

aural language   listening; receptive verbal language.

authentic assessment   assessment that takes place while children are engaged in contextual learning situations (actual vs. contrived) or that requires children to engage in tasks that reflect "real-life" situations.

bodies of evidence   many sources of assessment data collected in a variety of contexts over a period of time.

checklist   a list of observable child behaviors or performances that serve as benchmarks of progress toward an identified classroom, school, or district goal; used to keep track of a child's work or progress.

child-sensitive curriculum   a curriculum that respects and responds to individual developmental differences and cultural and linguistic diversity; relationships among adults and children are interactive, learning experiences emphasize planned interactions with concrete materials, and many of the learning experiences are child initiated.

cohesive curriculum   a curriculum that makes sense to children and helps them make sense of their world; a curriculum organized around topics that reflect the concerns, interests, experiences, and environments of children and that may draw on and address more than one content area or discipline.

concepts about print   understandings that emerging readers have about the reading process and the form that written language takes. Specific understandings include identifying the front of the book; understanding that the words, and not the pictures, relate the message; where to begin reading on a page; directionality; and wordness.

constancy of words   the understandings that (1) a given word consists of the same sequence of letters each time it appears in print and (2) when writing a word, it is spelled with the same letters (and in the same letter sequence) the writer sees when reading the word in a book.

constructions   projects planned and constructed by children that may include painting, drawing, cutting, pasting, and woodworking.

constructivism   an aspect of Vygotsky's sociocultural theory of development that refers to children's attempts to create meaning based on their experiences; experiences become meaningful because of the interpretation children give them;

children are involved in making connections between new information and their existing understandings.

content objectives   critical knowledge that children are required to understand about the subject areas under study.

content subjects   the disciplines such as science, social studies, math, language arts, music, and art; the various perspectives, structures, and ways of organizing what one knows about the world.

criterion-referenced assessments   assessments with a predetermined level of mastery used to measure the extent to which a child is mastering *specific* content, regardless of the achievement of other children.

critical friend   an individual respected and trusted by the teacher and invited into the classroom by the teacher to observe, listen, share insights, ask thought-provoking questions, share helpful information, help generate instructional alternatives, and problem-solve with the teacher.

critical knowledge   specified information, concepts, or processes that children are expected to learn.

cues   sources of information a reader uses to construct meaning and to identify words when reading; the sources of information include semantics (meaning/vocabulary), syntax (sentence structure), and graphophonics (sound/symbol associations).

curriculum   what is to be taught and how it is to be taught.

democratic classroom   a classroom in which democratic values and behaviors are reflected and experienced throughout each day; children learn to relate ideas to behaviors appropriate for members of a democratic society (cooperative learning, open discussion, democratic decision making, respect for self and others).

developmental   occurring along a continuum, roughly correlated with age and directly related to previous experiences.

developmentally appropriate practices   those practices that take into consideration the aspects of teaching, learning, and assessment that change with the age and experiences of the individual learners.

diagnostic assessments   assessments designed to provide in-depth understanding of children's strengths and needs in specific areas (e.g., literacy, math, oral language development).

dictated language experience (DLE)   a sentence, paragraph, or story dictated by a child or group of children to an adult after a discussion of an experience; the adult writes the dictation in such a way as to deliberately model or demonstrate specific concepts about print, reading, and/or writing; becomes initial reading material for emerging readers.

directionality   the understanding that print is read or written from left to right with a return sweep and from top to bottom.

disciplines   the various perspectives, structures, and ways of organizing what one knows about the world; see also *content subjects*.

dispositions   inclinations (curiosity, friendliness, cynicism, creativity, generosity, aggressiveness) to respond to certain situations in certain ways.

emergent literacy   literacy development prior to the ability to read and write conventionally; indicated by a range of reading and writing conceptualizations and behaviors that begin long before children enter school.

emergent storybook reading   children's attempts to "reread" familiar storybooks; pretend reading. Children demonstrate a range of reading-like behaviors based on their prior literacy experiences and their familiarity with the book.

enchantment   an innocent and wonder-filled state of being by which children interact and connect intimately with other people and things.

equilibration   a Piagetian concept that refers to a child's continual process of cognitive self-correction and clarification. Assimilation and accommodation are the two subcategories of equilibration.

ESL   English as a second language; often used to identify students who are learning English as a second language.

evaluation   the process of making sense of, drawing conclusions about, and making judgments or decisions based on many sources of assessment data (*bodies of evidence*).

explicit instruction   a type of instructional interaction used to directly teach specific strategies, skills, or information. It is followed by opportunities for the student to try out the new learning with support and then independently.

facilitator   teacher or other adult who sets up the learning environment, structures it for independent learning, and supports learning.

fine arts   the visual and performing arts (e.g., drawing, painting, sculpting, using mixed media, dancing, singing, dramatizing) that represent media by which children may choose to express themselves.

formal measures   measures used to collect data under controlled conditions; all norm-referenced and standardized measures. Other assessments conducted under controlled conditions, such as performance samples, standards-referenced assessments, and criterion-referenced assessments can also be considered formal measures.

gender equity   equal opportunity for, equal treatment of, and equal acknowledgement of the accomplishments of girls and boys.

habits of mind   internalized dispositions, cognitive processes, and attitudes that come to control or guide an individual's ways of behaving and ways of thinking.

HyperStudio   a multimedia computer tool that lets children develop creatively expressive projects by combining information in text form with graphics, movies, and sound.

immersion   an instructional approach in which ESL students learn English by being completely immersed in English to the exclusion of their native language.

immersion stage of an integrated unit   the first stage of an integrated unit during which the teacher determines what children already know, creates enough familiarity and curiosity about the topic that children are able to generate interesting investigations, builds a common language and basic concepts with shared experiences; and teaches any new skills the children will need to conduct their investigations.

inclusion   the provision of special education support and services to children within the general classroom, as opposed to the provision of such support and services outside the classroom environment; the practice of including children with developmental delays and disabilities in day-to-day classroom learning experiences; provisions are made for all class members to succeed academically and socially.

individualized education program (IEP)   an individual educational program designed by a multidisciplinary team for a child who may receive special services; the IEP identifies specific instructional goals, targeted standards for performance, and who will be responsible for helping the child achieve the identified goals within a specified time frame.

informal assessments   nonstandardized measures primarily designed to inform classroom instruction through observation; often teacher constructed.

innovations of a text   new versions of patterned, predictable texts written or dictated by children.

instructional interactions   interactions that occur between teachers and children and that are intended to help the children construct new knowledge and become self-regulated learners.

instructional objectives   the knowledge, processes, and abilities children need to become increasingly informed and proficient learners.

instruction–assessment–instruction feedback loop   the continuous collection and use of information during assessment and instruction by the teacher to inform (design, or modify) both current/future instruction and current/future assessment; instruction is used as an opportunity for assessment, and assessment is used as an opportunity for learning about instruction.

integrated curriculum   learning events and opportunities organized around topics or concepts within children's range of understanding that is based on connections between and among disciplines or subject areas, materials, and strategies.

invented spelling   see *sound spelling.*

investigations   planned opportunities, both active (asking questions, interviewing, researching) and receptive (listening and reading), for children to develop new ideas and understandings.

language predictable books   books with one or two sentences per page that are written in the natural language of most children (everyday syntax, rather than literary language and syntax).

learning cycle   a constantly recurring process in which children acquire an interest in something, ponder and explore it, and evaluate, use, and apply what they learn.

lending library books, magazines, videotapes, computer programs, educational games, and other resources collected and organized to be lent to parents of students.

literacy events planned opportunities for children to read, write, listen, and speak within a meaningful context designed to result in increased proficiency or new understandings.

logico-mathematical knowledge knowledge of objects that comes from identifying a relationship between objects (e.g., longer than, similar in color).

long-term instructional goals goals grounded in the philosophy of the school community that serve as the filter through which all decisions about curriculum, instruction, assessment, and funding are funneled; the habits of mind that have been identified as the desired results of participation in an educational system.

maintenance an instructional approach in which ESL students are taught in their native language to facilitate their cognitive development. Proponents of the maintenance approach believe that children will not be able to process information as effectively or to incorporate new information into the schemata grounded in their native language if they are taught exclusively in a new language.

manipulative materials materials that provide the children handling and using them with concrete references to explore and think about; materials that provide children with tactile and visual opportunities for discovering relationships and concepts.

mathematical power the extent to which children value mathematics, are confident in their ability to do mathematics, are able to solve mathematical problems, are able to communicate mathematically, and can reason mathematically.

mathematics the study of number, form, arrangement, and associated relationships, using a formal system of symbols. Mathematics consists of questioning, posing and testing various strategies for drawing conclusions, and determining the accuracy of results.

maturation genetically predisposed patterns of change in development that occur as individuals become older—aging from the moment of conception through childhood, adolescence, and early adulthood to late adulthood.

mediation a teacher's use of wait time, questioning, prompting, and scaffolding to help children apply what they know to new situations and to become capable, self-regulated learners.

mini-lesson a short, concise, episode of explicit instruction of a strategy or skill related to an observed need of a group of children.

miscue a reader's deviation from the printed text when reading.

multiple intelligences as proposed by Howard Gardner, at least seven different ways of thinking (verbal/linguistic, logical/mathematical, bodily/kinesthetic, visual/spatial, musical/rhythmic, interpersonal/intrapersonal). Children differ in terms of which intelligences they favor and excel in.

norm-referenced assessment an assessment designed to determine how a child or group of children perform in relation to other children of the same age and grade.

oral language speaking, expressive verbal language.

pedagogical content knowledge (PCK) effective ways to help children understand a particular content area; includes knowledge of strategies for teaching a topic, knowledge of children's understanding of the topic, and knowledge of curriculum.

perceptual learning the redefining of concepts through the subconscious processes of assimilation and accommodation.

performance sampling an assessment procedure that requires active engagement of children in carefully designed, open-ended learning activities; systematic observation and evaluation of both the process and the product are conducted to draw conclusions regarding children's level of development and instructional needs.

personal word bank printed words generated from familiar materials and personal writing (including dictated language experience), as well as words that are personally significant to the child.

phonemic awareness the conscious awareness that words are made up of phonemes, or sounds, and the ability to segment the spoken word into those sounds, but not necessarily the ability to identify the letters that can represent those sounds.

play   a natural, essentially anxiety-free, spontaneous, relatively goal-free, child-initiated process that children engage in largely out of personal impulse, desire, and motivation.

primary context   a learning environment designed to address the interests and needs of children ages four to eight; children may be organized on a same-age basis or on the basis of mixed ages, whereby children two or three years apart in age play and work together in the same classroom.

process objectives   the processes and abilities that children need to develop to become increasingly proficient learners.

process subjects   those subjects or skills that serve as the tools or vehicles with which children develop and conduct their investigations, think about and construct understanding, and communicate their learnings with others (reading, writing, math, technology, art, music).

project approach   an approach to teaching and learning designed by Katz and Chard that seeks to engage children's minds in ways that deepen their understanding of their own experiences and environments and in ways that enhance their emotional, moral, and aesthetic sensibilities. Projects focus exploration on a broad theme or topic of interest to children; provide for the integration of content areas; and extend over a period of two weeks or more.

reciprocal interactions   collaboration between child and teacher whereby control, decision making, power, voice, and knowledge are shared.

Reggio Emilia approach   an approach to learning in which children are engaged in cooperative investigations of long-term projects, curriculum is integrated, decision making is shared among children and teachers, the use of a variety of means of expressing one's feelings and understandings is promoted, and continuous evaluation and refinement of work are encouraged (named after a municipality in Italy).

rubric   clear descriptions of all the dimensions of child behaviors or performance being assessed; descriptions are organized along a continuum with scoring guidelines.

scaffolded interactions   instructional interactions between a teacher and child intended to help the child do something he or she is capable of understanding but cannot accomplish without support.

scaffolding   assistance from supportive adults by which a framework for guiding children's learning is created. The framework that is created usually takes the form of a learning experience that helps form an intellectual and conceptual "bridge" between children's current level of understanding about a concept and a new or clearer level of understanding.

schema   (*pl. schemata*) a child's background knowledge (internalized cognitive structures) related to specific concepts or topics.

science   the systematized knowledge of nature and the physical world derived from observation, study, and experimentation.

self-expression   the variety of things children do or say to convey a personal feeling, opinion, or understanding about something or someone.

self-help tools   skills and materials that children can independently refer to or use to locate or figure out information they want or need to accomplish a task.

self-monitoring behaviors   behaviors that indicate children are independently noticing whether what they are doing (e.g., reading, writing, project work) is working as anticipated and attempting to correct or modify their behaviors to accomplish their goals.

shared reading   the repeated reading aloud of a patterned, predictable book to a child or children, with invitations for the child or children to join in the reading as they can.

short-term instructional goals   daily curriculum and instructional goals established by teachers, sometimes in conjunction with children and sometimes independently, so that children acquire a broad knowledge base while developing the skills and strategies they need to become self-regulated learners.

social studies   the integrated study of the social sciences and humanities for the purpose of helping children learn to make good decisions on behalf of the public good in a democratic society.

sociodramatic play   the highest level of play; defined by Sara Smilansky on the basis of six components (imitative role play, make-believe with objects, make-believe with actions and situations, persistence, interaction, and verbal communication).

sound spelling sometimes referred to as *temporary spelling* or *invented spelling;* the visual representation of a child's emerging ability to identify one or more sounds in a word and to represent the sound(s) with appropriate, but not necessarily the correct, letter(s).

standardized assessments assessments conducted under the same controlled conditions with consistent scoring procedures to ensure comparable interpretation of student performance.

standards-referenced assessments assessments used to measure the progress children are making along a continuum toward established goals or standards.

student portfolio a collection of materials (e.g., work samples, self-evaluations, learning process journals) selected and organized by a child to reflect on personal learning strengths and needs.

supported reading interactive reading with a child during which the teacher reads only enough to help the child begin to anticipate the language or pattern of a book; less supportive than shared reading.

symbolic interactions interactions by which a child is able to use an object or person in the "real" world and create a signifier, or symbol. A child might pretend that a craft stick is a toothbrush; a child might pretend to be a classroom teacher and "teach" her stuffed animal "pupils."

transformational curriculum curriculum for which children have been involved in the planning, implementation, and assessment. The curriculum affects the learner, and the learner affects and changes the curriculum.

validity the degree to which an assessment (1) measures what it is intended to measure, (2) addresses a specific instructional goal, and (3) reflects the instructional processes employed in the classroom.

voices various ways or means by which children express their feelings, understandings, and opinions (e.g., movement, drama, storytelling, poetry, drawing, humor, play).

wordness the understanding that there is one spoken word for every written word, that the written word is bounded by spaces, and that the spoken word may be constructed of more than one syllable.

working portfolio a folder, created by the teacher, containing documentation (e.g., anecdotal records, work samples, checklists) to indicate a child's strengths and needs, as well as the most appropriate instructional and mediational strategies to use with the child.

writing vocabulary words a child can independently write, read, and spell correctly.

zone of proximal development the relationship between development and learning; represents the difference between what a child is able to do and understand independently and what the child is able to do and understand with varying degrees of support.

Name Index

Subject Index